Ao Haru Ride

The scent of air after rain...
In the light around us, I felt your heartbeat.

3

IO SAKISAKA

C O N T E N T S

3

S T O R Y
T H U S
F A R

In junior high, Futaba Yoshioka was quiet and disliked all boys, except for Tanaka, her first love. Their romance was cut short when he suddenly transferred schools, leaving behind an unresolved misunderstanding. As a tomboy in high school, Futaba is reunited with Tanaka, who's been going by the name Kou Mabuchi since his parents' divorce. Futaba is disturbed to see how much his personality has changed...

Now in her second year of high school, Futaba decides to start over with new friendships. She and Kou become class representatives, and Yuri, Murao and Kominato join the event committee. Thanks to a mishap during a school retreat, these five start to bond.

On the way home from the retreat, Yuri texts Futaba: "I think I like Mabuchi!" But where does that leave Futaba...?

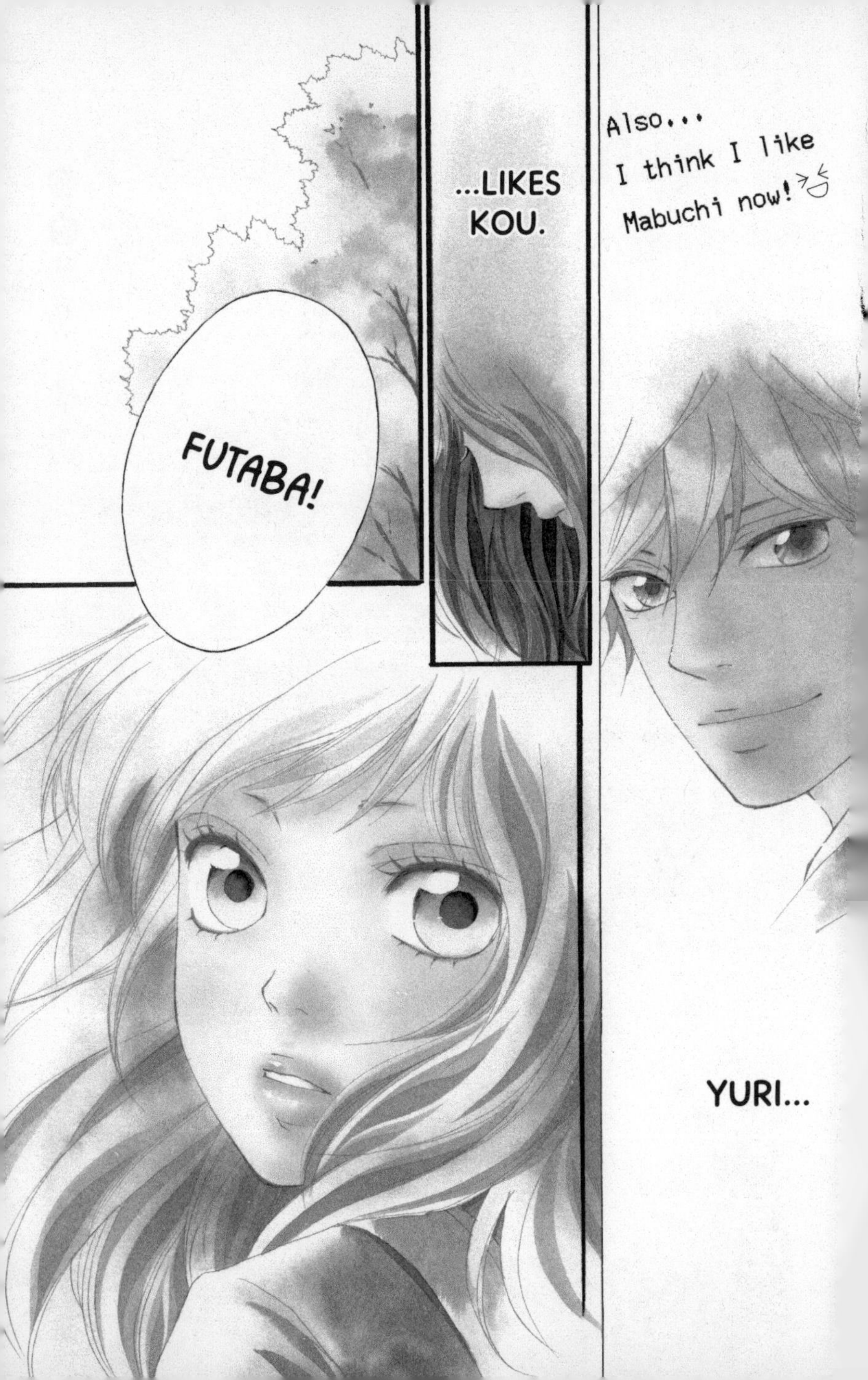
Also...
I think I like Mabuchi now!
YURI...
...LIKES KOU.
FUTABA!

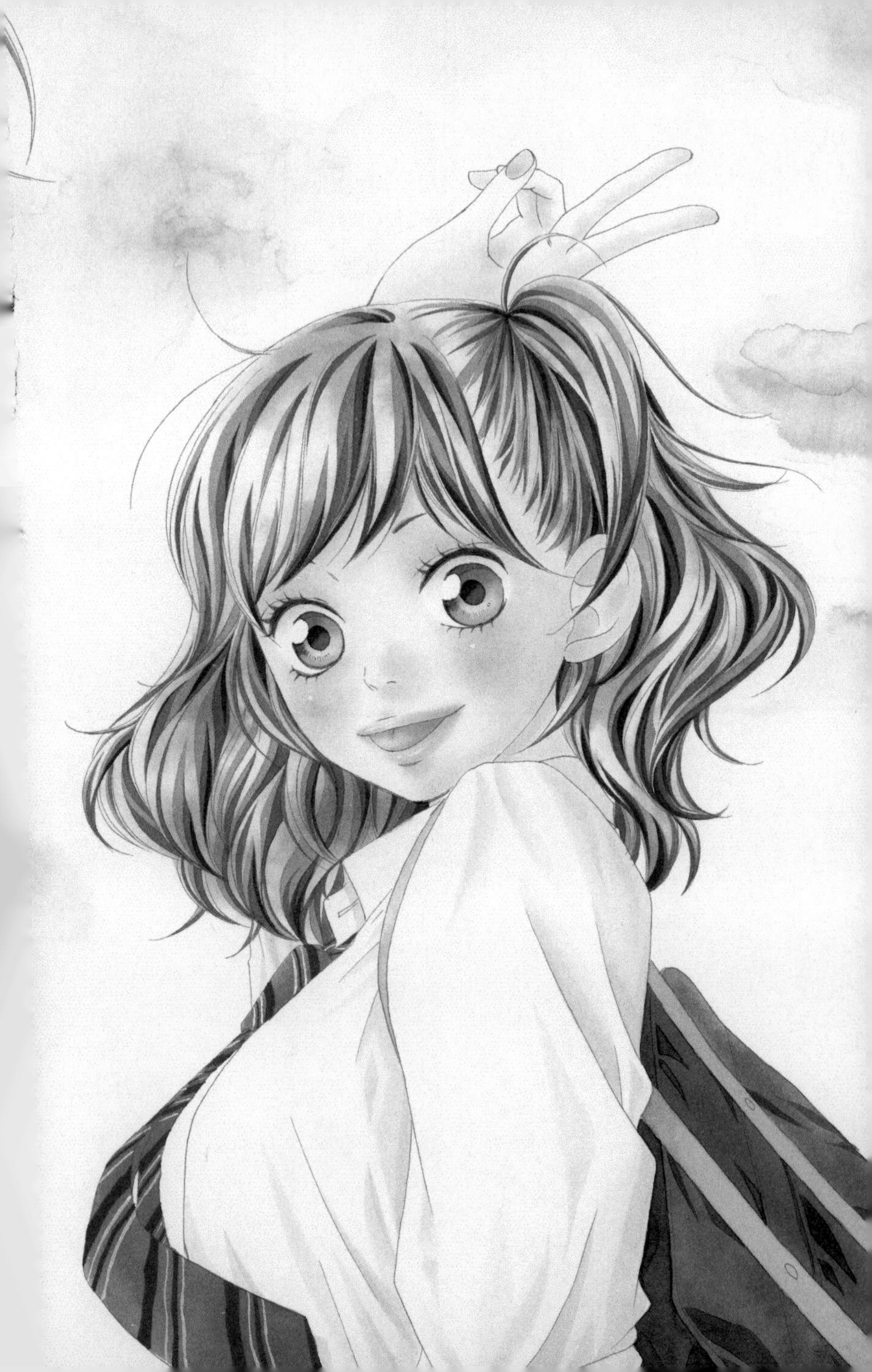

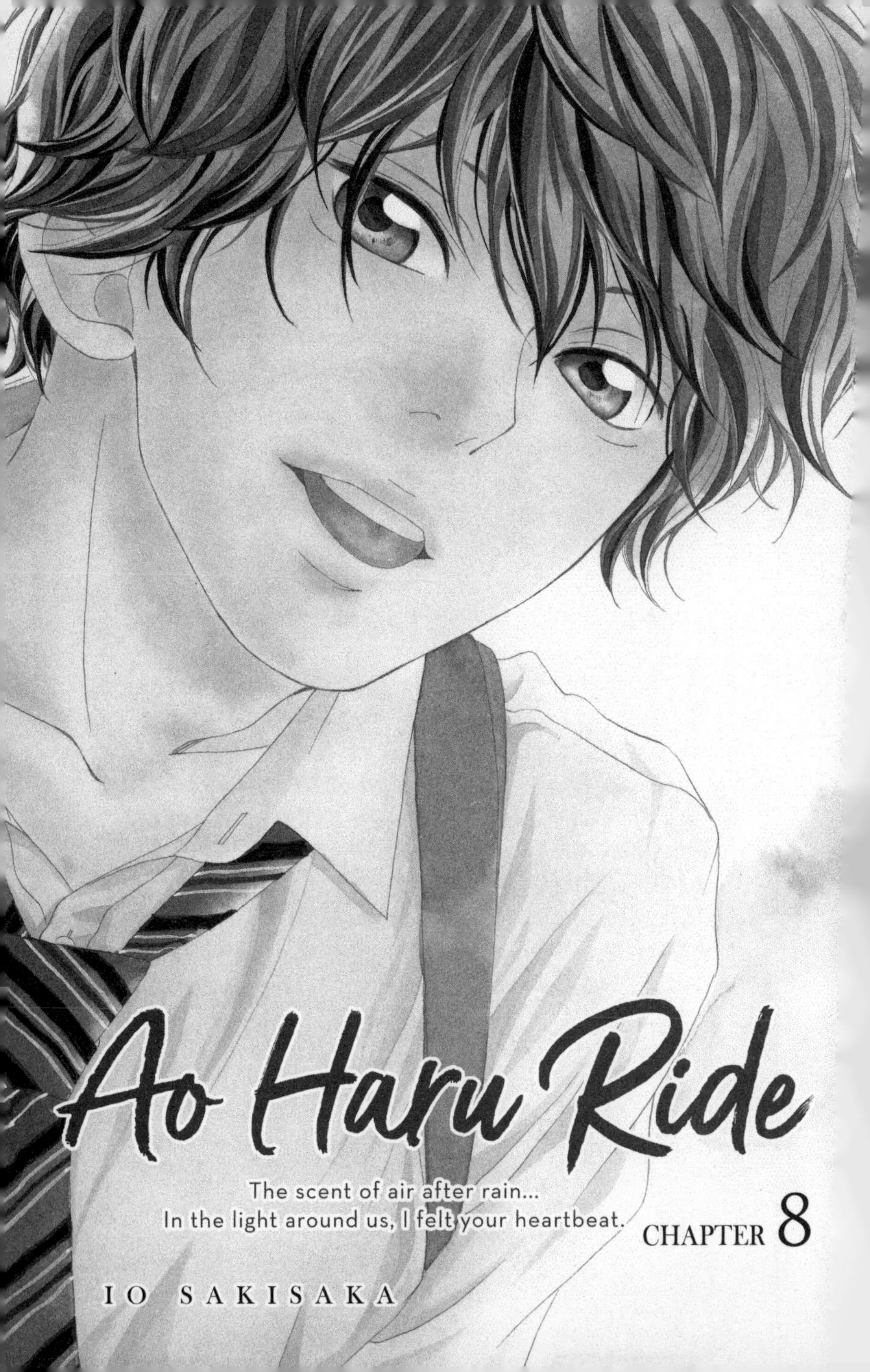
Ao Haru Ride
The scent of air after rain...
In the light around us, I felt your heartbeat.
CHAPTER 8
IO SAKISAKA

GREETINGS

Hi! I'm Io Sakisaka. Thank you for picking up a copy of *Ao Haru Ride* volume 3.

It's been a whole year since *Ao Haru Ride* started serialization. Yet the characters haven't quite taken to me, which makes drawing them a constant challenge.
(Especially you, Kou! Hurry up and love me already! MEOW)

There are many parts that I want to draw, but stringing them all together is tricky and exciting. I'm constantly thinking about the order I should present things in to make it the most exciting and wondering whether the timing is right in a certain chapter. Sometimes branches of the story develop, but I'm forced to prune them back so that other parts—ones that I either really want to draw or have to draw—can stand out. (← This leaves me very conflicted because I'm cutting out content that I came up with...) Really, I just want everyone to enjoy the story!

So, through much fuss and grinding of teeth, I have somehow completed volume 3. I hope for nothing more than that my readers can relax and enjoy it. On that note, I hope you'll read this volume through to the end!

 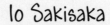 Io Sakisaka

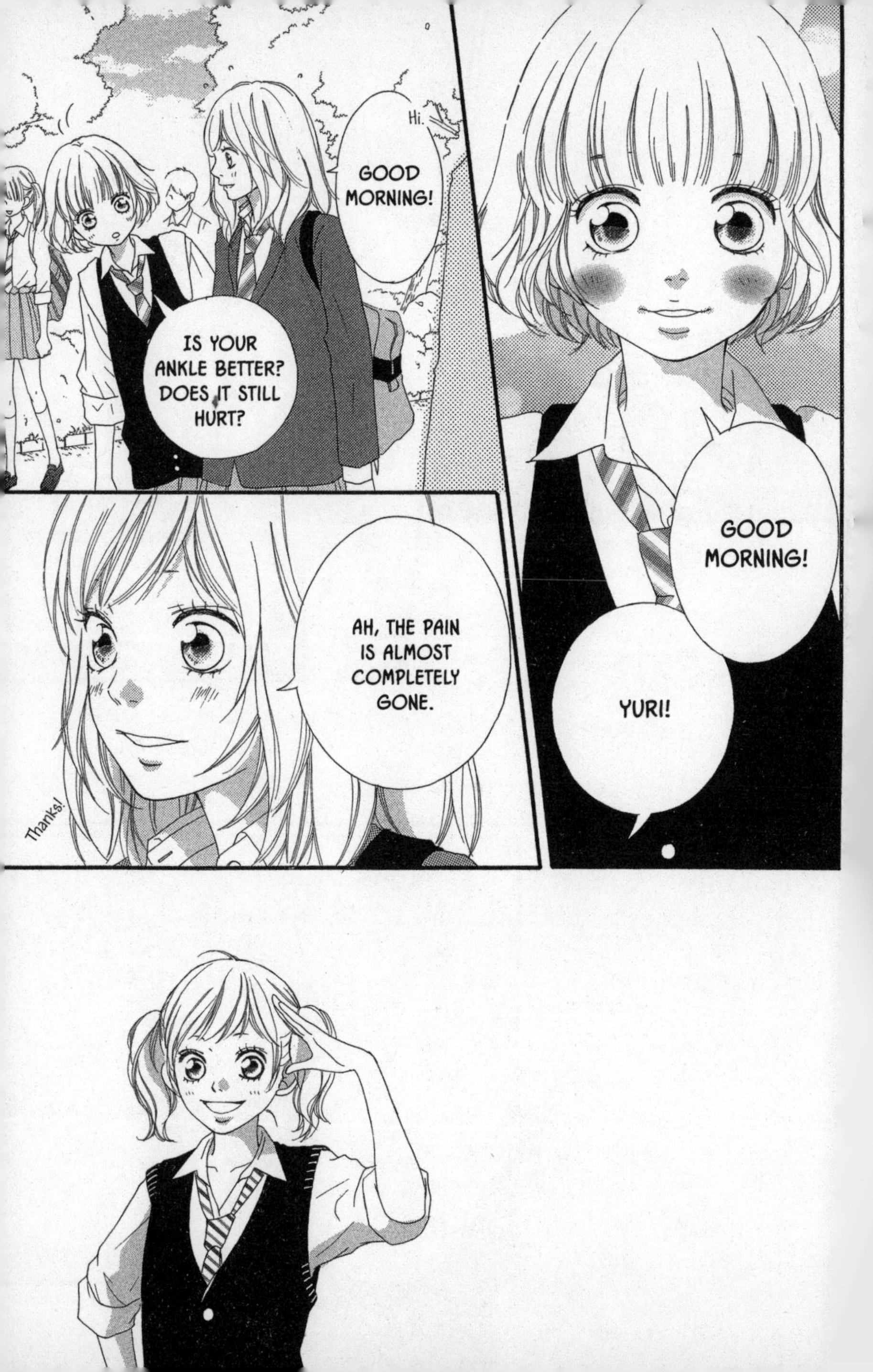
GOOD MORNING!
YURI!
Hi.
GOOD MORNING!
IS YOUR ANKLE BETTER? DOES IT STILL HURT?
AH, THE PAIN IS ALMOST COMPLETELY GONE.
Thanks!

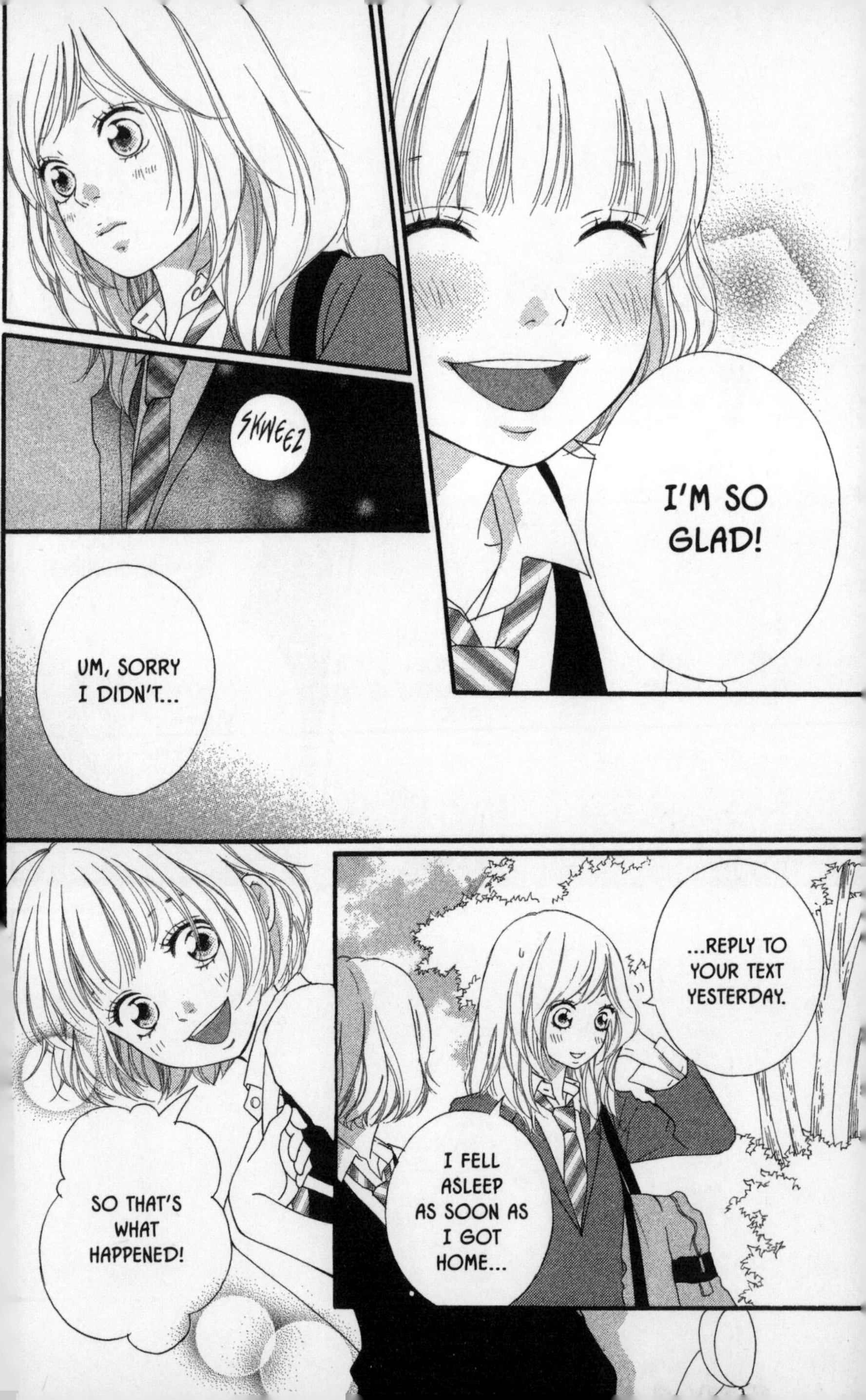
I'M SO GLAD!
SKWEEZ
UM, SORRY I DIDN'T...
...REPLY TO YOUR TEXT YESTERDAY.
I FELL ASLEEP AS SOON AS I GOT HOME...
SO THAT'S WHAT HAPPENED!

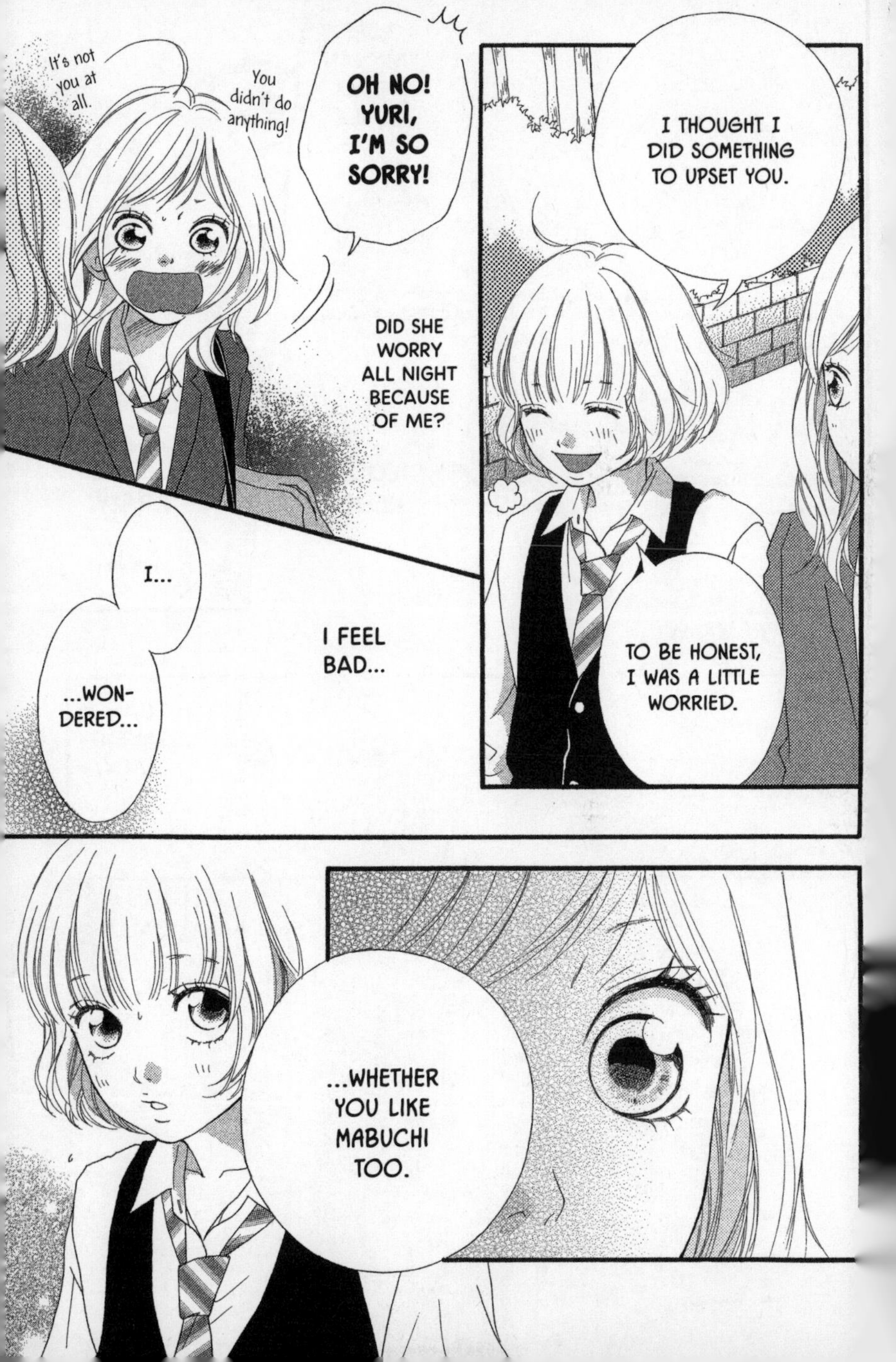
I THOUGHT I DID SOMETHING TO UPSET YOU.
TO BE HONEST, I WAS A LITTLE WORRIED.
OH NO! YURI, I'M SO SORRY!
You didn't do anything!
It's not you at all.
DID SHE WORRY ALL NIGHT BECAUSE OF ME?
I FEEL BAD...
I...
...WON-DERED...
...WHETHER YOU LIKE MABUCHI TOO.

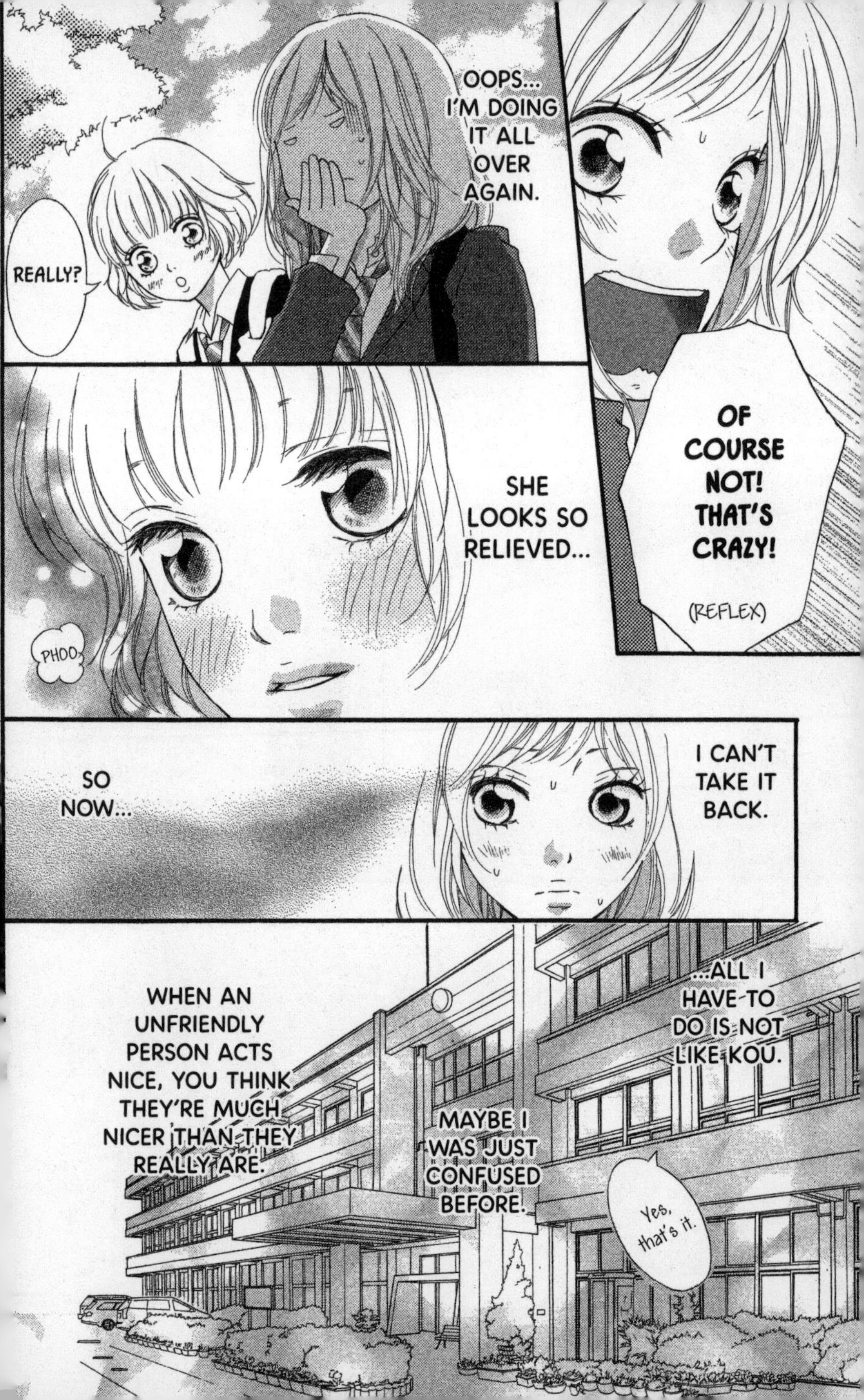
OF COURSE NOT! THAT'S CRAZY!
(REFLEX)
OOPS... I'M DOING IT ALL OVER AGAIN.
REALLY?
SHE LOOKS SO RELIEVED...
PHOO
I CAN'T TAKE IT BACK.
SO NOW...
...ALL I HAVE TO DO IS NOT LIKE KOU.
Yes, that's it.
MAYBE I WAS JUST CONFUSED BEFORE.
WHEN AN UNFRIENDLY PERSON ACTS NICE, YOU THINK THEY'RE MUCH NICER THAN THEY REALLY ARE.

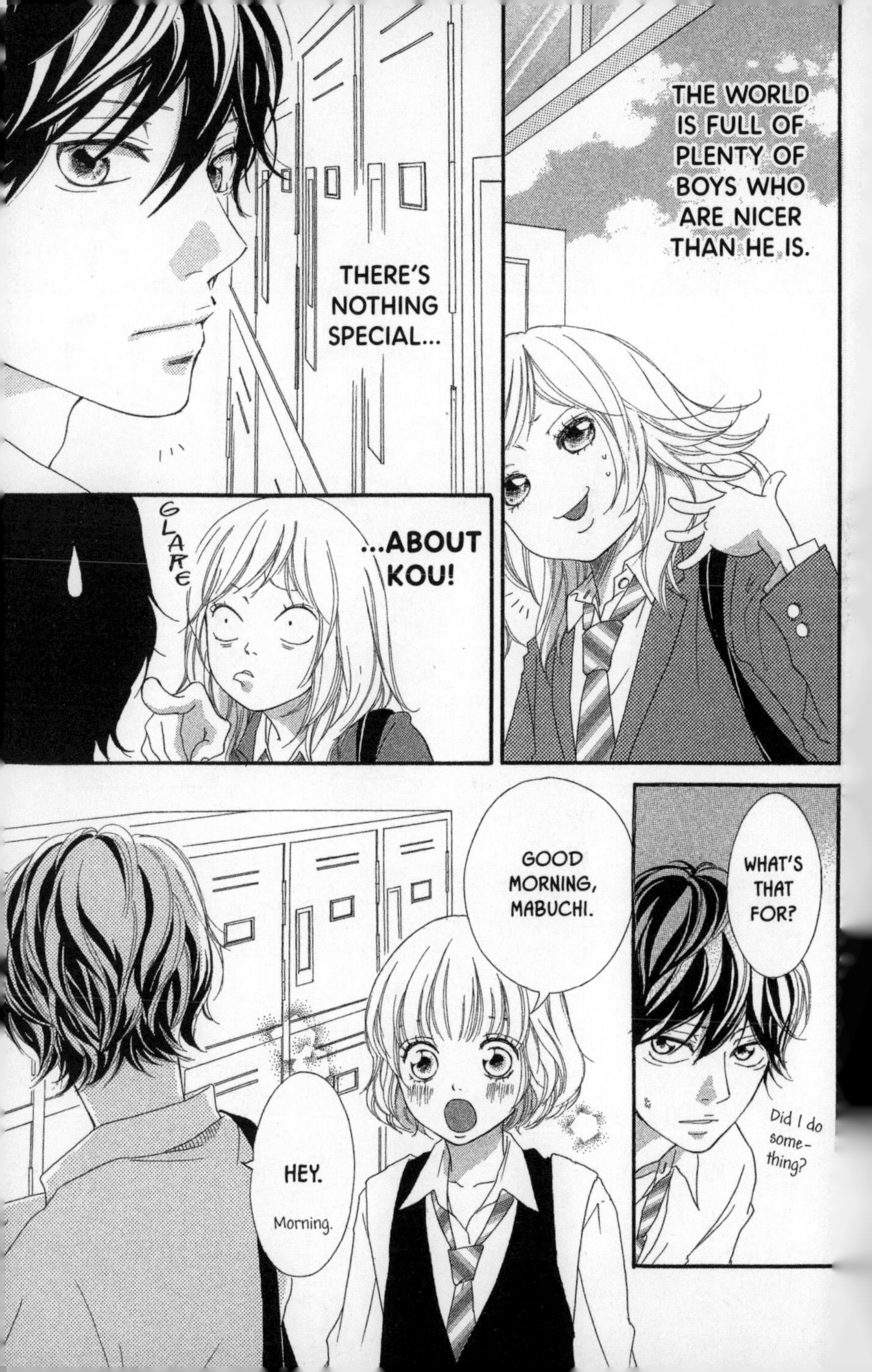
THE WORLD IS FULL OF PLENTY OF BOYS WHO ARE NICER THAN HE IS.
THERE'S NOTHING SPECIAL...
GLARE
...ABOUT KOU!
WHAT'S THAT FOR?
Did I do some-thing?
GOOD MORNING, MABUCHI.
HEY.
Morning.

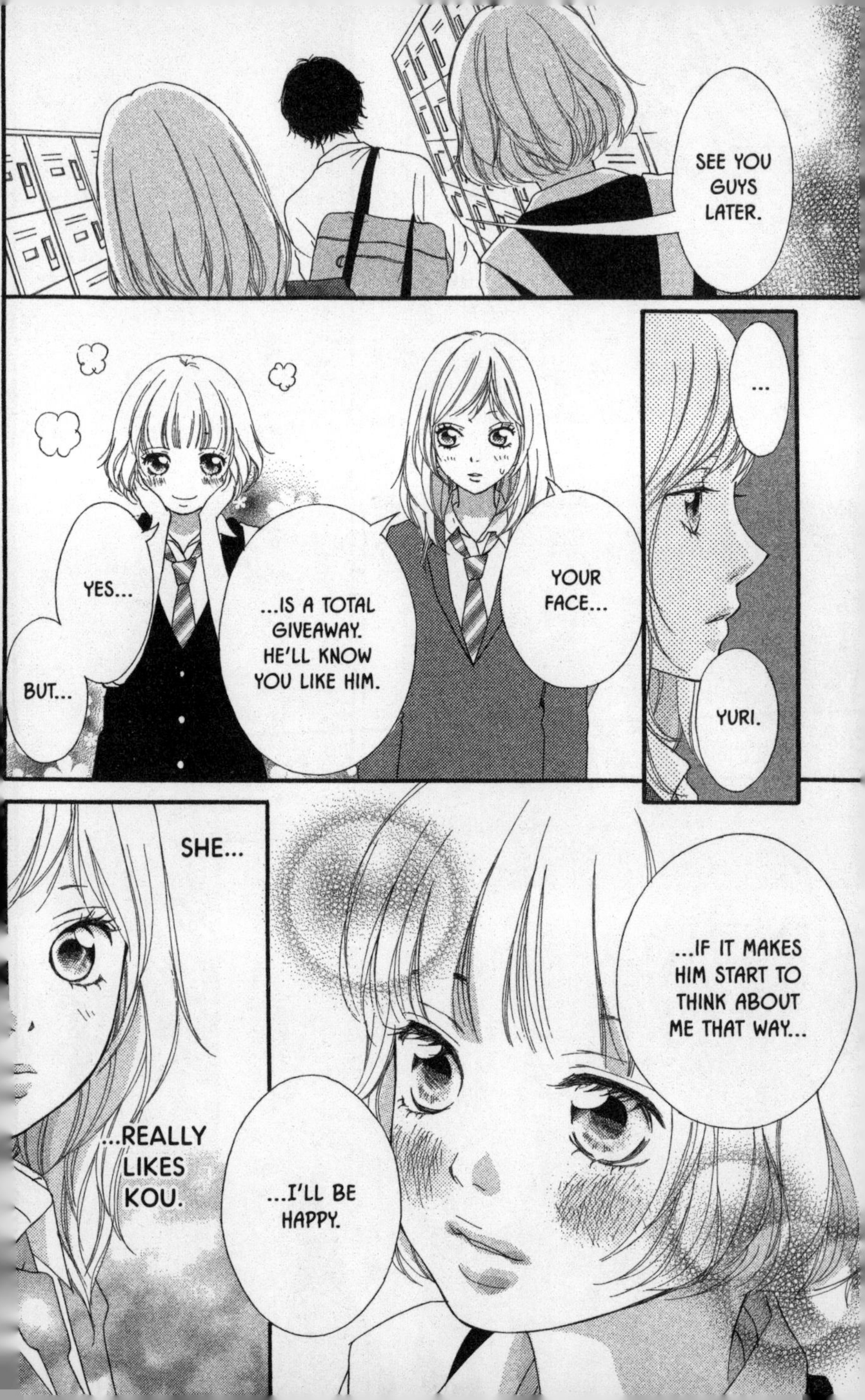
SEE YOU GUYS LATER.
...
YURI.
YOUR FACE...
...IS A TOTAL GIVEAWAY. HE'LL KNOW YOU LIKE HIM.
YES...
BUT...
...IF IT MAKES HIM START TO THINK ABOUT ME THAT WAY...
...I'LL BE HAPPY.
SHE...
...REALLY LIKES KOU.

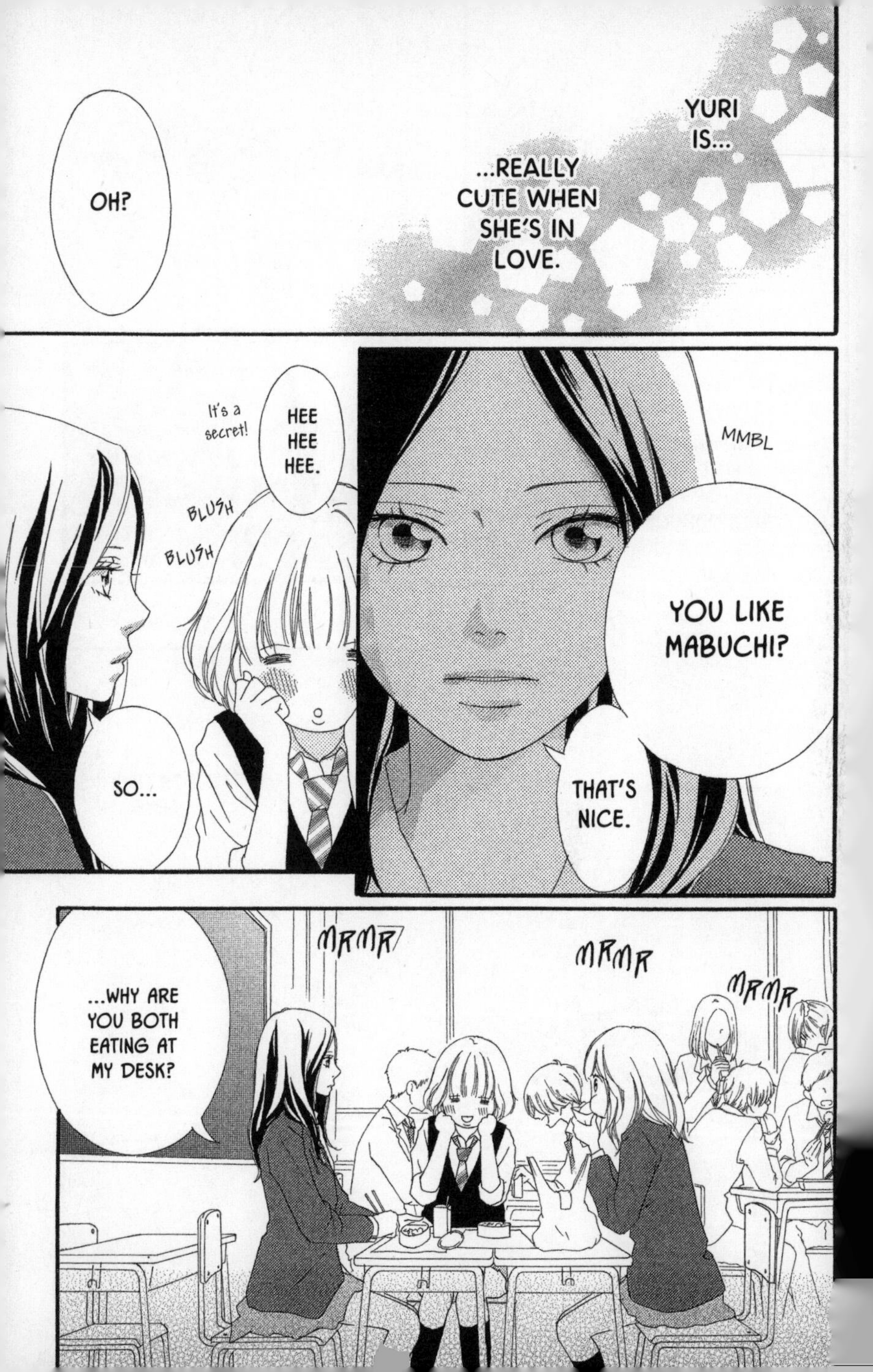
YURI IS...
...REALLY CUTE WHEN SHE'S IN LOVE.
OH?
MMBL
YOU LIKE MABUCHI?
THAT'S NICE.
HEE HEE HEE.
It's a secret!
BLUSH
BLUSH
SO...
MRMR
MRMR
MRMR
...WHY ARE YOU BOTH EATING AT MY DESK?

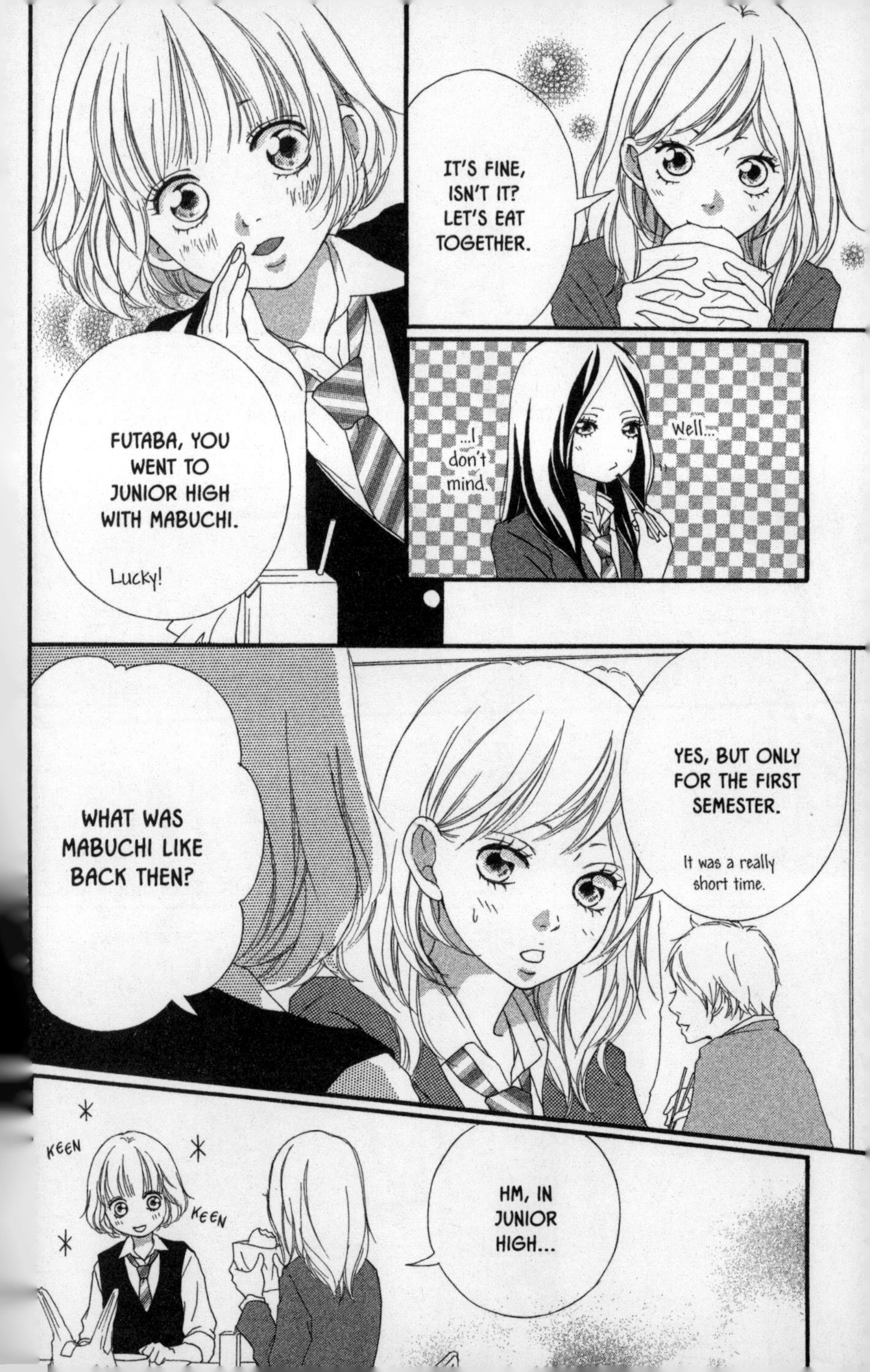
IT'S FINE, ISN'T IT? LET'S EAT TOGETHER.
Well...
...I don't mind.
FUTABA, YOU WENT TO JUNIOR HIGH WITH MABUCHI.
Lucky!
YES, BUT ONLY FOR THE FIRST SEMESTER.
It was a really short time.
WHAT WAS MABUCHI LIKE BACK THEN?
HM, IN JUNIOR HIGH...
KEEN
KEEN

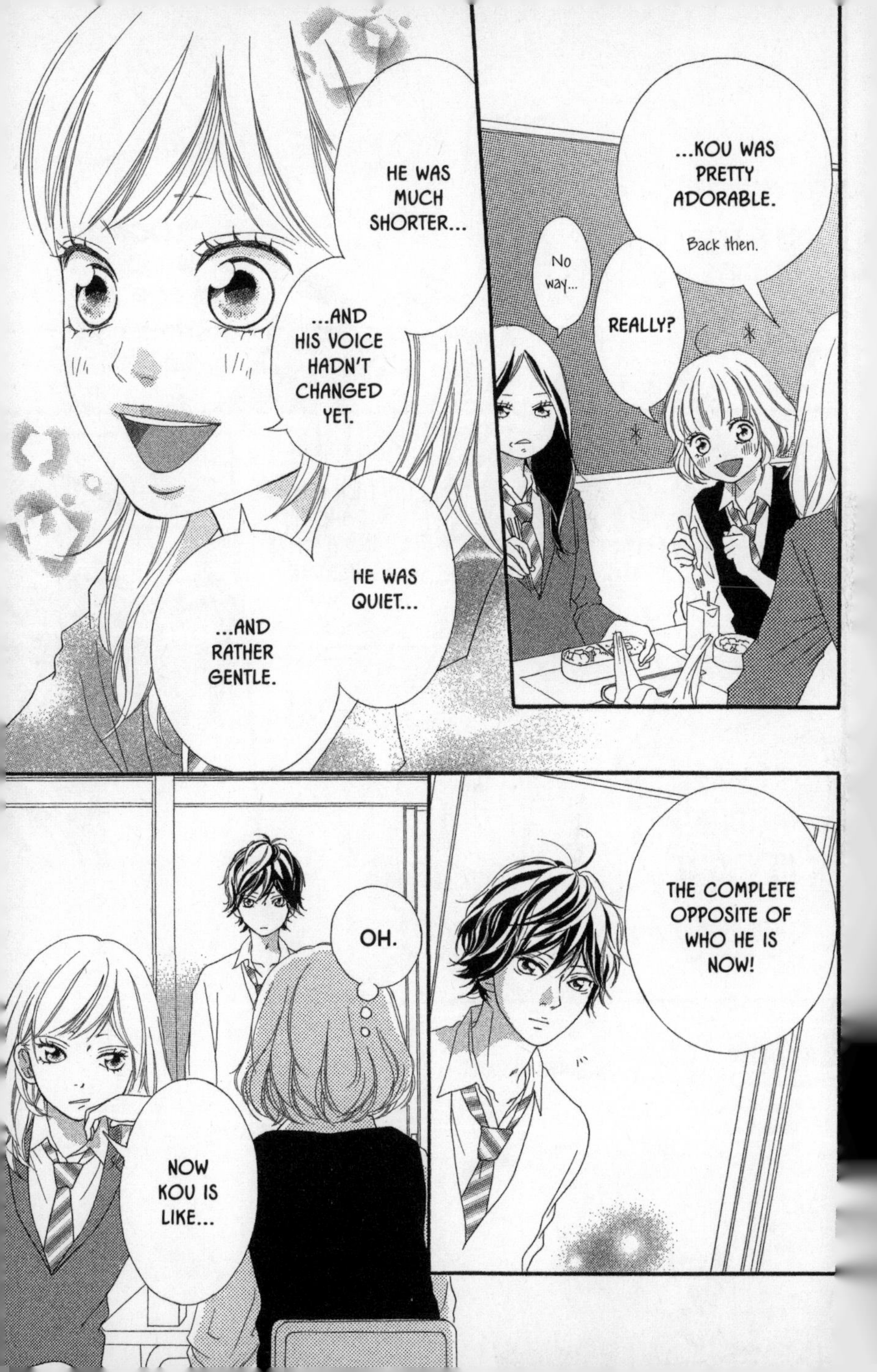
...KOU WAS PRETTY ADORABLE.
Back then.
REALLY?
No way...
HE WAS MUCH SHORTER...
...AND HIS VOICE HADN'T CHANGED YET.
HE WAS QUIET...
...AND RATHER GENTLE.
THE COMPLETE OPPOSITE OF WHO HE IS NOW!
OH.
NOW KOU IS LIKE...

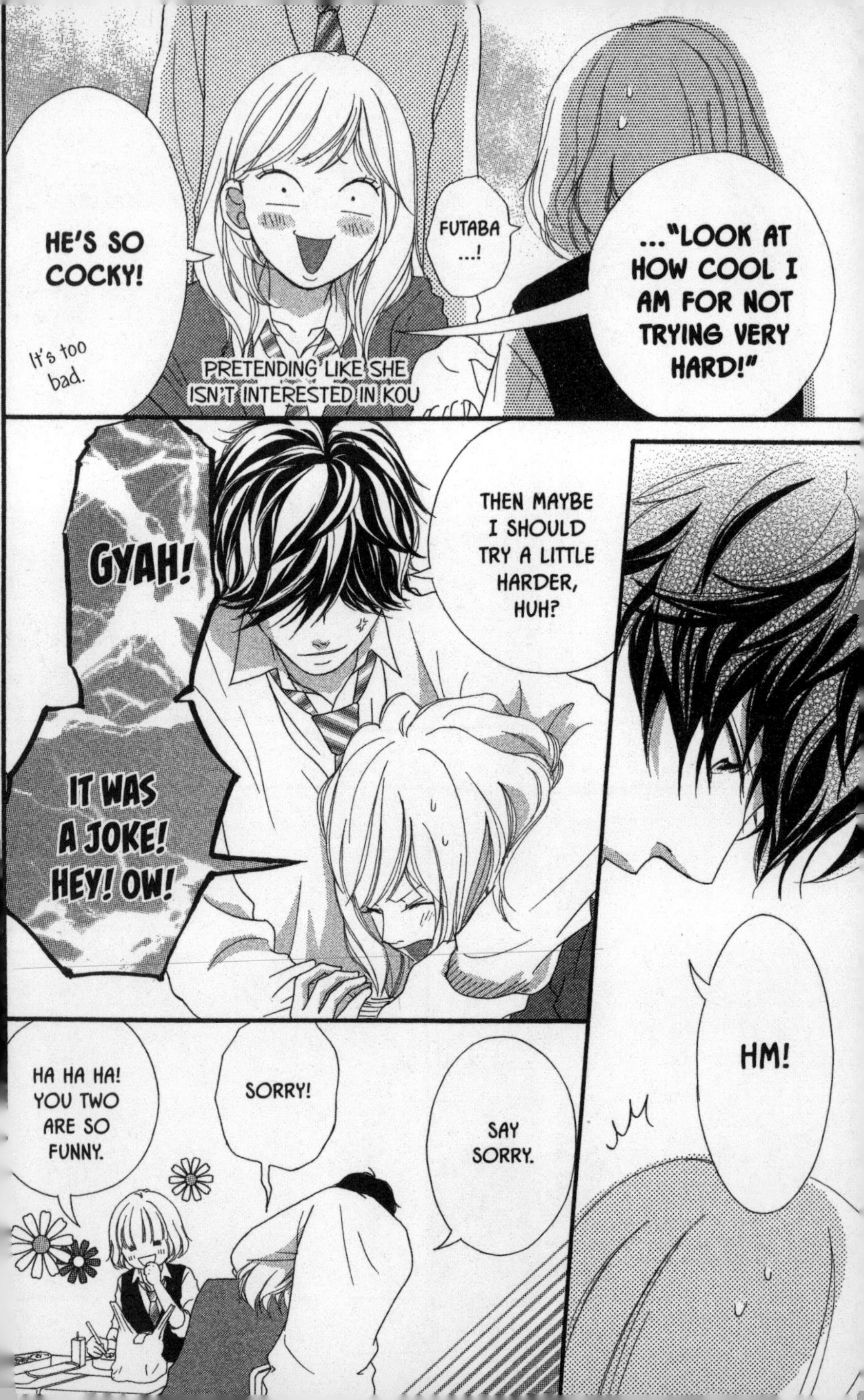
..."LOOK AT HOW COOL I AM FOR NOT TRYING VERY HARD!"
FUTABA ...!
HE'S SO COCKY!
PRETENDING LIKE SHE ISN'T INTERESTED IN KOU
It's too bad.
HM!
THEN MAYBE I SHOULD TRY A LITTLE HARDER, HUH?
GYAH!
IT WAS A JOKE! HEY! OW!
SAY SORRY.
SORRY!
HA HA HA! YOU TWO ARE SO FUNNY.

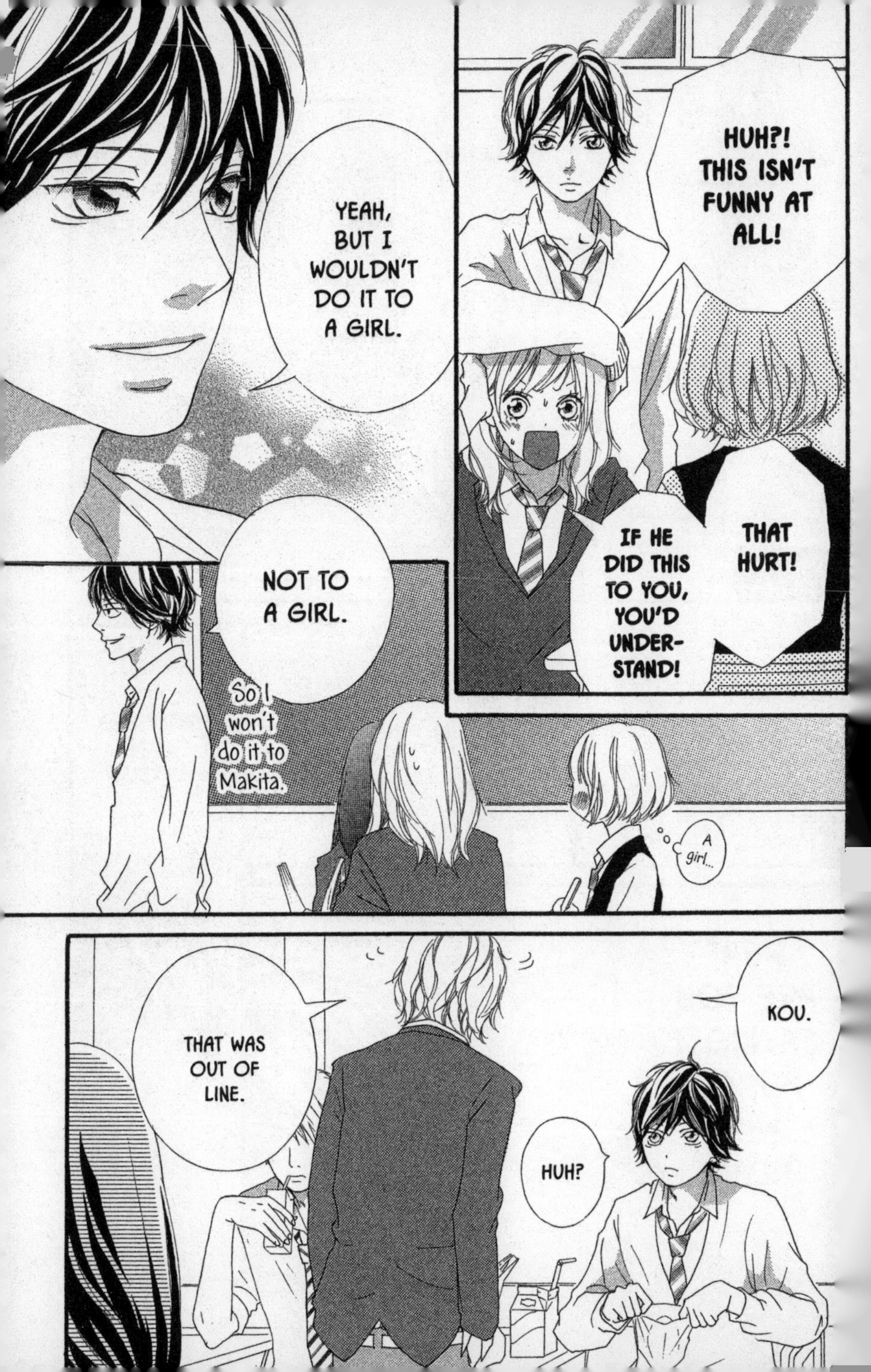
HUH?! THIS ISN'T FUNNY AT ALL!
THAT HURT!
IF HE DID THIS TO YOU, YOU'D UNDER-STAND!
YEAH, BUT I WOULDN'T DO IT TO A GIRL.
NOT TO A GIRL.
So I won't do it to Makita.
A girl...
KOU.
HUH?
THAT WAS OUT OF LINE.

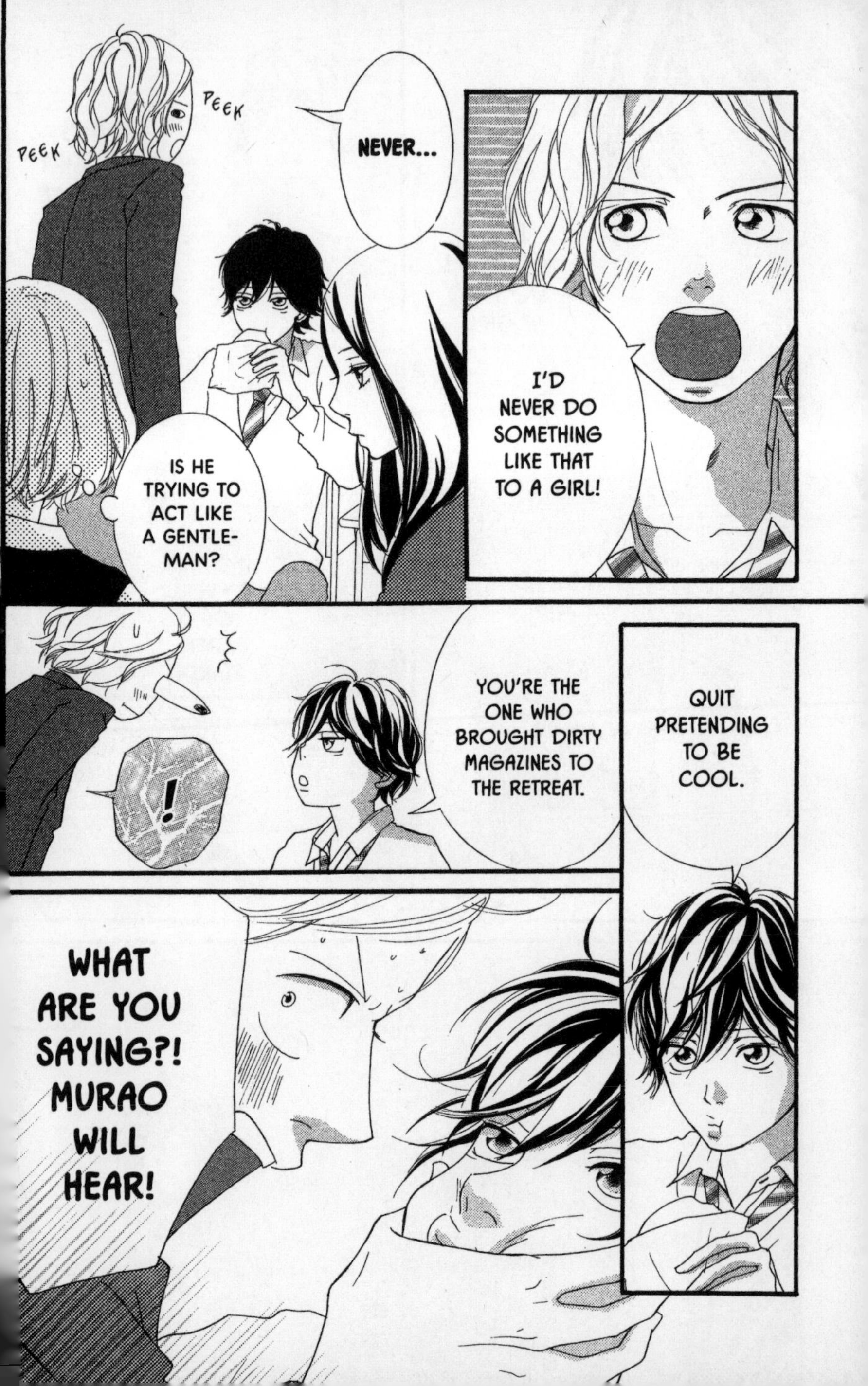
I'D NEVER DO SOMETHING LIKE THAT TO A GIRL!
NEVER...
PEEK
PEEK
IS HE TRYING TO ACT LIKE A GENTLE-MAN?
QUIT PRETENDING TO BE COOL.
YOU'RE THE ONE WHO BROUGHT DIRTY MAGAZINES TO THE RETREAT.
!
WHAT ARE YOU SAYING?! MURAO WILL HEAR!

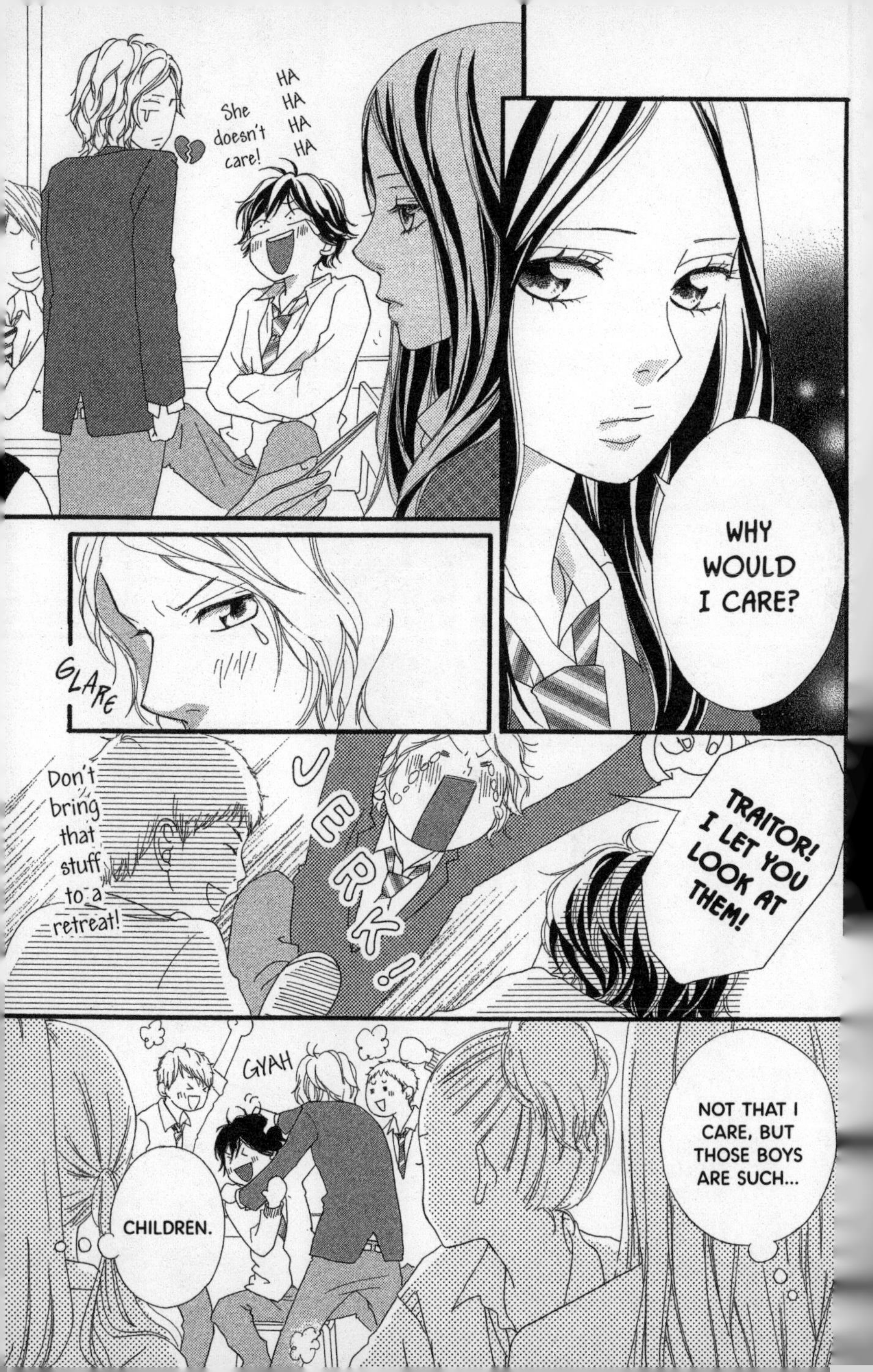
HA HA HA HA
She doesn't care!
WHY WOULD I CARE?
GLARE
TRAITOR! I LET YOU LOOK AT THEM!
JERK!
Don't bring that stuff to a retreat!
NOT THAT I CARE, BUT THOSE BOYS ARE SUCH...
GYAH
CHILDREN.

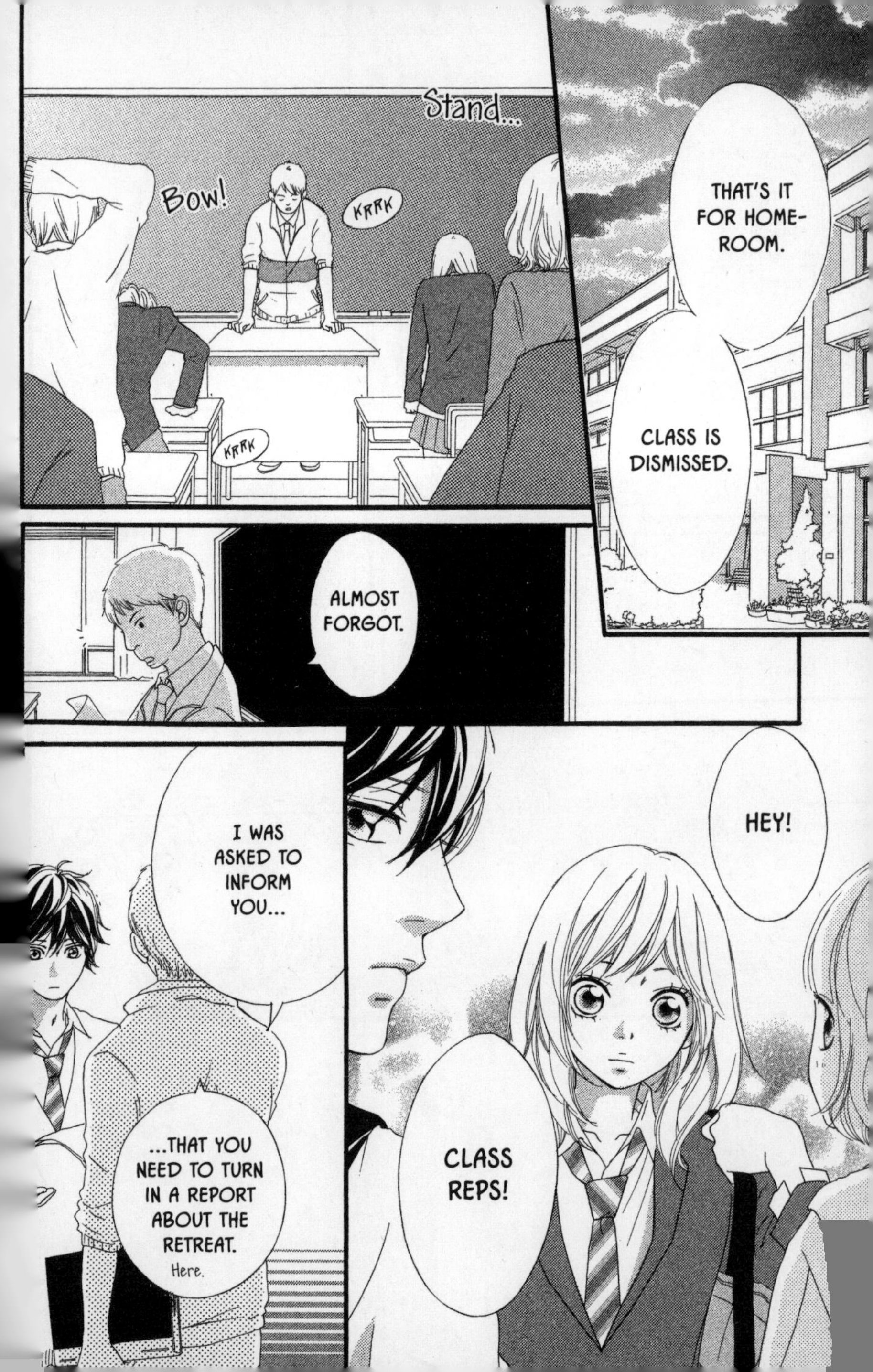
THAT'S IT FOR HOME-ROOM.
CLASS IS DISMISSED.
Stand...
Bow!
KRRK
KRRK
ALMOST FORGOT.
HEY!
CLASS REPS!
I WAS ASKED TO INFORM YOU...
...THAT YOU NEED TO TURN IN A REPORT ABOUT THE RETREAT.
Here.

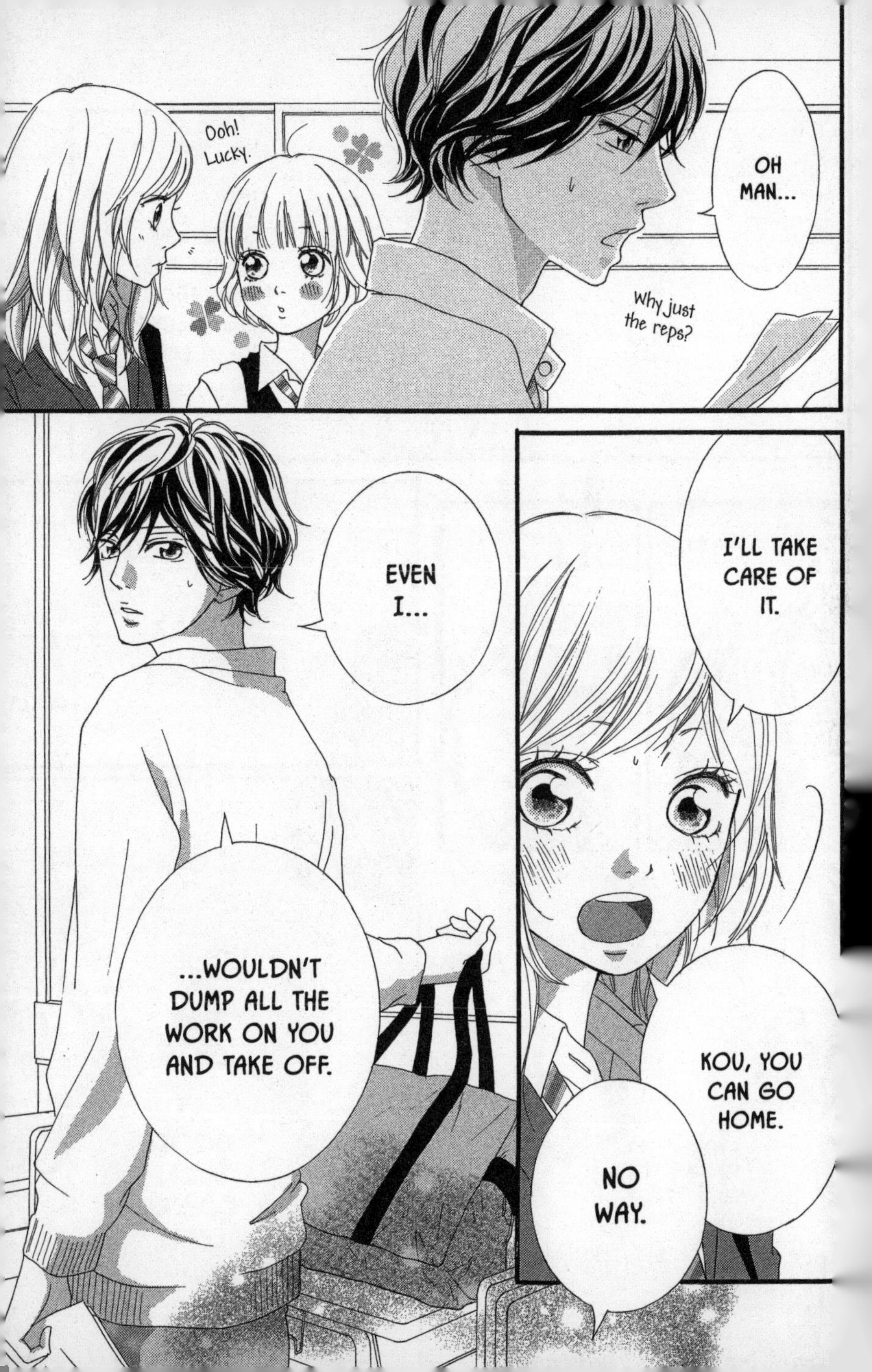
OH MAN...
Why just the reps?
Ooh! Lucky.
I'LL TAKE CARE OF IT.
KOU, YOU CAN GO HOME.
NO WAY.
EVEN I...
...WOULDN'T DUMP ALL THE WORK ON YOU AND TAKE OFF.

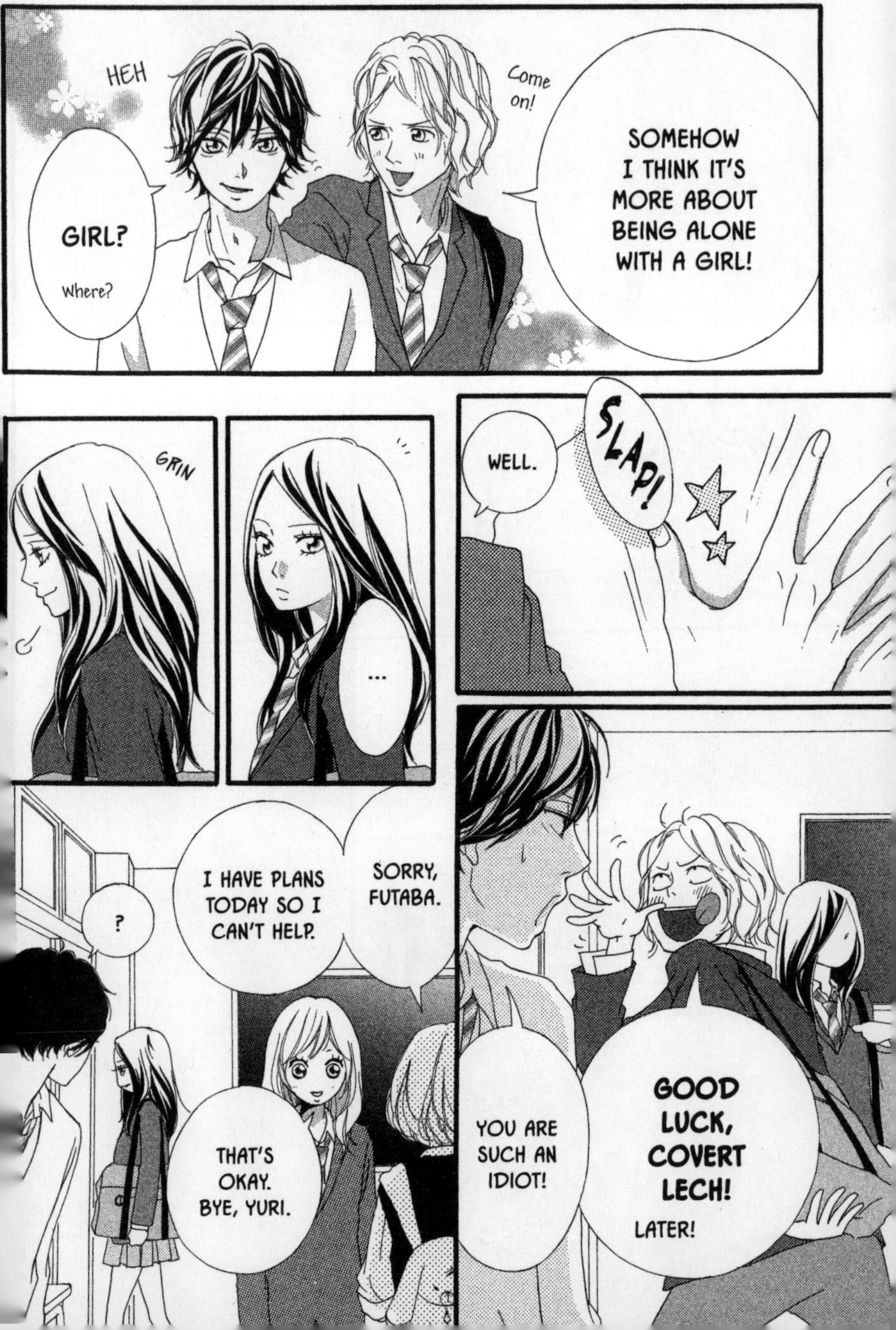
SOMEHOW I THINK IT'S MORE ABOUT BEING ALONE WITH A GIRL!
Come on!
HEH
GIRL? Where?
SLAP!
WELL.
GOOD LUCK, COVERT LECH! LATER!
YOU ARE SUCH AN IDIOT!
...
GRIN
SORRY, FUTABA.
I HAVE PLANS TODAY SO I CAN'T HELP.
?
THAT'S OKAY. BYE, YURI.

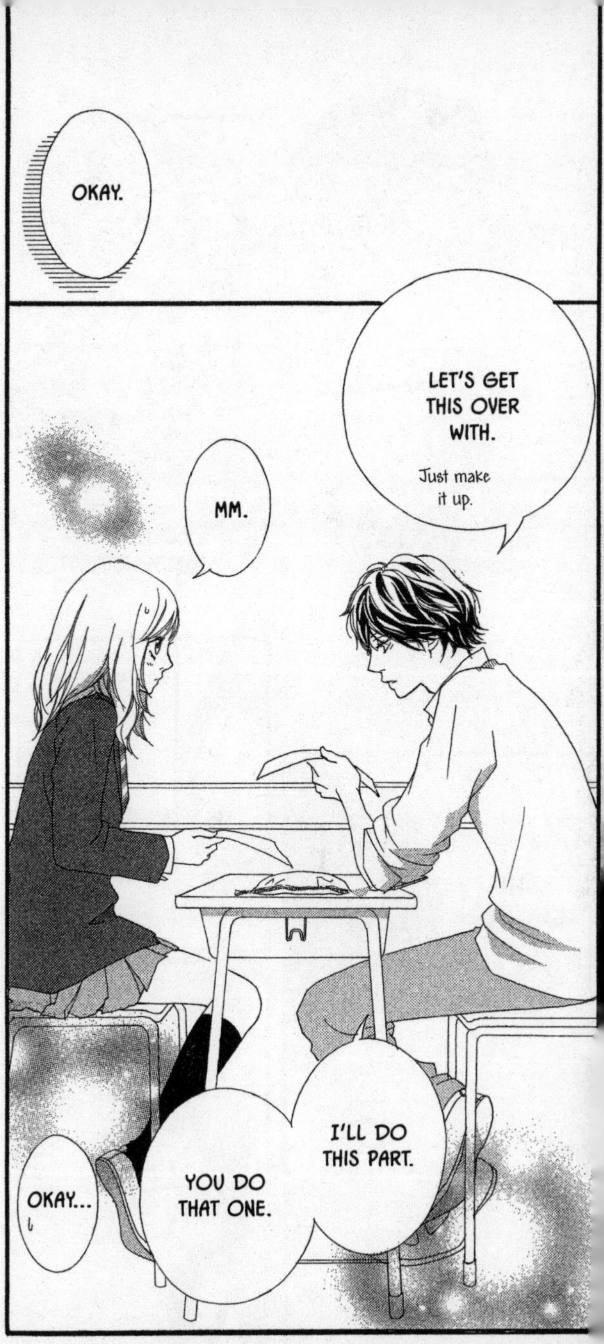
OKAY.
LET'S GET THIS OVER WITH.
Just make it up.
MM.
I'LL DO THIS PART.
YOU DO THAT ONE.
OKAY...

The other day, I overslept an insane amount. And on the worst day possible—the day of a big deadline! Want to know how much? Six hours. When I awoke, I was so baffled by what I saw on the clock that I had to have some coffee first. Slowly I started to realize how bad the situation was. But I didn't panic like usual. Instead I started to giggle and laugh at myself. When I thought about why I was able to remain calm, I determined that it was because the consequences of what I had done were so extreme that if I focused on them too much, my psyche would crumble. Somehow I was instinctively defending myself. After some time, I slowly revved up and in the last hour I worked like a madwoman and finished. I was exhausted.

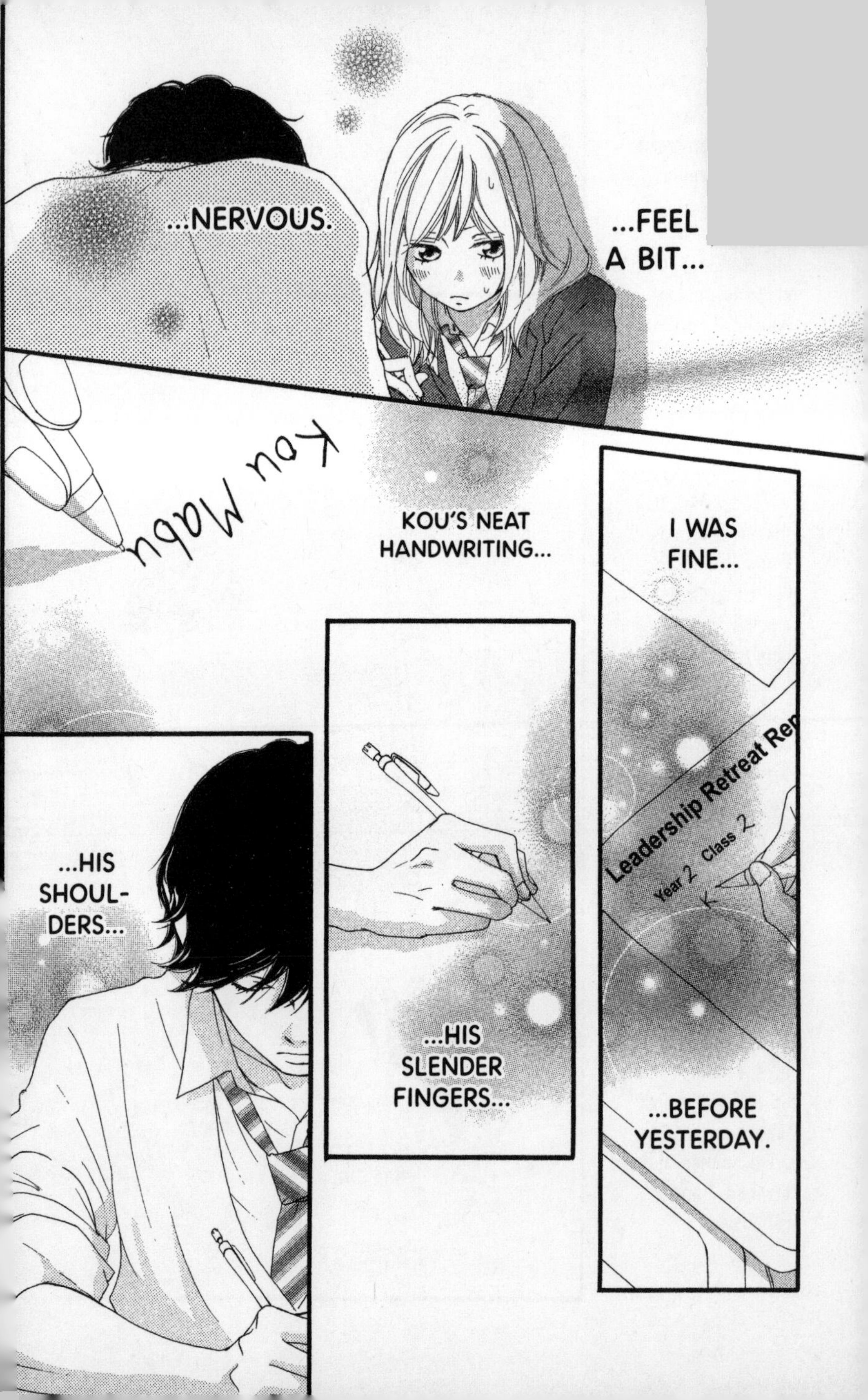
...FEEL A BIT...
...NERVOUS.
I WAS FINE...
Leadership Retreat Rep
Year 2 Class 2
...BEFORE YESTERDAY.
Kou Mabu
KOU'S NEAT HANDWRITING...
...HIS SLENDER FINGERS...
...HIS SHOULDERS...

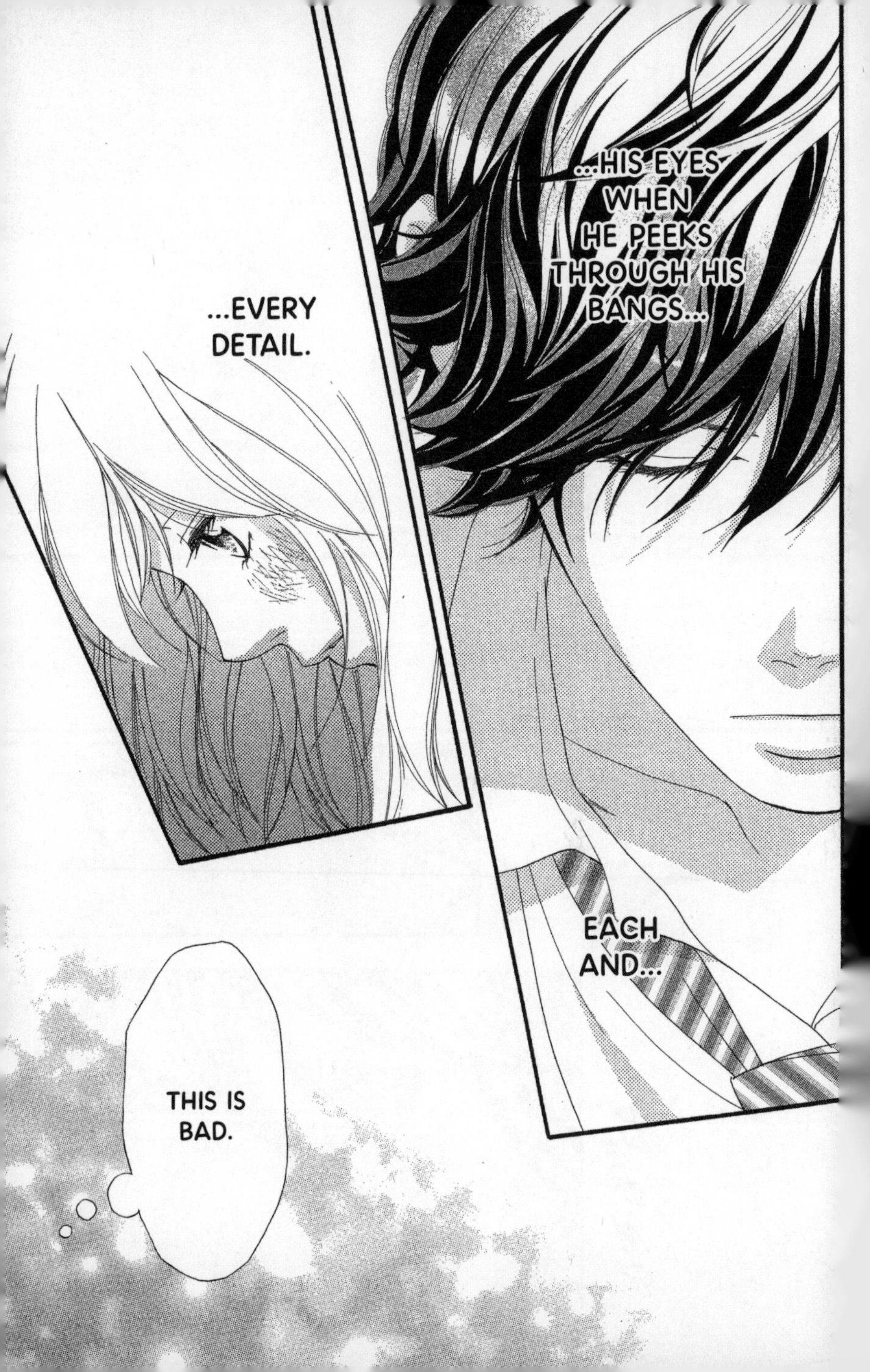
...HIS EYES WHEN HE PEEKS THROUGH HIS BANGS...
EACH AND...
...EVERY DETAIL.
THIS IS BAD.

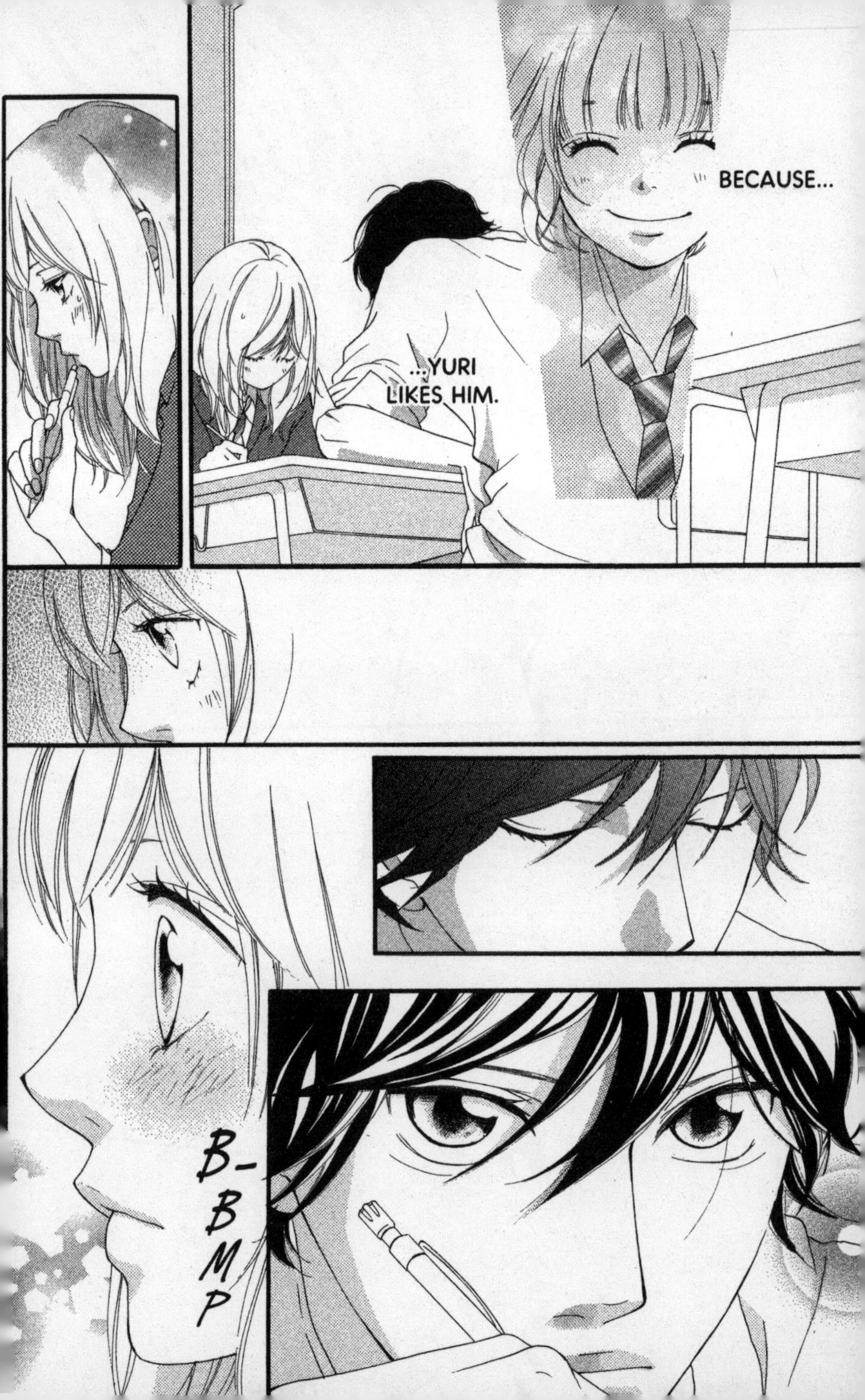
BECAUSE...
...YURI LIKES HIM.
B-BMP

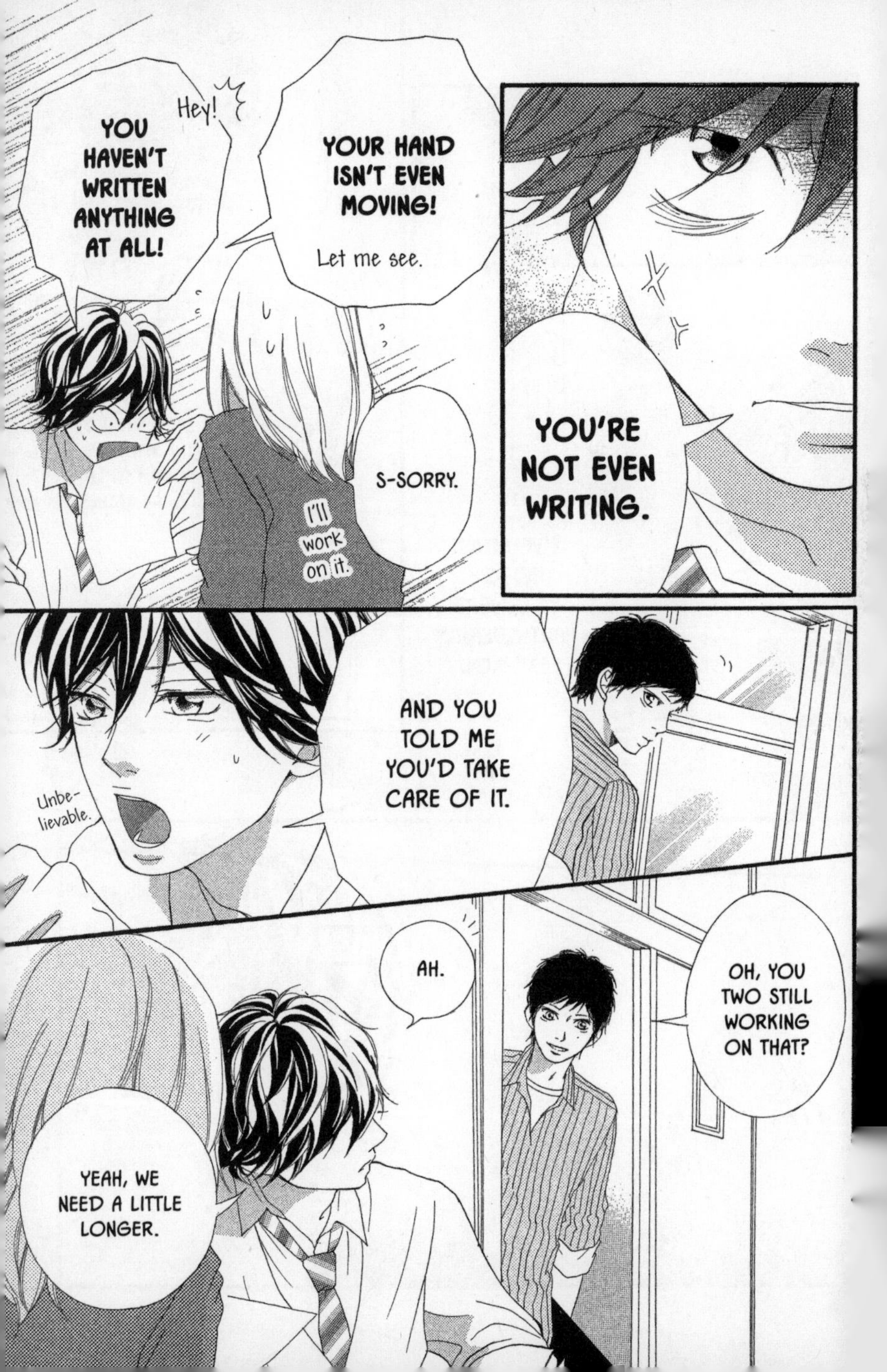
YOU'RE NOT EVEN WRITING.
YOUR HAND ISN'T EVEN MOVING!
Let me see.
Hey!
YOU HAVEN'T WRITTEN ANYTHING AT ALL!
S-SORRY.
I'll work on it.
AND YOU TOLD ME YOU'D TAKE CARE OF IT.
Unbelievable.
OH, YOU TWO STILL WORKING ON THAT?
AH.
YEAH, WE NEED A LITTLE LONGER.

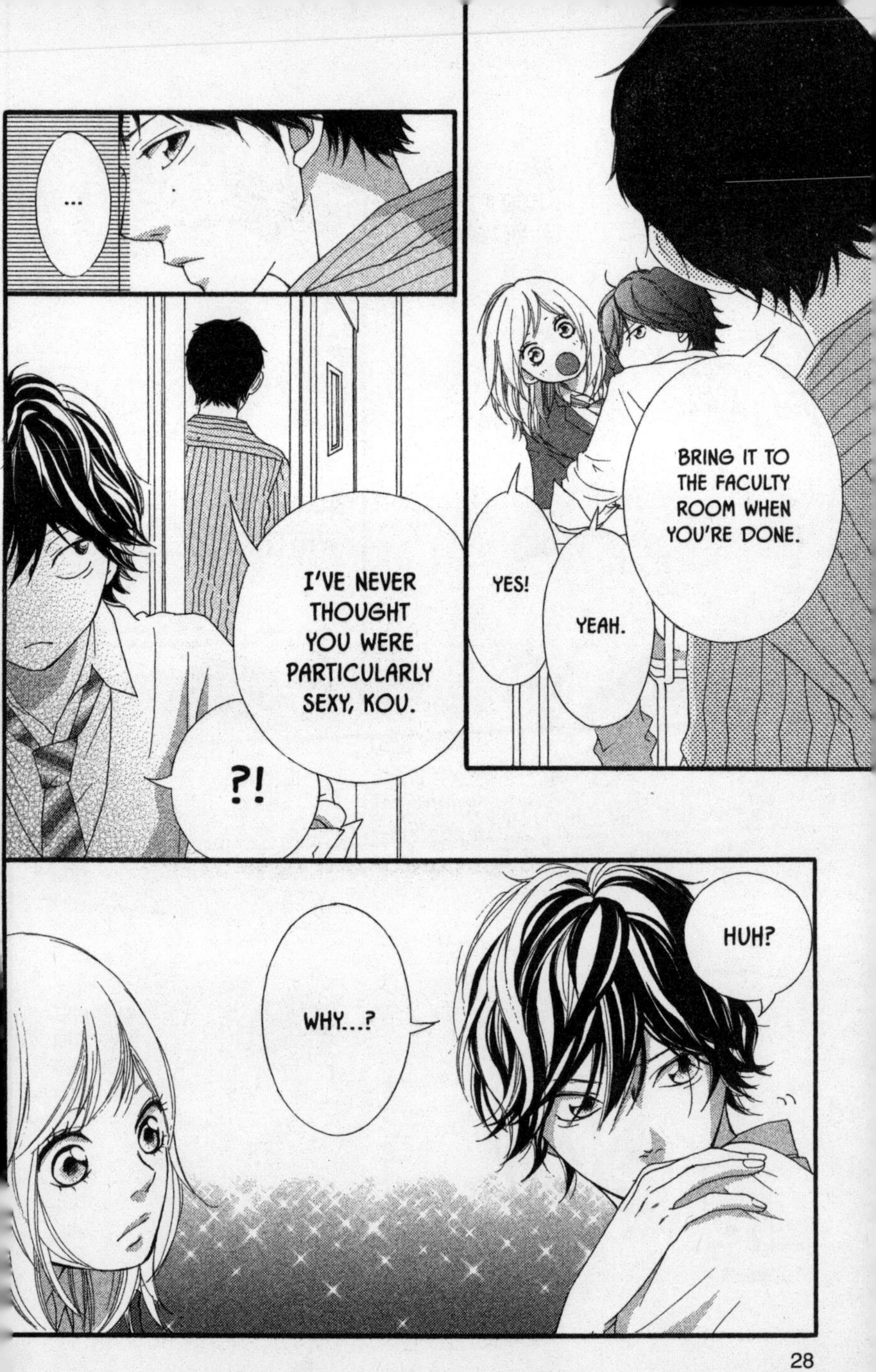
BRING IT TO THE FACULTY ROOM WHEN YOU'RE DONE.
YEAH.
YES!
...
I'VE NEVER THOUGHT YOU WERE PARTICULARLY SEXY, KOU.
?!
HUH?
WHY...?

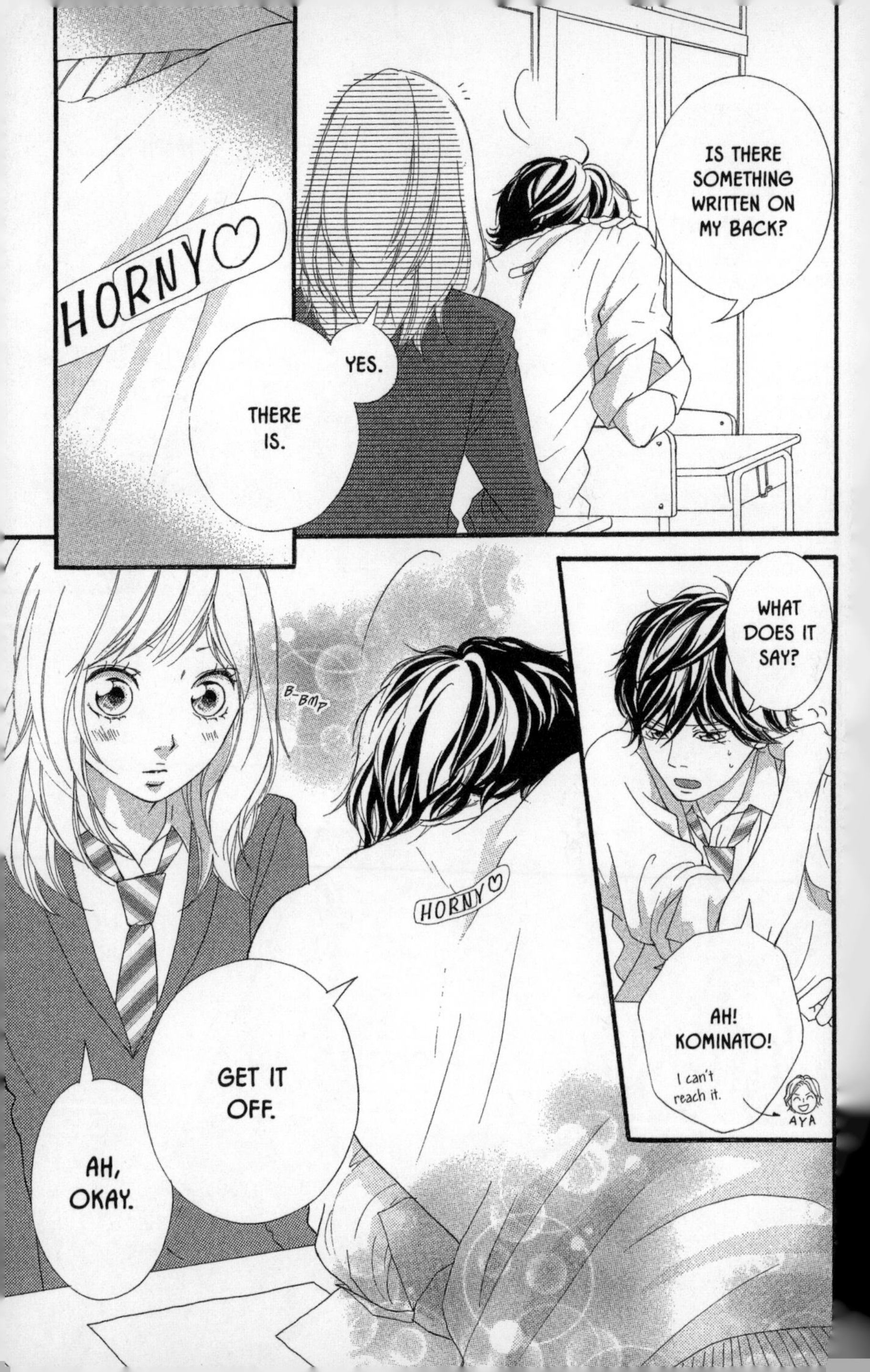
IS THERE SOMETHING WRITTEN ON MY BACK?
HORNY
YES.
THERE IS.
WHAT DOES IT SAY?
AH! KOMINATO!
I can't reach it.
AYA
B-BMP
HORNY
GET IT OFF.
AH, OKAY.

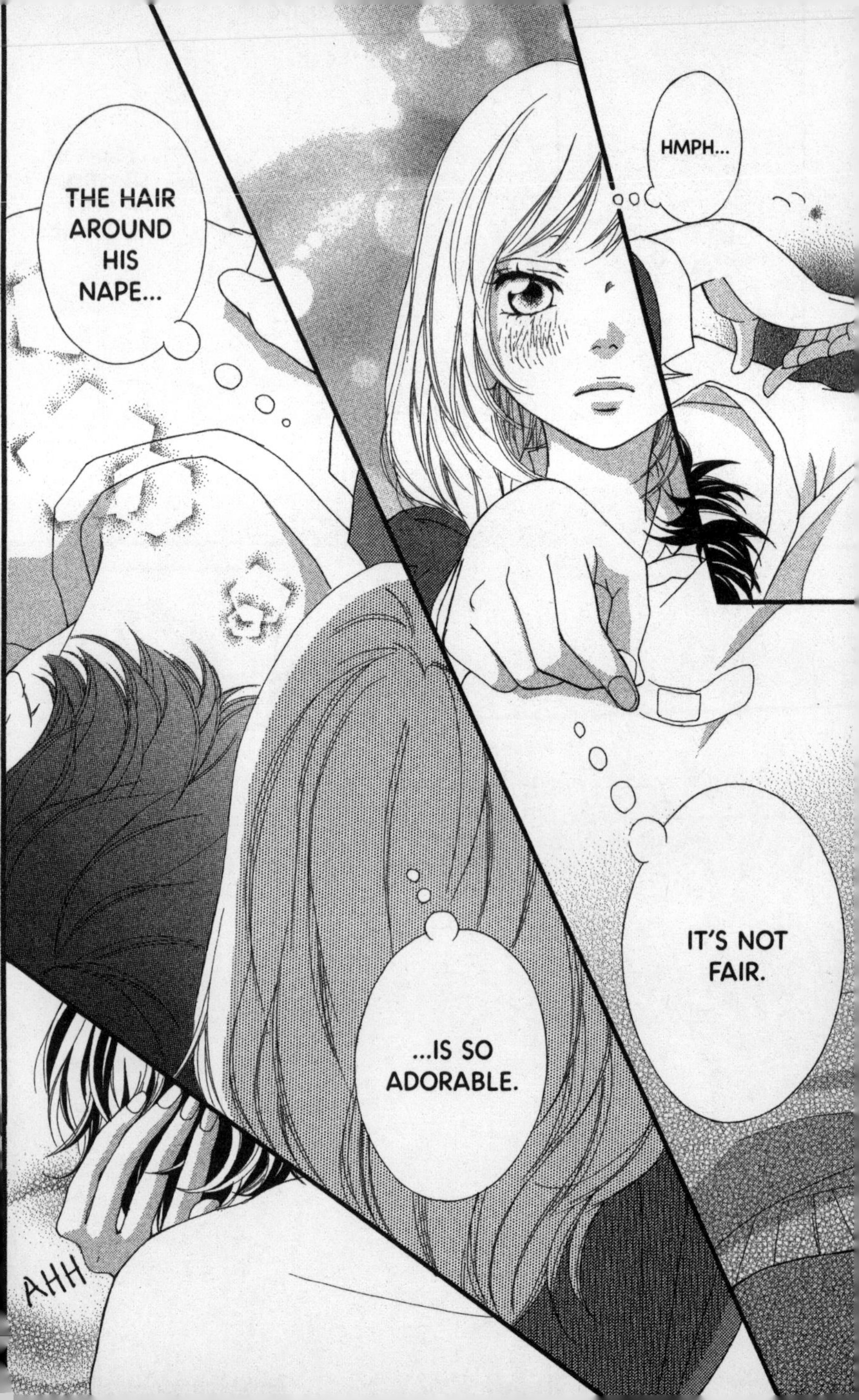
HMPH...
IT'S NOT FAIR.
THE HAIR AROUND HIS NAPE...
...IS SO ADORABLE.
AHH

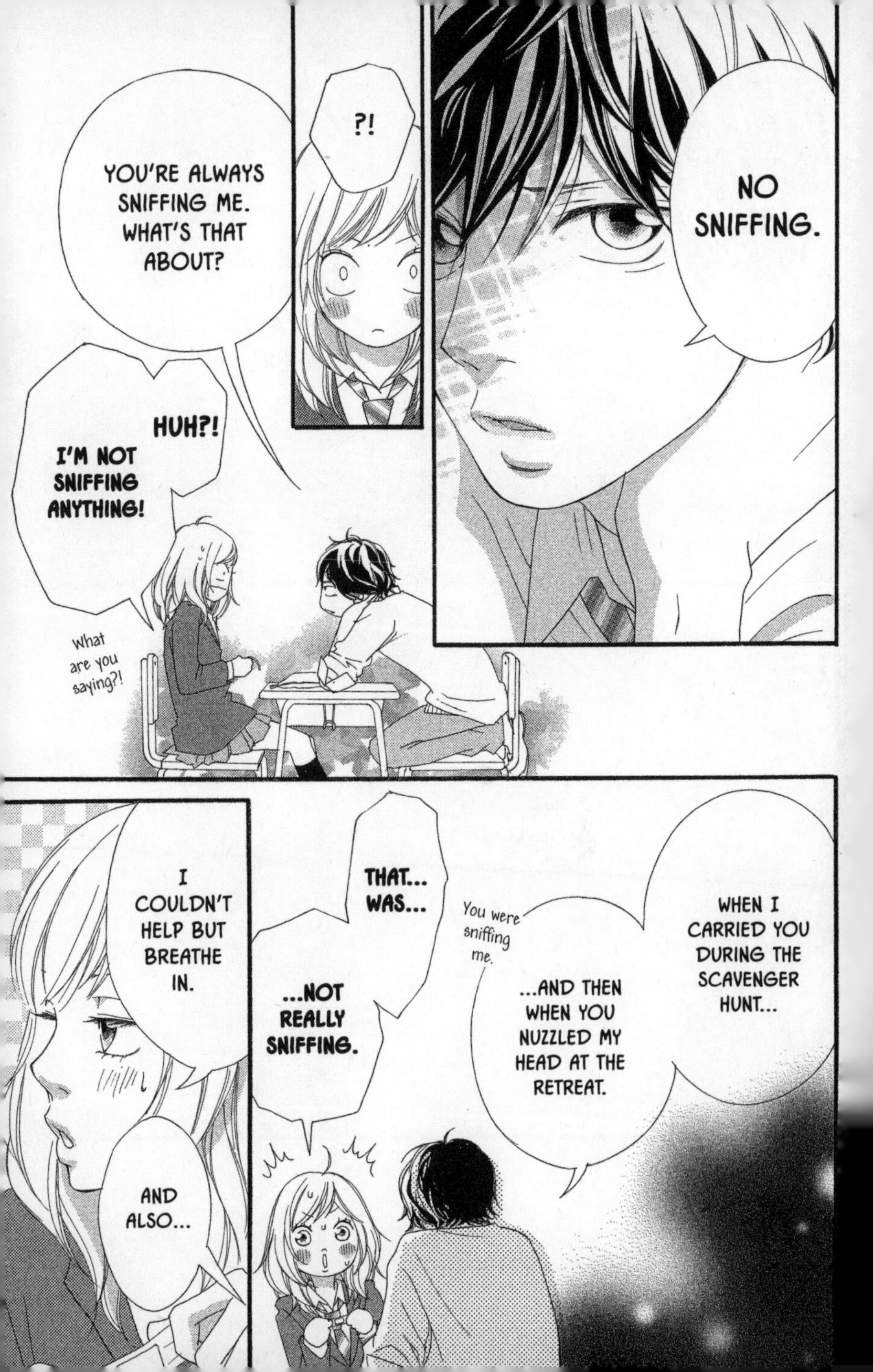
NO SNIFFING.
?!
YOU'RE ALWAYS SNIFFING ME. WHAT'S THAT ABOUT?
HUH?! I'M NOT SNIFFING ANYTHING!
What are you saying?!
WHEN I CARRIED YOU DURING THE SCAVENGER HUNT...
...AND THEN WHEN YOU NUZZLED MY HEAD AT THE RETREAT.
You were sniffing me.
THAT... WAS...
...NOT REALLY SNIFFING.
I COULDN'T HELP BUT BREATHE IN.
AND ALSO...

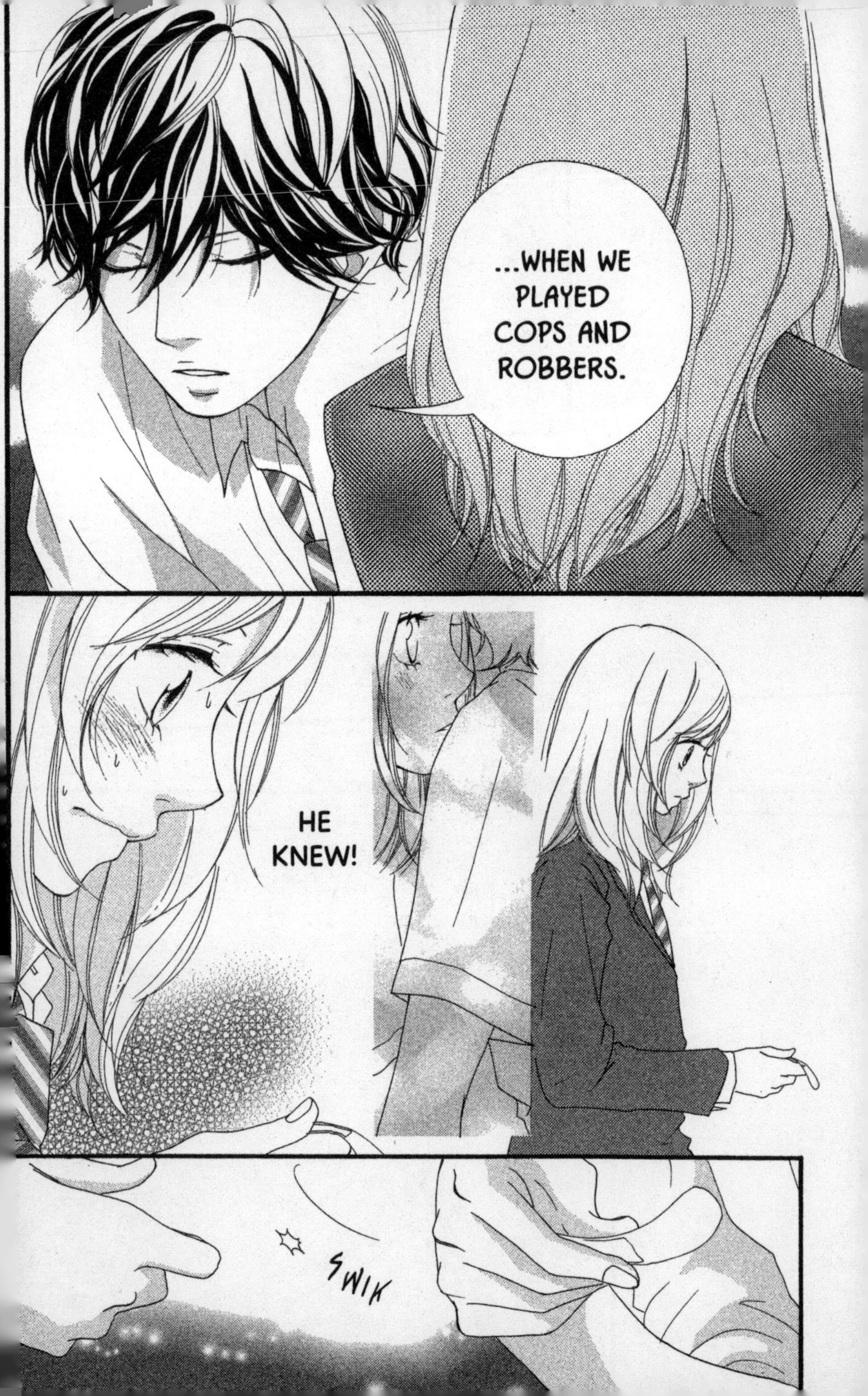
...WHEN WE PLAYED COPS AND ROBBERS.
HE KNEW!
SWIK

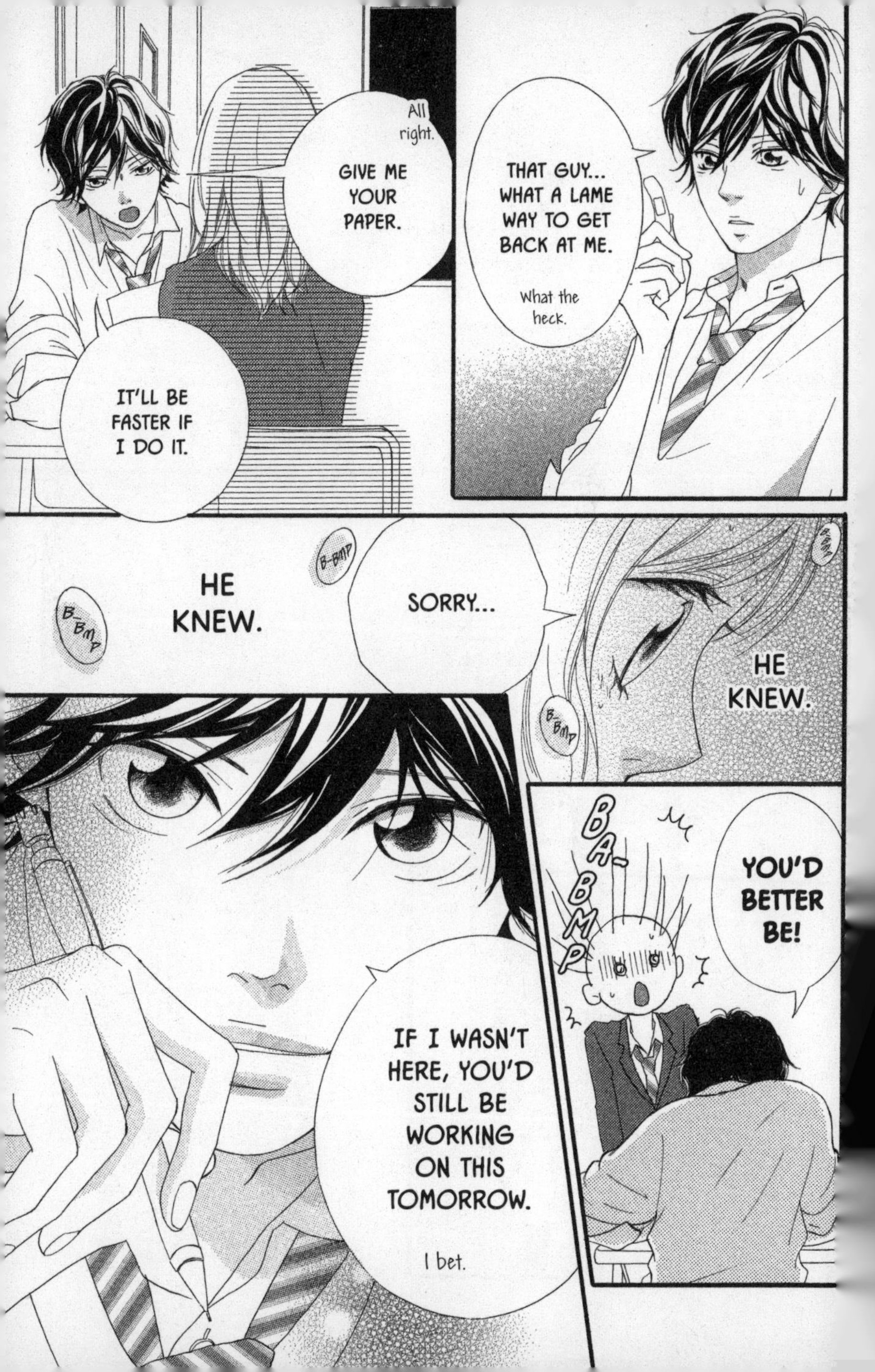
THAT GUY... WHAT A LAME WAY TO GET BACK AT ME.
What the heck.
All right.
GIVE ME YOUR PAPER.
IT'LL BE FASTER IF I DO IT.
HE KNEW.
B-BMP
SORRY...
B-BMP
HE KNEW.
B-BMP
BA-BMP
YOU'D BETTER BE!
IF I WASN'T HERE, YOU'D STILL BE WORKING ON THIS TOMORROW.
I bet.

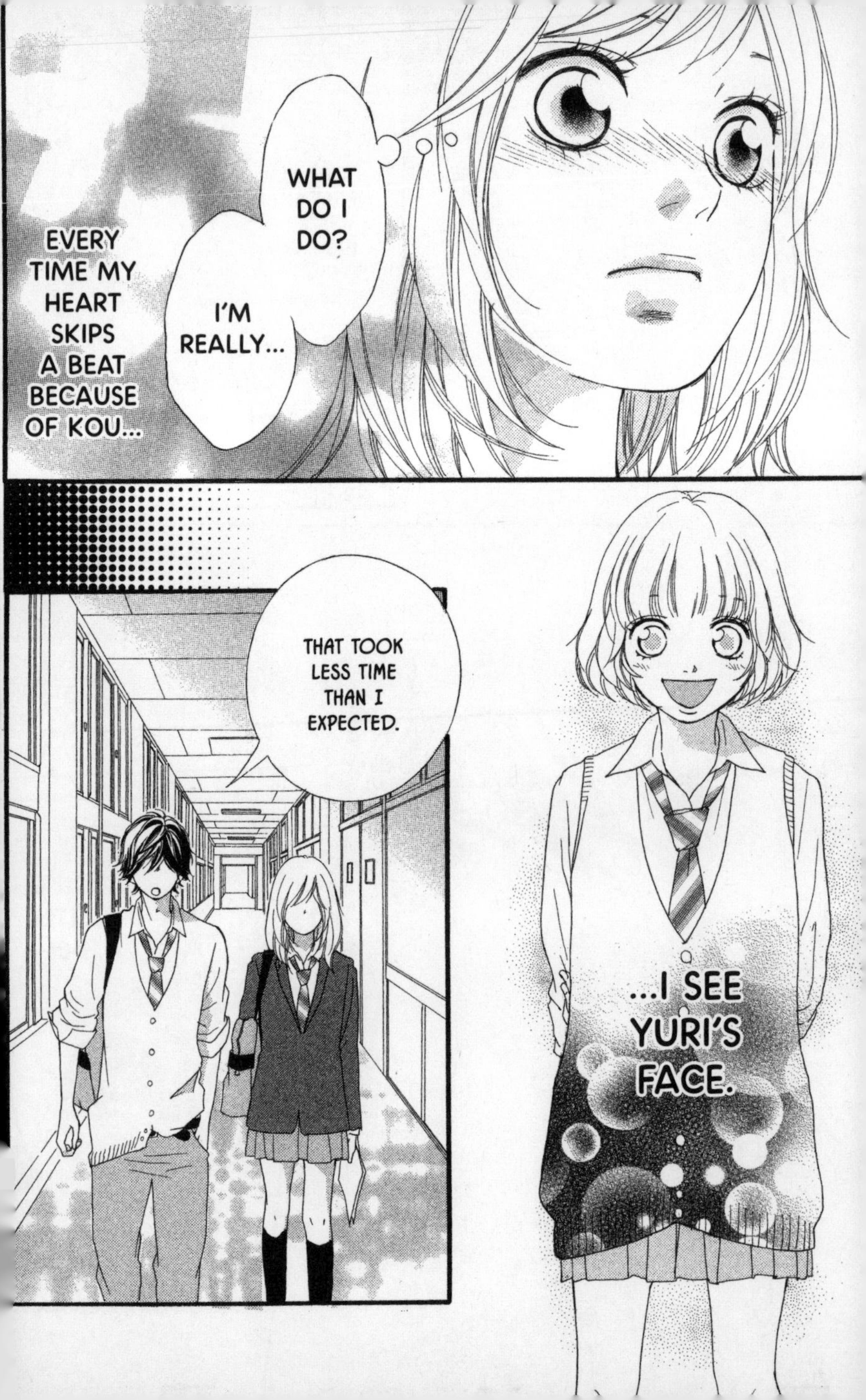
WHAT DO I DO?
I'M REALLY...
EVERY TIME MY HEART SKIPS A BEAT BECAUSE OF KOU...
...I SEE YURI'S FACE.
THAT TOOK LESS TIME THAN I EXPECTED.

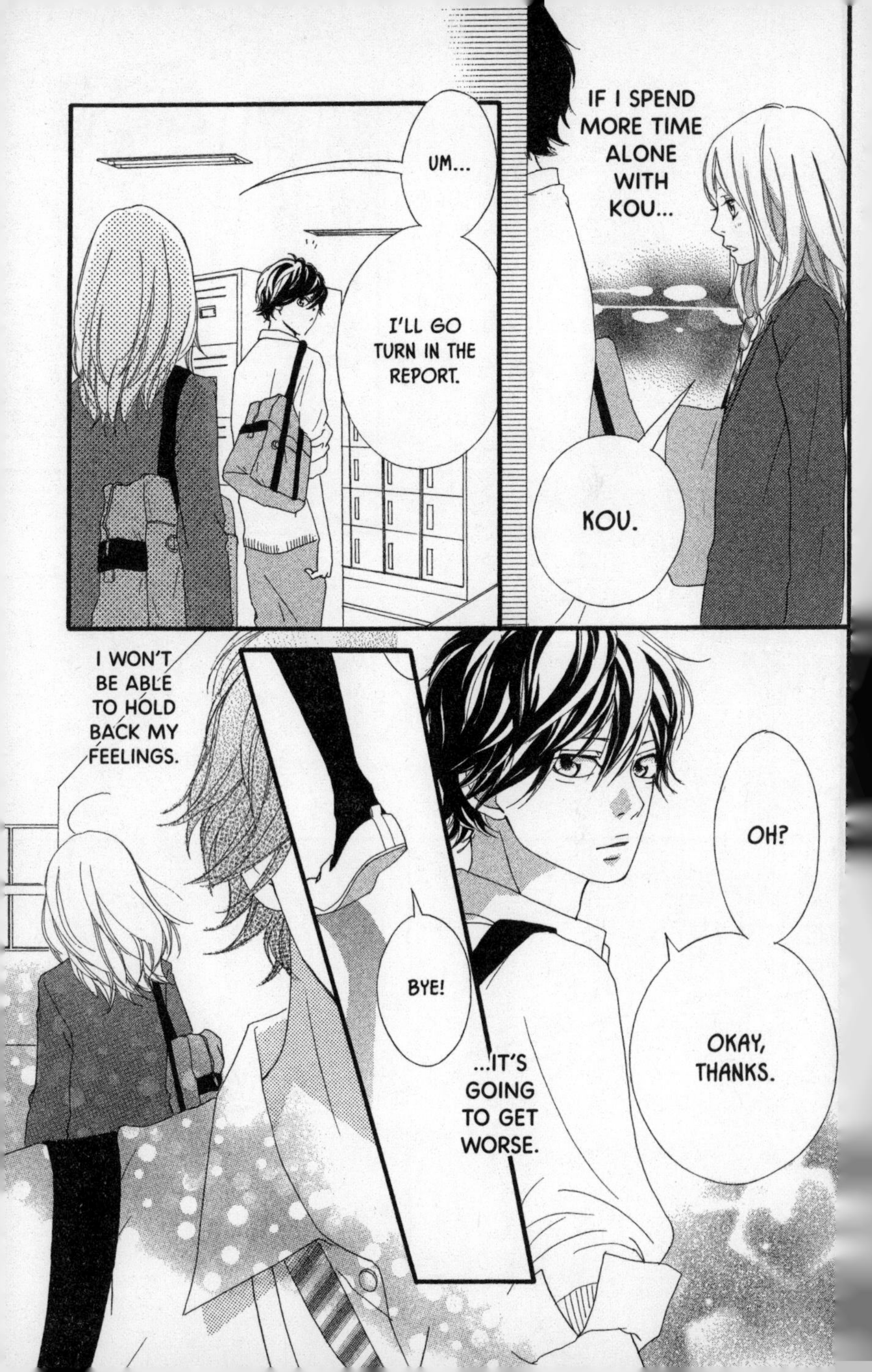
IF I SPEND MORE TIME ALONE WITH KOU...
KOU.
UM...
I'LL GO TURN IN THE REPORT.
OH?
OKAY, THANKS.
BYE!
...IT'S GOING TO GET WORSE.
I WON'T BE ABLE TO HOLD BACK MY FEELINGS.

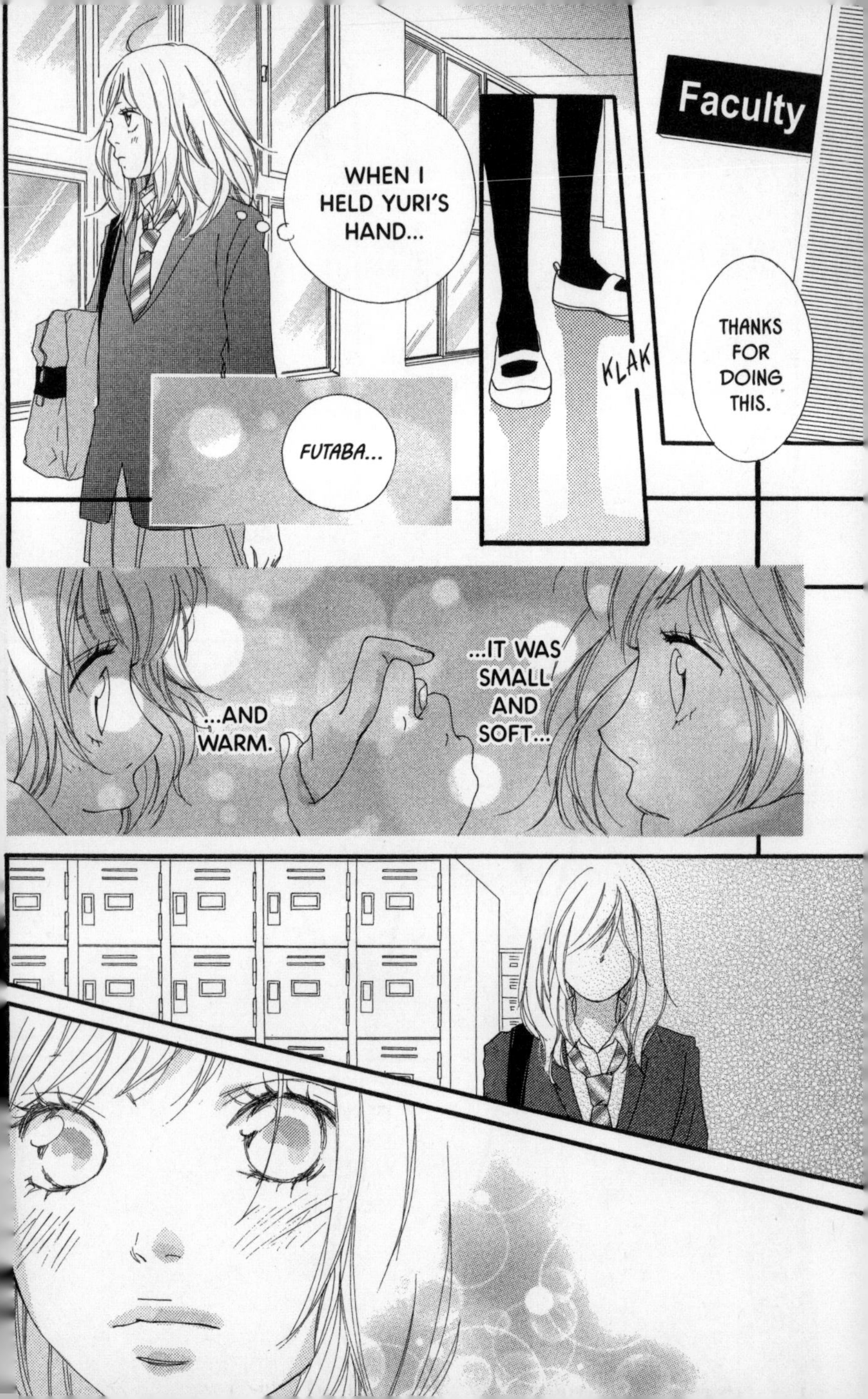
Faculty
THANKS FOR DOING THIS.
KLAK
WHEN I HELD YURI'S HAND...
FUTABA...
...IT WAS SMALL AND SOFT...
...AND WARM.

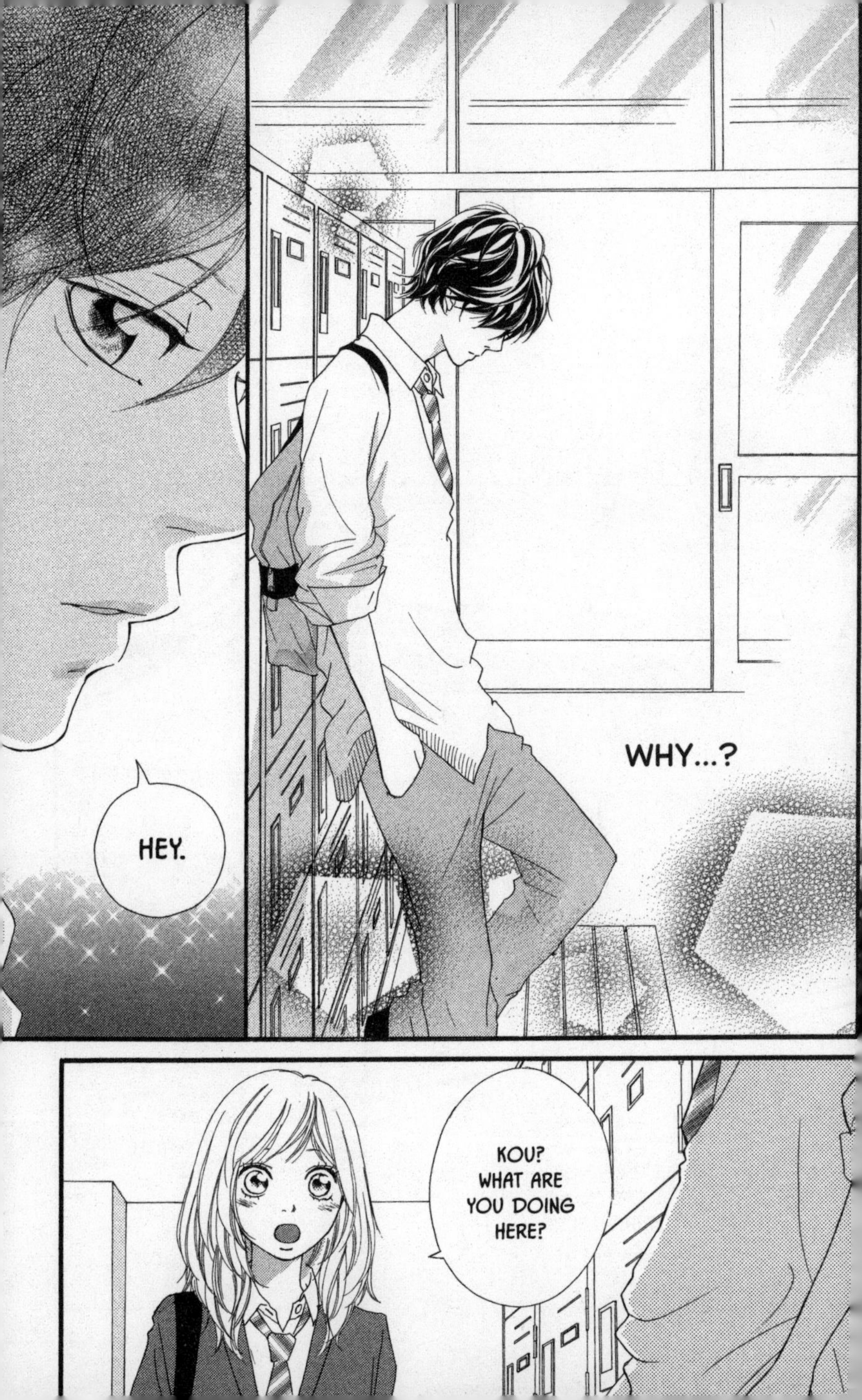
WHY...?
HEY.
KOU? WHAT ARE YOU DOING HERE?

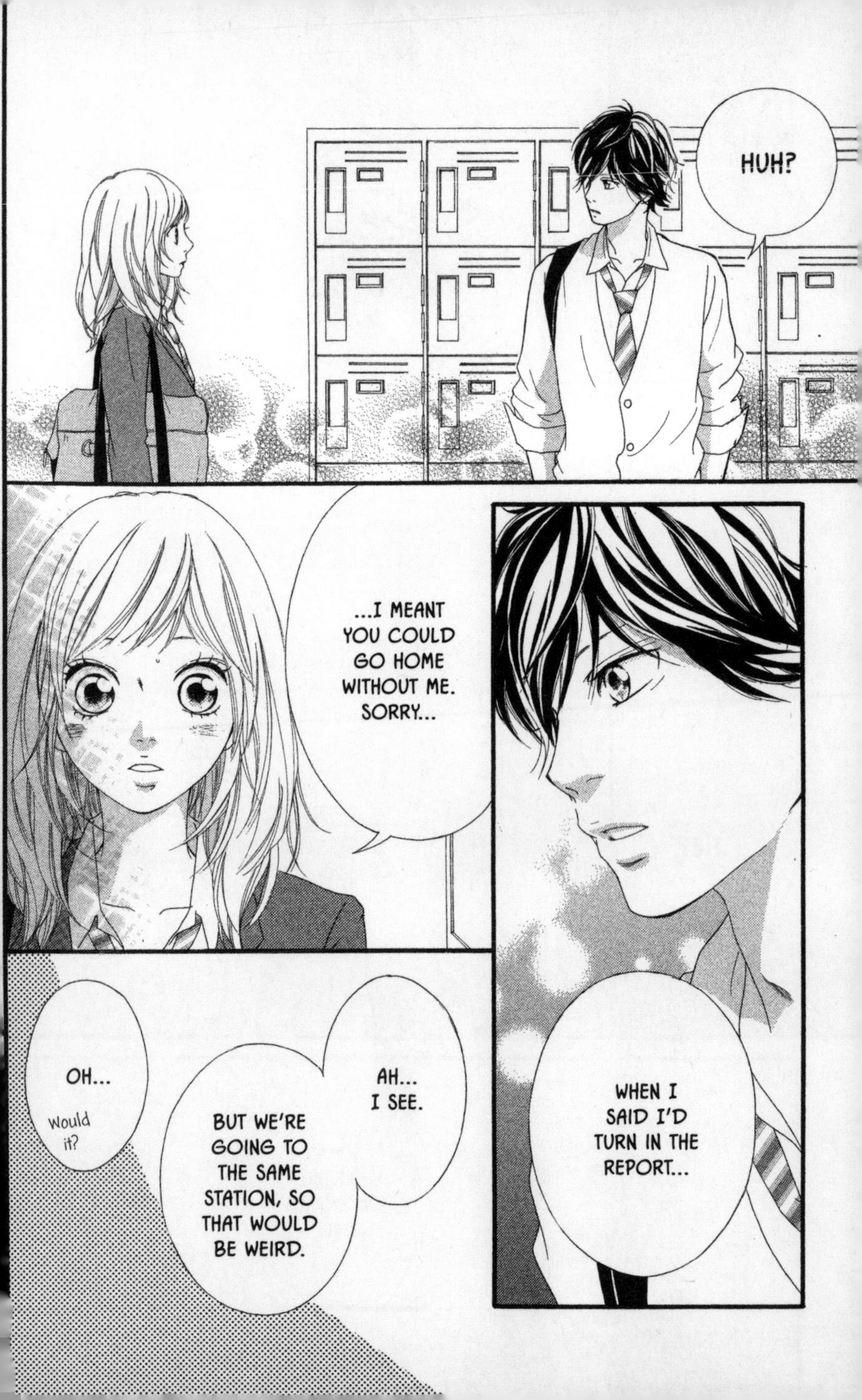
HUH?
WHEN I SAID I'D TURN IN THE REPORT...
...I MEANT YOU COULD GO HOME WITHOUT ME. SORRY...
AH... I SEE.
BUT WE'RE GOING TO THE SAME STATION, SO THAT WOULD BE WEIRD.
OH...
Would it?

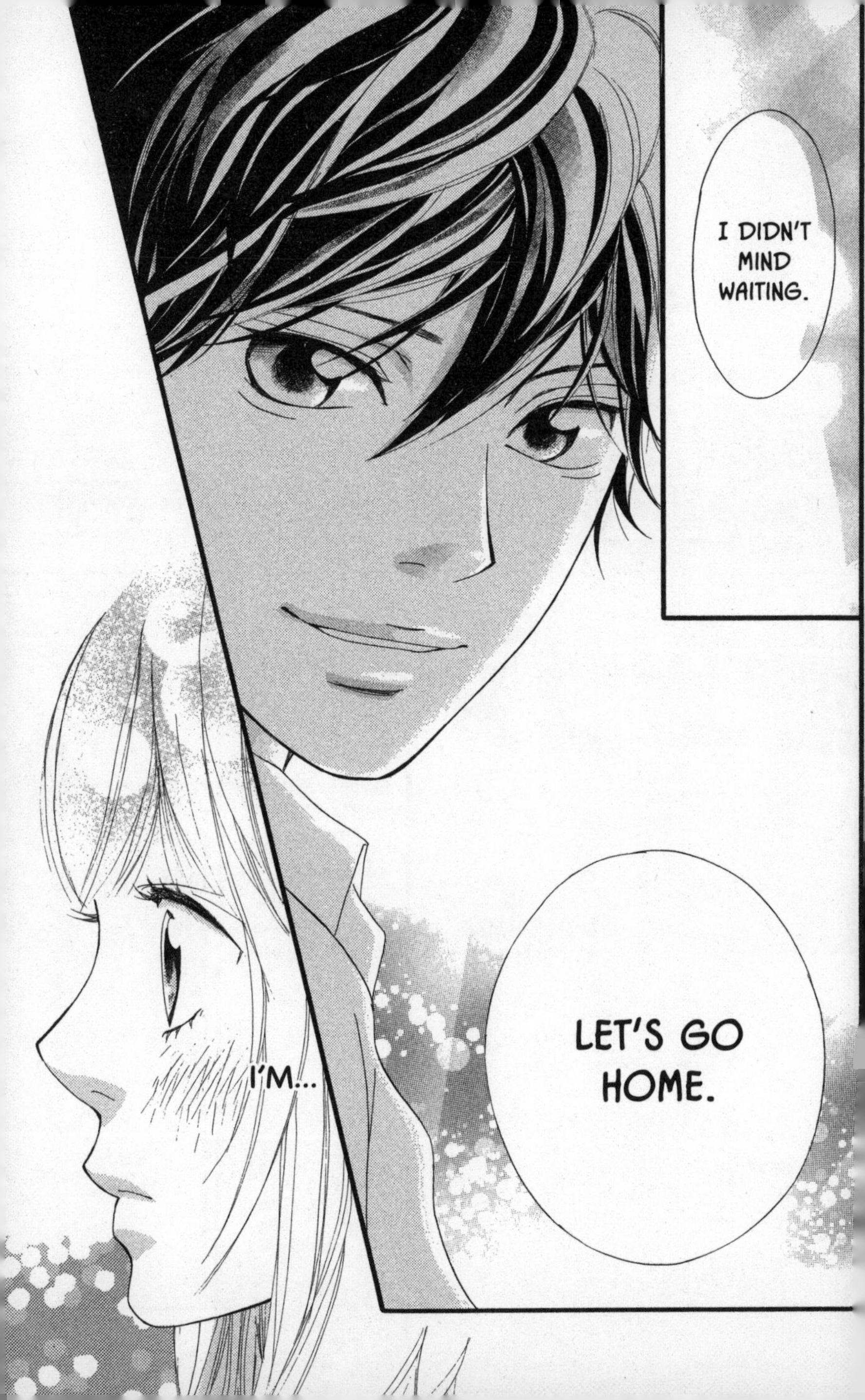
I DIDN'T MIND WAITING.
LET'S GO HOME.
I'M...

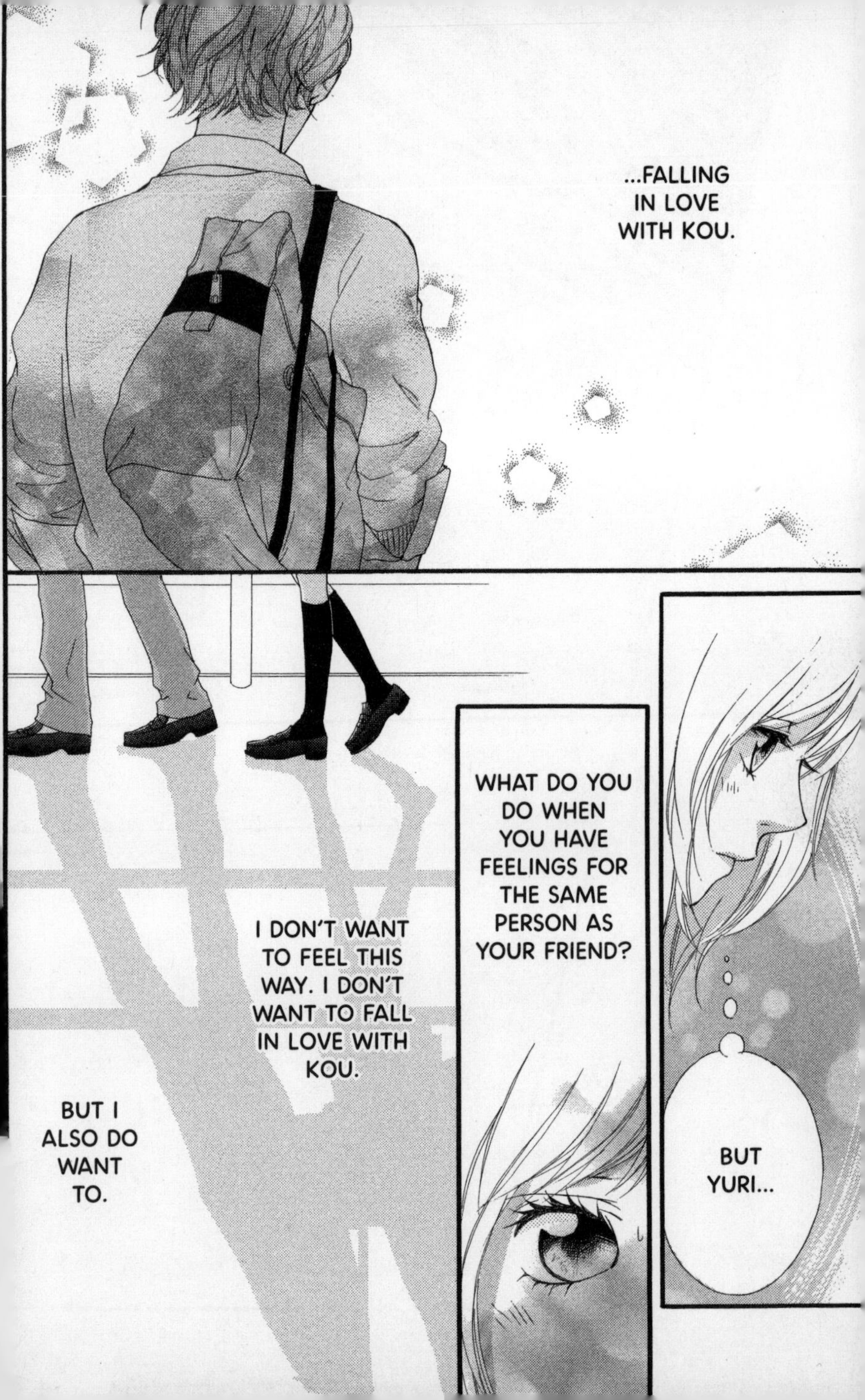
...FALLING IN LOVE WITH KOU.
BUT YURI...
WHAT DO YOU DO WHEN YOU HAVE FEELINGS FOR THE SAME PERSON AS YOUR FRIEND?
I DON'T WANT TO FEEL THIS WAY. I DON'T WANT TO FALL IN LOVE WITH KOU.
BUT I ALSO DO WANT TO.

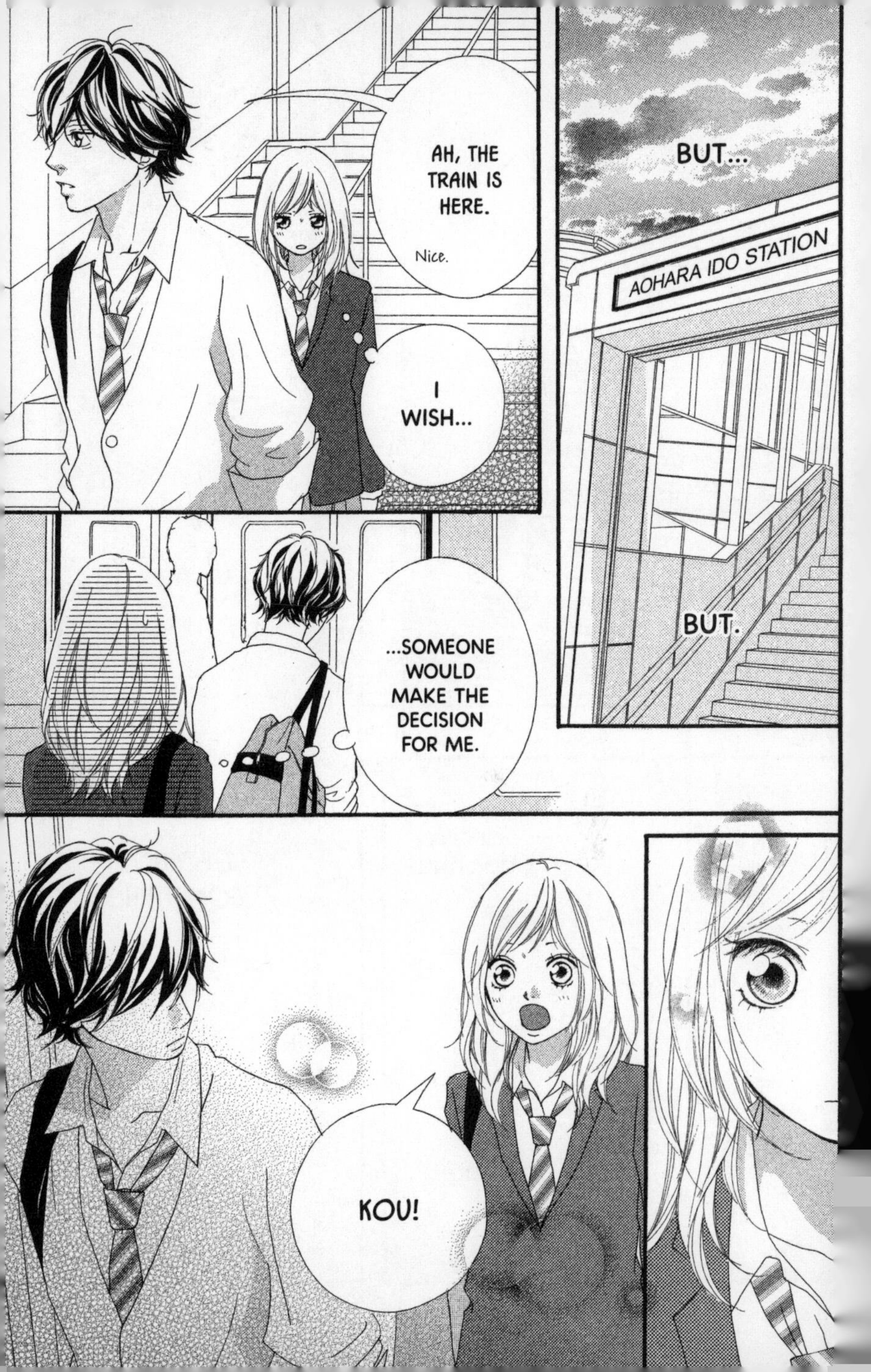
BUT...
AOHARA IDO STATION
BUT.
AH, THE TRAIN IS HERE.
Nice.
I WISH...
...SOMEONE WOULD MAKE THE DECISION FOR ME.
KOU!

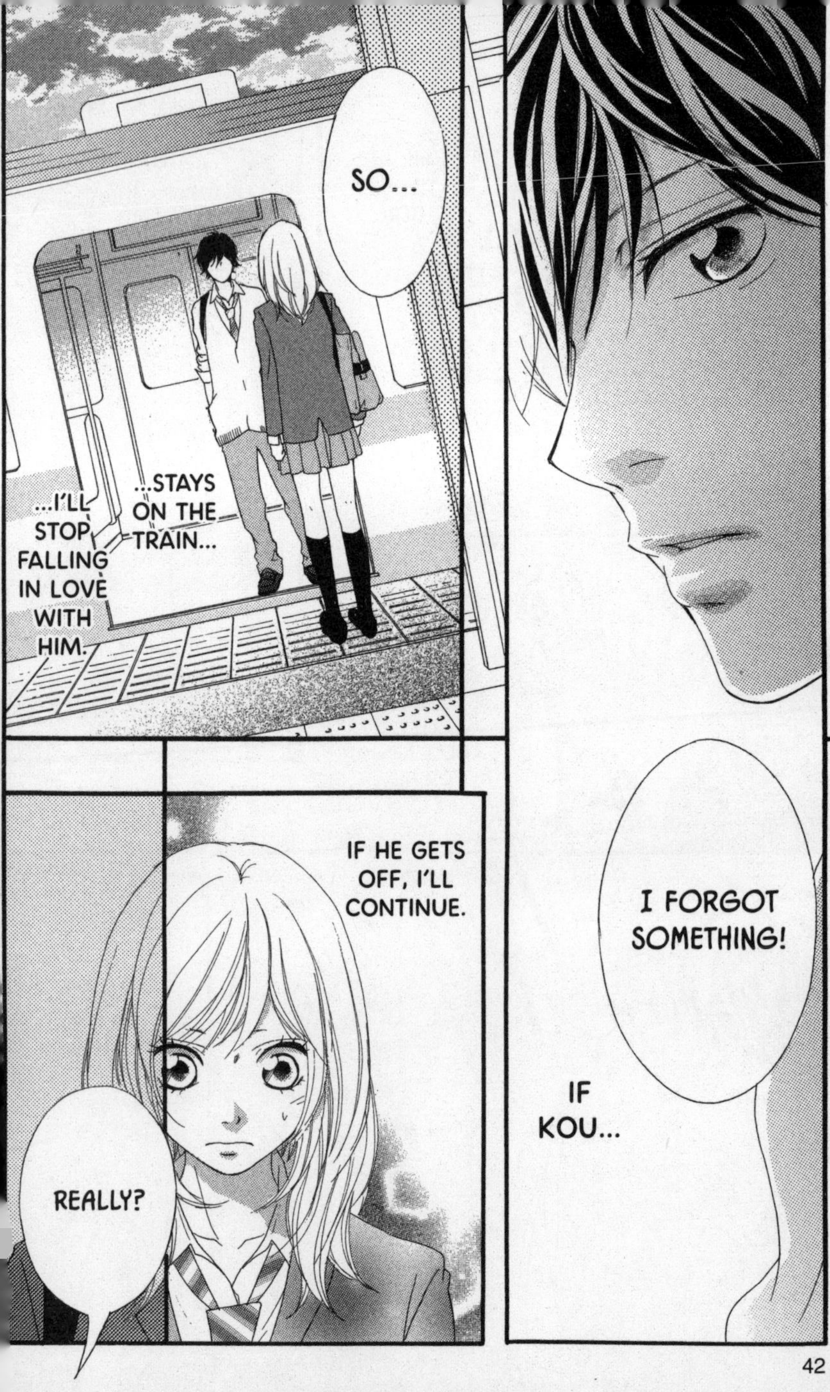
I FORGOT SOMETHING!
IF KOU...
SO...
...STAYS ON THE TRAIN...
...I'LL STOP FALLING IN LOVE WITH HIM.
IF HE GETS OFF, I'LL CONTINUE.
REALLY?

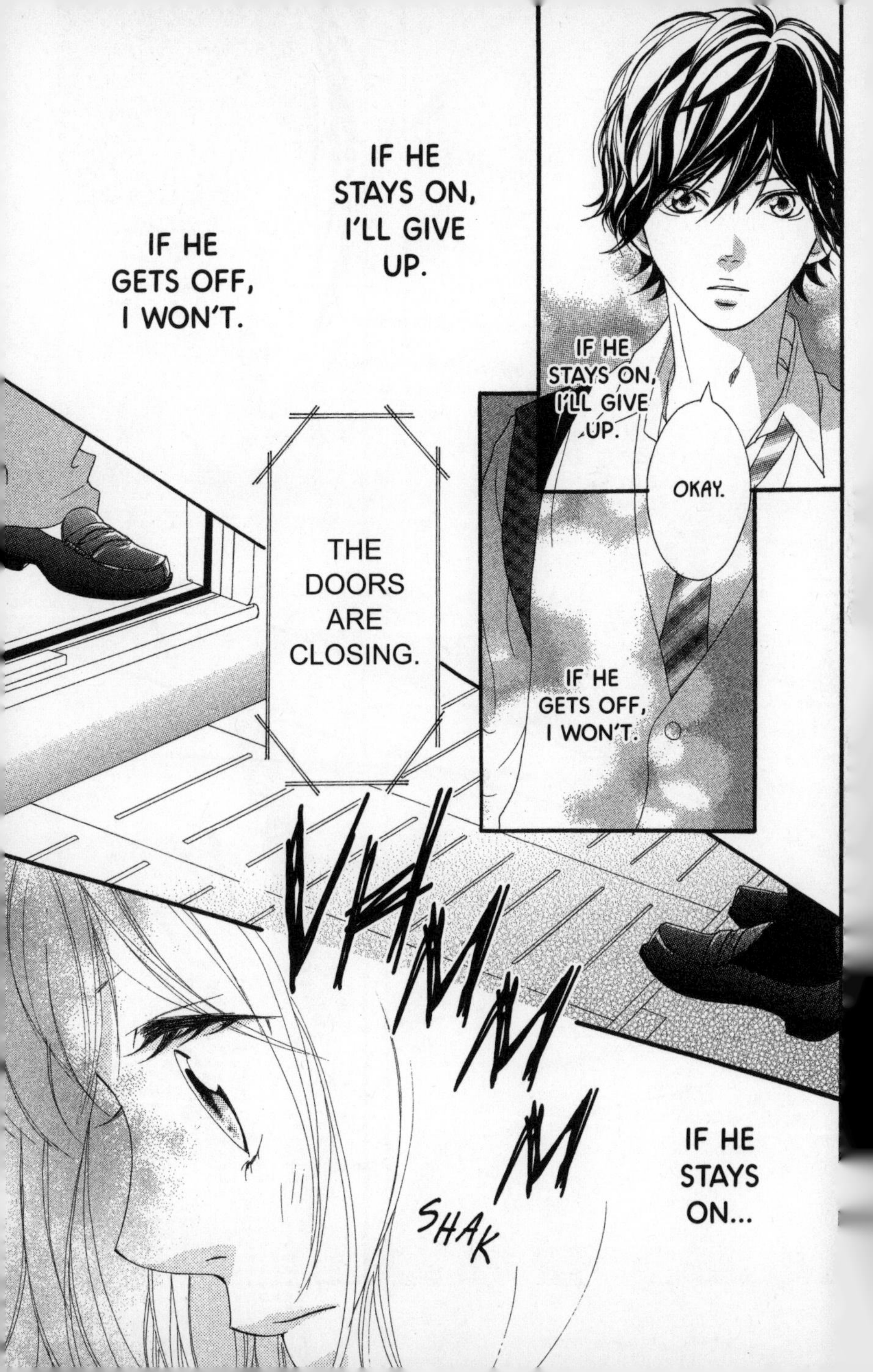
IF HE STAYS ON, I'LL GIVE UP.
OKAY.
IF HE GETS OFF, I WON'T.
IF HE STAYS ON, I'LL GIVE UP.
IF HE GETS OFF, I WON'T.
THE DOORS ARE CLOSING.
VHMMM
SHAK
IF HE STAYS ON...

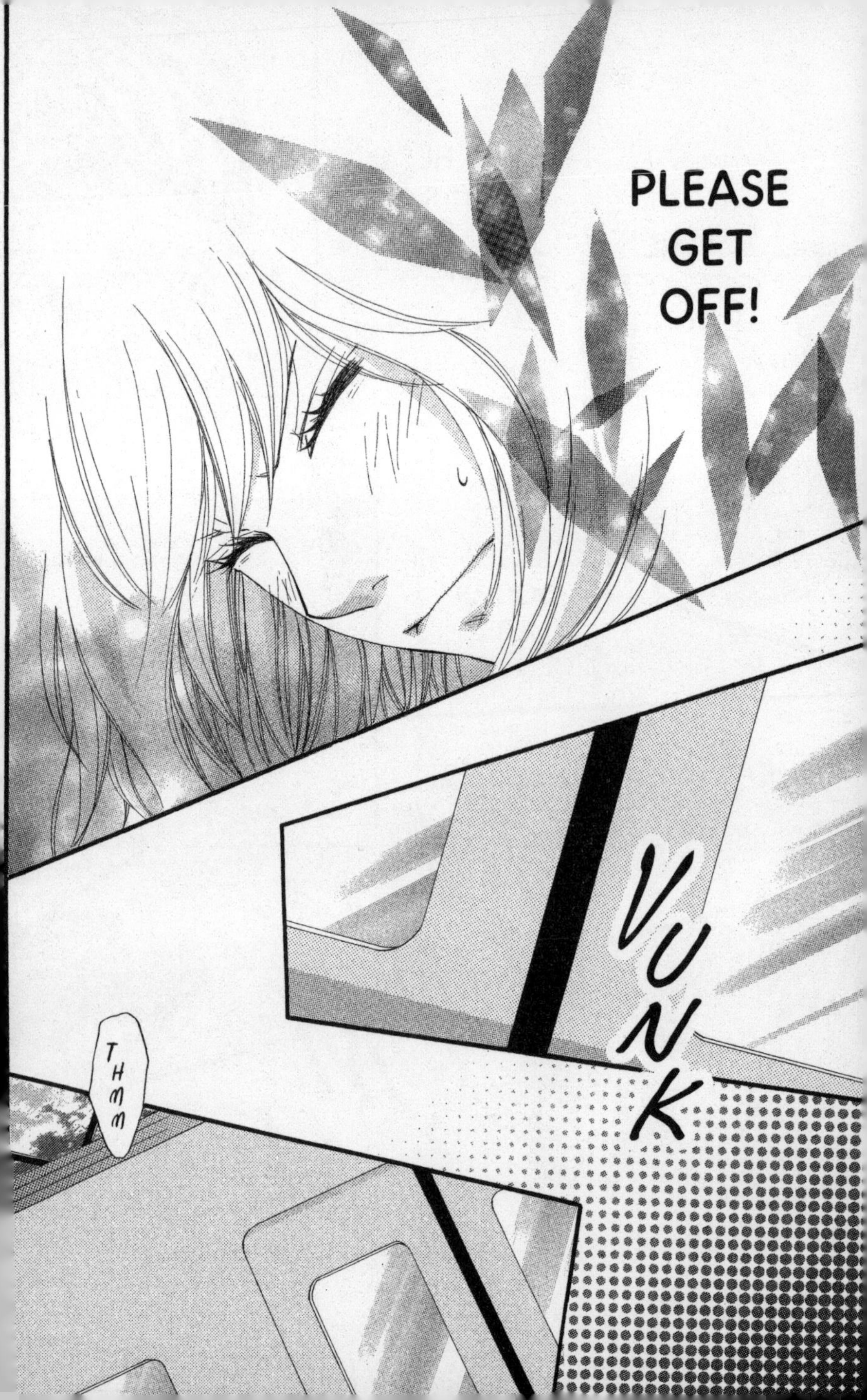
PLEASE GET OFF!
VUNK
THMM

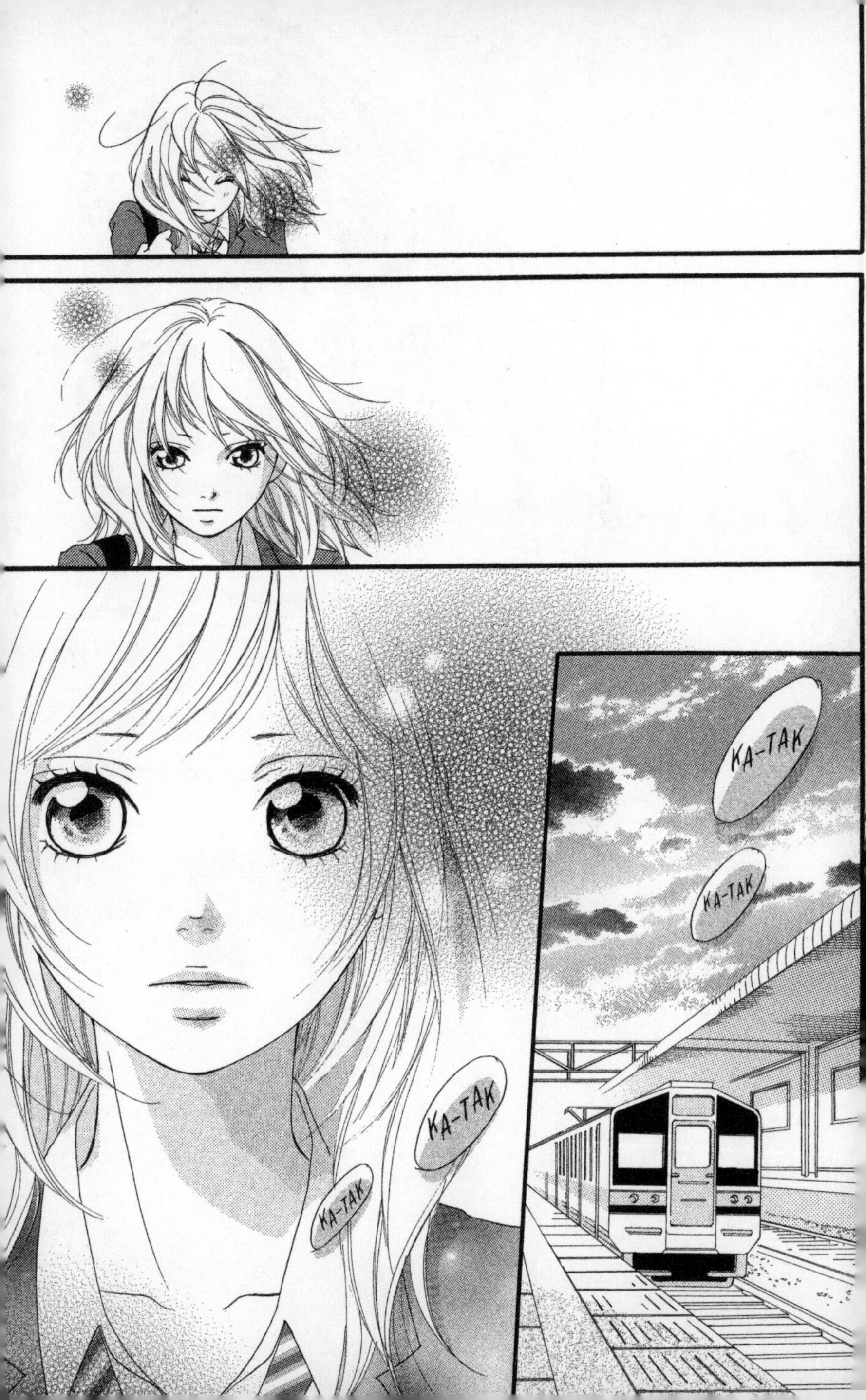
KA-TAK
KA-TAK
KA-TAK
KA-TAK

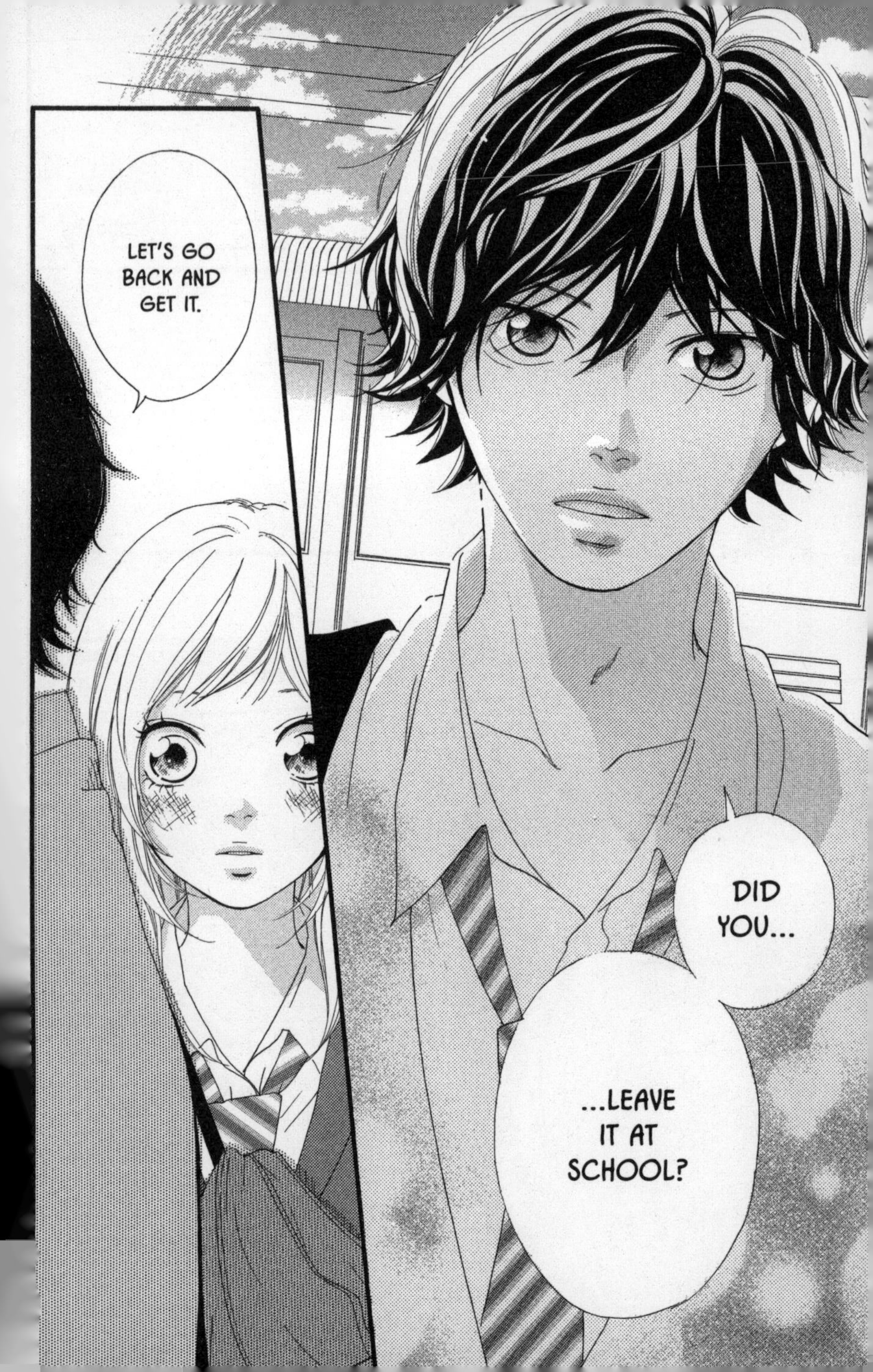
DID YOU...
...LEAVE IT AT SCHOOL?
LET'S GO BACK AND GET IT.

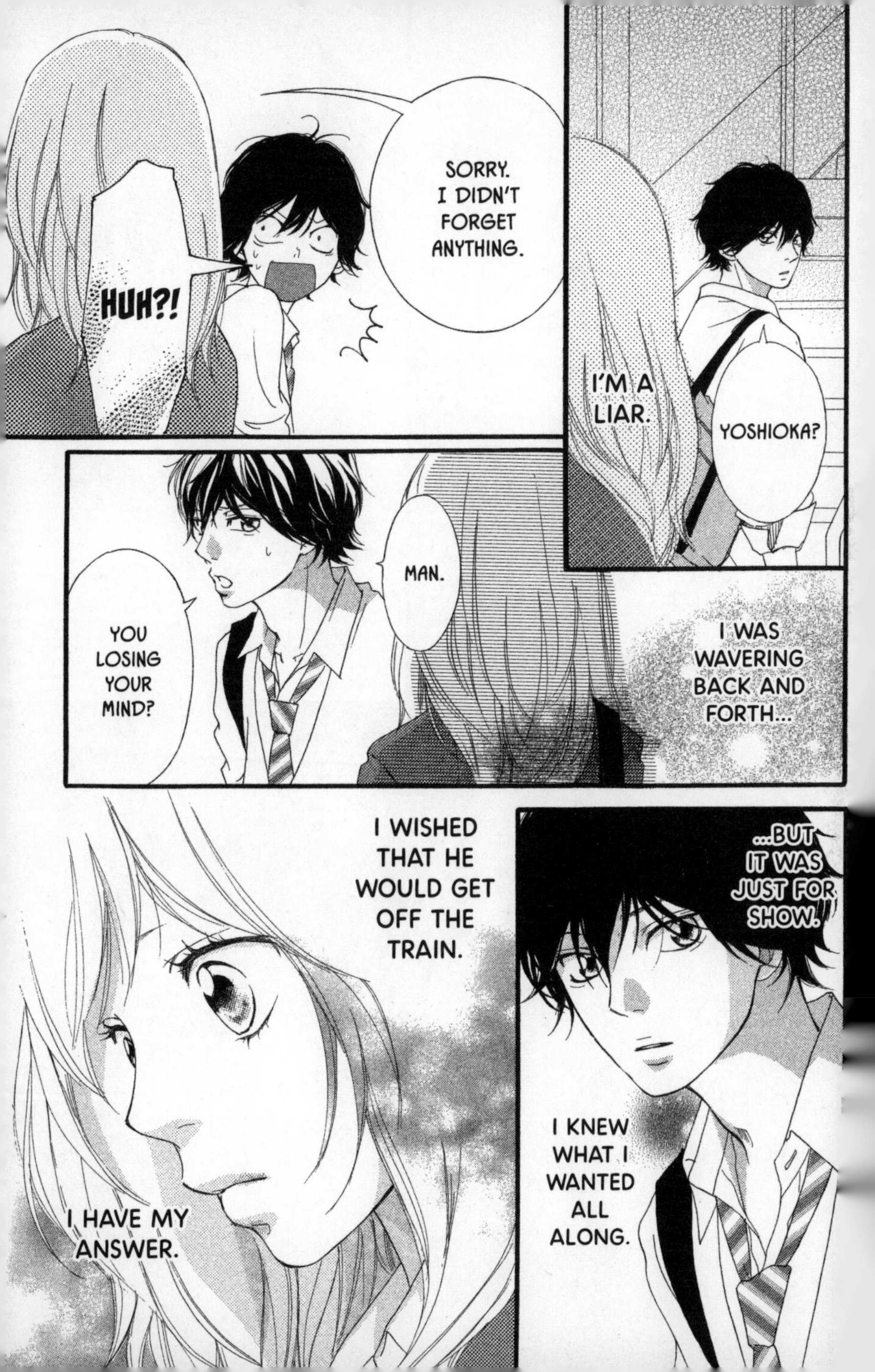
YOSHIOKA?
I'M A LIAR.
SORRY. I DIDN'T FORGET ANYTHING.
HUH?!
I WAS WAVERING BACK AND FORTH...
MAN.
YOU LOSING YOUR MIND?
...BUT IT WAS JUST FOR SHOW.
I KNEW WHAT I WANTED ALL ALONG.
I WISHED THAT HE WOULD GET OFF THE TRAIN.
I HAVE MY ANSWER.

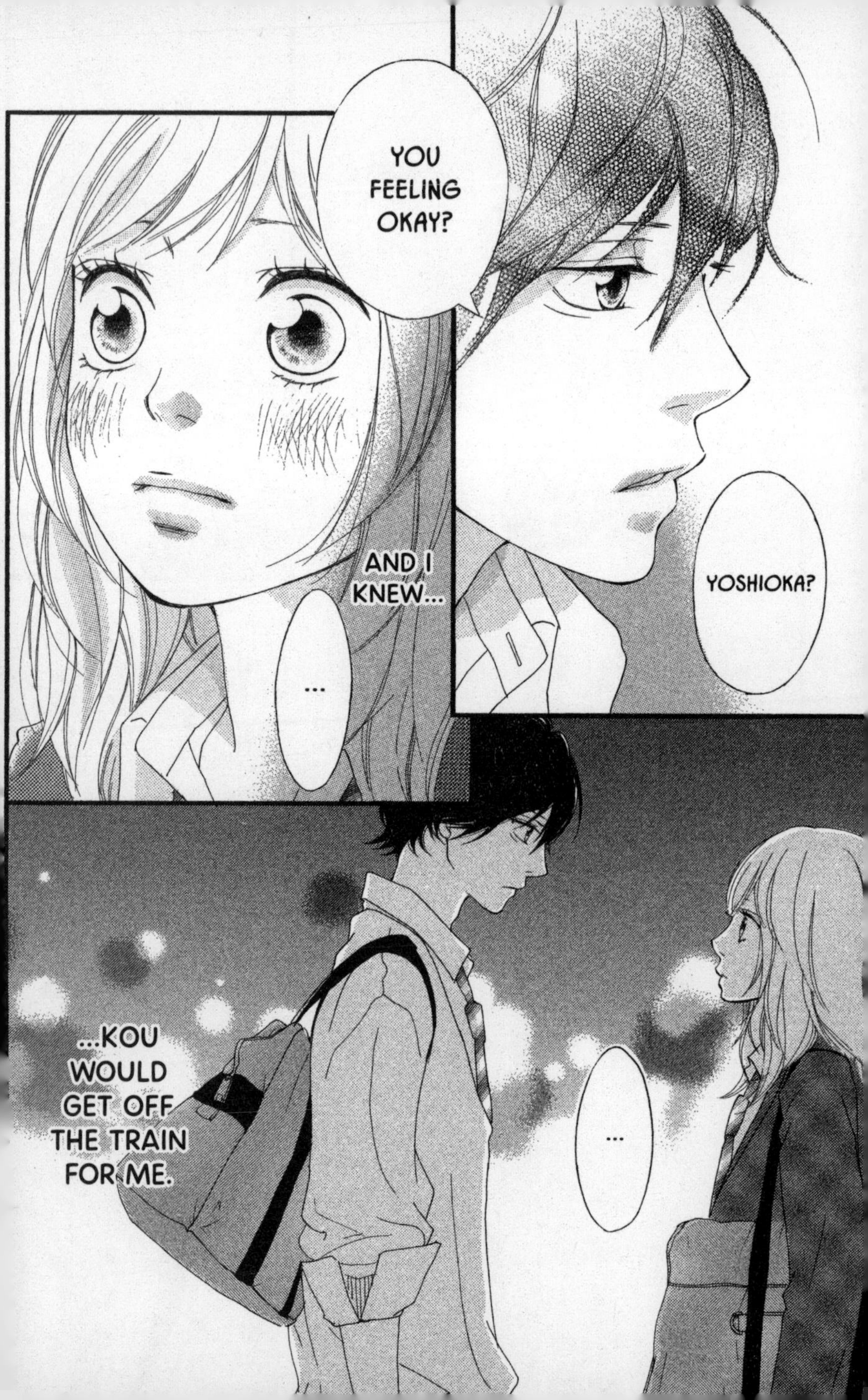
YOU FEELING OKAY?
YOSHIOKA?
AND I KNEW...
...
...
...KOU WOULD GET OFF THE TRAIN FOR ME.

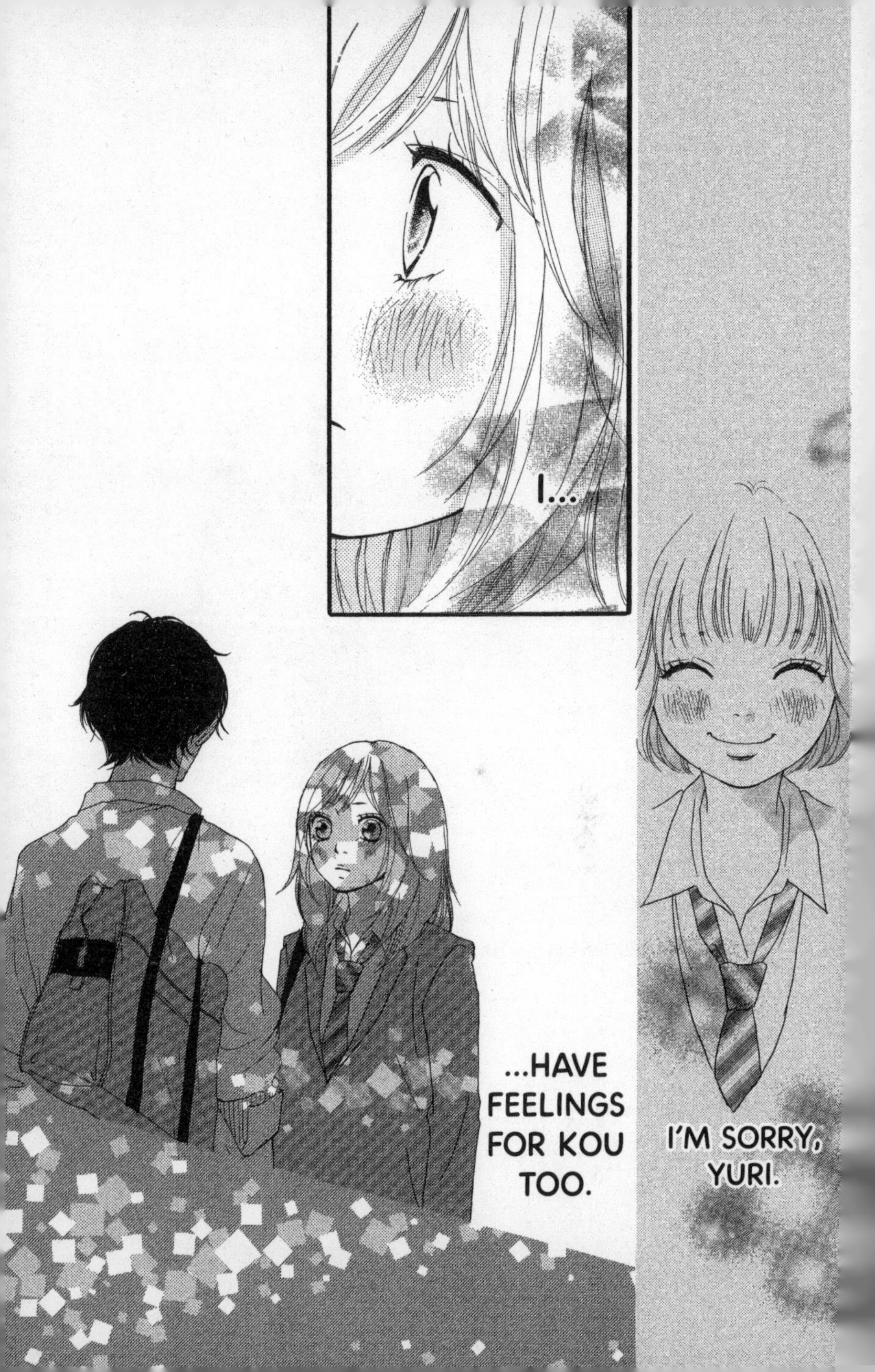

I'M SORRY, YURI.
I...
...HAVE FEELINGS FOR KOU TOO.

AO HARU RIDE CHARACTERS ❸

Yuri Makita

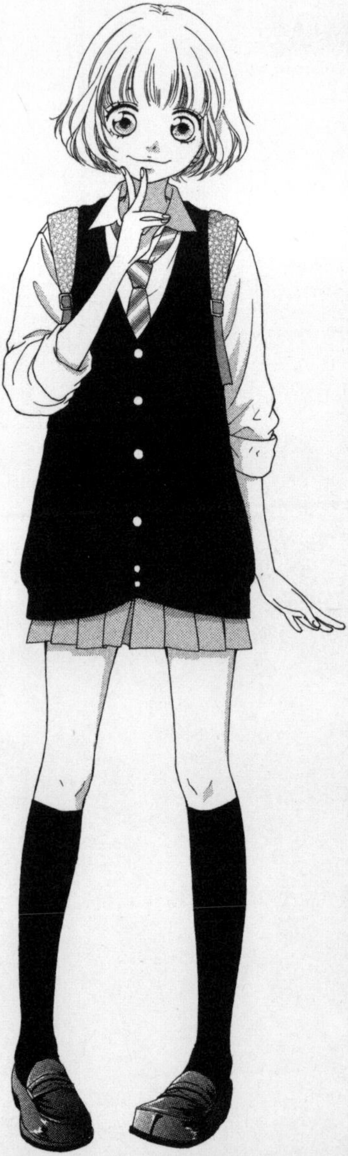

- **Birthday:**
  September 10th
- **Astrological Sign, Blood Type:**
  Virgo, type B
- **Height, Weight:**
  5'1", 97 lbs.
- **Favorite Subject:**
  Japanese
- **Least Favorite Subject:**
  Physical education
- **Favorite Food:**
  Lasagna
- **Least Favorite Food:**
  Raisins
- **Favorite Music:**
  NEGOTO
- **Siblings:**
  Younger brother
- **Age When First Crush Happened:**
  Age 4
- **Fun Fact:**
  I've never had a cavity.
- **Favorite Snack:**
  Haribo
- **Favorite Drink:**
  Milk tea
- **Favorite Color:**
  Pink

Ao Haru Ride

The scent of air after rain...
In the light around us, I felt your heartbeat.

CHAPTER 9

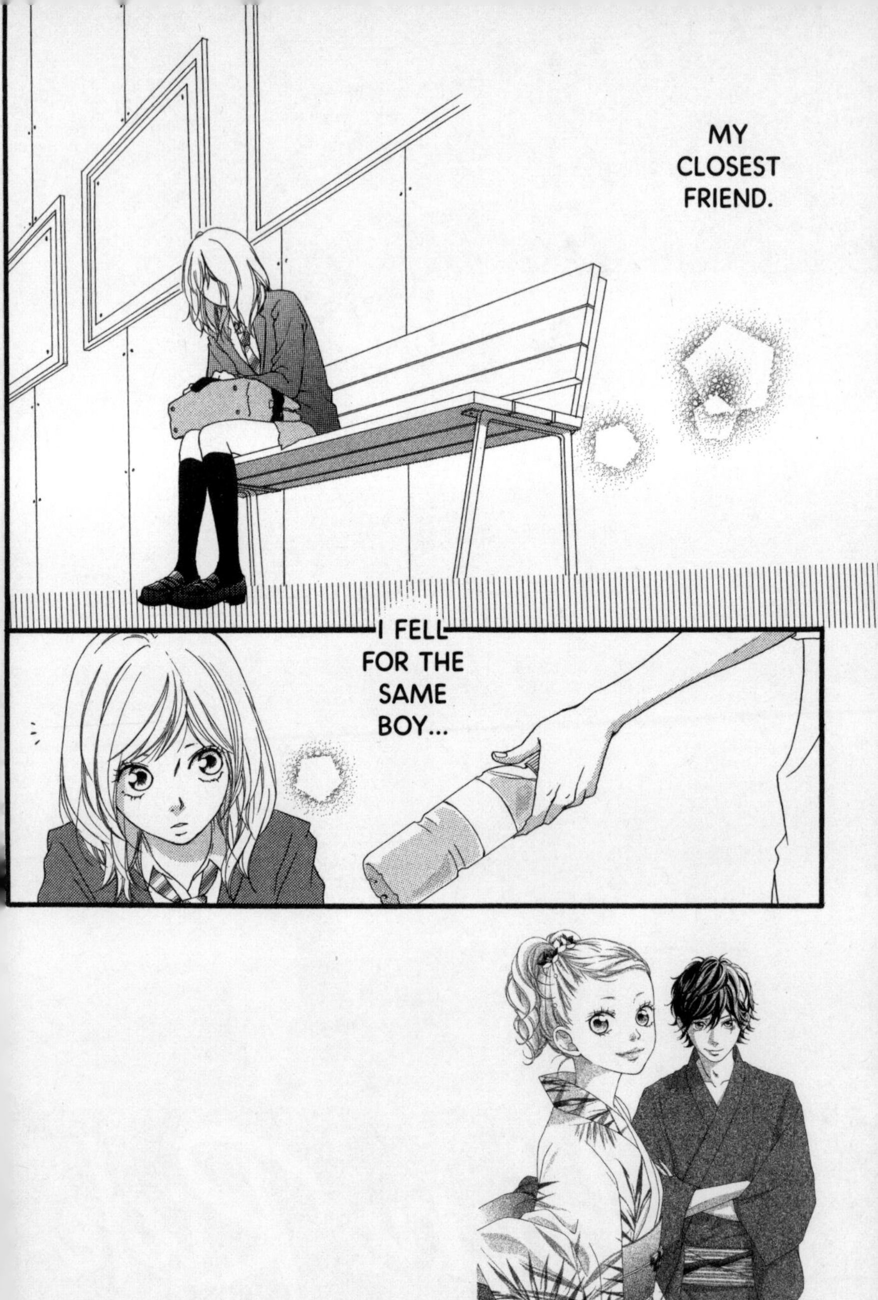
MY CLOSEST FRIEND.
I FELL FOR THE SAME BOY...

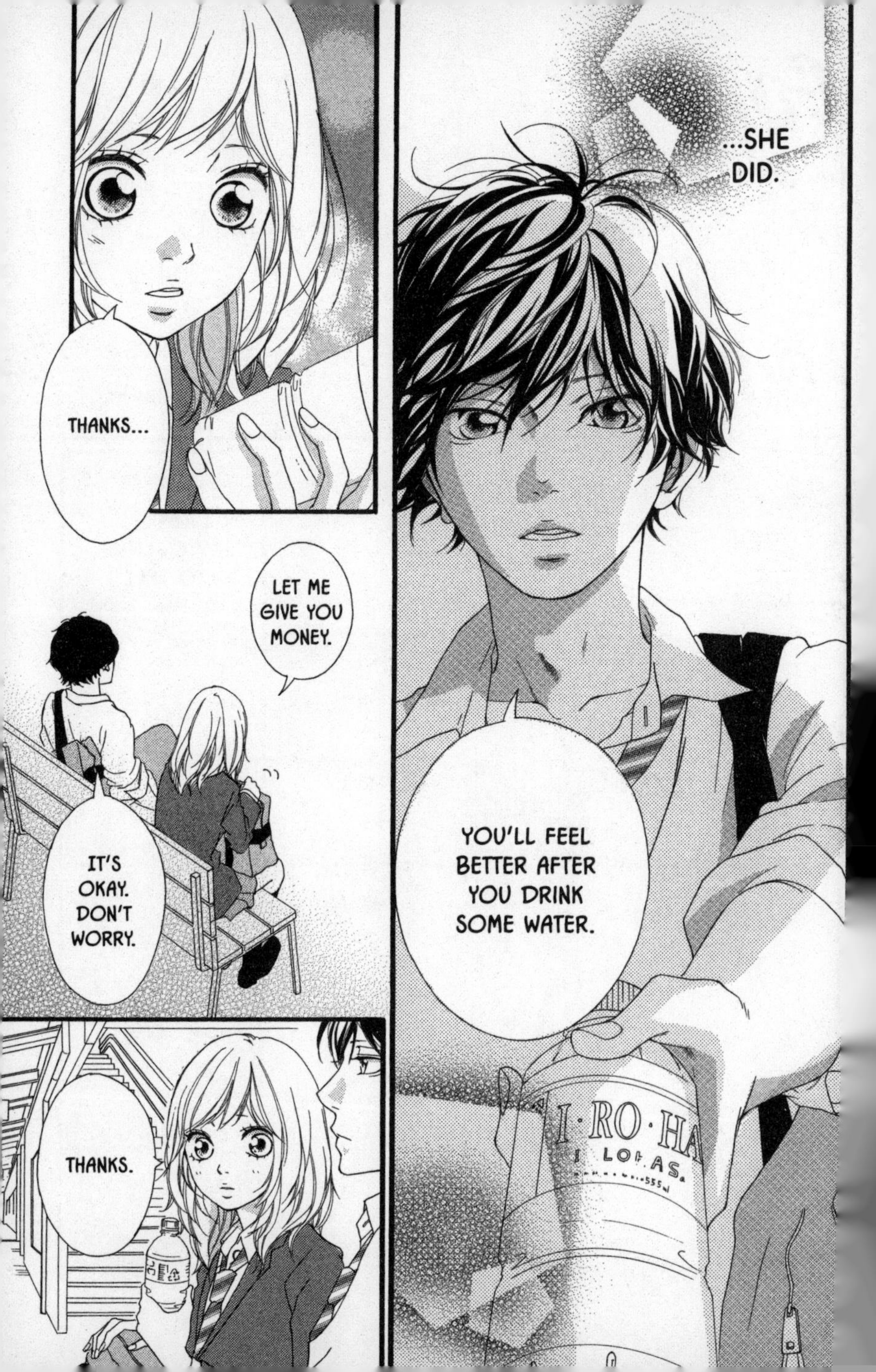
...SHE DID.
YOU'LL FEEL BETTER AFTER YOU DRINK SOME WATER.
THANKS...
LET ME GIVE YOU MONEY.
IT'S OKAY. DON'T WORRY.
THANKS.

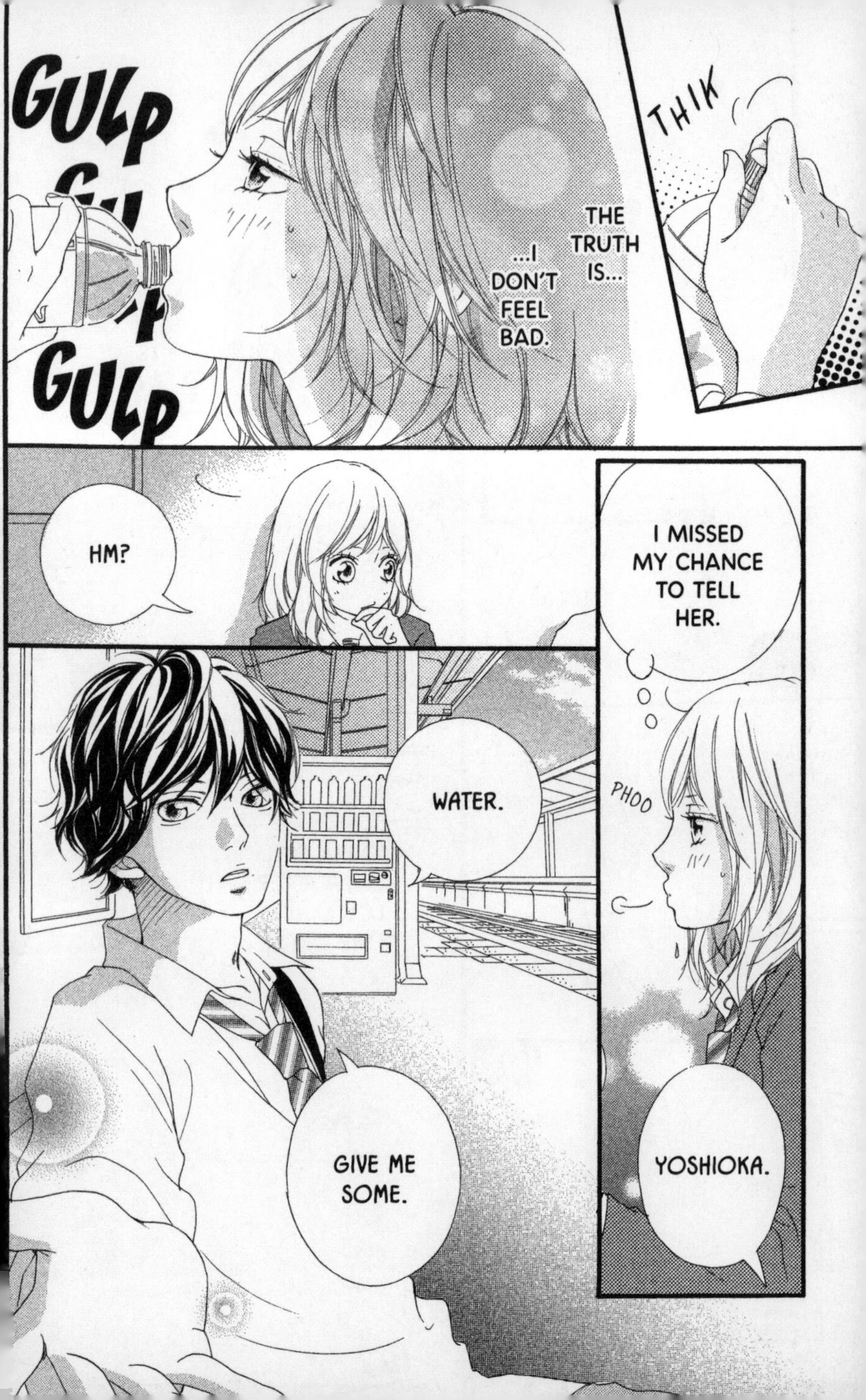
THIK
GULP
GULP
THE TRUTH IS...
...I DON'T FEEL BAD.
I MISSED MY CHANCE TO TELL HER.
PHOO
YOSHIOKA.
HM?
WATER.
GIVE ME SOME.

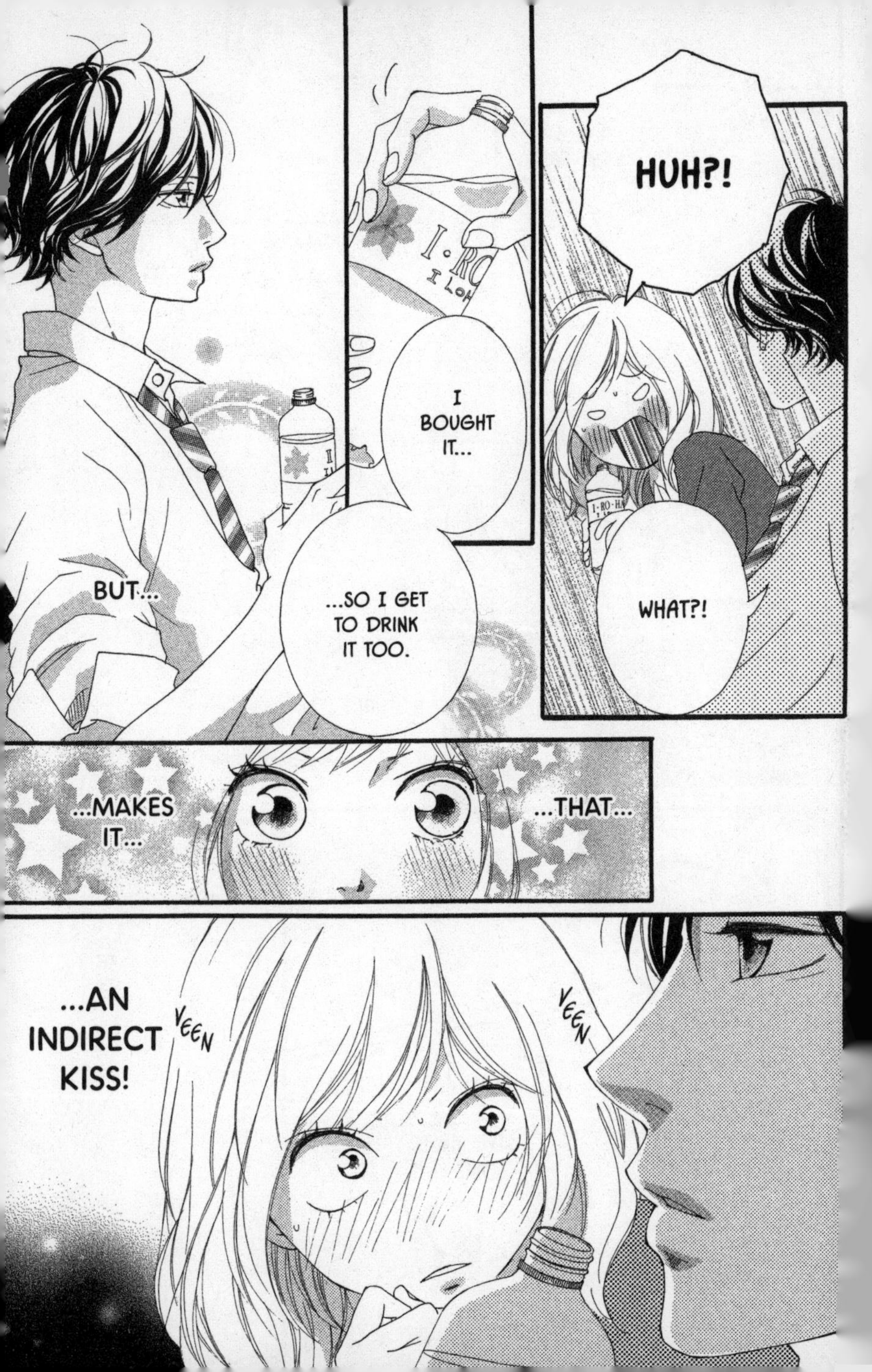
HUH?!
WHAT?!
I BOUGHT IT...
BUT...
...SO I GET TO DRINK IT TOO.
...THAT...
...MAKES IT...
VEEN
...AN INDIRECT KISS!
VEEN

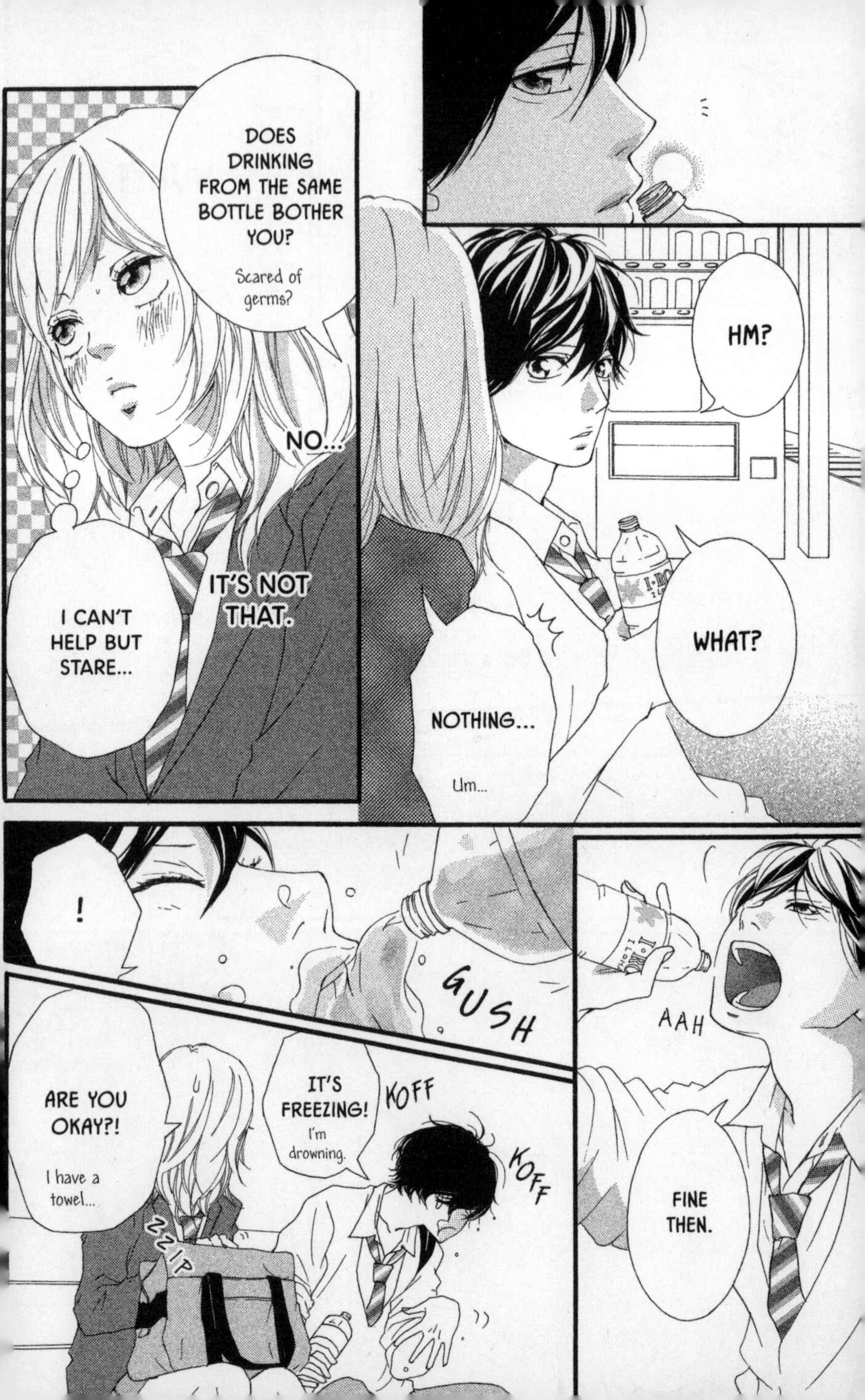
HM?
WHAT?
NOTHING...
Um...
DOES DRINKING FROM THE SAME BOTTLE BOTHER YOU?
Scared of germs?
NO...
IT'S NOT THAT.
I CAN'T HELP BUT STARE...
AAH
FINE THEN.
!
GUSH
IT'S FREEZING!
I'm drowning.
KOFF
KOFF
ARE YOU OKAY?!
I have a towel...
ZZIP

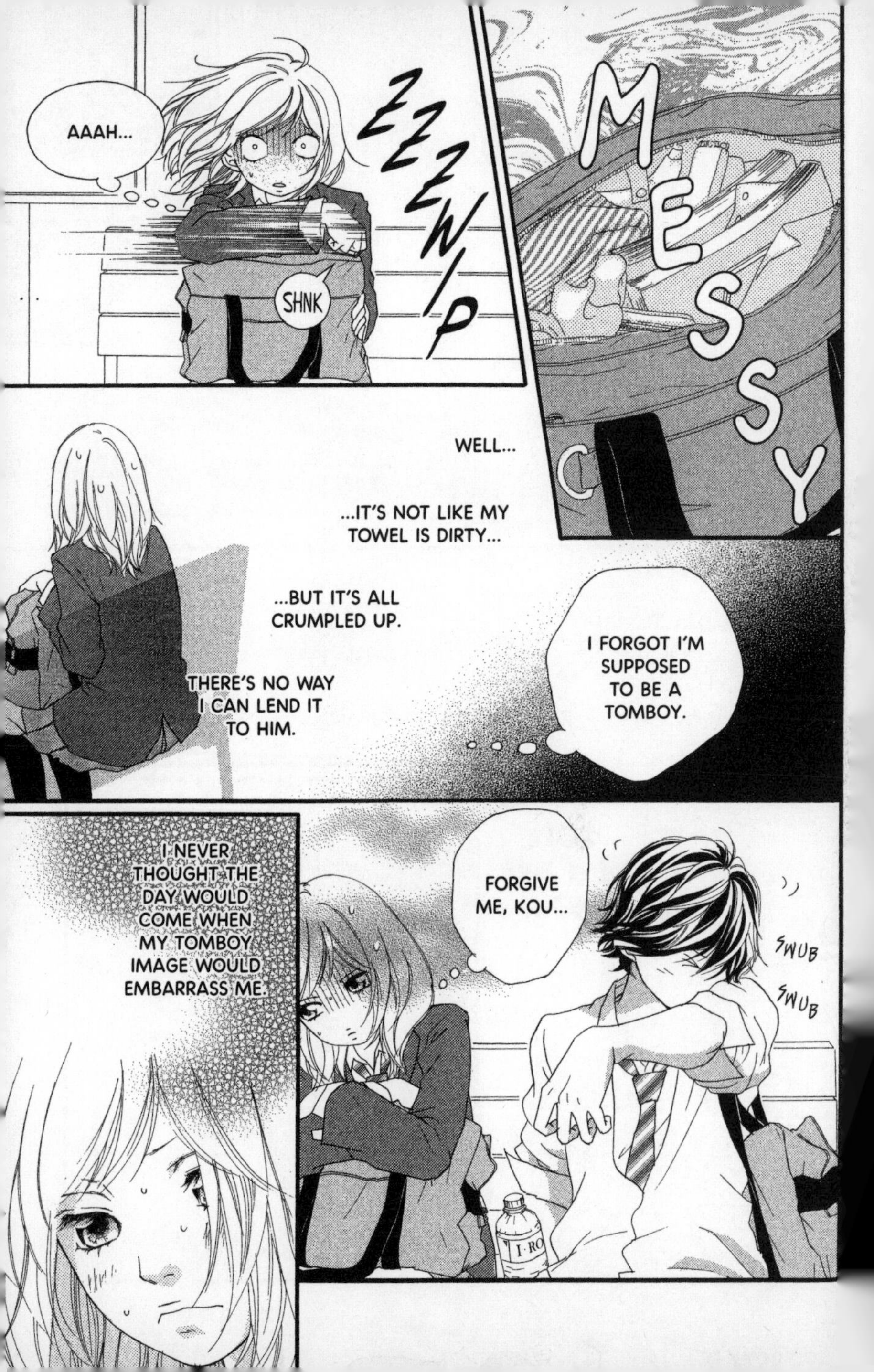
MESSY
ZZZWIP
AAAH...
SHNK
WELL...
...IT'S NOT LIKE MY TOWEL IS DIRTY...
...BUT IT'S ALL CRUMPLED UP.
THERE'S NO WAY I CAN LEND IT TO HIM.
I FORGOT I'M SUPPOSED TO BE A TOMBOY.
FORGIVE ME, KOU...
SWUB
SWUB
I NEVER THOUGHT THE DAY WOULD COME WHEN MY TOMBOY IMAGE WOULD EMBARRASS ME.
I·RO

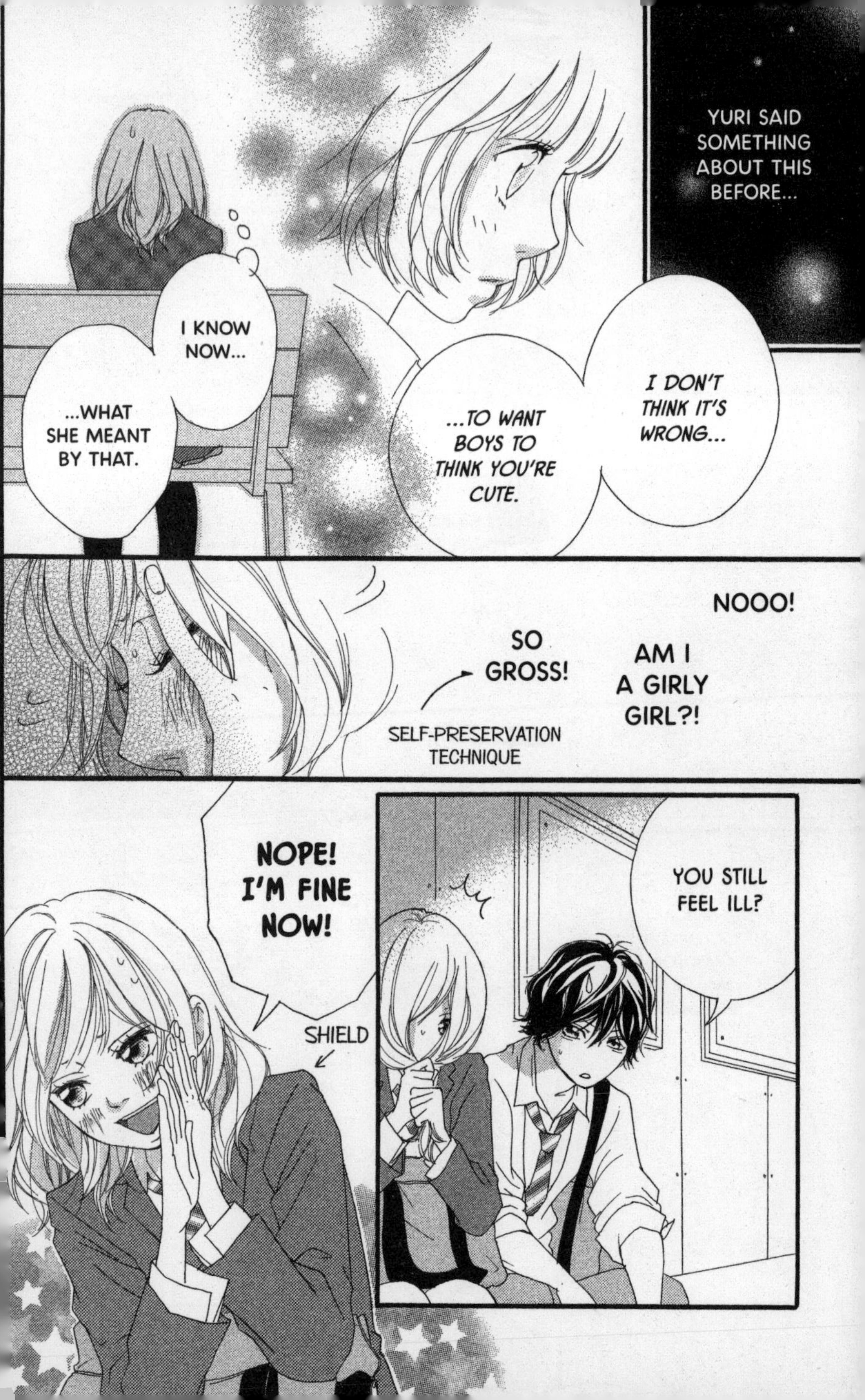
YURI SAID SOMETHING ABOUT THIS BEFORE...
I DON'T THINK IT'S WRONG...
...TO WANT BOYS TO THINK YOU'RE CUTE.
I KNOW NOW...
...WHAT SHE MEANT BY THAT.
NOOO!
AM I A GIRLY GIRL?!
SO GROSS!
SELF-PRESERVATION TECHNIQUE
YOU STILL FEEL ILL?
NOPE! I'M FINE NOW!
SHIELD

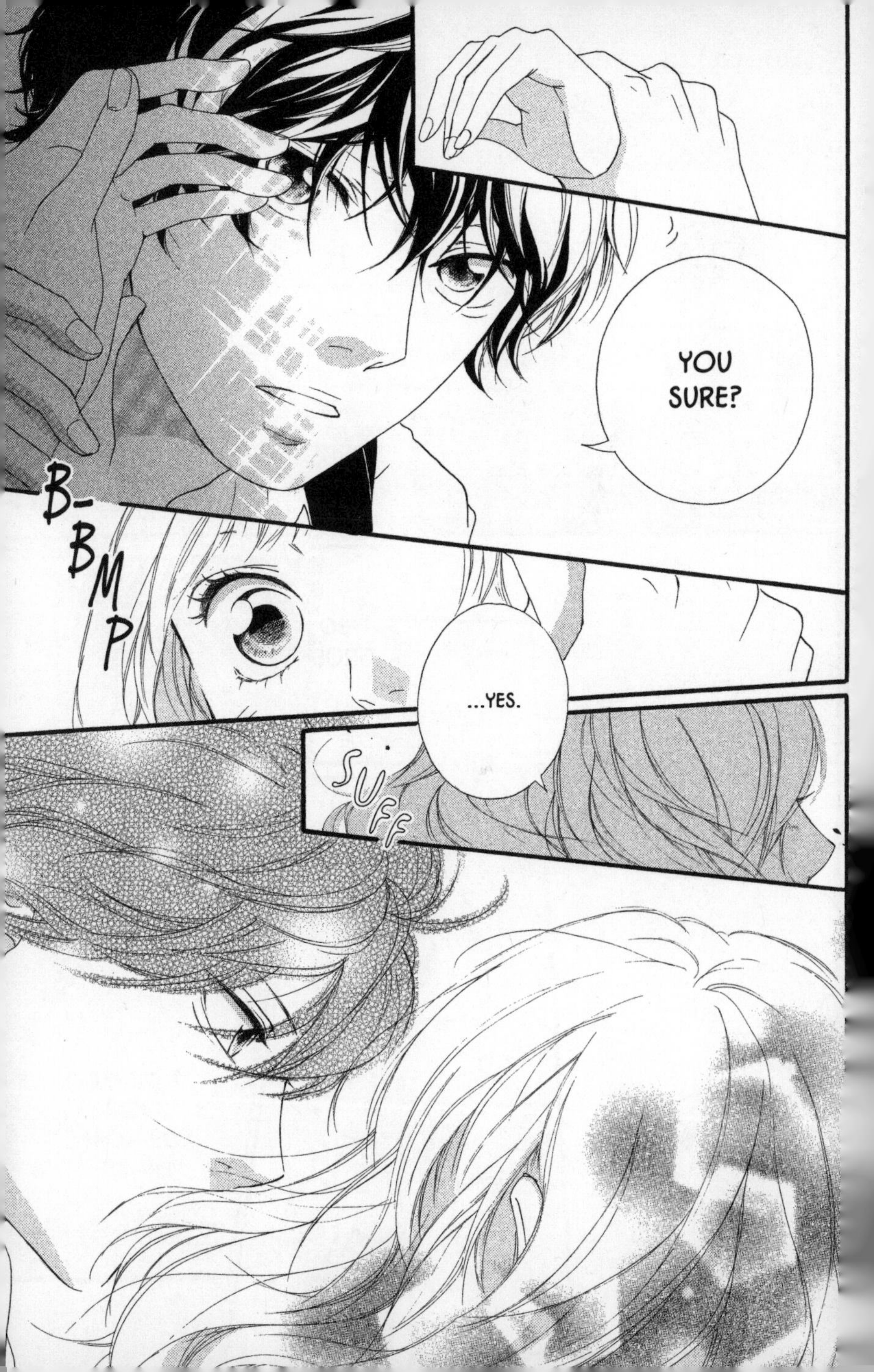
YOU SURE?
B-BMP
...YES.
SUFF

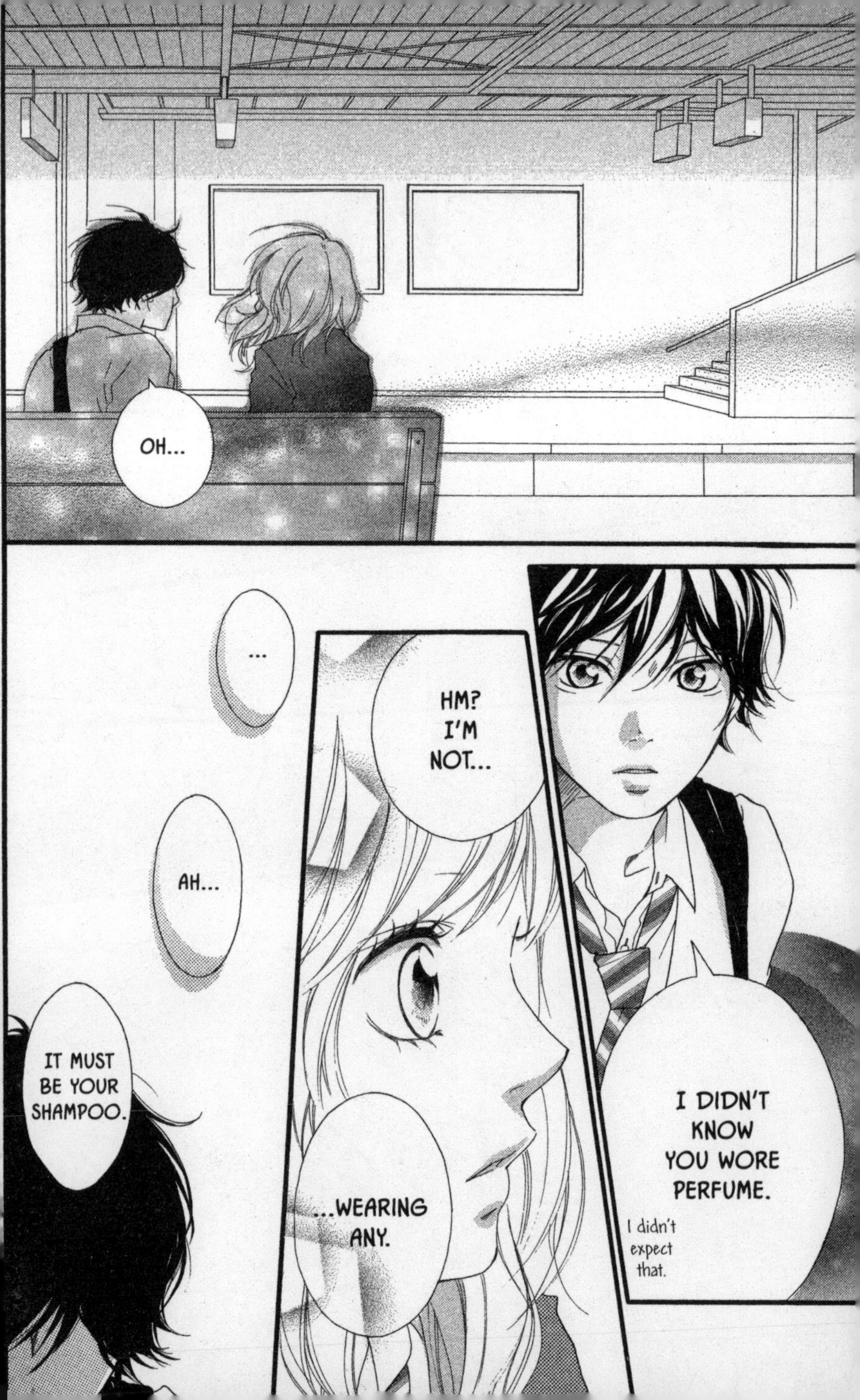
OH...
I DIDN'T KNOW YOU WORE PERFUME.
I didn't expect that.
HM? I'M NOT...
...WEARING ANY.
...
AH...
IT MUST BE YOUR SHAMPOO.

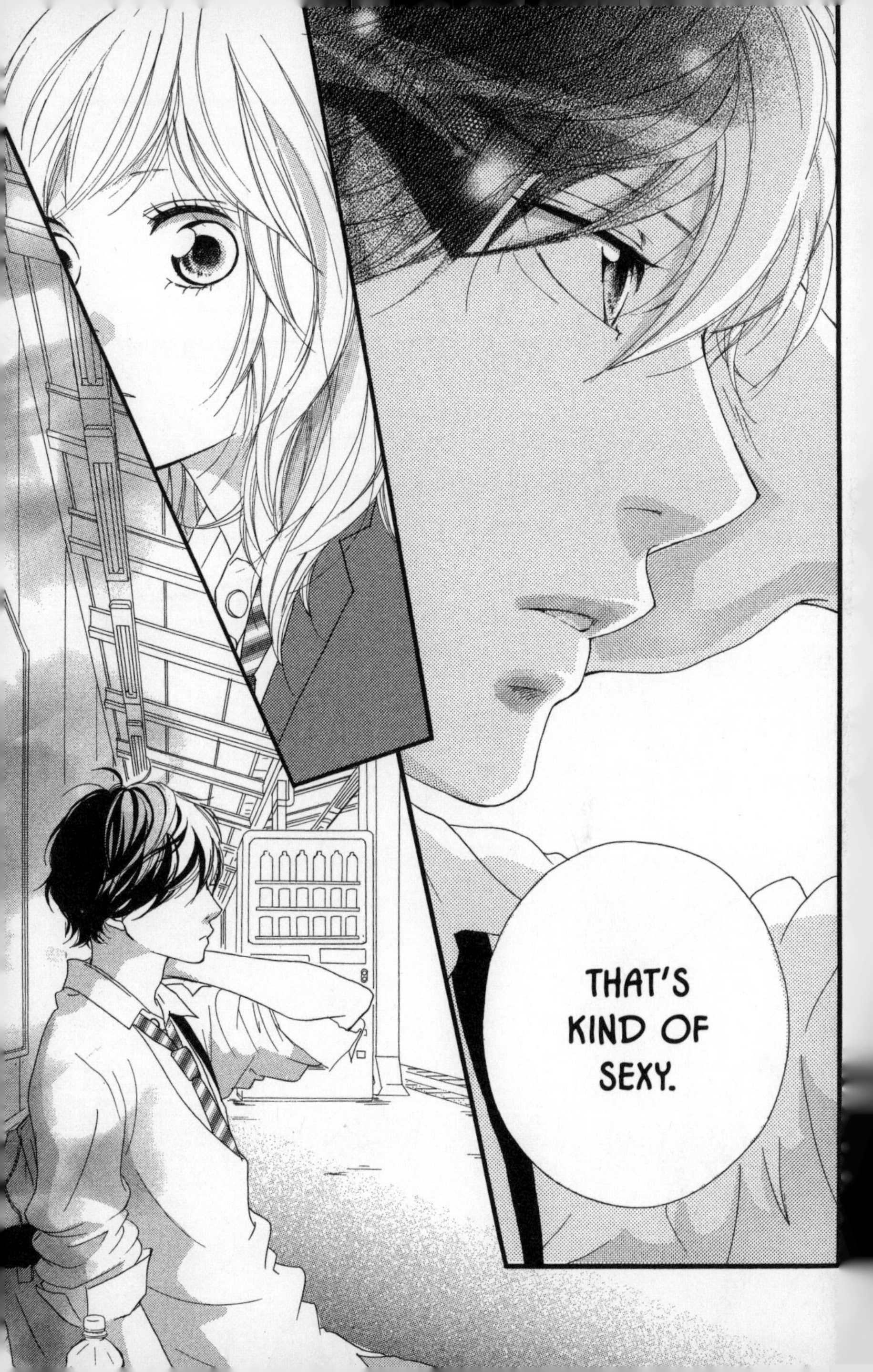
THAT'S KIND OF SEXY.

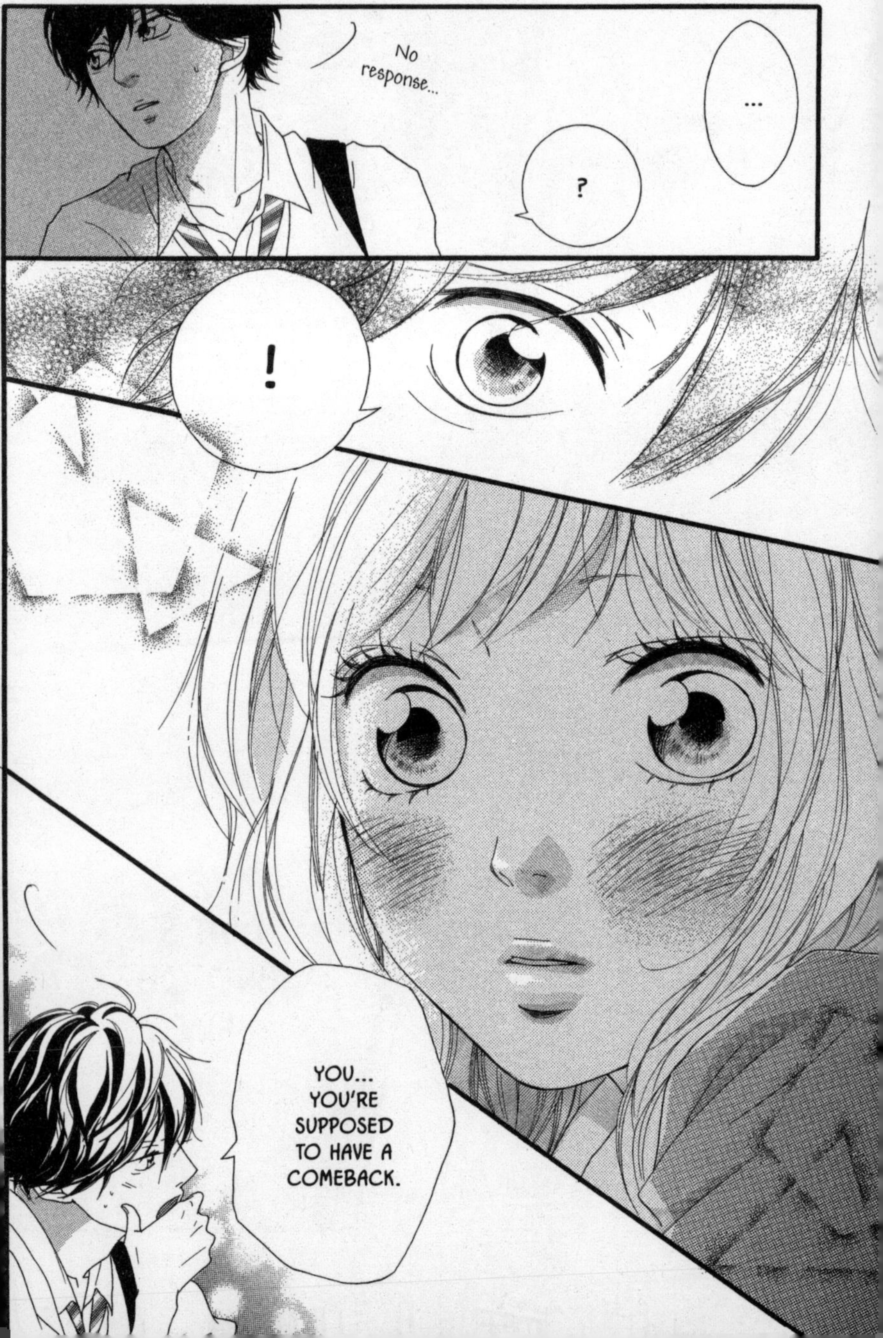
...
?
No response...
!
YOU... YOU'RE SUPPOSED TO HAVE A COMEBACK.

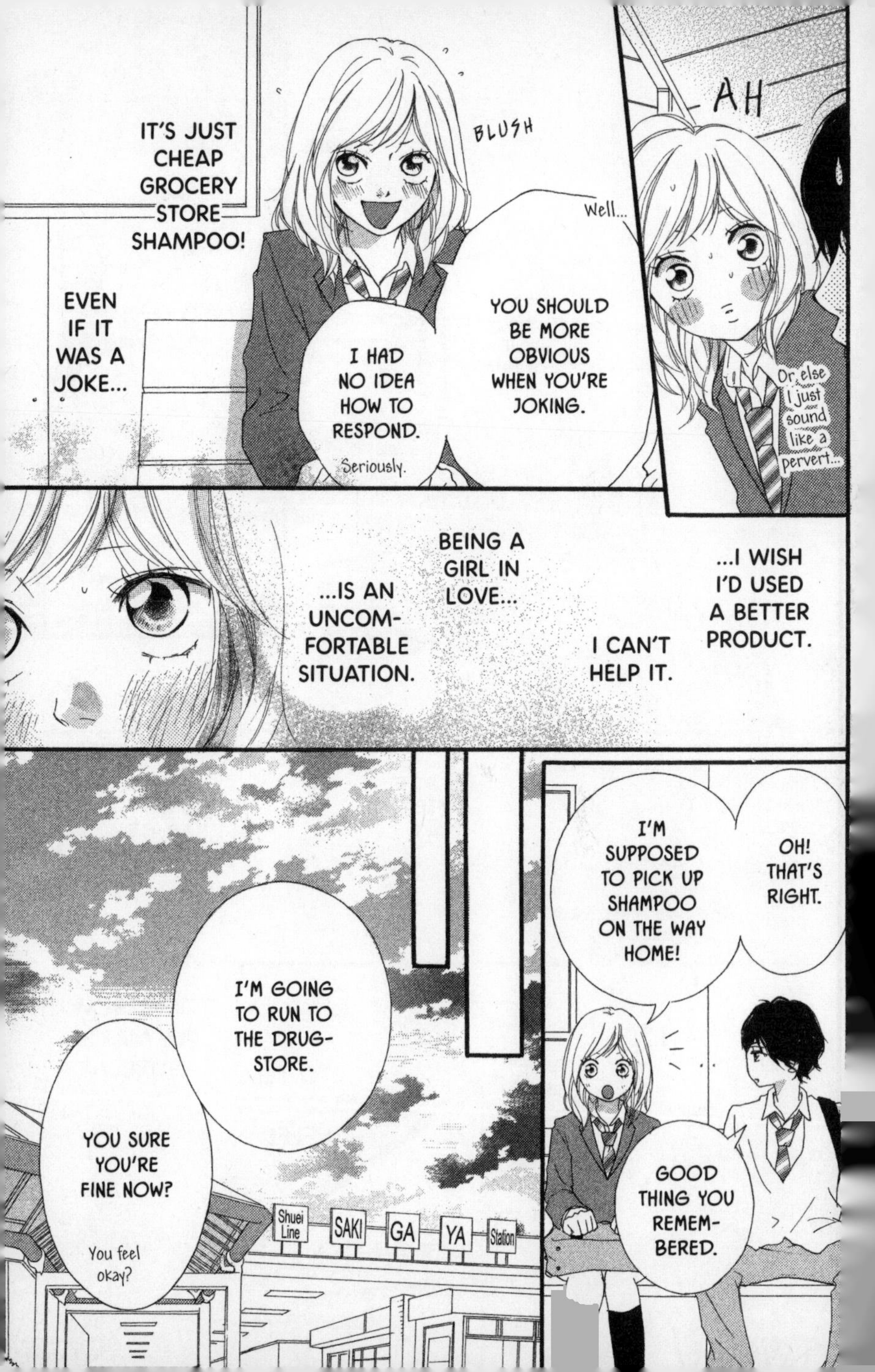
AH
Or, else I just sound like a pervert...
BLUSH
Well...
YOU SHOULD BE MORE OBVIOUS WHEN YOU'RE JOKING.
IT'S JUST CHEAP GROCERY STORE SHAMPOO!
I HAD NO IDEA HOW TO RESPOND.
Seriously.
EVEN IF IT WAS A JOKE...
...I WISH I'D USED A BETTER PRODUCT.
I CAN'T HELP IT.
BEING A GIRL IN LOVE...
...IS AN UNCOM-FORTABLE SITUATION.
OH! THAT'S RIGHT.
I'M SUPPOSED TO PICK UP SHAMPOO ON THE WAY HOME!
GOOD THING YOU REMEM-BERED.
I'M GOING TO RUN TO THE DRUG-STORE.
YOU SURE YOU'RE FINE NOW?
You feel okay?
Shuei Line SAKI GA YA Station

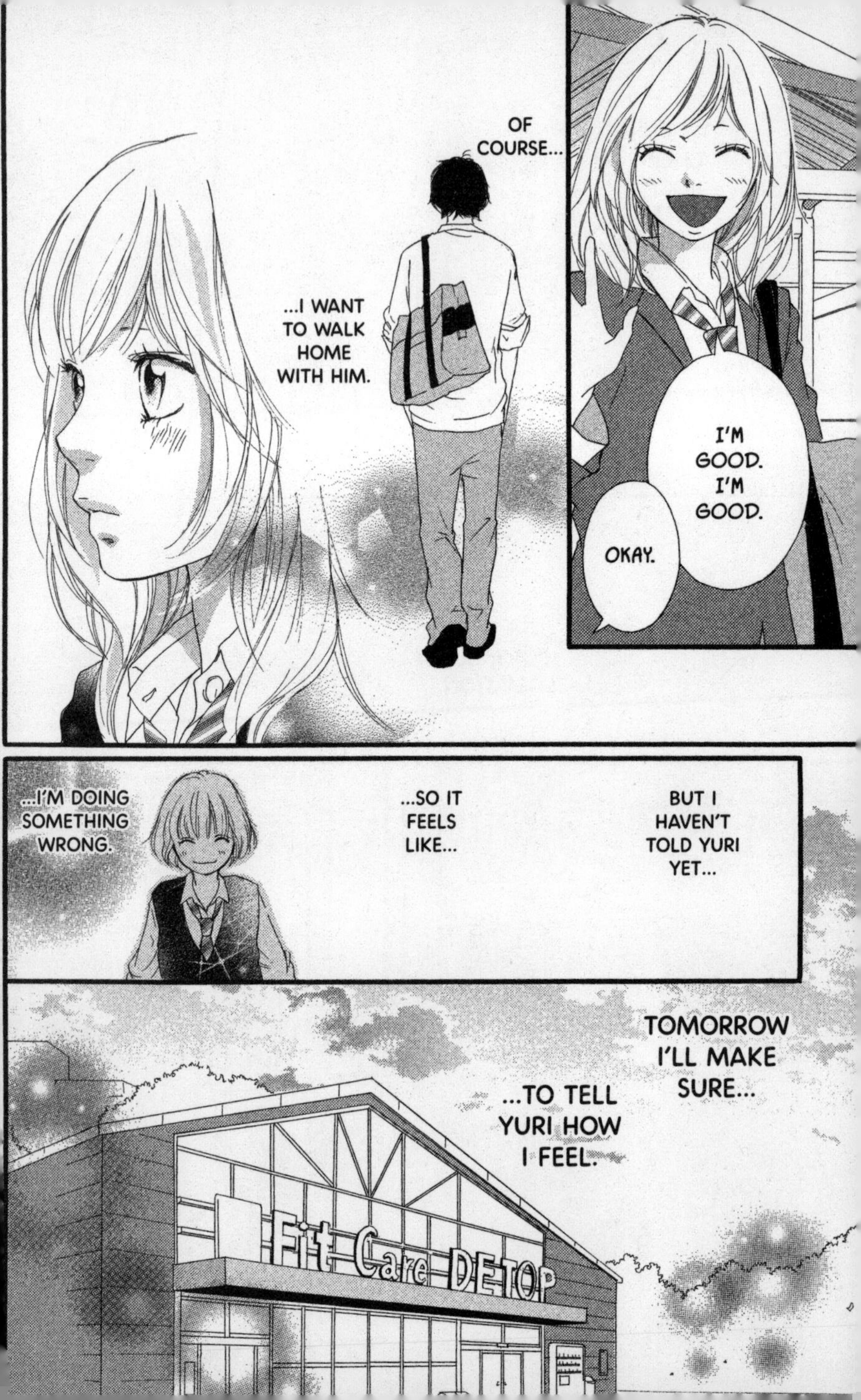
I'M GOOD. I'M GOOD.
OKAY.
OF COURSE...
...I WANT TO WALK HOME WITH HIM.
BUT I HAVEN'T TOLD YURI YET...
...SO IT FEELS LIKE...
...I'M DOING SOMETHING WRONG.
TOMORROW I'LL MAKE SURE...
...TO TELL YURI HOW I FEEL.
Fit Care DETOP

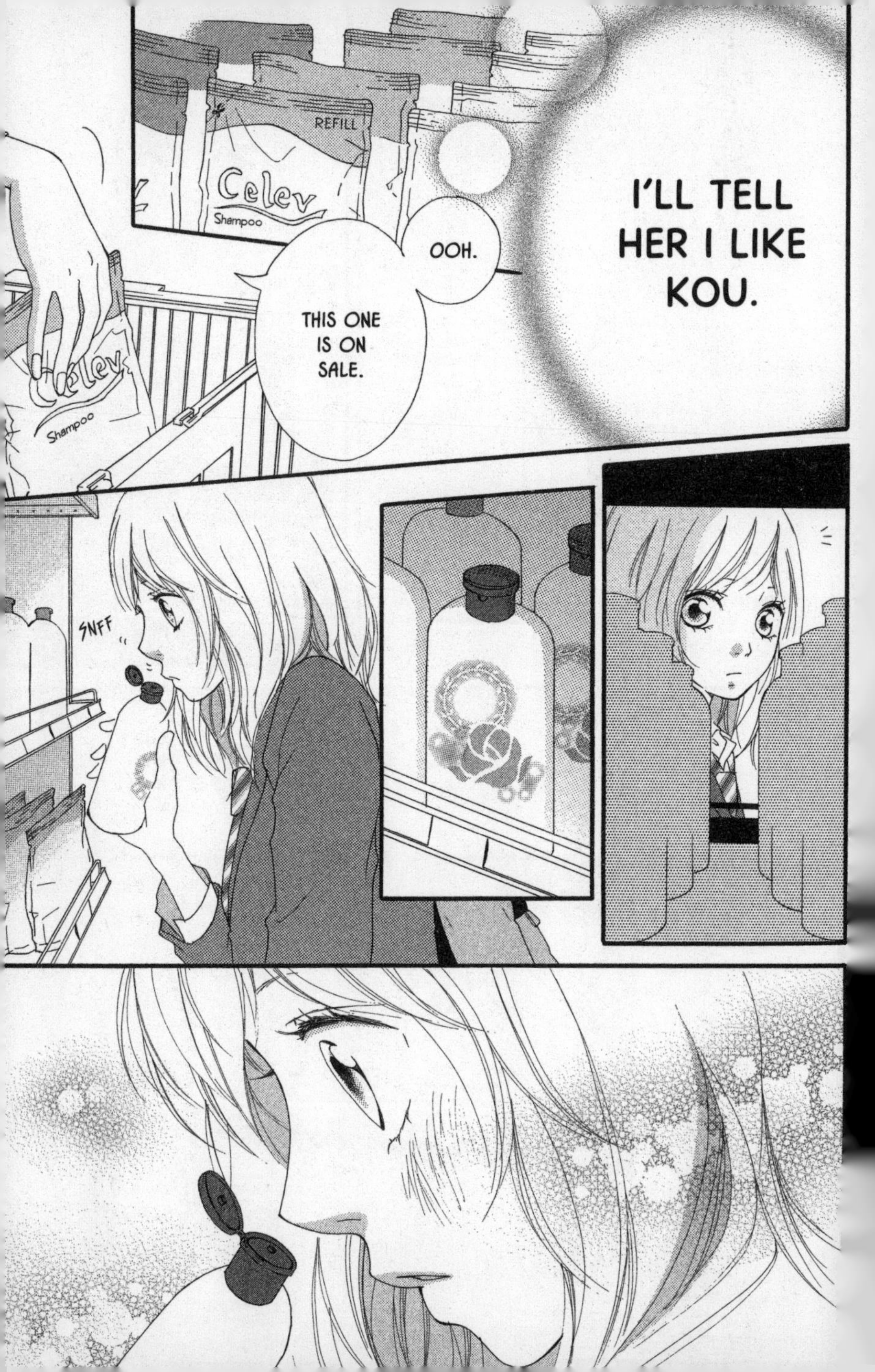
I'LL TELL HER I LIKE KOU.
OOH.
THIS ONE IS ON SALE.
REFILL
Celev
Shampoo
Celev
Shampoo
SNFF

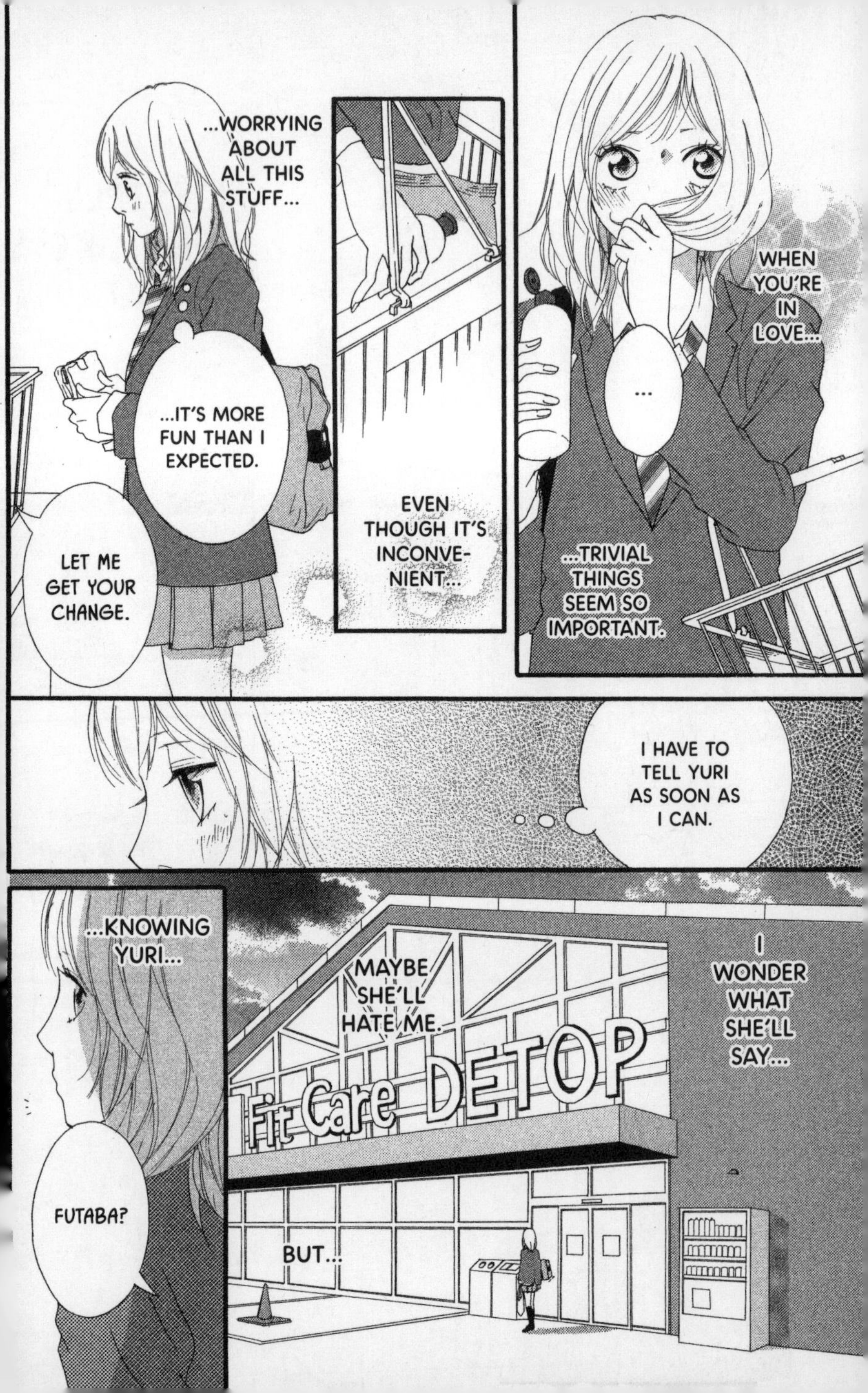

WHEN YOU'RE IN LOVE...
...
...TRIVIAL THINGS SEEM SO IMPORTANT.
EVEN THOUGH IT'S INCONVE-NIENT...
...WORRYING ABOUT ALL THIS STUFF...
...IT'S MORE FUN THAN I EXPECTED.
LET ME GET YOUR CHANGE.
I HAVE TO TELL YURI AS SOON AS I CAN.
I WONDER WHAT SHE'LL SAY...
MAYBE SHE'LL HATE ME.
Fit Care DETOP
BUT...
...KNOWING YURI...
FUTABA?

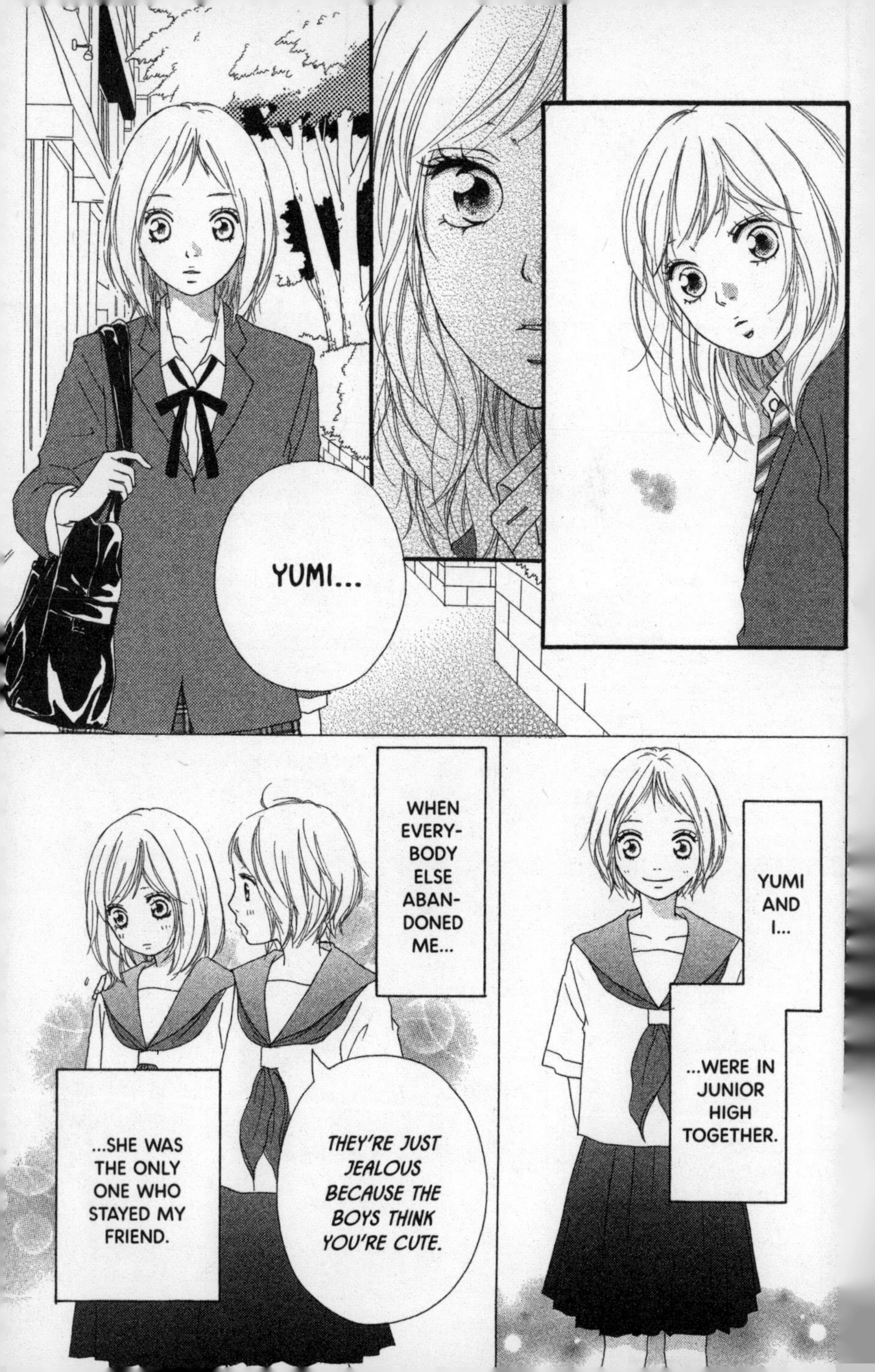
YUMI...
YUMI AND I...
...WERE IN JUNIOR HIGH TOGETHER.
WHEN EVERY-BODY ELSE ABAN-DONED ME...
THEY'RE JUST JEALOUS BECAUSE THE BOYS THINK YOU'RE CUTE.
...SHE WAS THE ONLY ONE WHO STAYED MY FRIEND.

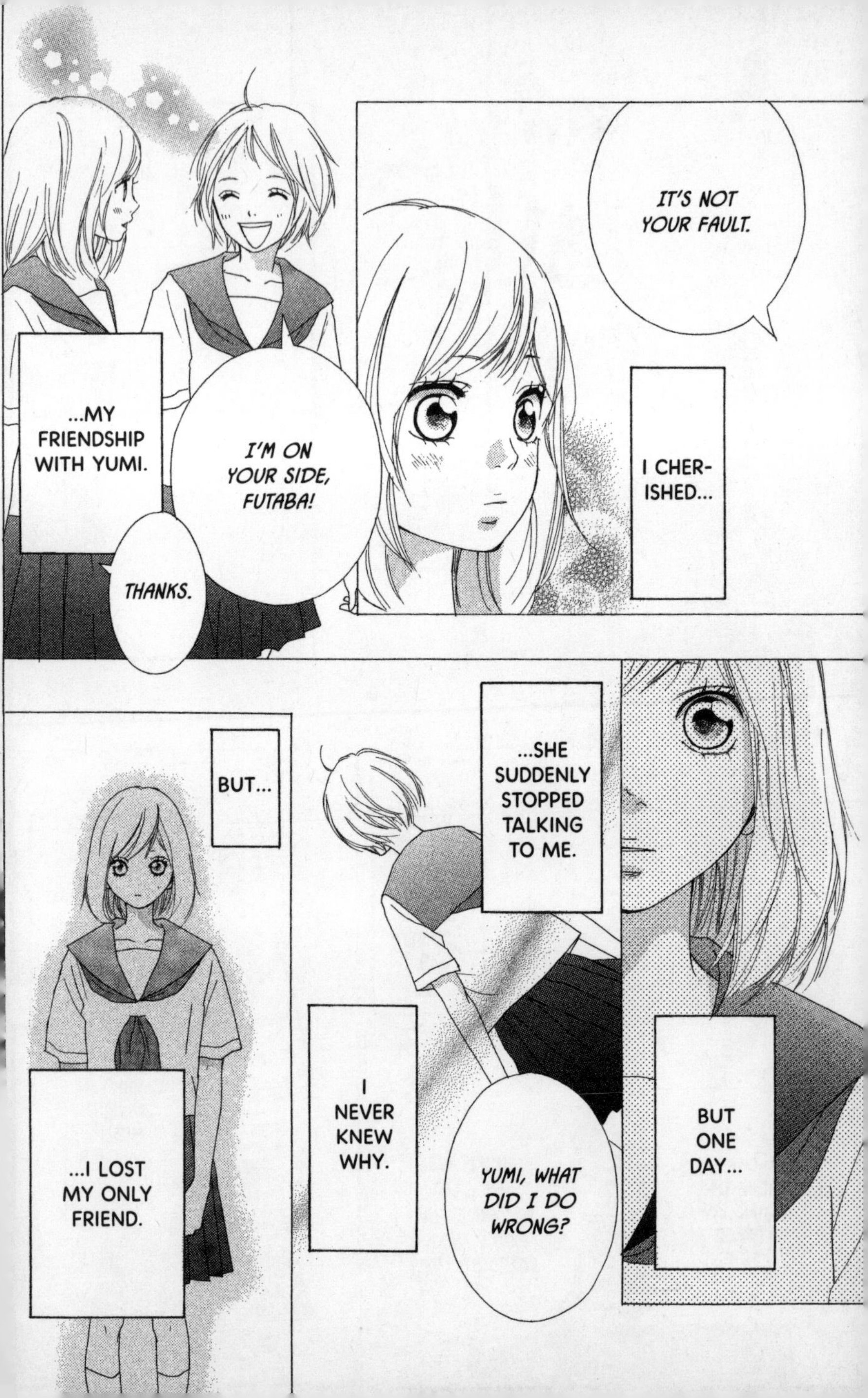
IT'S NOT YOUR FAULT.
I CHER-ISHED...
I'M ON YOUR SIDE, FUTABA!
...MY FRIENDSHIP WITH YUMI.
THANKS.
BUT ONE DAY...
...SHE SUDDENLY STOPPED TALKING TO ME.
YUMI, WHAT DID I DO WRONG?
I NEVER KNEW WHY.
BUT...
...I LOST MY ONLY FRIEND.

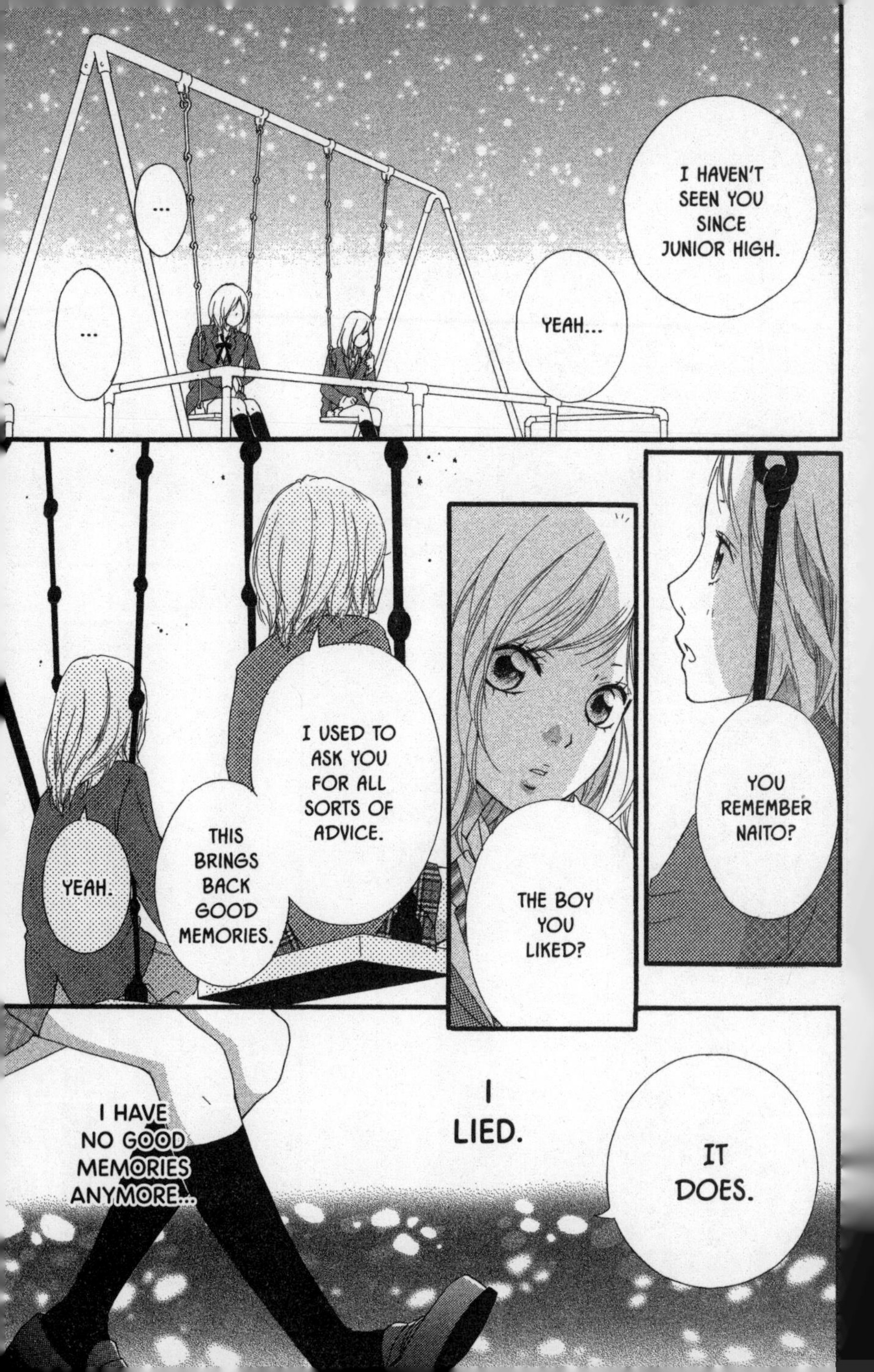
I HAVEN'T SEEN YOU SINCE JUNIOR HIGH.
YEAH...
...
...
YOU REMEMBER NAITO?
THE BOY YOU LIKED?
I USED TO ASK YOU FOR ALL SORTS OF ADVICE.
THIS BRINGS BACK GOOD MEMORIES.
YEAH.
IT DOES.
I LIED.
I HAVE NO GOOD MEMORIES ANYMORE...

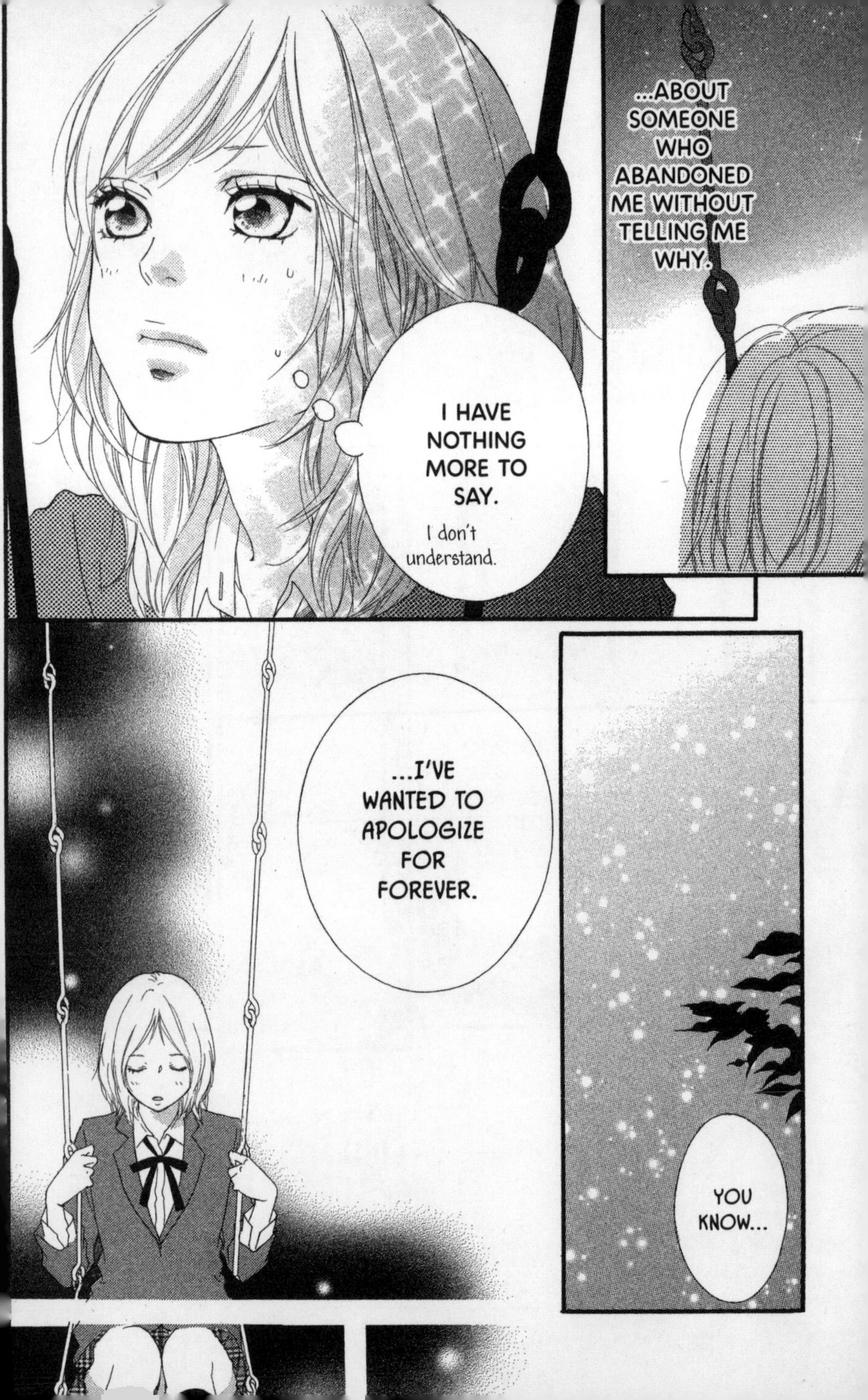
...ABOUT SOMEONE WHO ABANDONED ME WITHOUT TELLING ME WHY.
I HAVE NOTHING MORE TO SAY.
I don't understand.
YOU KNOW...
...I'VE WANTED TO APOLOGIZE FOR FOREVER.

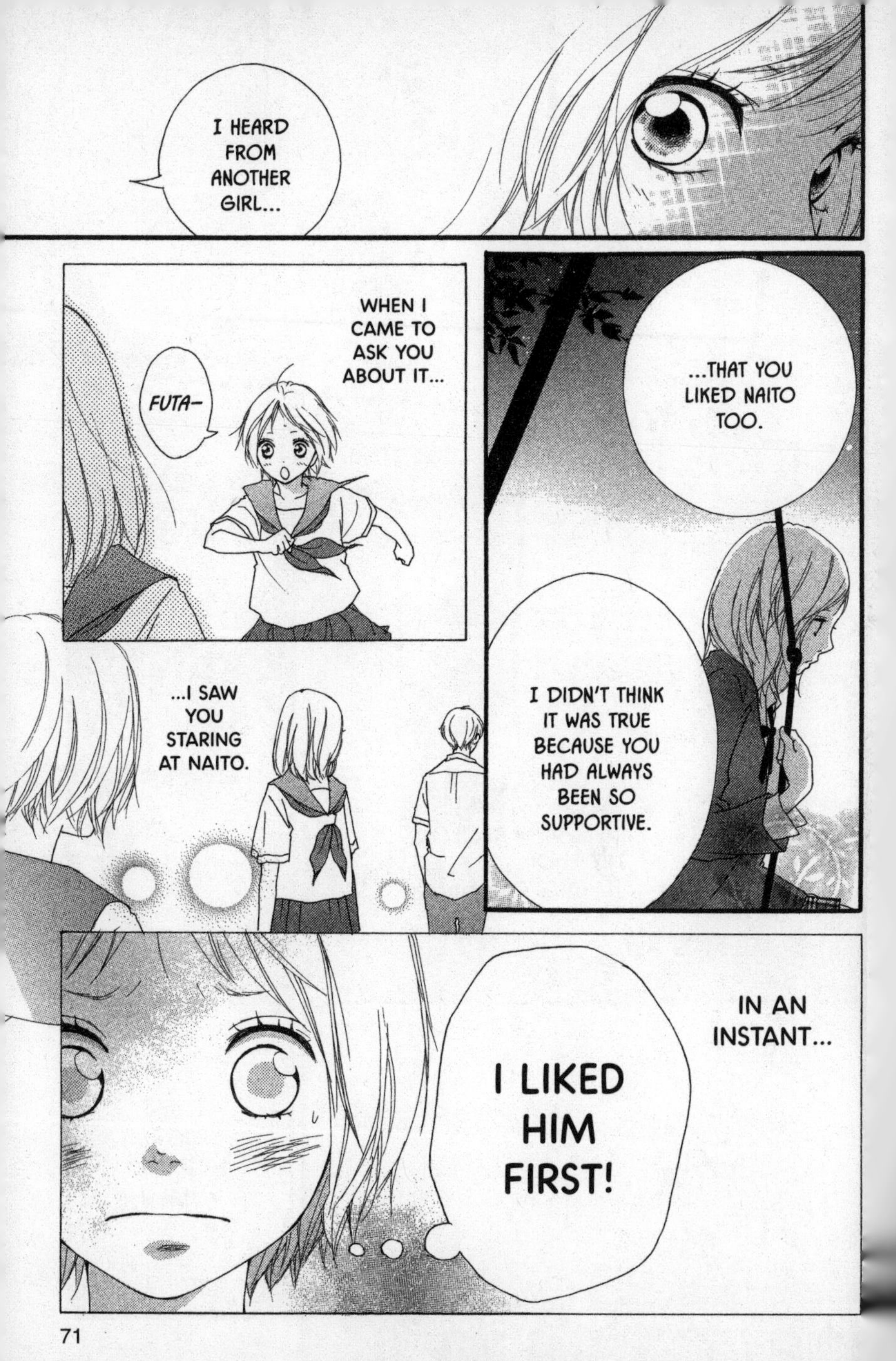
I HEARD FROM ANOTHER GIRL...
...THAT YOU LIKED NAITO TOO.
I DIDN'T THINK IT WAS TRUE BECAUSE YOU HAD ALWAYS BEEN SO SUPPORTIVE.
WHEN I CAME TO ASK YOU ABOUT IT...
FUTA-
...I SAW YOU STARING AT NAITO.
IN AN INSTANT...
I LIKED HIM FIRST!

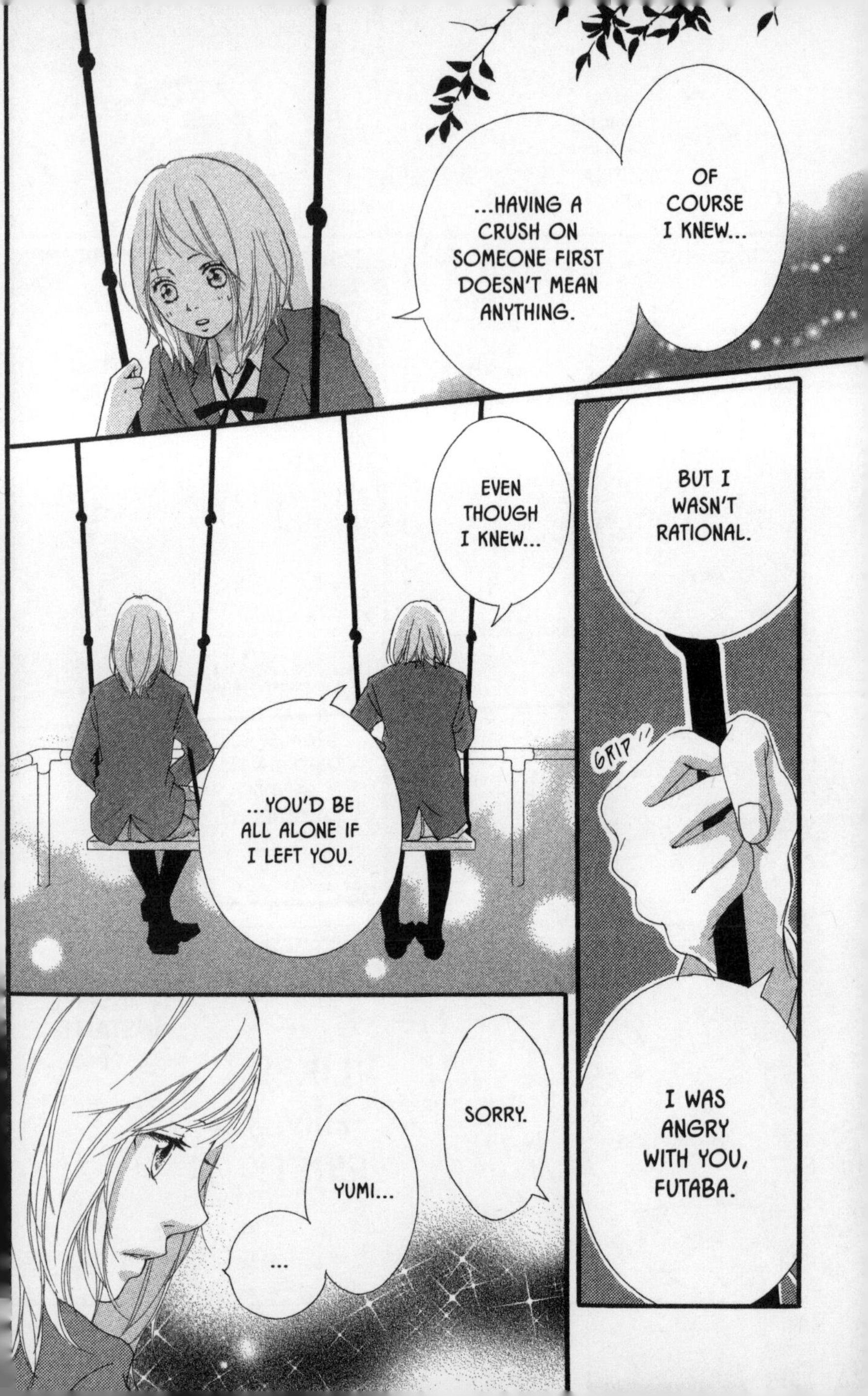
OF COURSE I KNEW...
...HAVING A CRUSH ON SOMEONE FIRST DOESN'T MEAN ANYTHING.
BUT I WASN'T RATIONAL.
GRIP
I WAS ANGRY WITH YOU, FUTABA.
EVEN THOUGH I KNEW...
...YOU'D BE ALL ALONE IF I LEFT YOU.
SORRY.
YUMI...
...

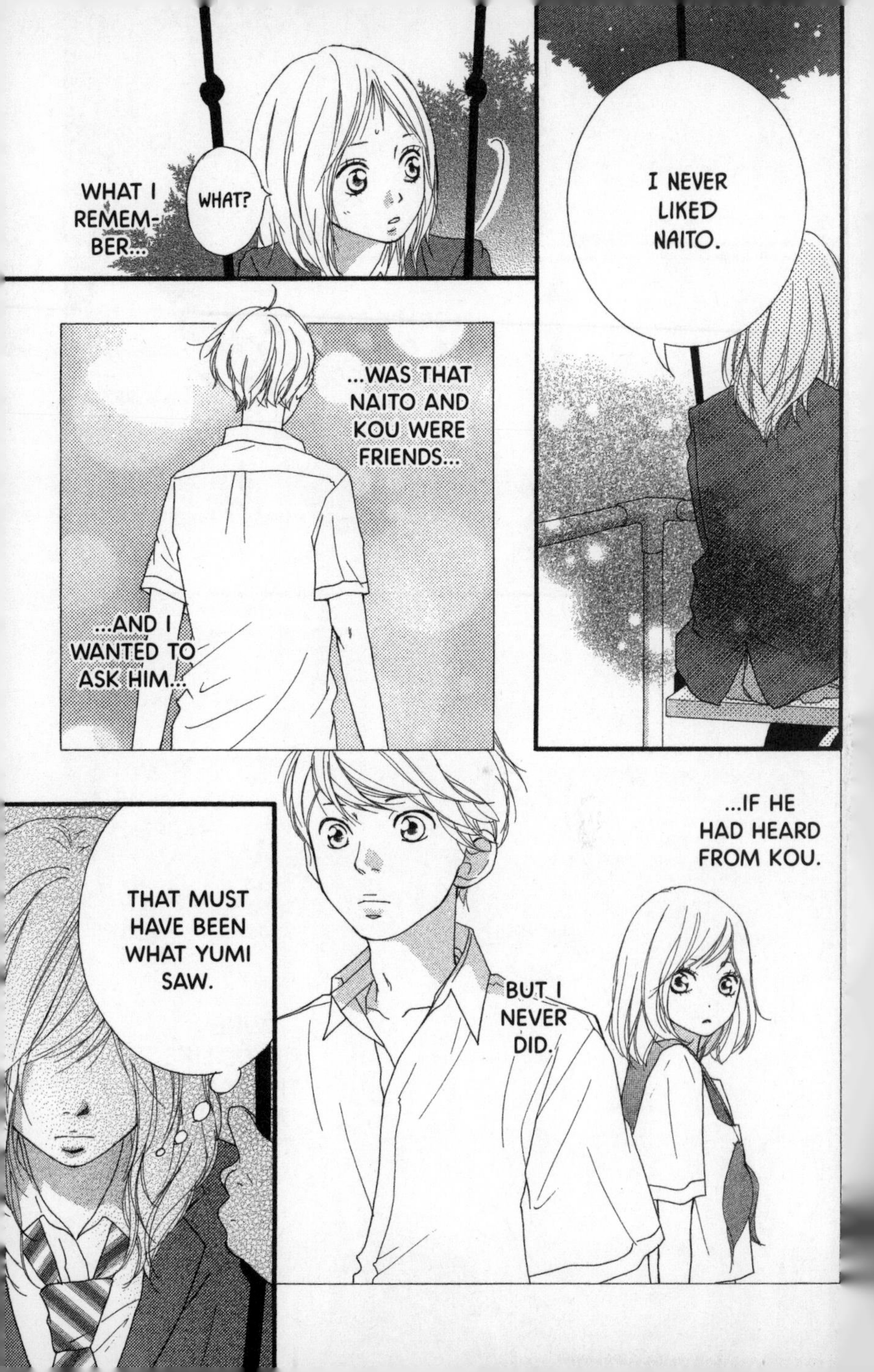
I NEVER LIKED NAITO.
WHAT?
WHAT I REMEMBER...
...WAS THAT NAITO AND KOU WERE FRIENDS...
...AND I WANTED TO ASK HIM...
...IF HE HAD HEARD FROM KOU.
BUT I NEVER DID.
THAT MUST HAVE BEEN WHAT YUMI SAW.

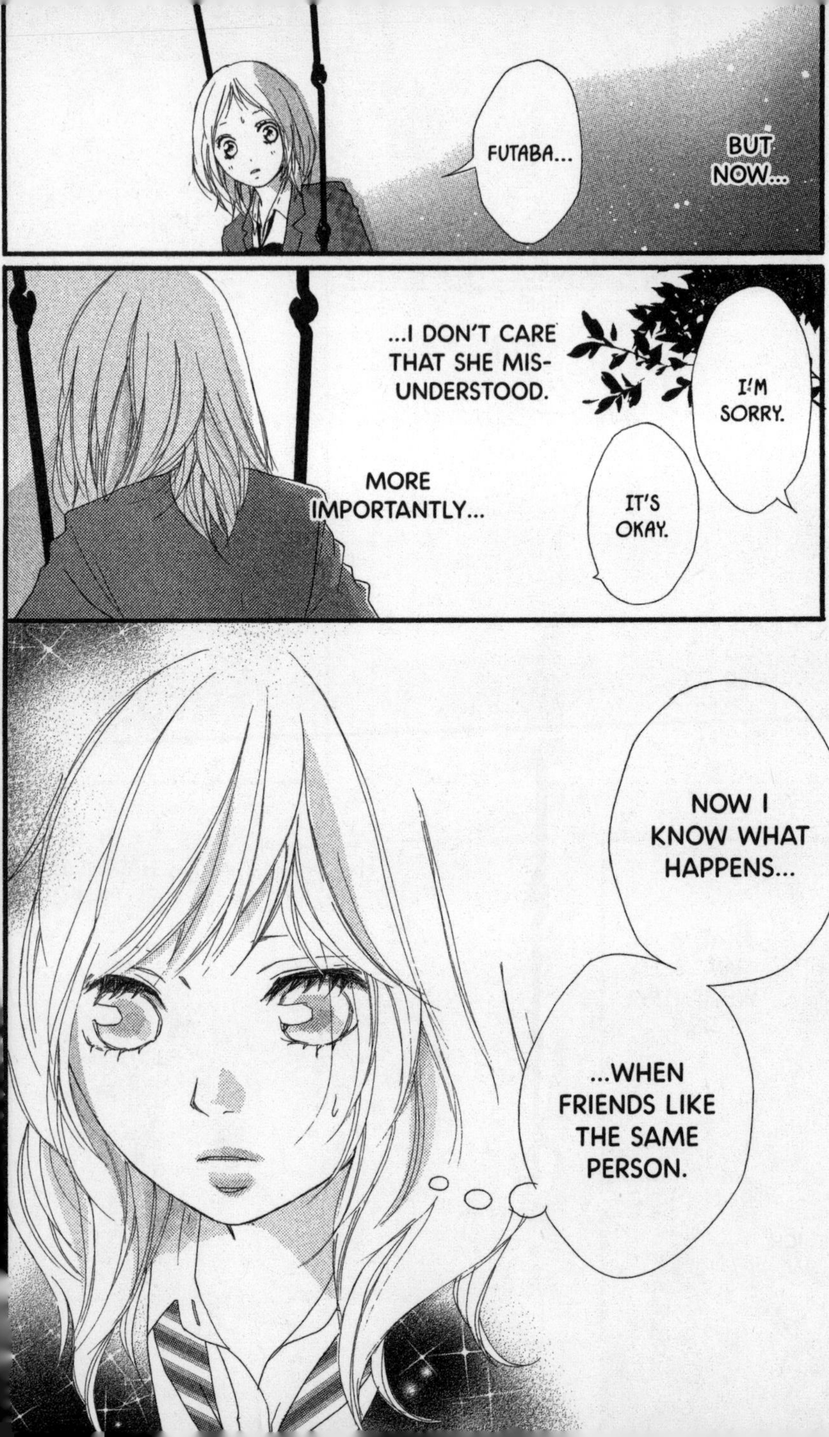
BUT NOW...
FUTABA...
I'M SORRY.
IT'S OKAY.
...I DON'T CARE THAT SHE MIS-UNDERSTOOD.
MORE IMPORTANTLY...
NOW I KNOW WHAT HAPPENS...
...WHEN FRIENDS LIKE THE SAME PERSON.

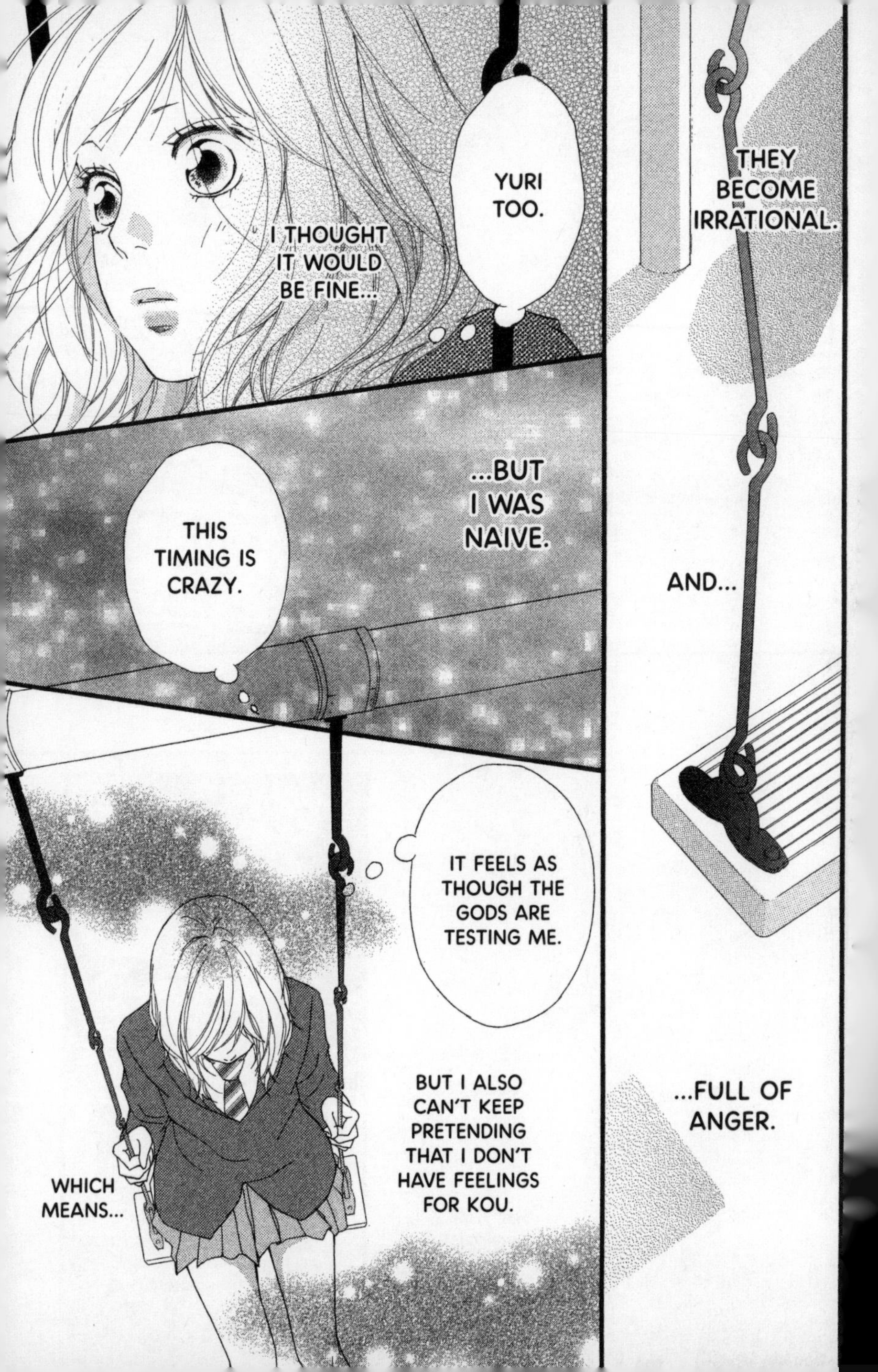
THEY BECOME IRRATIONAL.
AND...
...FULL OF ANGER.
YURI TOO.
I THOUGHT IT WOULD BE FINE...
...BUT I WAS NAIVE.
THIS TIMING IS CRAZY.
IT FEELS AS THOUGH THE GODS ARE TESTING ME.
BUT I ALSO CAN'T KEEP PRETENDING THAT I DON'T HAVE FEELINGS FOR KOU.
WHICH MEANS...

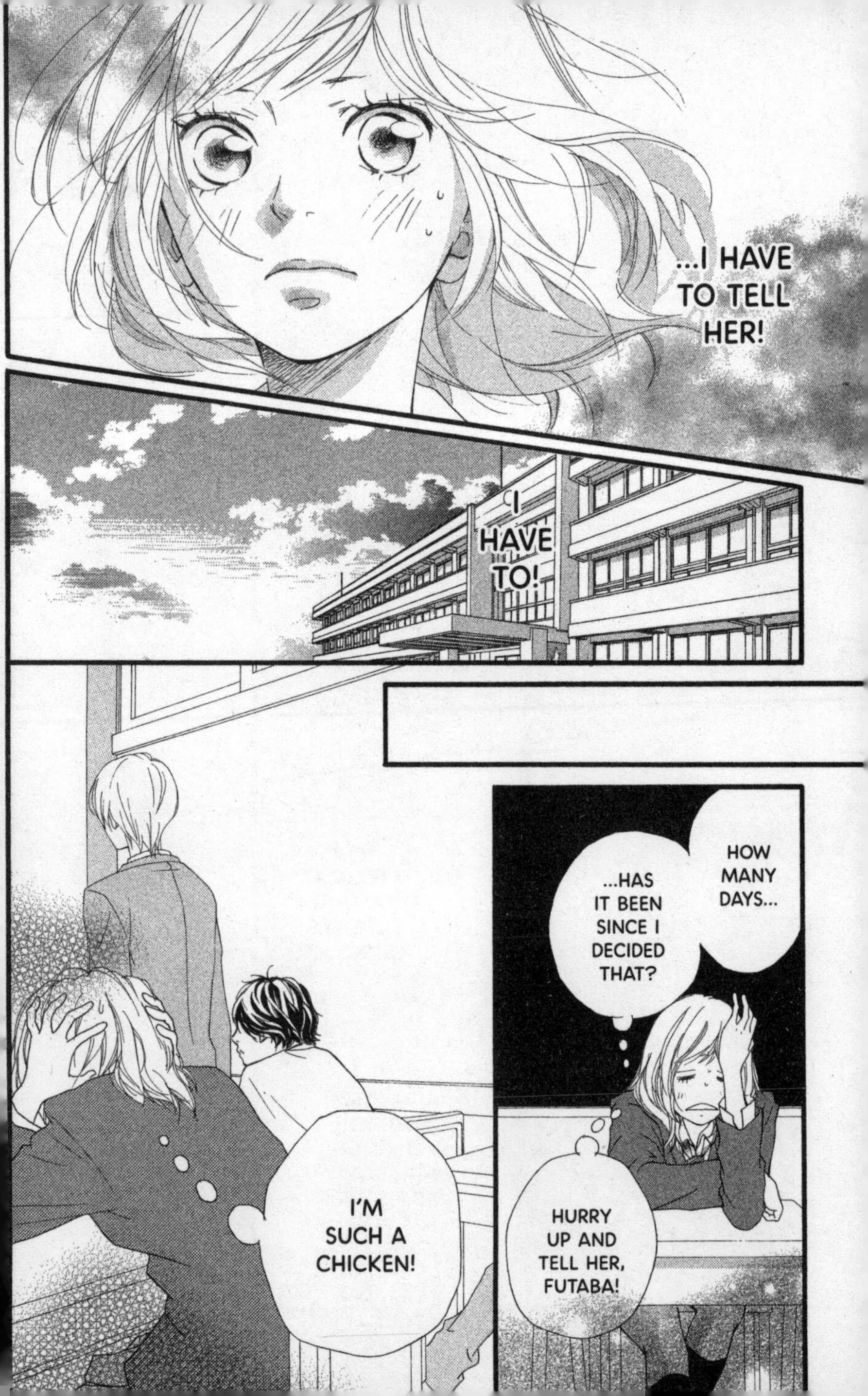
...I HAVE TO TELL HER!
I HAVE TO!
HOW MANY DAYS...
...HAS IT BEEN SINCE I DECIDED THAT?
HURRY UP AND TELL HER, FUTABA!
I'M SUCH A CHICKEN!

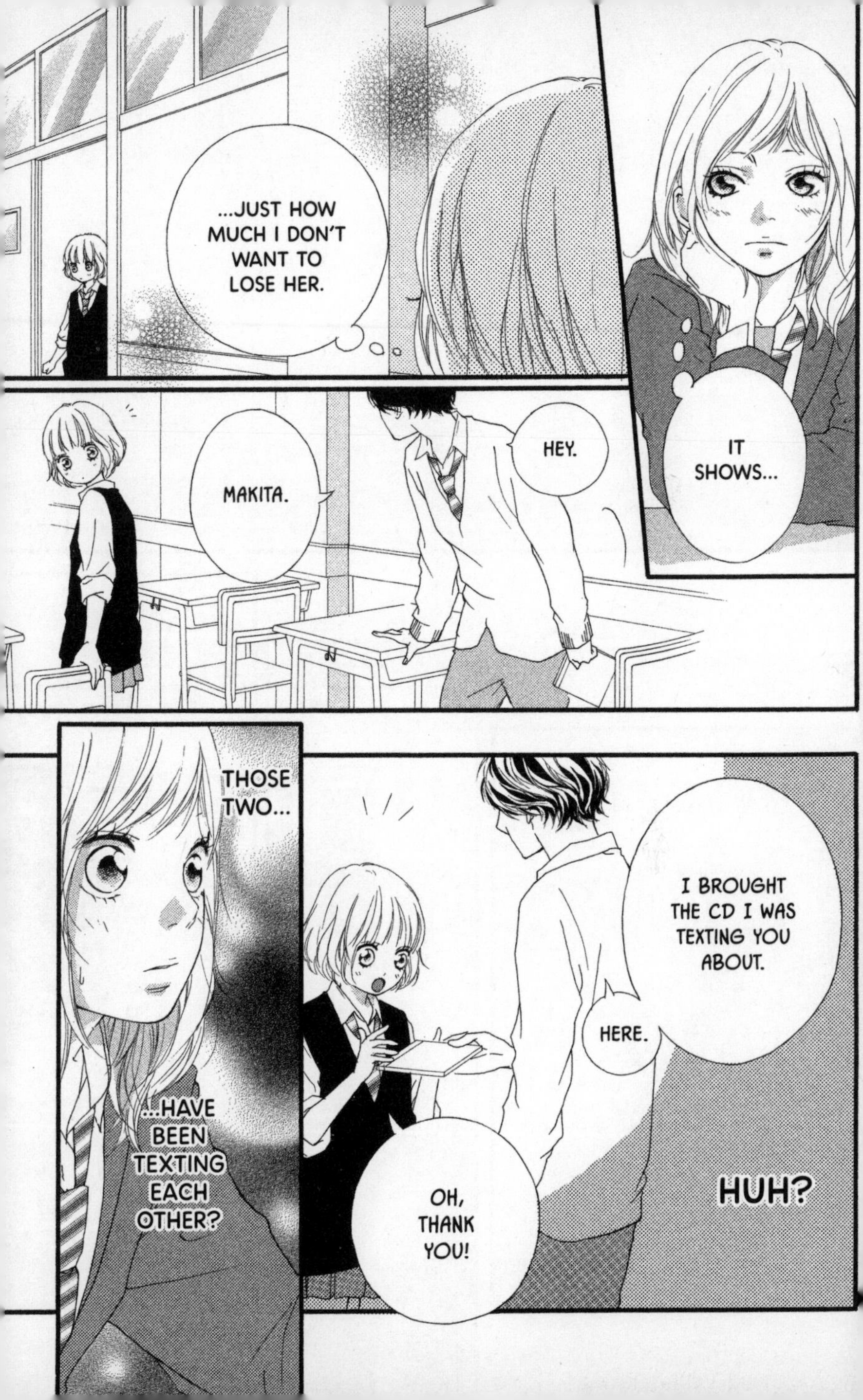
IT SHOWS...
...JUST HOW MUCH I DON'T WANT TO LOSE HER.
HEY.
MAKITA.
I BROUGHT THE CD I WAS TEXTING YOU ABOUT.
HERE.
HUH?
OH, THANK YOU!
THOSE TWO...
...HAVE BEEN TEXTING EACH OTHER?

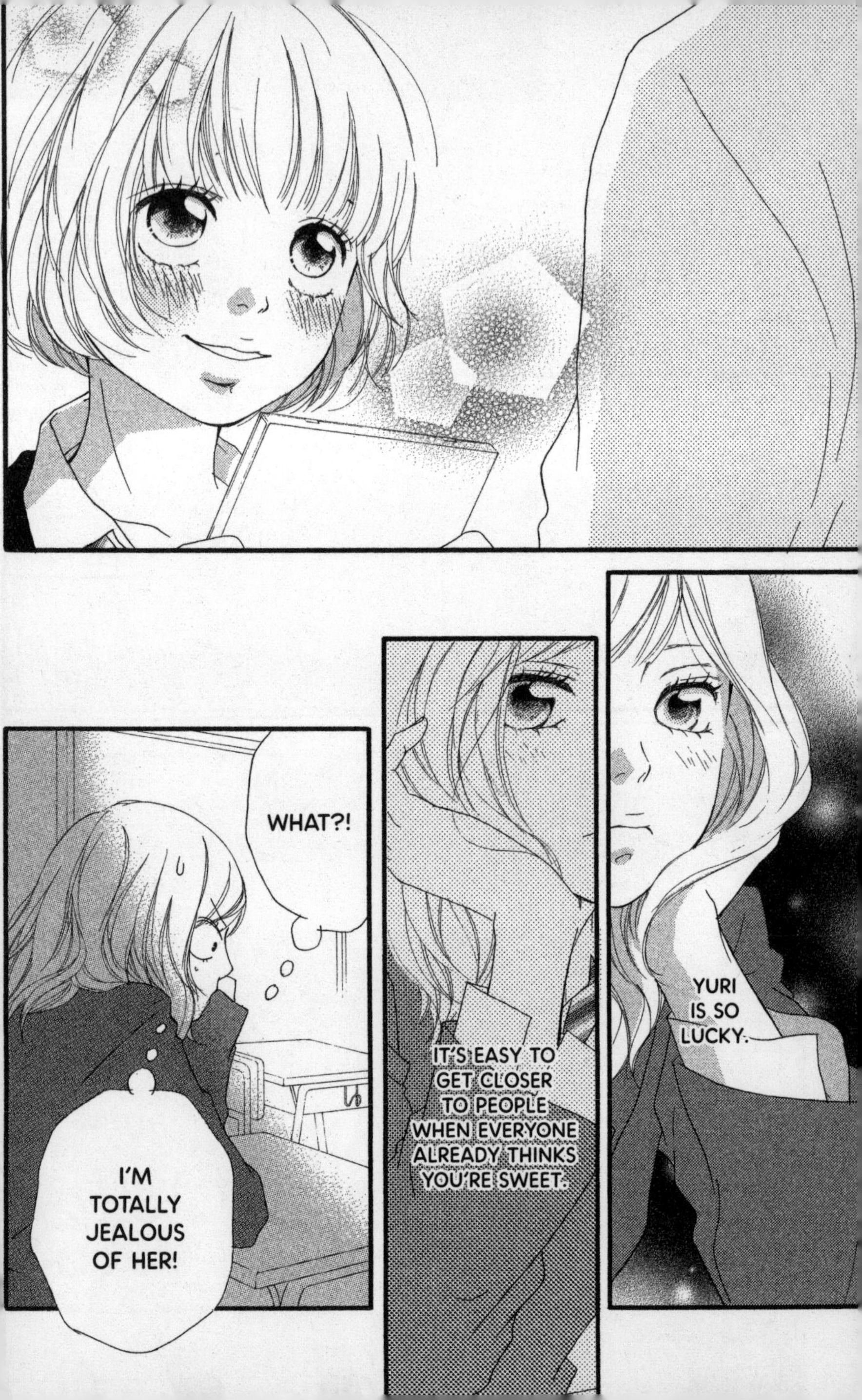
YURI IS SO LUCKY.
IT'S EASY TO GET CLOSER TO PEOPLE WHEN EVERYONE ALREADY THINKS YOU'RE SWEET.
WHAT?!
I'M TOTALLY JEALOUS OF HER!

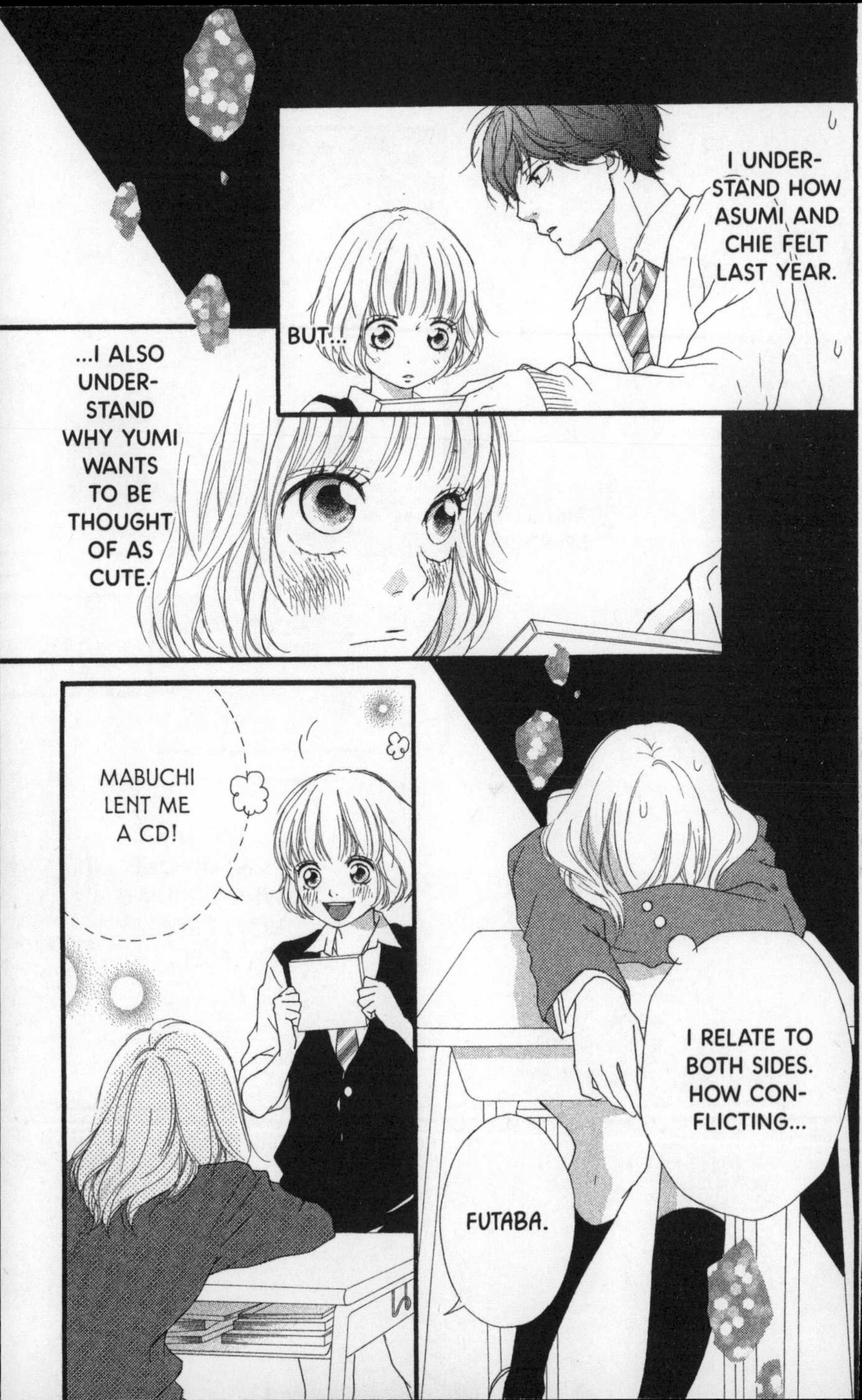
I UNDERSTAND HOW ASUMI AND CHIE FELT LAST YEAR.
BUT...
...I ALSO UNDERSTAND WHY YUMI WANTS TO BE THOUGHT OF AS CUTE.
I RELATE TO BOTH SIDES. HOW CONFLICTING...
FUTABA.
MABUCHI LENT ME A CD!

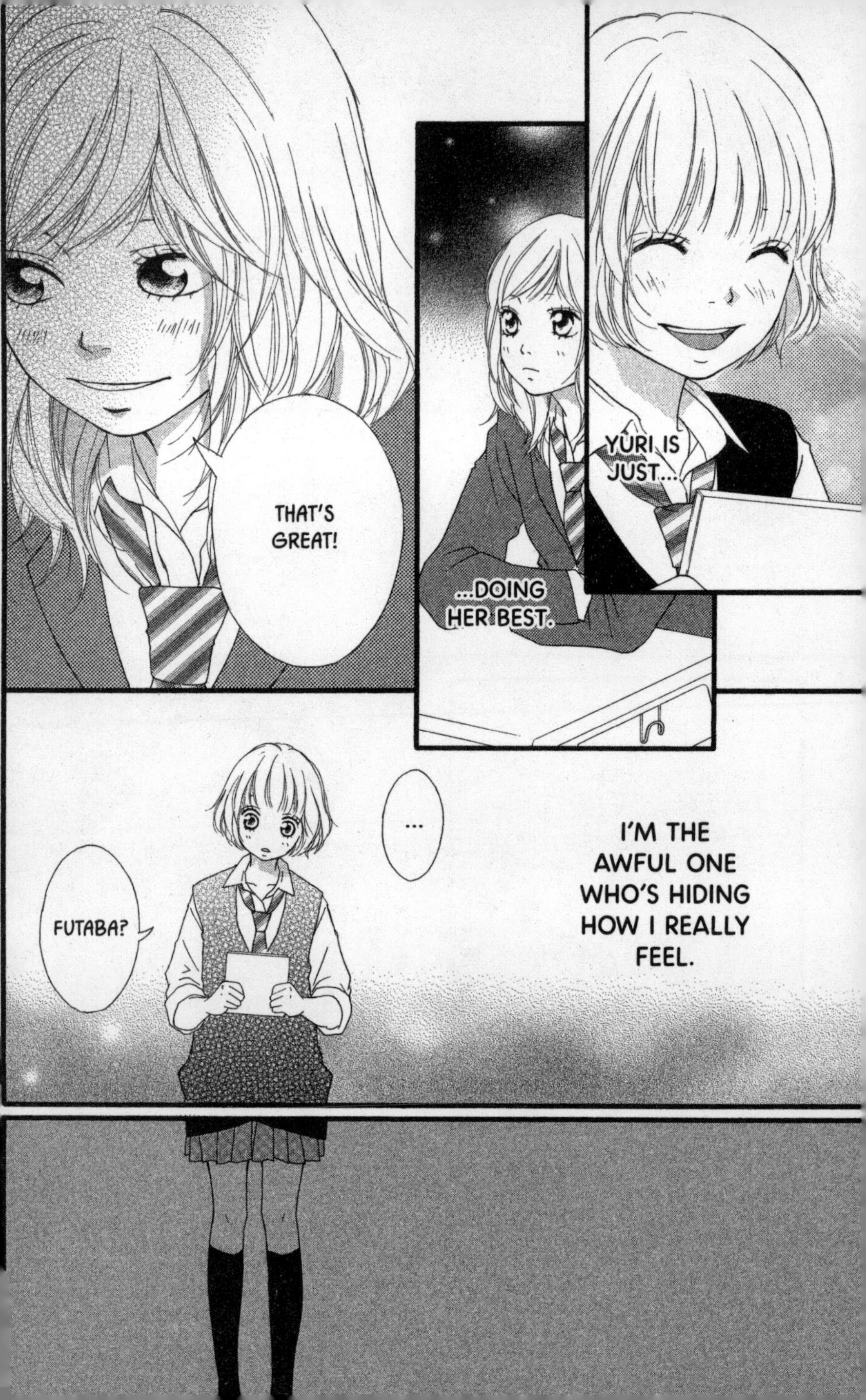
YURI IS JUST...
...DOING HER BEST.
THAT'S GREAT!
I'M THE AWFUL ONE WHO'S HIDING HOW I REALLY FEEL.
...
FUTABA?

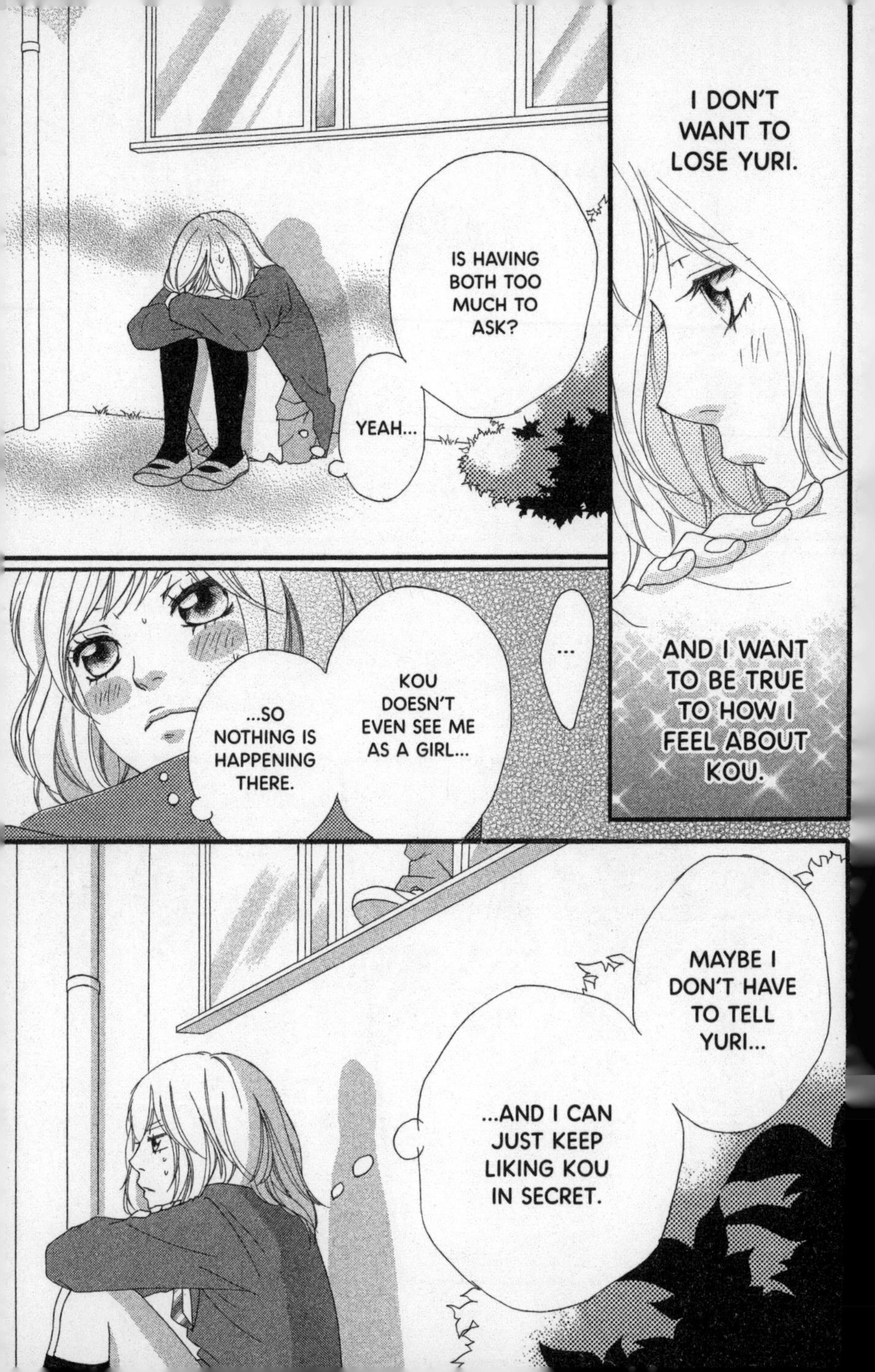
I DON'T WANT TO LOSE YURI.
AND I WANT TO BE TRUE TO HOW I FEEL ABOUT KOU.
IS HAVING BOTH TOO MUCH TO ASK?
YEAH...
...
KOU DOESN'T EVEN SEE ME AS A GIRL...
...SO NOTHING IS HAPPENING THERE.
MAYBE I DON'T HAVE TO TELL YURI...
...AND I CAN JUST KEEP LIKING KOU IN SECRET.

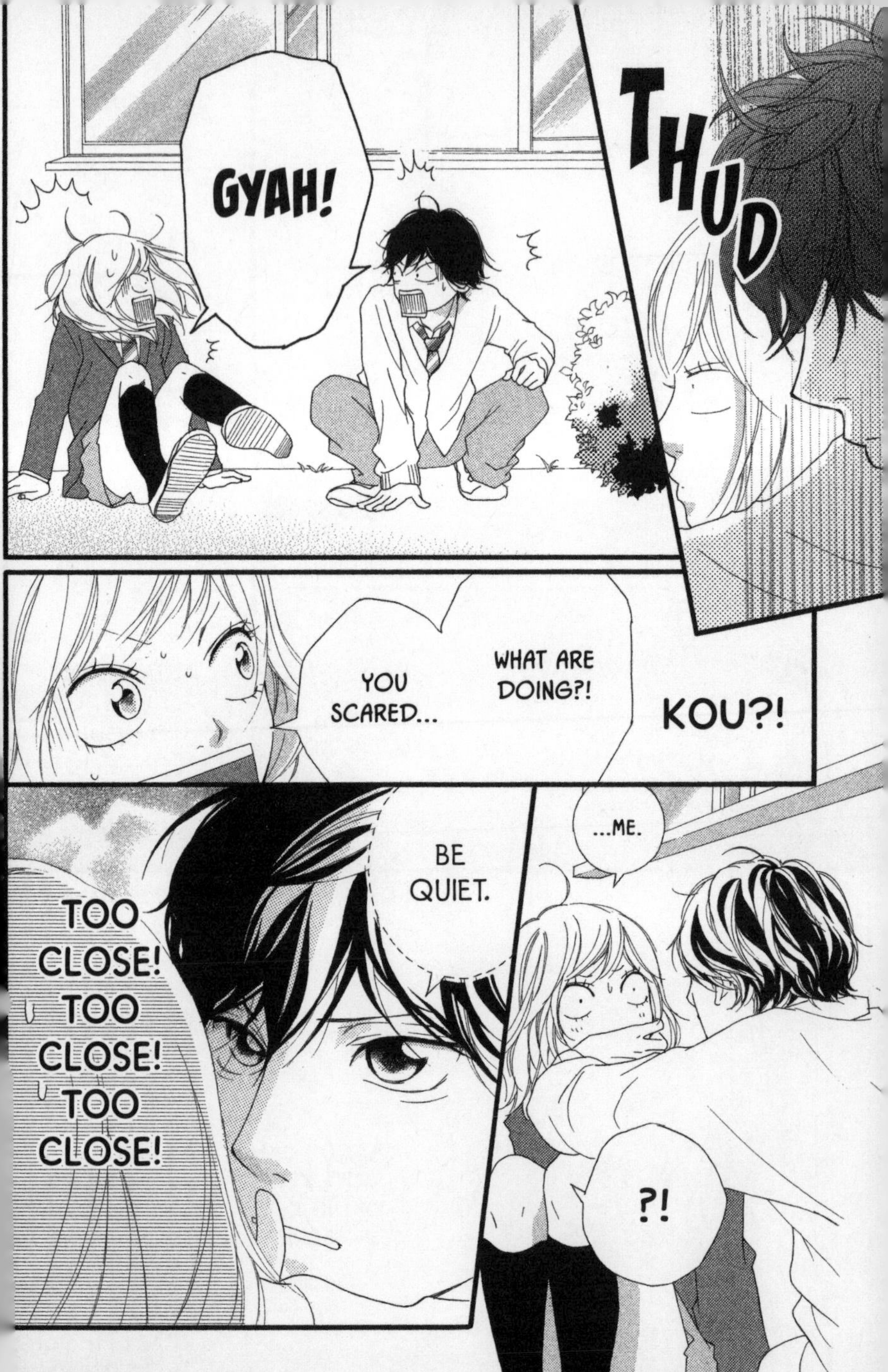
THUD
GYAH!
KOU?!
WHAT ARE DOING?!
YOU SCARED...
...ME.
?!
BE QUIET.
TOO CLOSE! TOO CLOSE! TOO CLOSE!

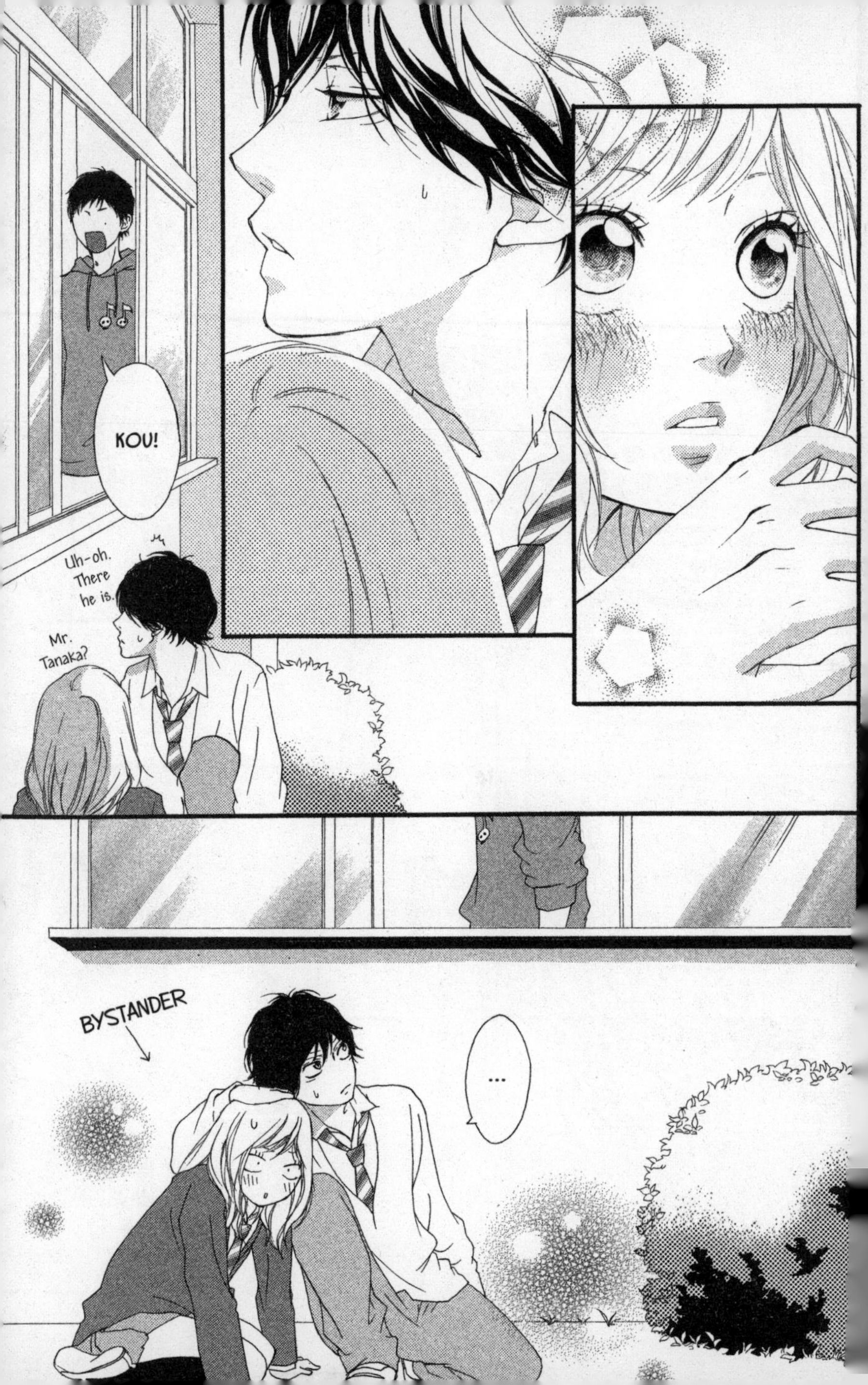
KOU!
Uh-oh. There he is.
Mr. Tanaka?
...
BYSTANDER

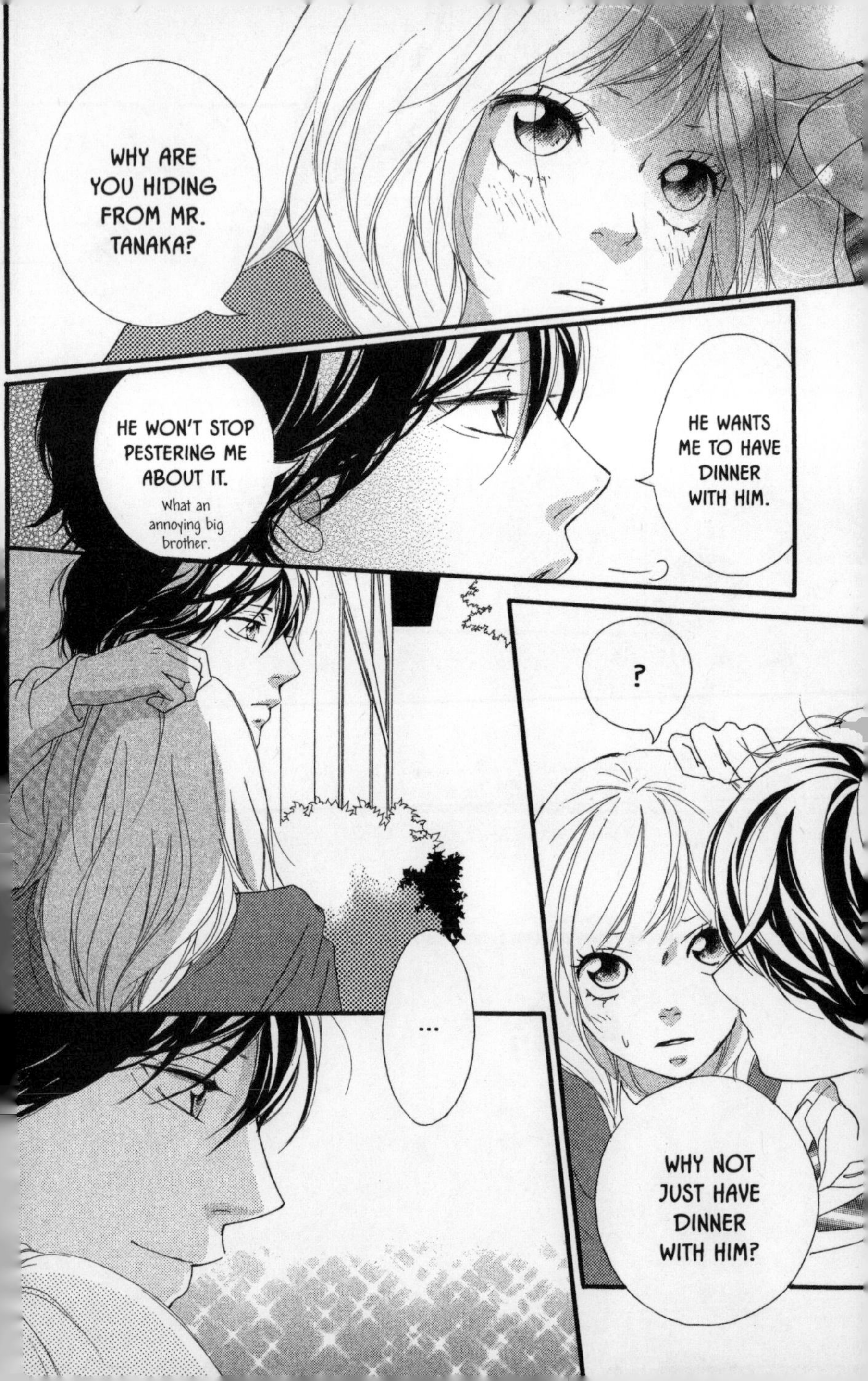
WHY ARE YOU HIDING FROM MR. TANAKA?
HE WANTS ME TO HAVE DINNER WITH HIM.
HE WON'T STOP PESTERING ME ABOUT IT.
What an annoying big brother.
?
WHY NOT JUST HAVE DINNER WITH HIM?
...

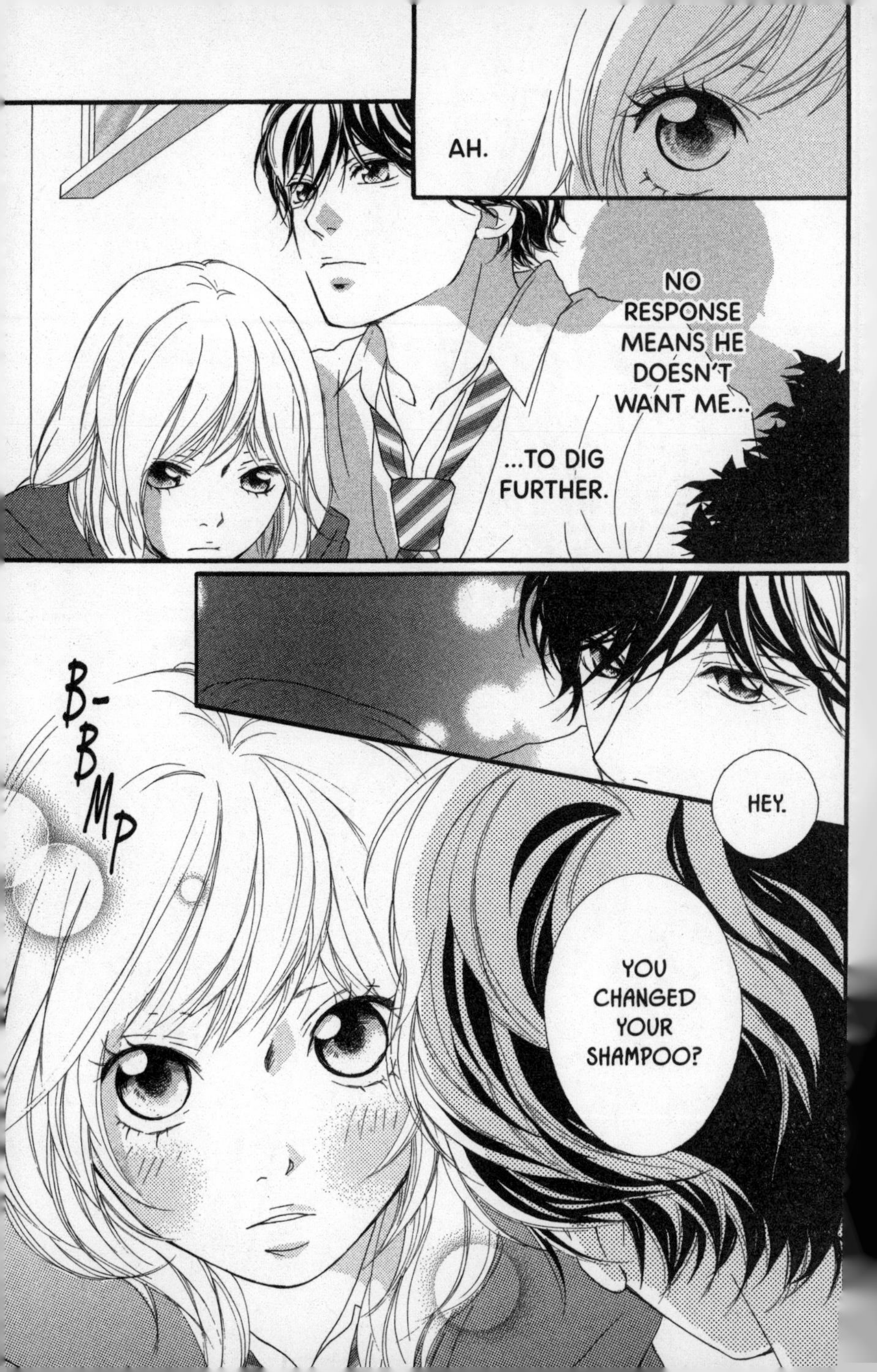
AH.
NO RESPONSE MEANS HE DOESN'T WANT ME...
...TO DIG FURTHER.
HEY.
B-BMP
YOU CHANGED YOUR SHAMPOO?

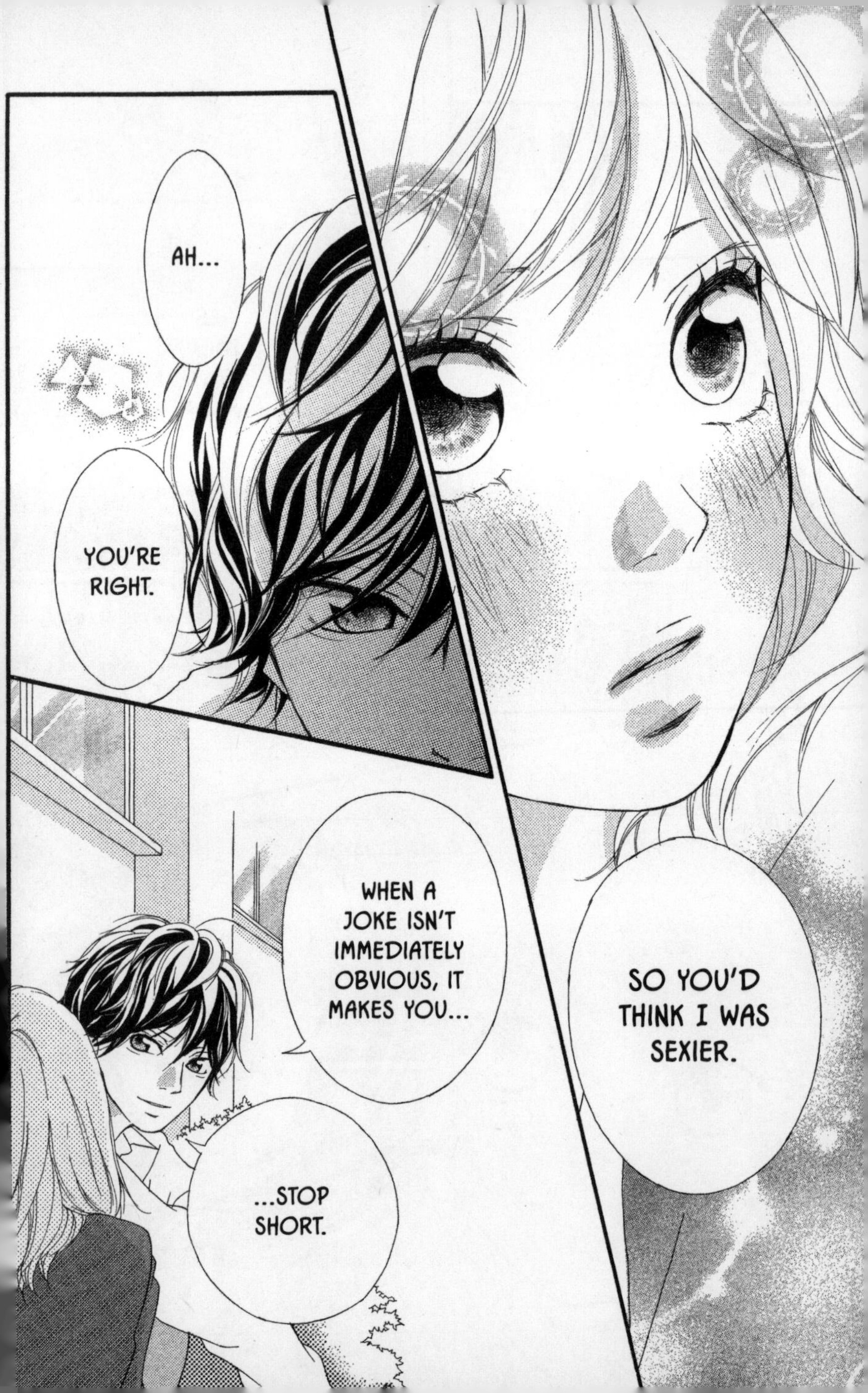
SO YOU'D THINK I WAS SEXIER.
AH...
YOU'RE RIGHT.
WHEN A JOKE ISN'T IMMEDIATELY OBVIOUS, IT MAKES YOU...
...STOP SHORT.

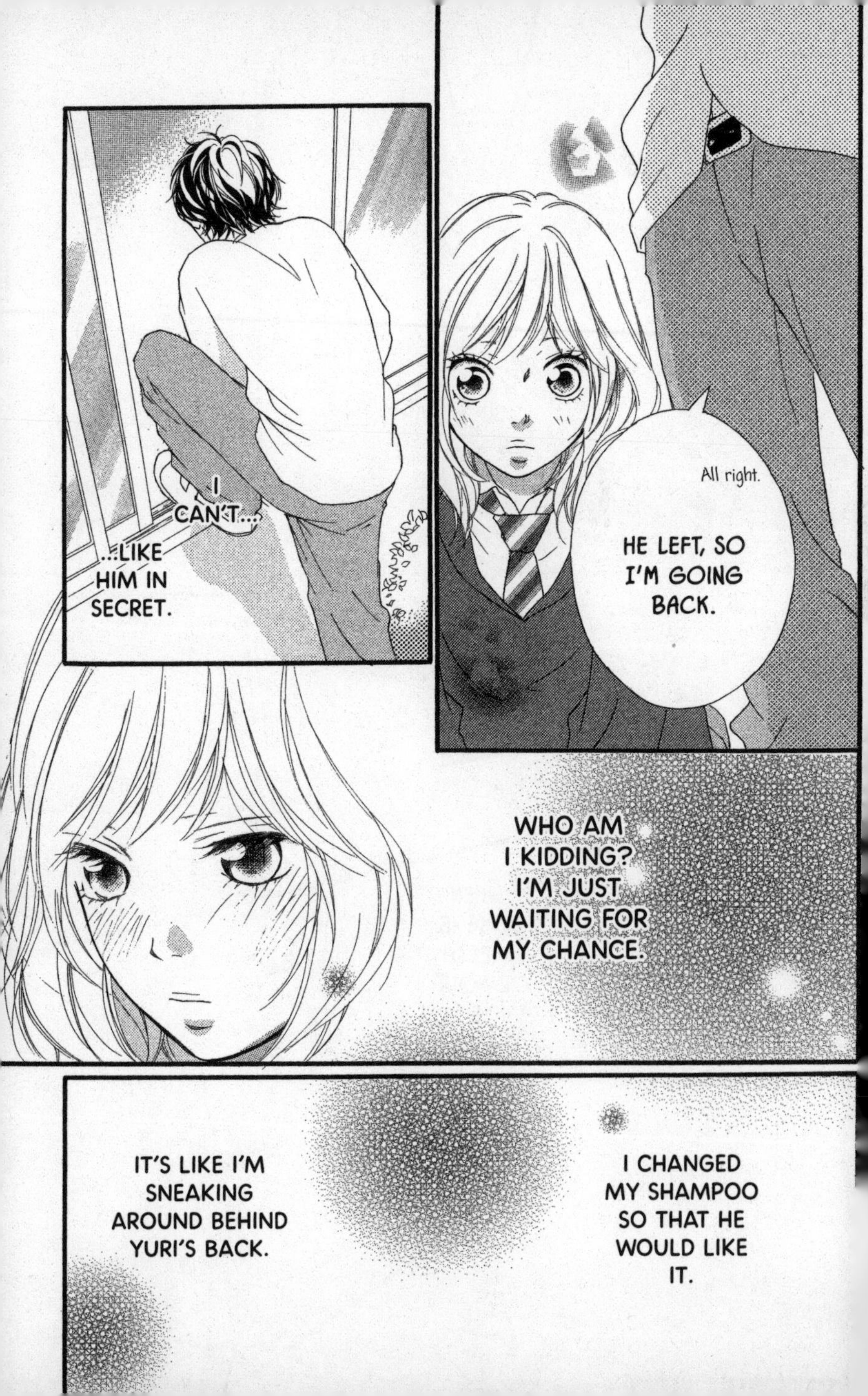
All right.
HE LEFT, SO I'M GOING BACK.
I CAN'T...
...LIKE HIM IN SECRET.
WHO AM I KIDDING? I'M JUST WAITING FOR MY CHANCE.
I CHANGED MY SHAMPOO SO THAT HE WOULD LIKE IT.
IT'S LIKE I'M SNEAKING AROUND BEHIND YURI'S BACK.

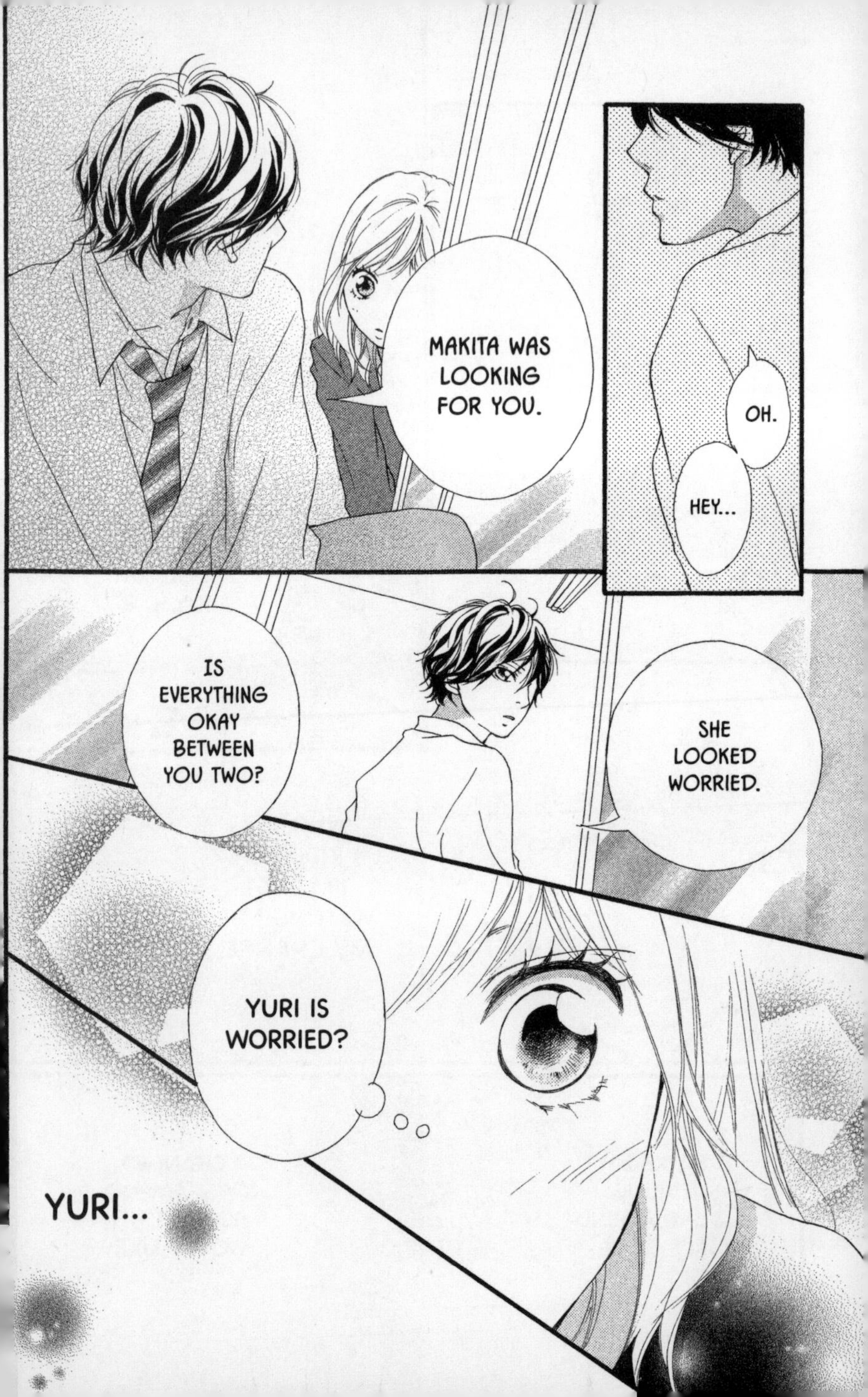
OH.
HEY...
MAKITA WAS LOOKING FOR YOU.
SHE LOOKED WORRIED.
IS EVERYTHING OKAY BETWEEN YOU TWO?
YURI IS WORRIED?
YURI...

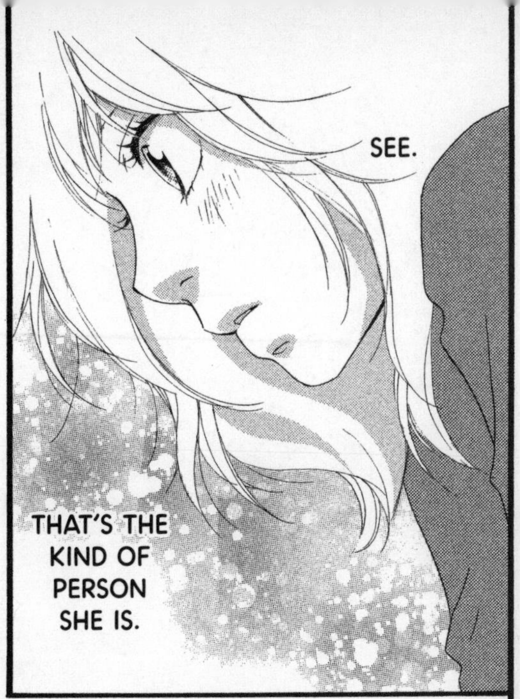
SEE.
THAT'S THE KIND OF PERSON SHE IS.

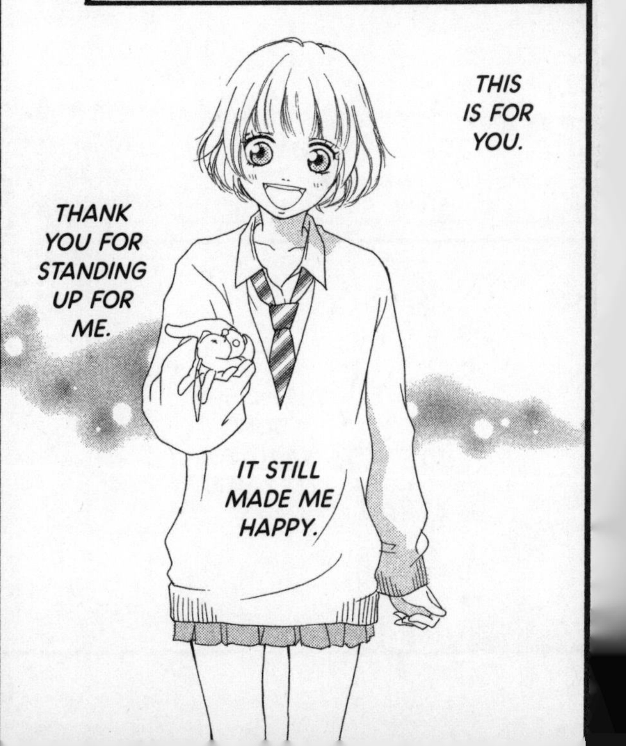
THIS IS FOR YOU.
THANK YOU FOR STANDING UP FOR ME.
IT STILL MADE ME HAPPY.

My lifestyle is rather irregular. My eating habits are especially erratic. Someone told me, "I'm really worried about the way you eat." It led me to realize that I'm no longer at an age when I can eat snacks instead of a meal. I committed to eating more vegetables! I got excited about it and bought a silicone steamer. I ate heaps of vegetables... But a few weeks later I got tired of it. I didn't want to eat vegetables all the time, and I got really tired of chopping them up. Supermarkets are a bother too. After this, I realized just how amazing all the moms out there are. There's nothing harder than preparing good meals for your family every day. And to change up the menu too... That's incredible!! Having someone else cook for you is a blessing.

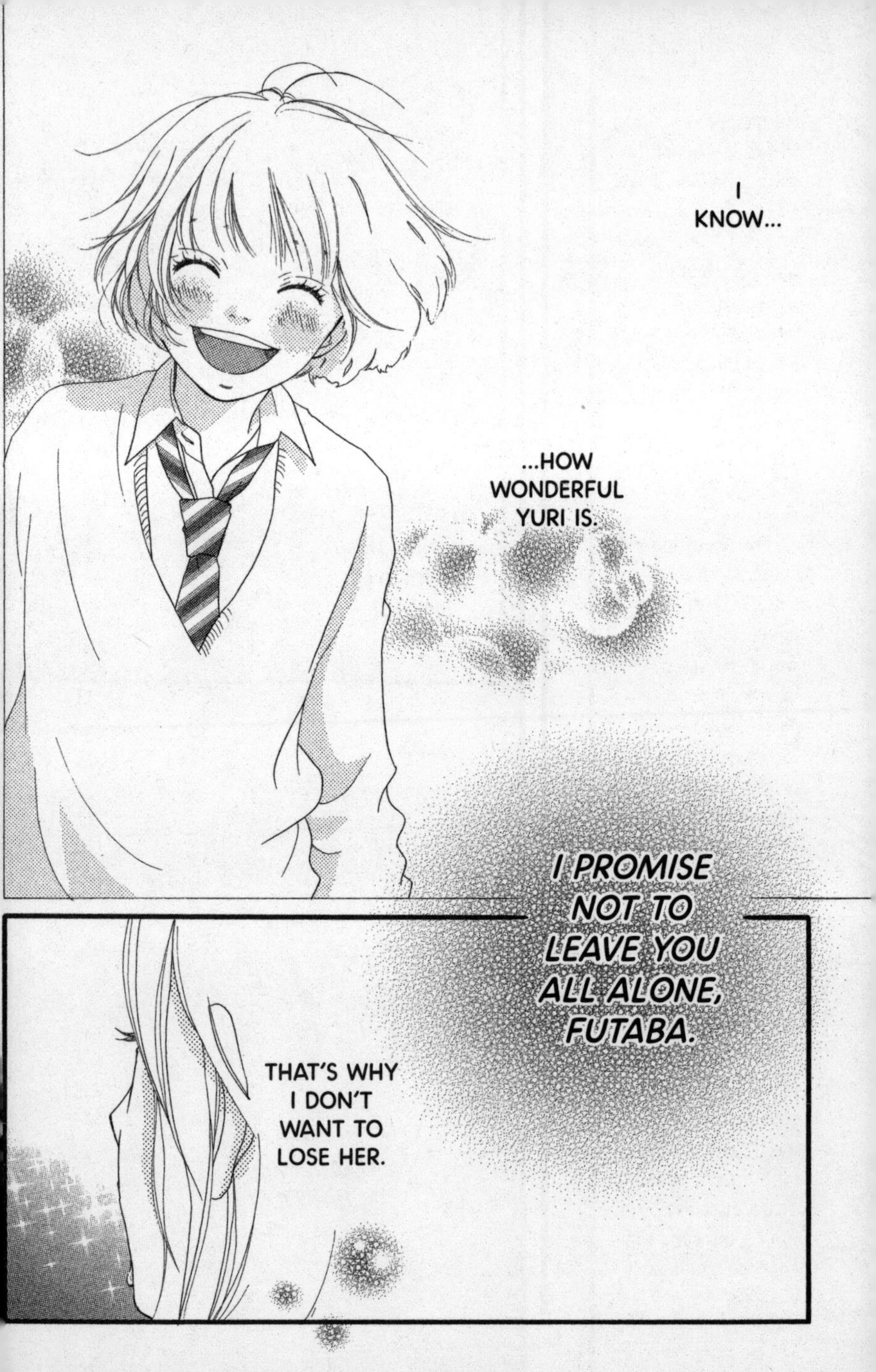
I KNOW...
...HOW WONDERFUL YURI IS.
I PROMISE NOT TO LEAVE YOU ALL ALONE, FUTABA.
THAT'S WHY I DON'T WANT TO LOSE HER.

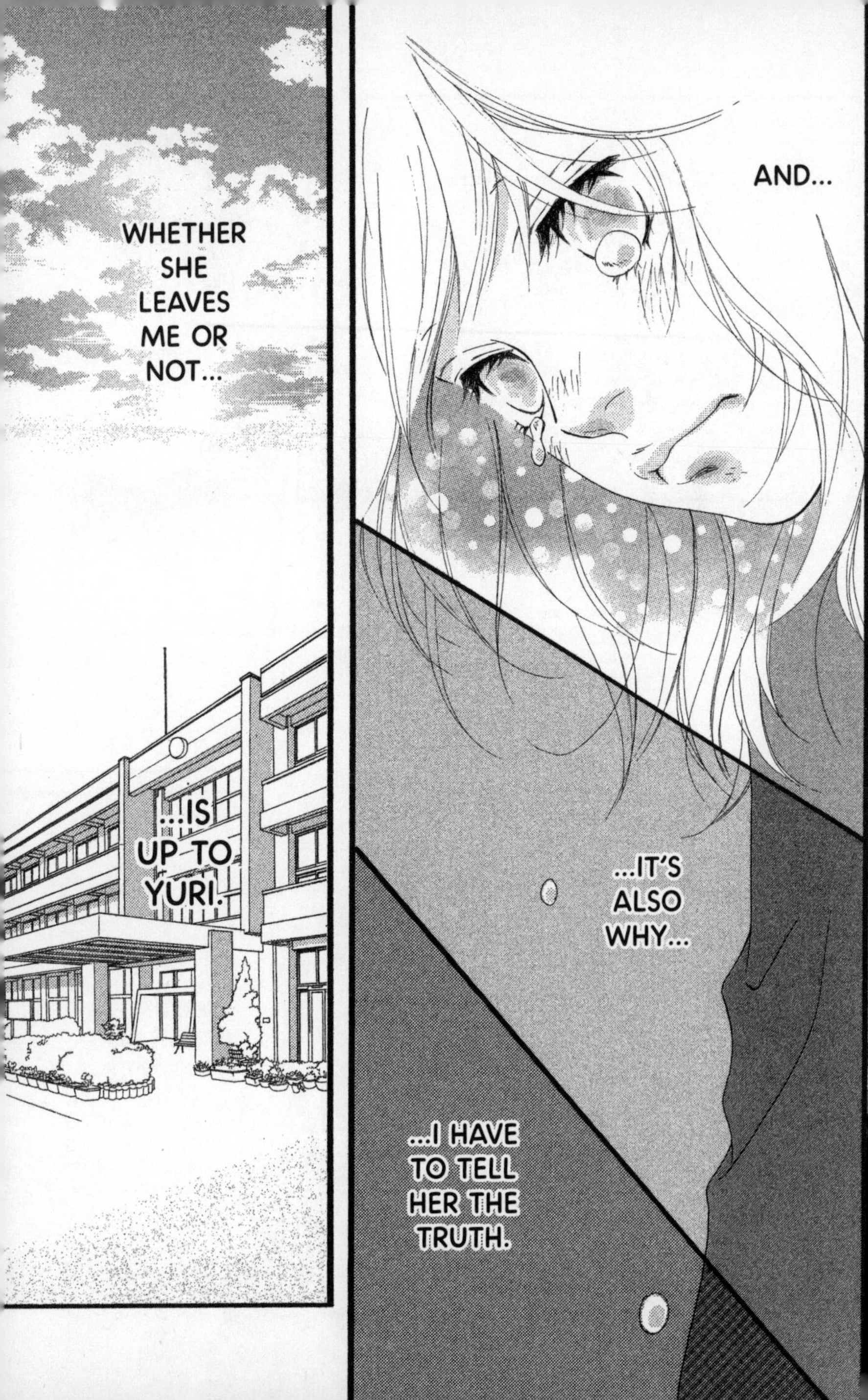
AND...
...IT'S ALSO WHY...
...I HAVE TO TELL HER THE TRUTH.
WHETHER SHE LEAVES ME OR NOT...
...IS UP TO YURI.

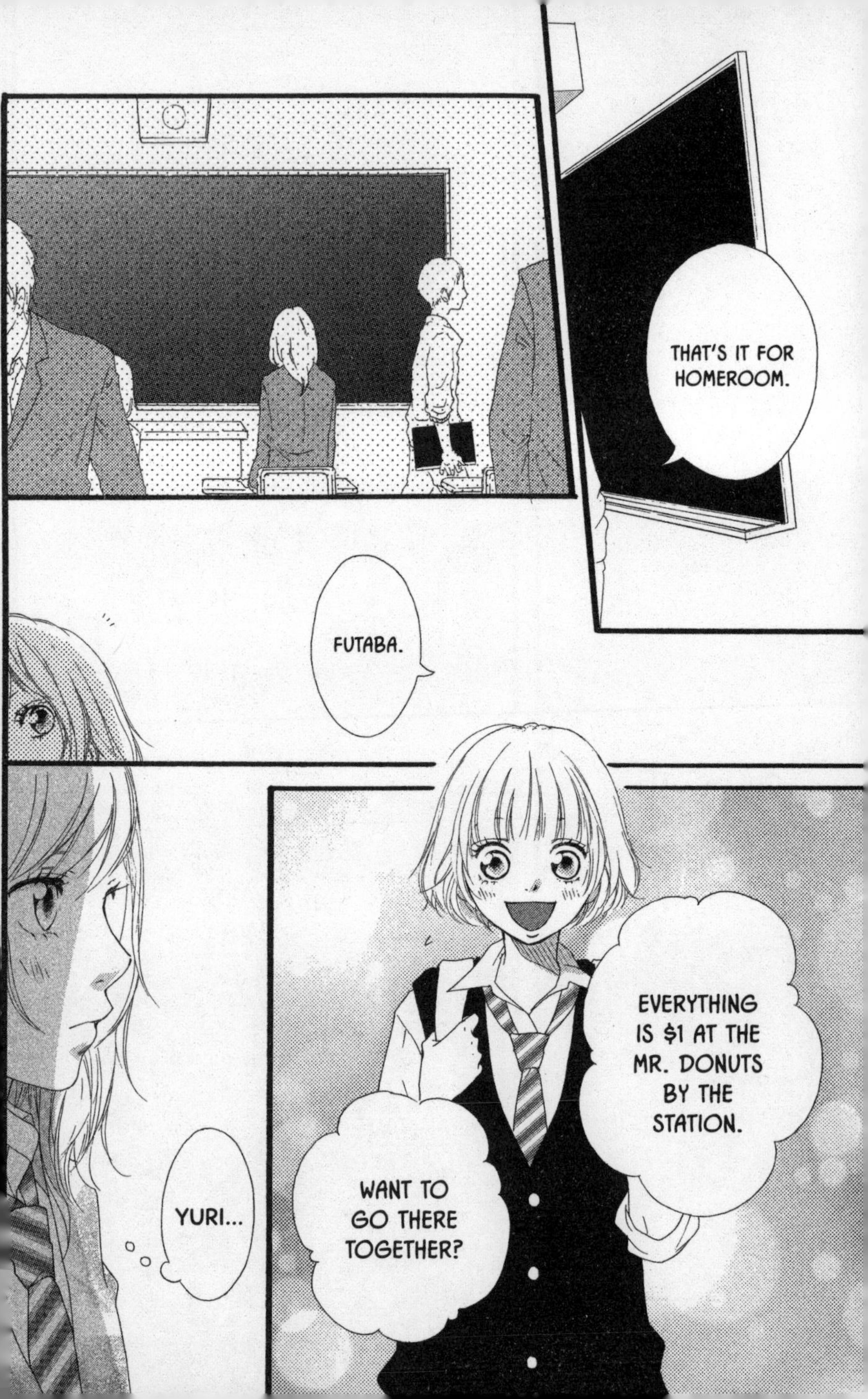
THAT'S IT FOR HOMEROOM.
FUTABA.
EVERYTHING IS $1 AT THE MR. DONUTS BY THE STATION.
WANT TO GO THERE TOGETHER?
YURI...

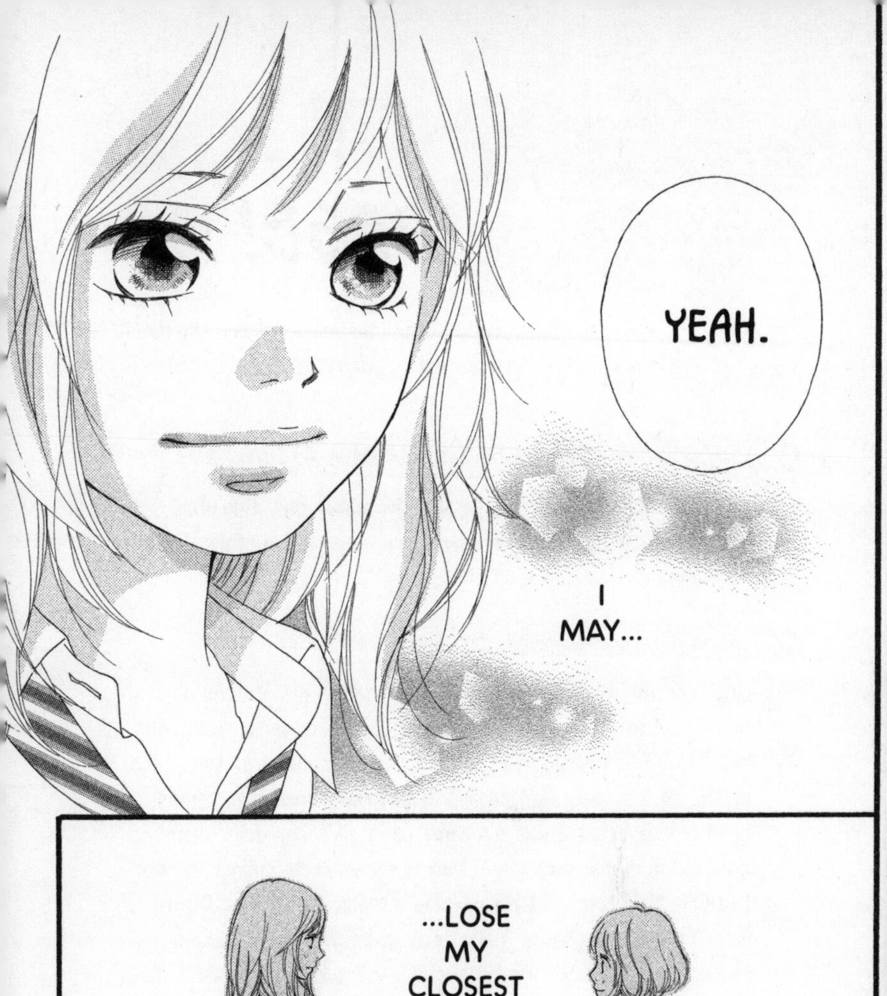
YEAH.
I MAY...

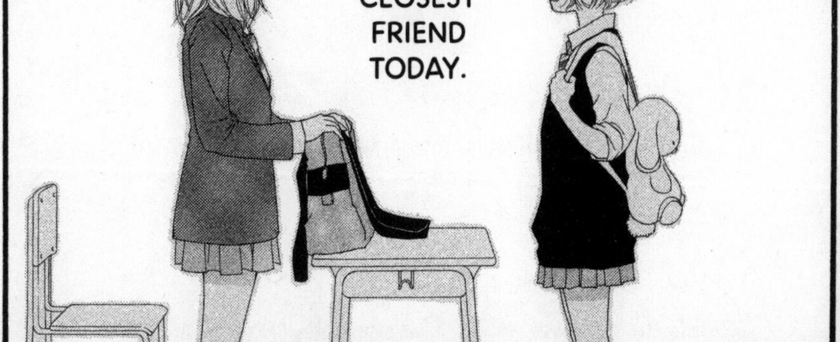
...LOSE MY CLOSEST FRIEND TODAY.

Q & A PAGE! PART 1

I'm going to answer as many of your questions as I can! For starters, I'll answer your questions about *Ao Haru Ride*. ☆

Q: Which characters are the hardest to draw in *Ao Haru Ride*?

A: Kou and Mr. Tanaka. Kou's personality makes him difficult to draw. But visually, the brothers are both hard. I really hate them...

Q: Where did the character names come from?

A: Until recently I had a notebook full of names I had made up, and I would use them based on each new character's personality. But I lost that notebook, so lately I've been coming up with them on the fly. Kou actually had a different name in the beginning, but I realized that it was the same name as a character from another *Betsuma* series, so I had to scramble to change it. Now I rather like "Kou," which I think is a better fit for him. By the way, "Futaba" is a name that's borrowed from one of my old teachers. Even back then I thought it was a cute name. And she was beautiful. And adorable. And amazing. Ha ha.

Q: Are there any true stories in *Ao Haru Ride*?

A: There are a few, although they've been modified. I've added and subtracted here and there to make them a bit more dramatic.

Q: Is Mr. Tanaka married?

A: He's still single. In volume 3, he's probably 25 years old. Unless I decide to change that.

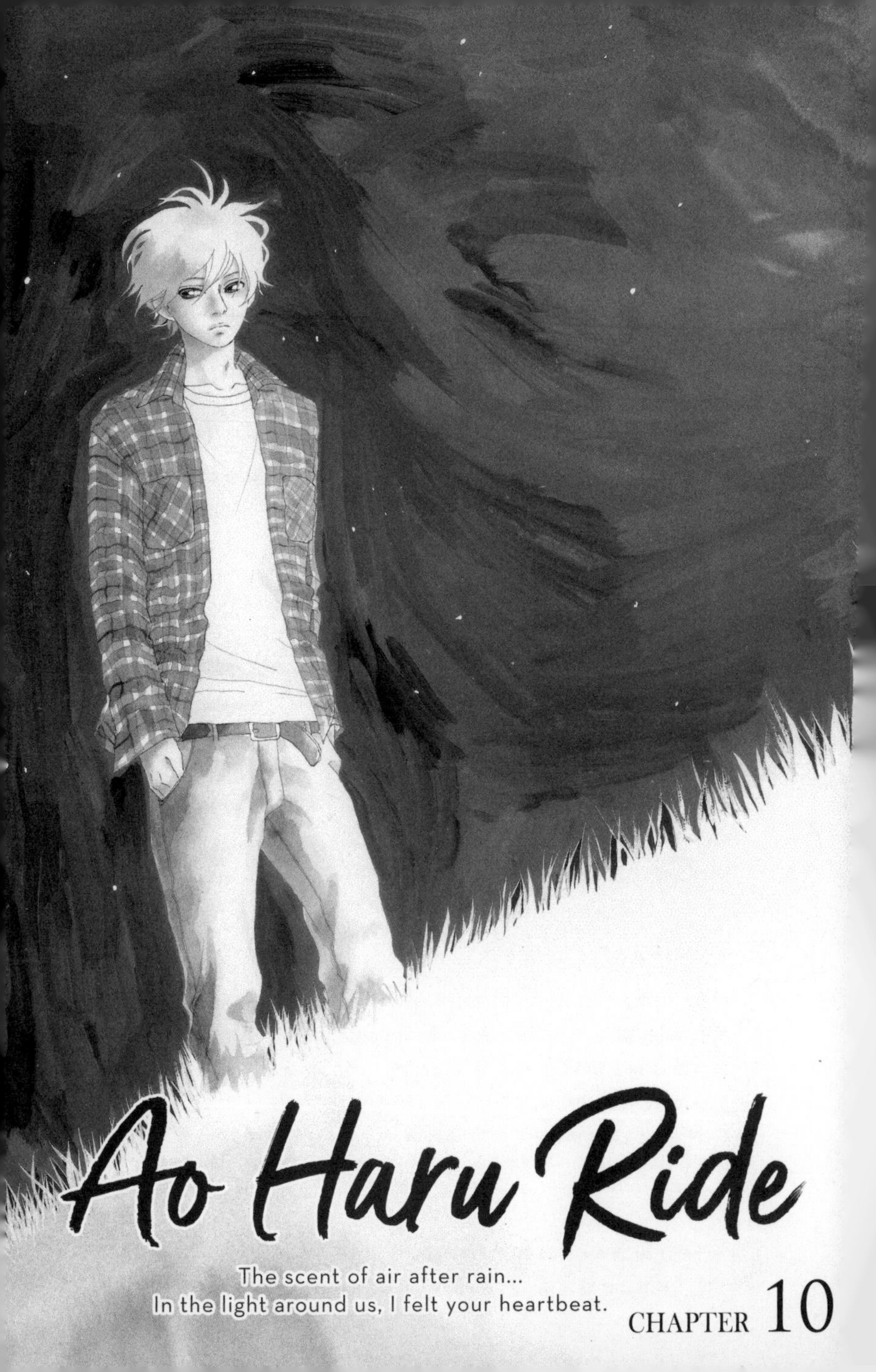
Ao Haru Ride
The scent of air after rain...
In the light around us, I felt your heartbeat.
CHAPTER 10

Q & A PAGE! PART 2

In this part I'm going to answer as many questions about me as I can.

Q : Why did you decide to become a mangaka?

A : If I had to say why, the catalyst was my disdain for riding on crowded trains. I thought, "If I can work at home, I can escape all this." It sounds like a silly reason, but I am who I am now thanks to those crowded trains!

Q : What order do you draw people in?

A : Face shape → eyes → eyebrows → nose → mouth → hair. That's it. ○

Q : What do you want right now?

A : A spacious room to work in! The room I currently work in is unbelievably cramped. A mere 5.75 tatami mats. I'm packed in here with two assistants. We're like sardines!

Q : What do you like to eat?

A : I like anything that can be eaten. The other day I ended my obsession with *dora yaki*, and now I'm onto *champon*, although it is also nearing the end of its reign. I wonder what I'll be obsessed with next.

(*Dora yaki* is a Japanese sweet that resembles two pancakes with red beans in the middle. *Champon* is a meat and vegetable soup that is a regional dish from Nagasaki.)

I didn't get to answer as many questions as I'd hoped. Please keep sending them along and I'll continue to do more Q&As in the future!

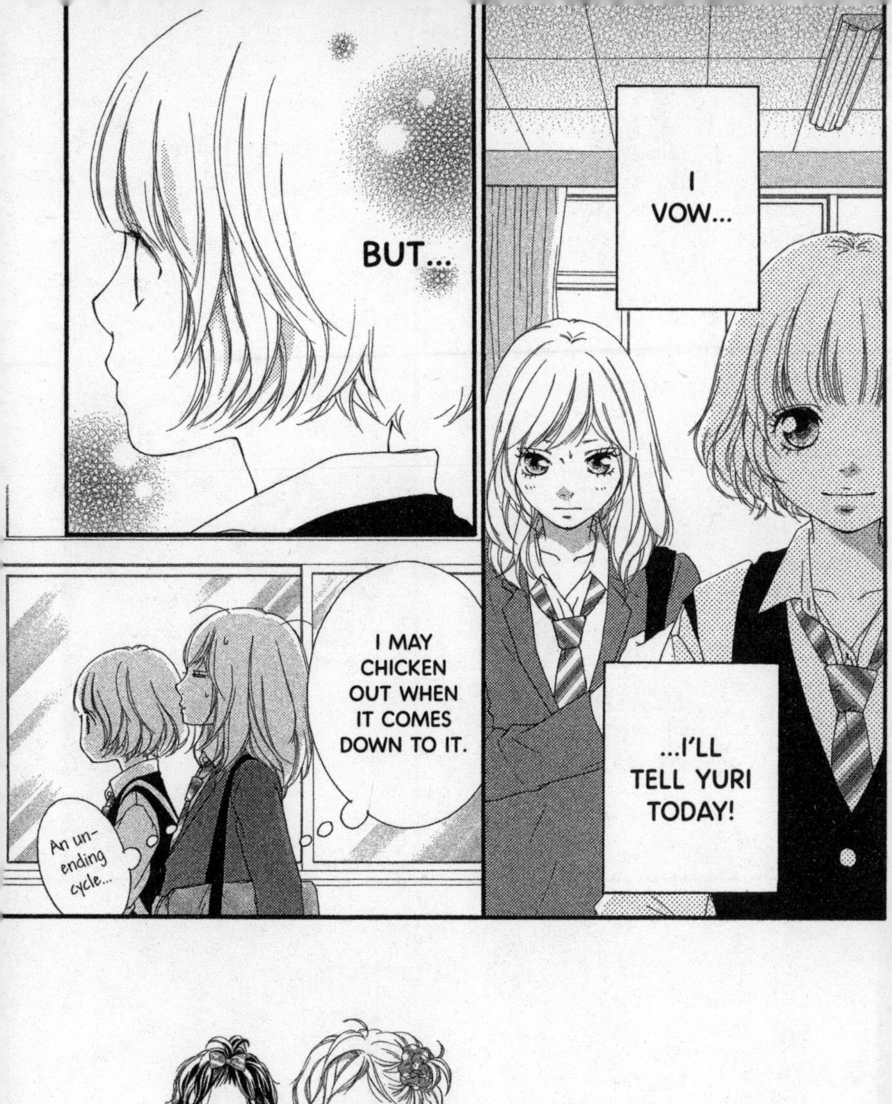
I VOW...
...I'LL TELL YURI TODAY!
BUT...
I MAY CHICKEN OUT WHEN IT COMES DOWN TO IT.
An un-ending cycle...

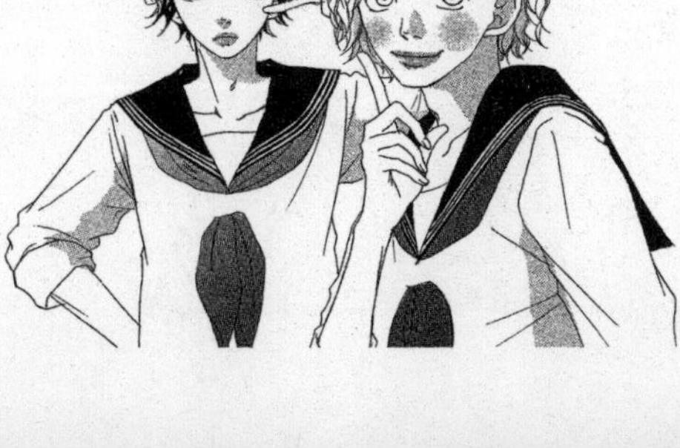

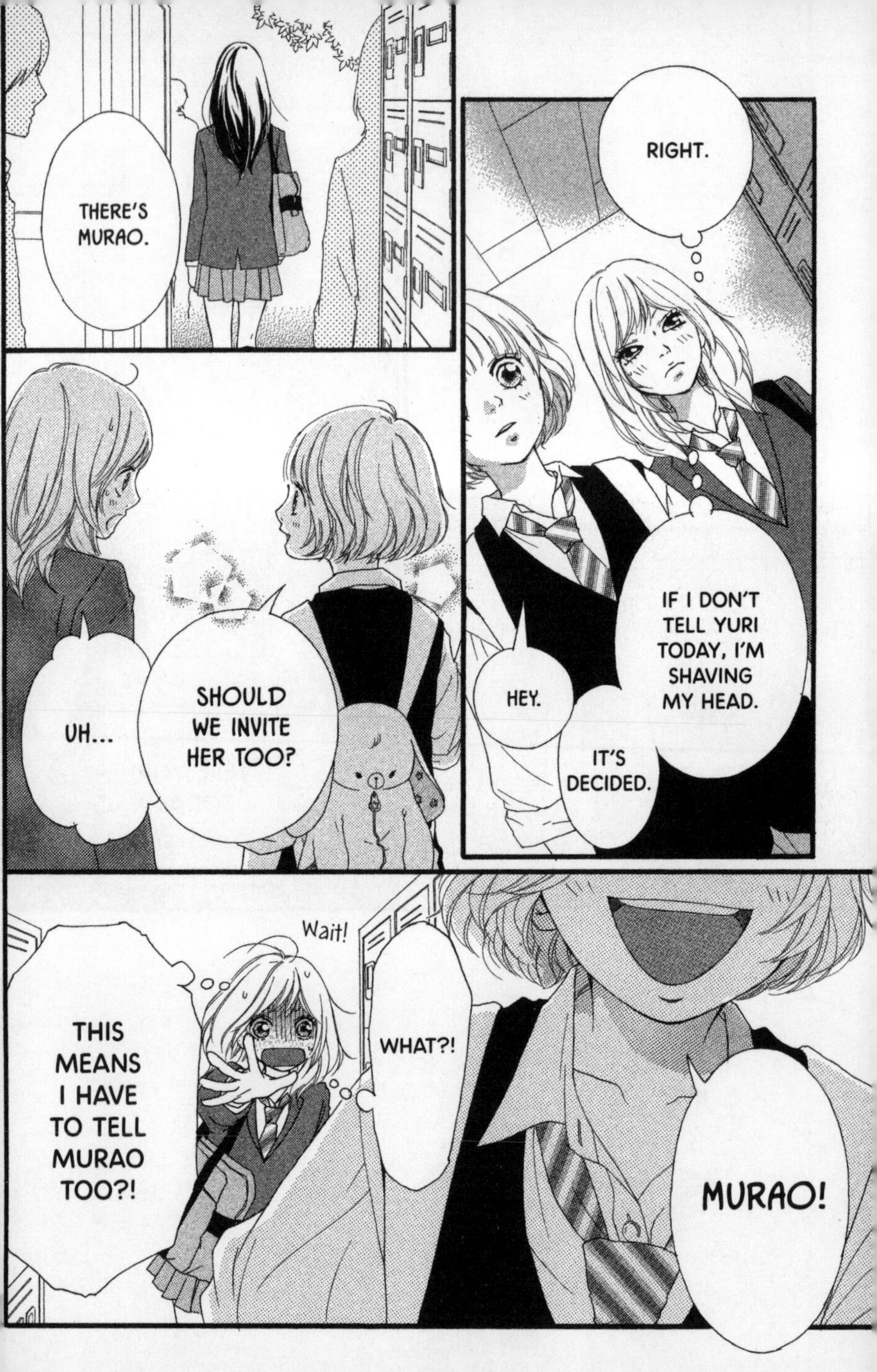
RIGHT.
IF I DON'T TELL YURI TODAY, I'M SHAVING MY HEAD.
IT'S DECIDED.
HEY.
THERE'S MURAO.
SHOULD WE INVITE HER TOO?
UH...
MURAO!
WHAT?!
Wait!
THIS MEANS I HAVE TO TELL MURAO TOO?!

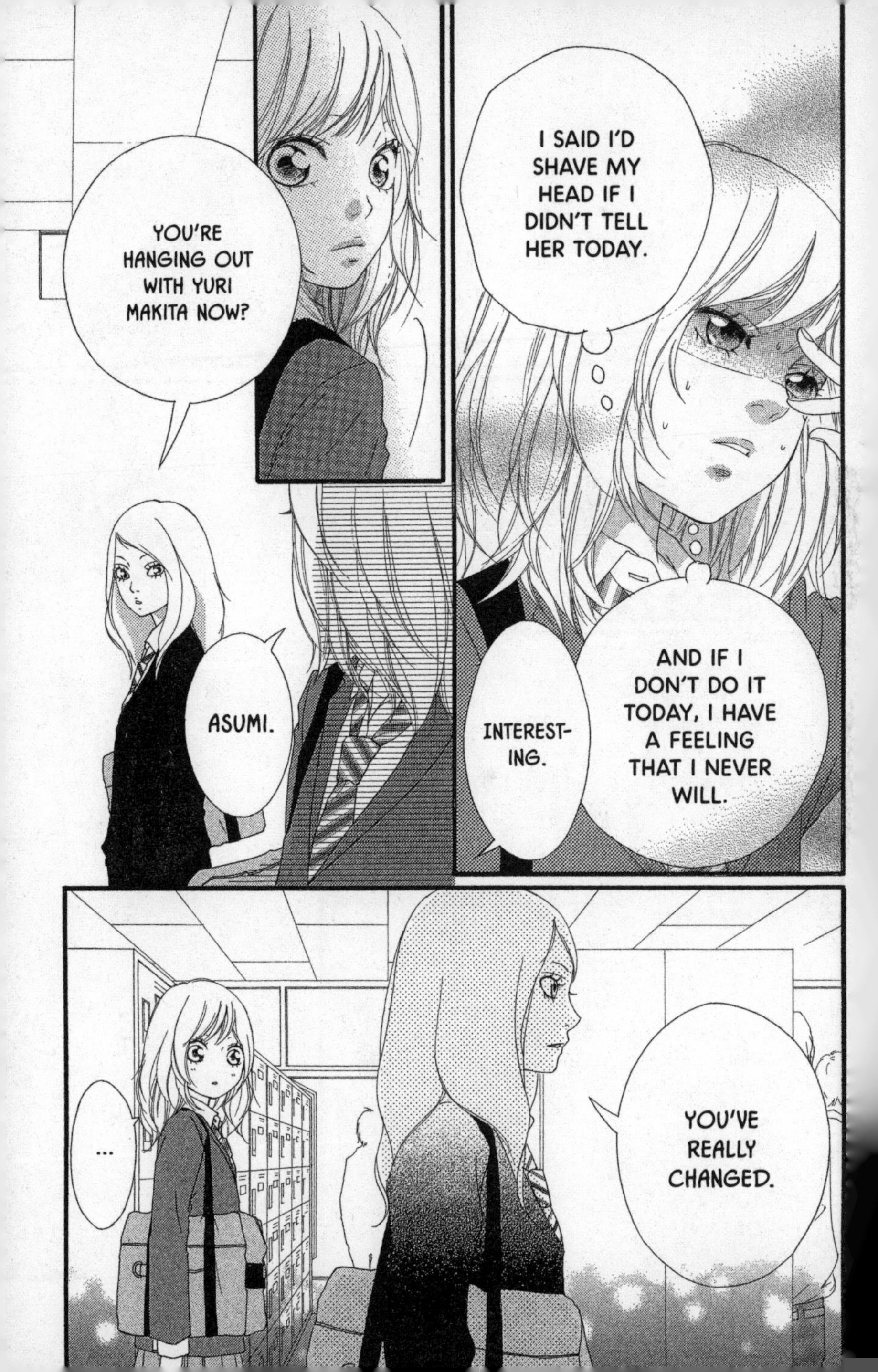
I SAID I'D SHAVE MY HEAD IF I DIDN'T TELL HER TODAY.
AND IF I DON'T DO IT TODAY, I HAVE A FEELING THAT I NEVER WILL.
INTERESTING.
YOU'RE HANGING OUT WITH YURI MAKITA NOW?
ASUMI.
YOU'VE REALLY CHANGED.
...

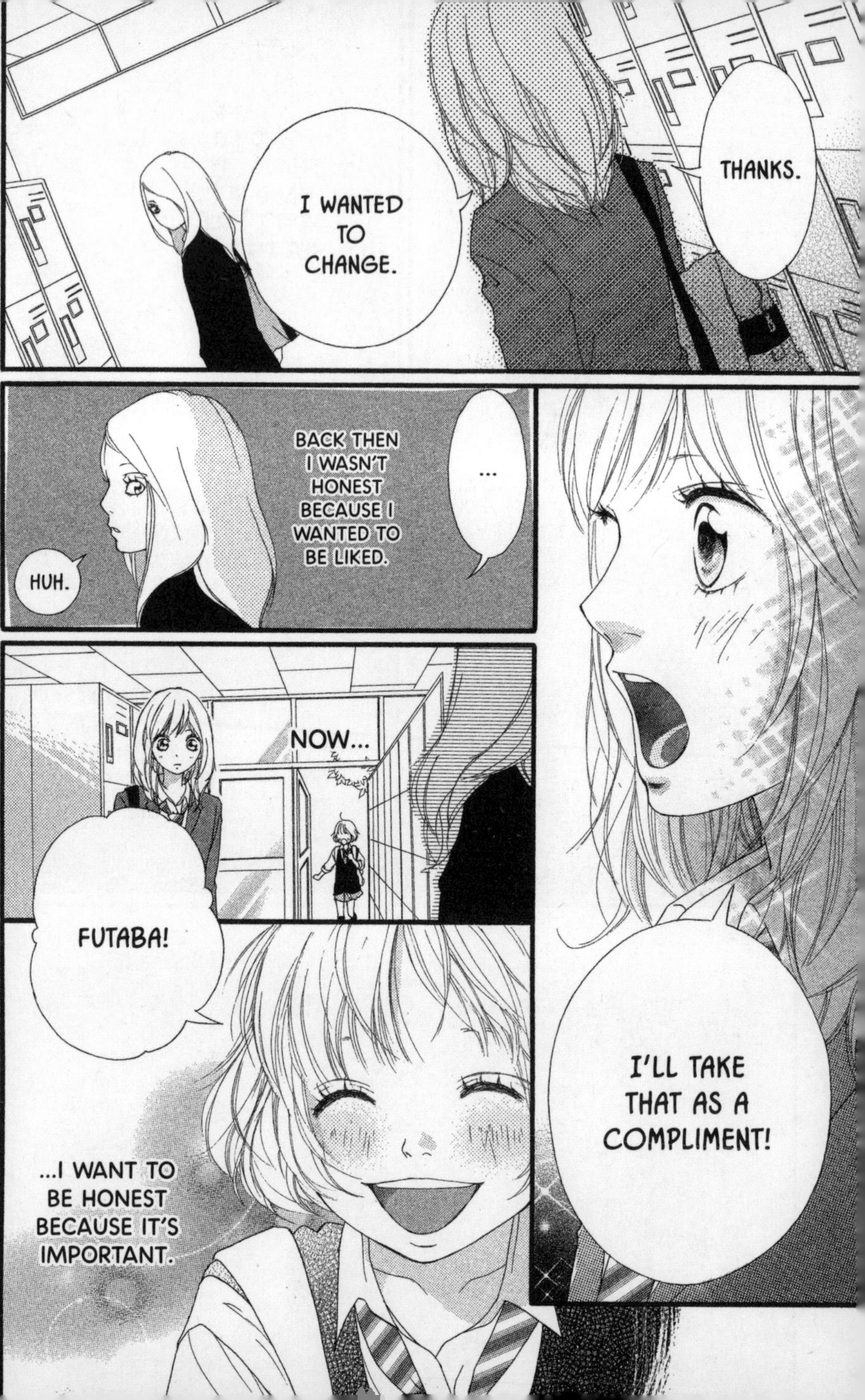
THANKS.
I WANTED TO CHANGE.
I'LL TAKE THAT AS A COMPLIMENT!
...
BACK THEN I WASN'T HONEST BECAUSE I WANTED TO BE LIKED.
HUH.
NOW...
FUTABA!
...I WANT TO BE HONEST BECAUSE IT'S IMPORTANT.

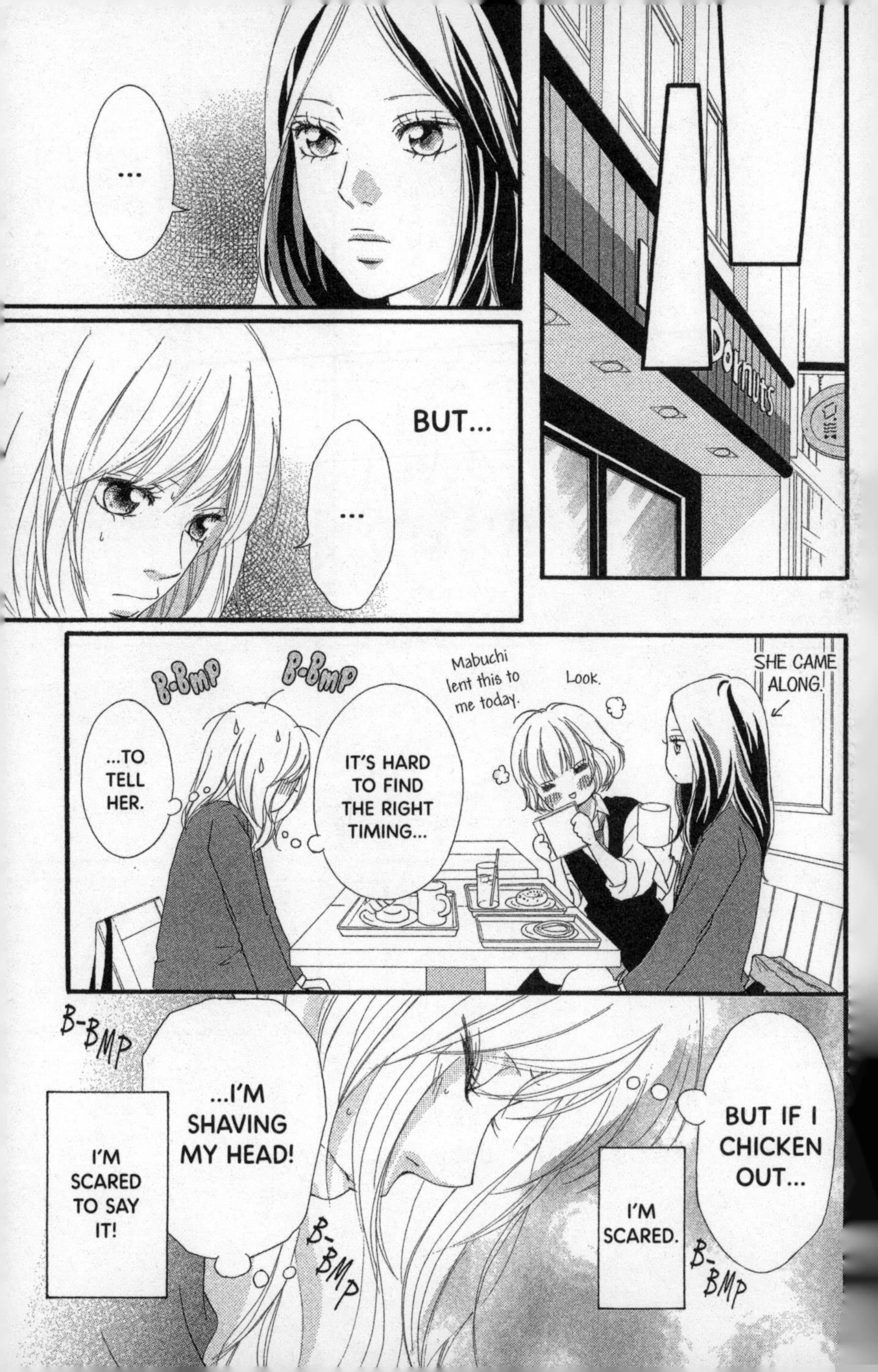
Donuts
...
BUT...
...
SHE CAME ALONG.
Look.
Mabuchi lent this to me today.
B-BMP
IT'S HARD TO FIND THE RIGHT TIMING...
B-BMP
...TO TELL HER.
BUT IF I CHICKEN OUT...
B-BMP
I'M SCARED.
...I'M SHAVING MY HEAD!
B-BMP
I'M SCARED TO SAY IT!
B-BMP

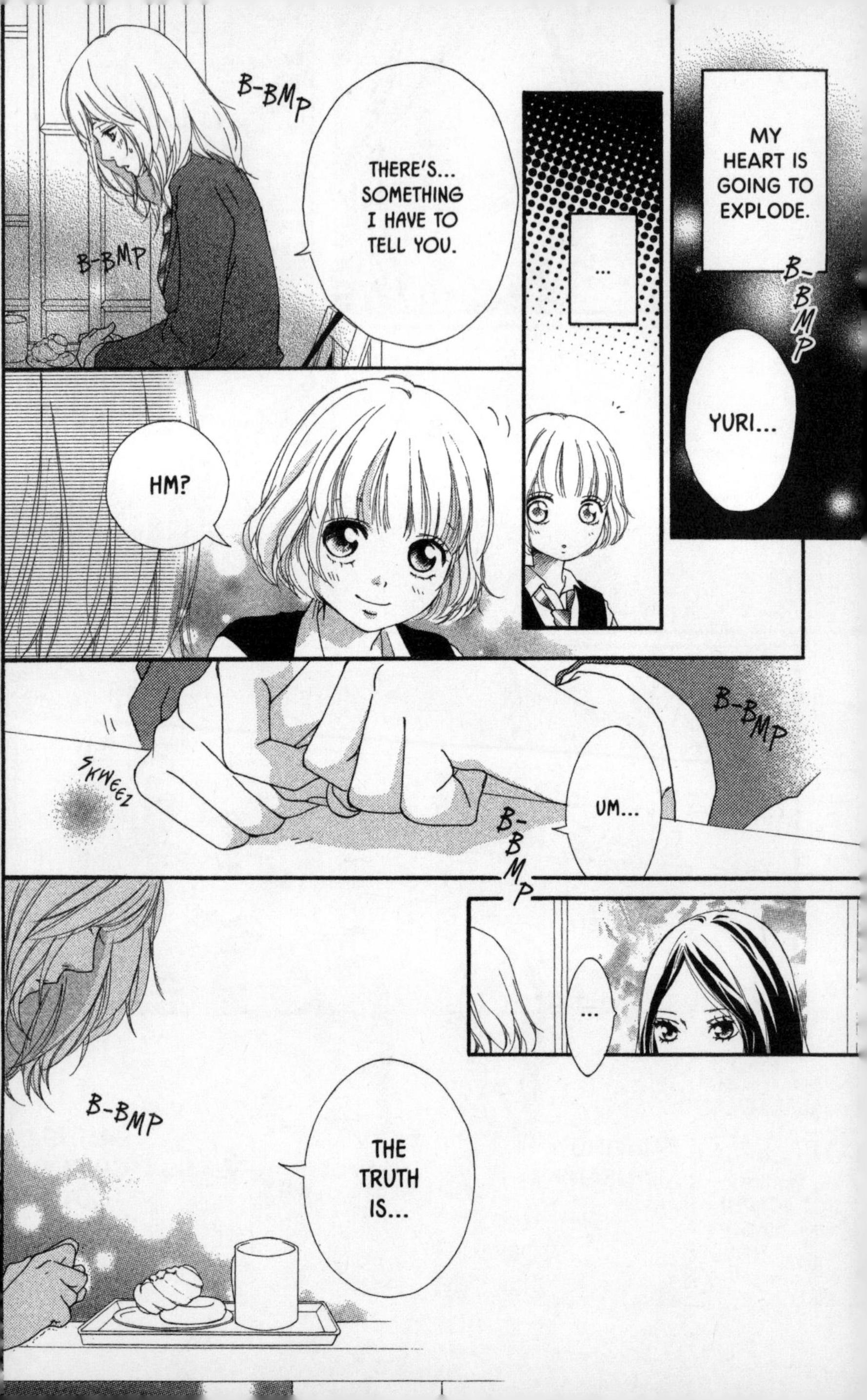

MY HEART IS GOING TO EXPLODE.
B-BMP
YURI...
...
B-BMP
THERE'S... SOMETHING I HAVE TO TELL YOU.
B-BMP
HM?
B-BMP
UM...
B-BMP
SKWEEZ
...
B-BMP
THE TRUTH IS...

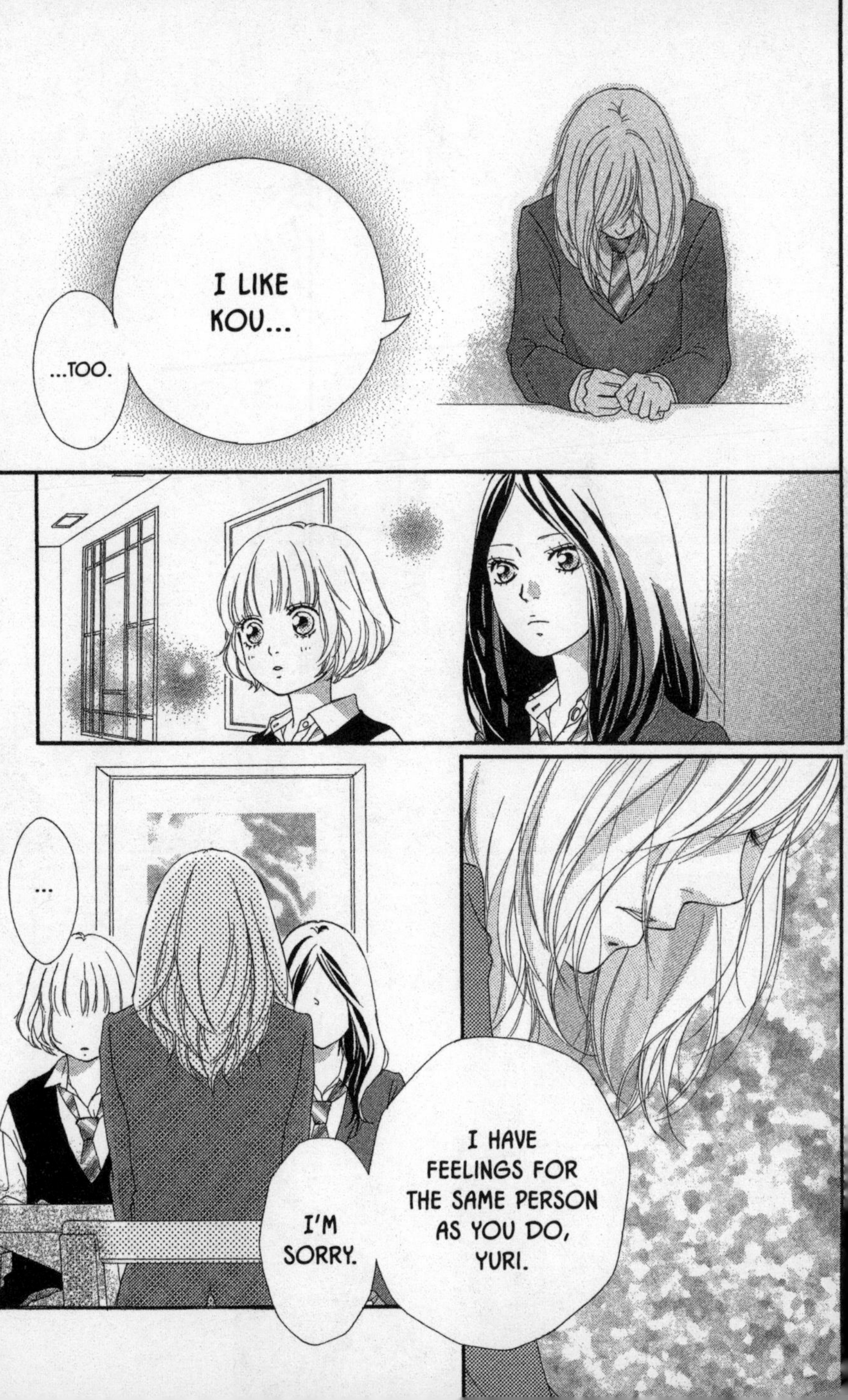
I LIKE KOU...
...TOO.
I HAVE FEELINGS FOR THE SAME PERSON AS YOU DO, YURI.
I'M SORRY.
...

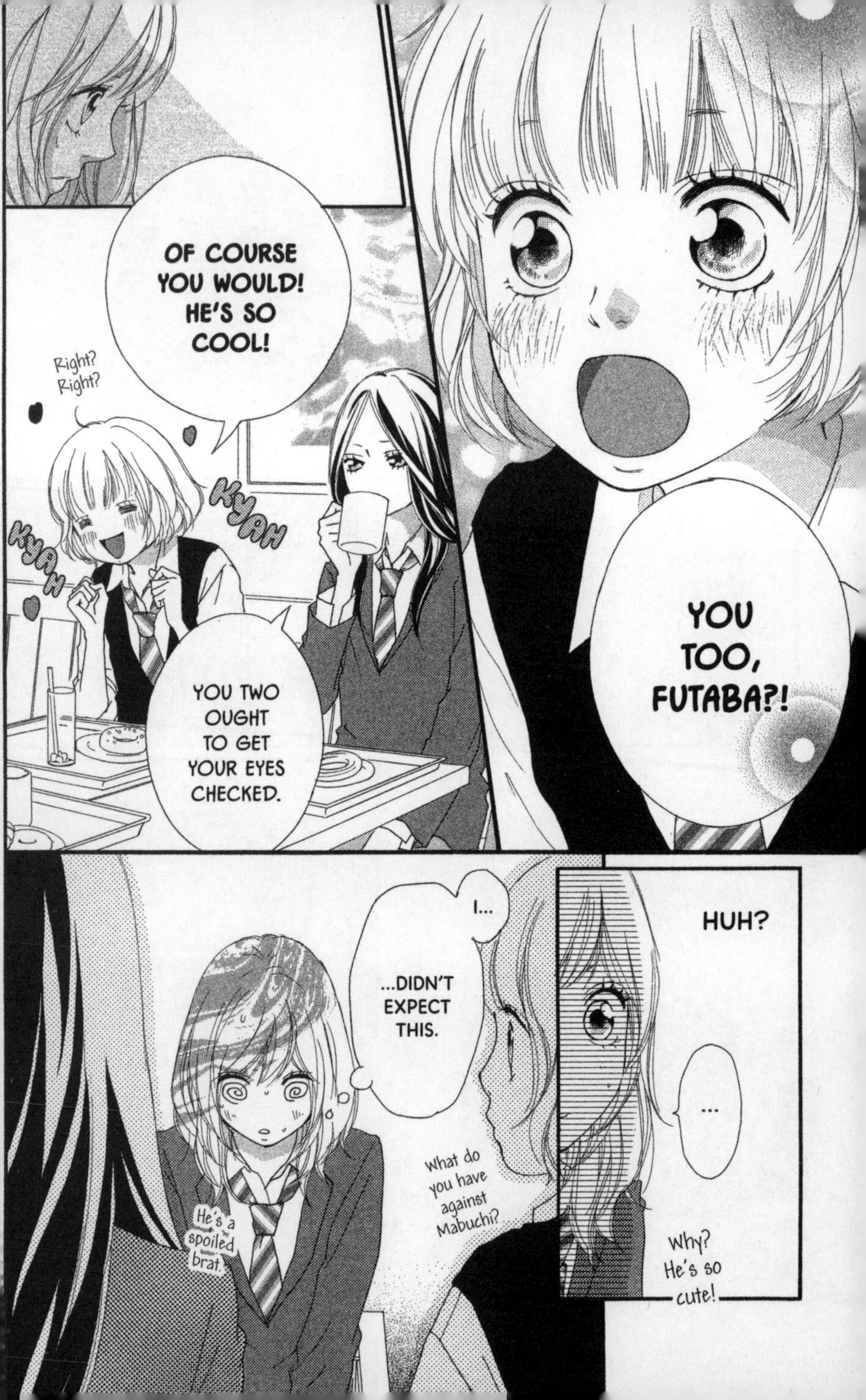
YOU TOO, FUTABA?!
OF COURSE YOU WOULD! HE'S SO COOL!
Right? Right?
KYAH
KYAH
YOU TWO OUGHT TO GET YOUR EYES CHECKED.
HUH?
...
Why? He's so cute!
I...
...DIDN'T EXPECT THIS.
What do you have against Mabuchi?
He's a spoiled brat.

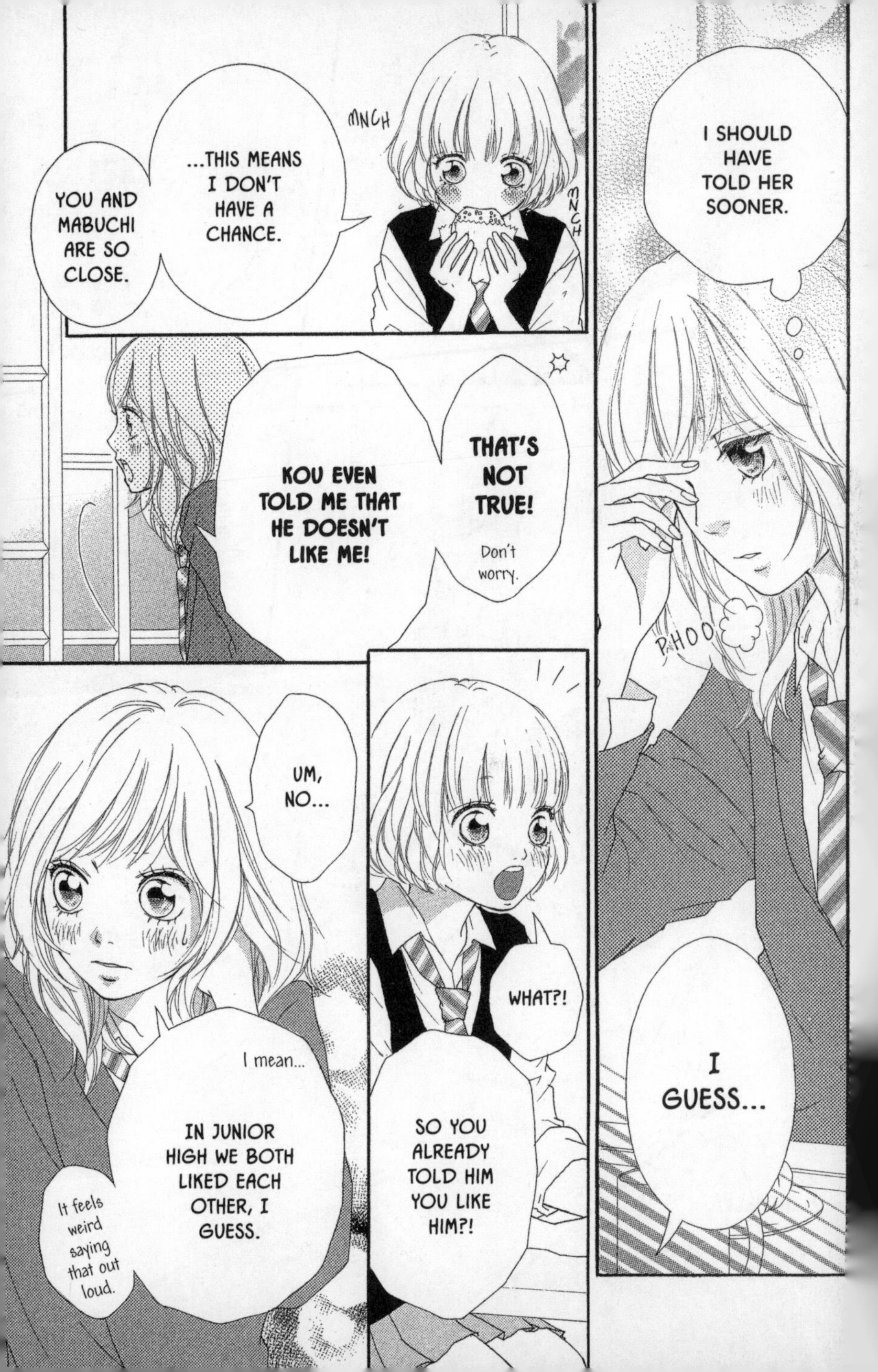
I SHOULD HAVE TOLD HER SOONER.
PHOO
I GUESS...
MNCH
MNCH
...THIS MEANS I DON'T HAVE A CHANCE.
YOU AND MABUCHI ARE SO CLOSE.
THAT'S NOT TRUE!
Don't worry.
KOU EVEN TOLD ME THAT HE DOESN'T LIKE ME!
WHAT?!
SO YOU ALREADY TOLD HIM YOU LIKE HIM?!
UM, NO...
I mean...
IN JUNIOR HIGH WE BOTH LIKED EACH OTHER, I GUESS.
It feels weird saying that out loud.

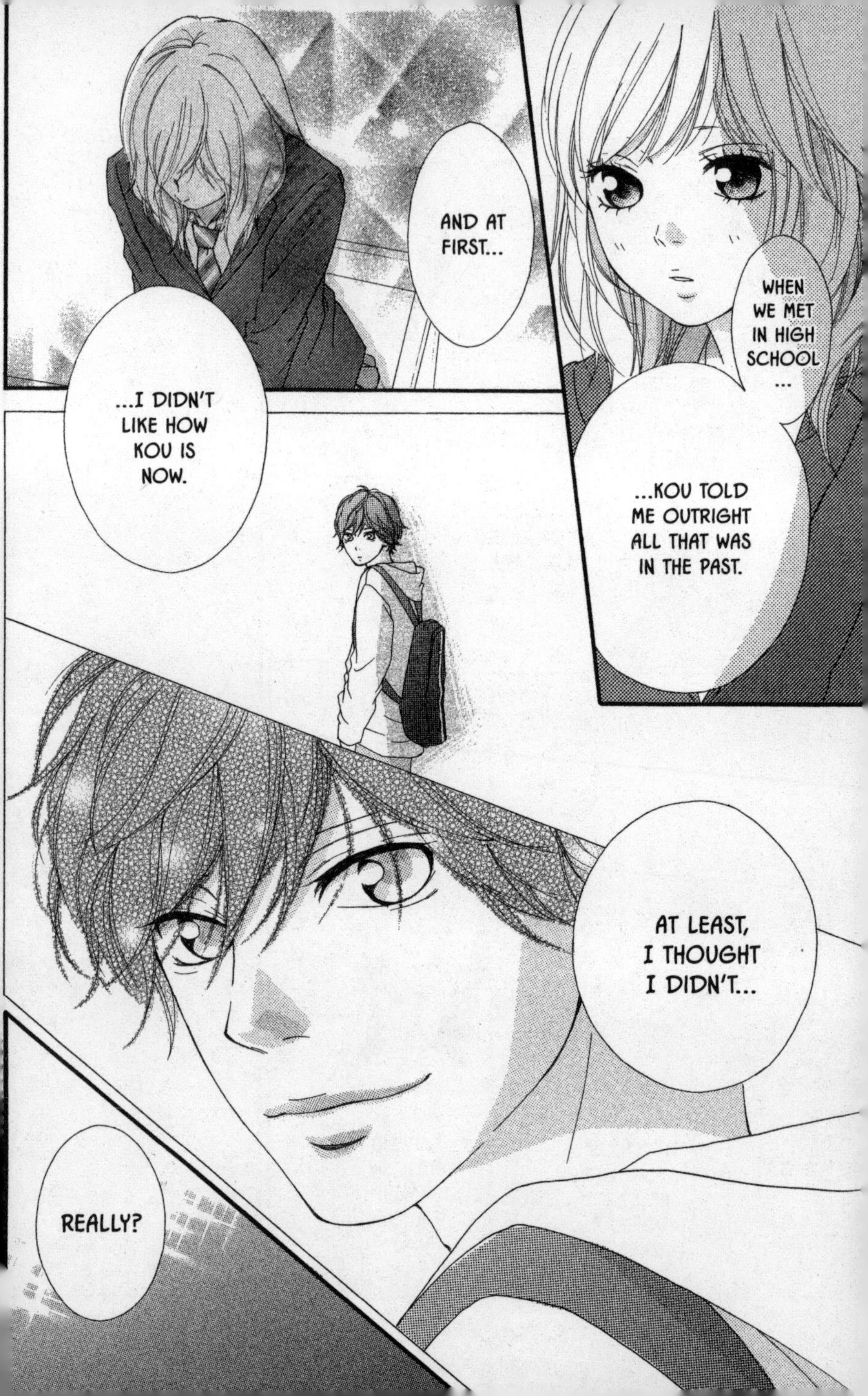
WHEN WE MET IN HIGH SCHOOL ...
...KOU TOLD ME OUTRIGHT ALL THAT WAS IN THE PAST.
AND AT FIRST...
...I DIDN'T LIKE HOW KOU IS NOW.
AT LEAST, I THOUGHT I DIDN'T...
REALLY?

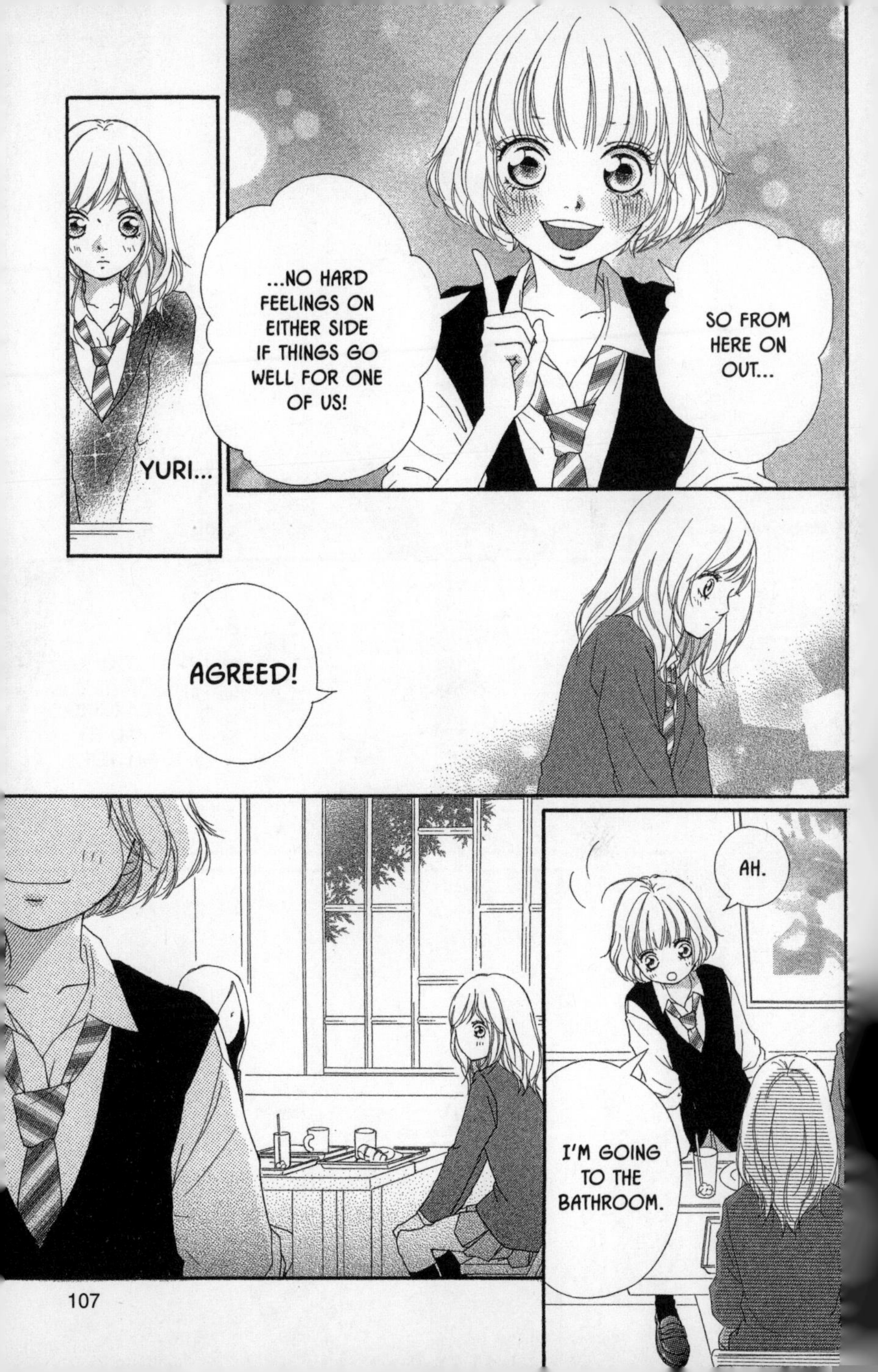
SO FROM HERE ON OUT...
...NO HARD FEELINGS ON EITHER SIDE IF THINGS GO WELL FOR ONE OF US!
YURI...
AGREED!
AH.
I'M GOING TO THE BATHROOM.

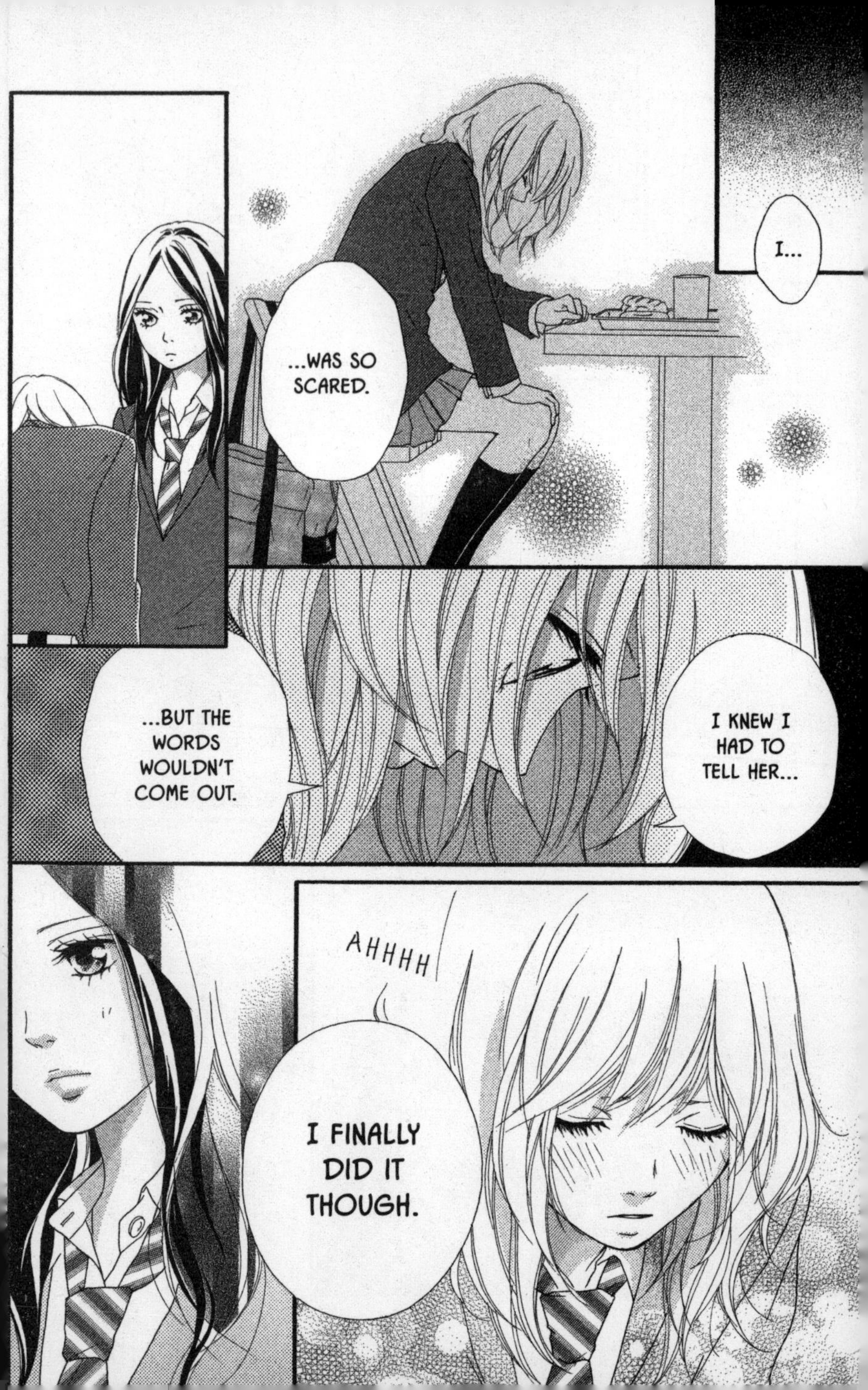
I...
...WAS SO SCARED.
I KNEW I HAD TO TELL HER...
...BUT THE WORDS WOULDN'T COME OUT.
AHHHH
I FINALLY DID IT THOUGH.

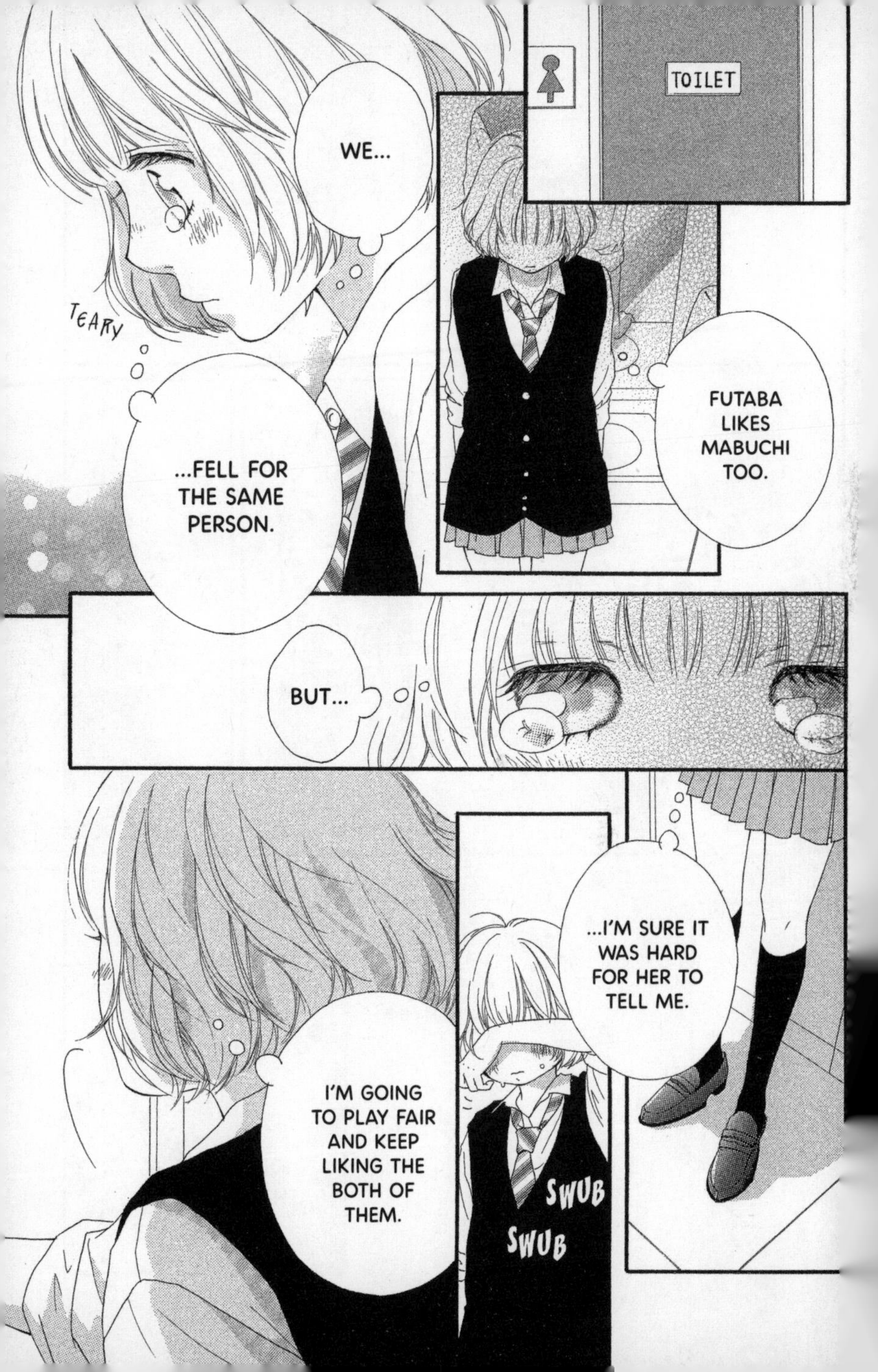
TOILET
FUTABA LIKES MABUCHI TOO.
WE...
TEARY
...FELL FOR THE SAME PERSON.
BUT...
...I'M SURE IT WAS HARD FOR HER TO TELL ME.
SWUB
SWUB
I'M GOING TO PLAY FAIR AND KEEP LIKING THE BOTH OF THEM.

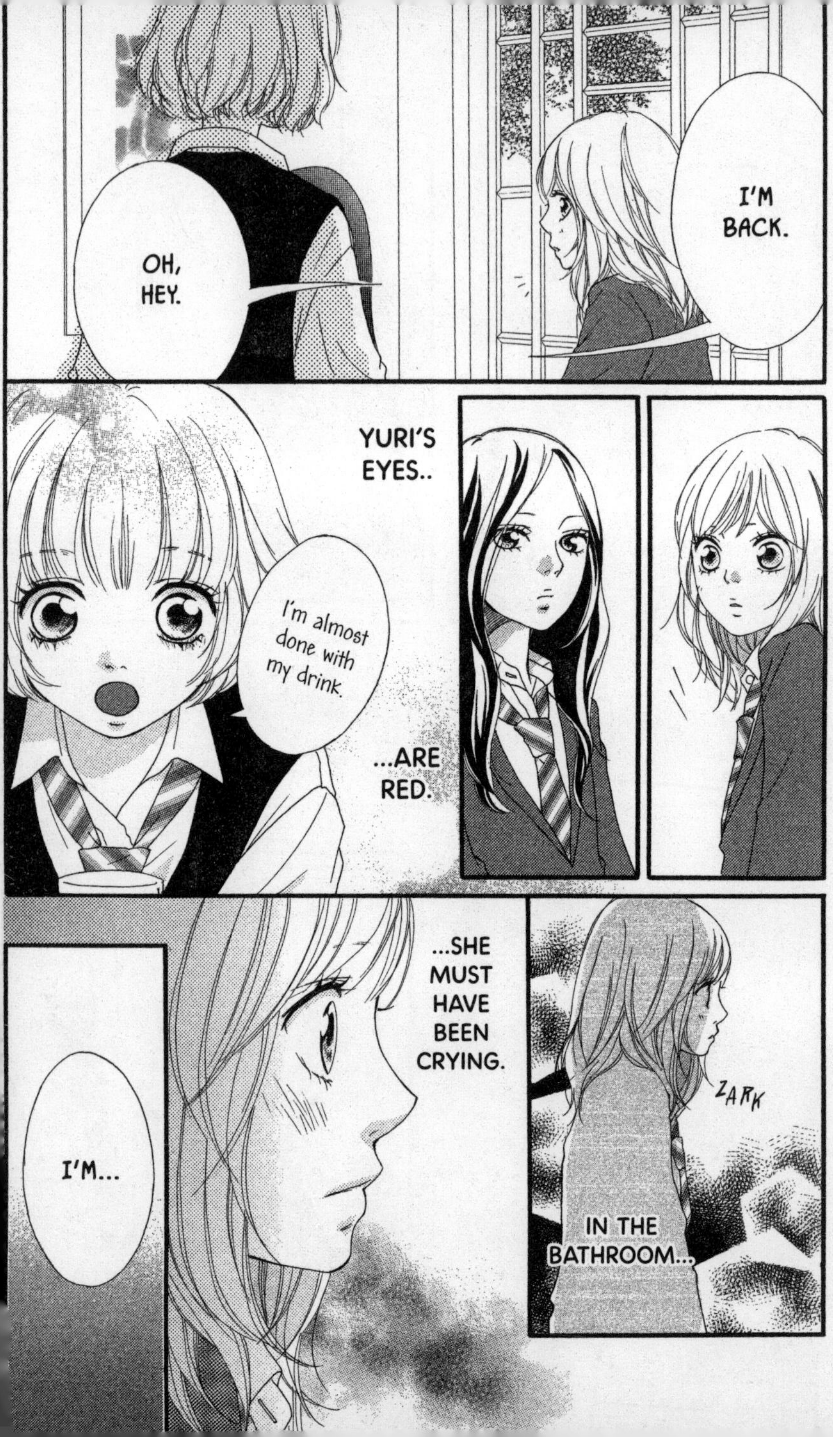
I'M BACK.
OH, HEY.
YURI'S EYES..
I'm almost done with my drink.
...ARE RED.
ZARK
IN THE BATHROOM...
...SHE MUST HAVE BEEN CRYING.
I'M...

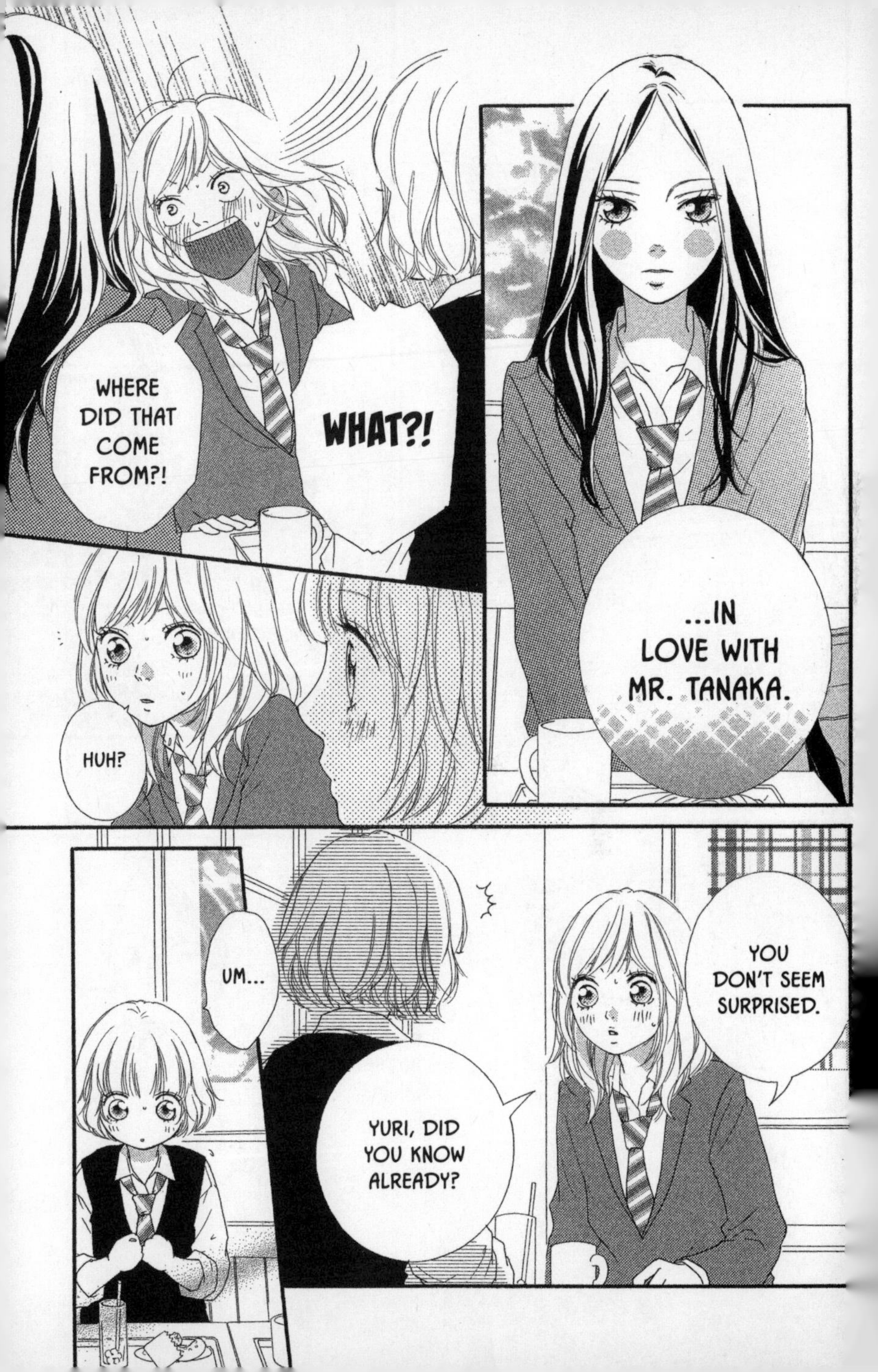
...IN LOVE WITH MR. TANAKA.
WHAT?!
WHERE DID THAT COME FROM?!
HUH?
YOU DON'T SEEM SURPRISED.
YURI, DID YOU KNOW ALREADY?
UM...

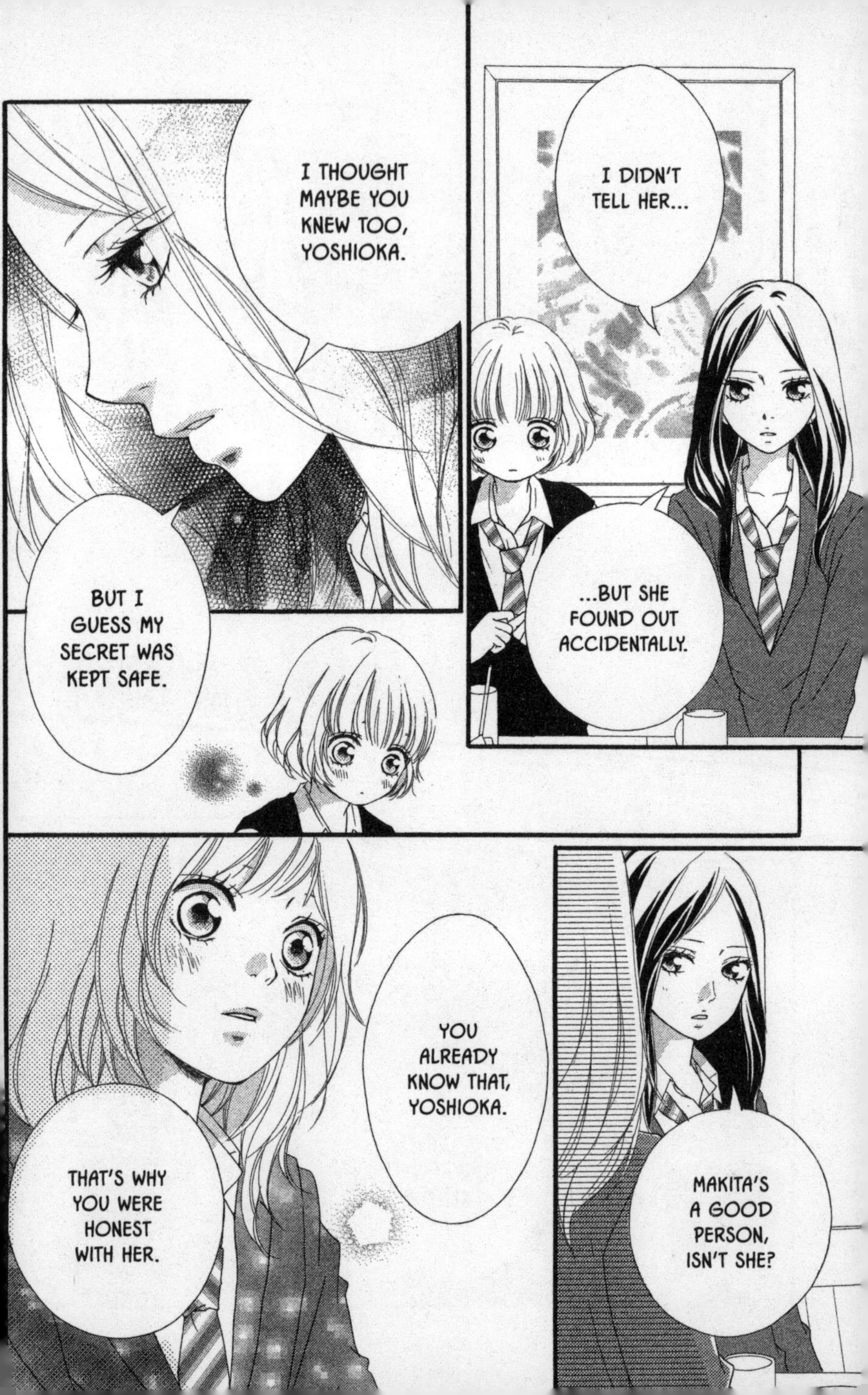
I DIDN'T TELL HER...
...BUT SHE FOUND OUT ACCIDENTALLY.
I THOUGHT MAYBE YOU KNEW TOO, YOSHIOKA.
BUT I GUESS MY SECRET WAS KEPT SAFE.
MAKITA'S A GOOD PERSON, ISN'T SHE?
YOU ALREADY KNOW THAT, YOSHIOKA.
THAT'S WHY YOU WERE HONEST WITH HER.

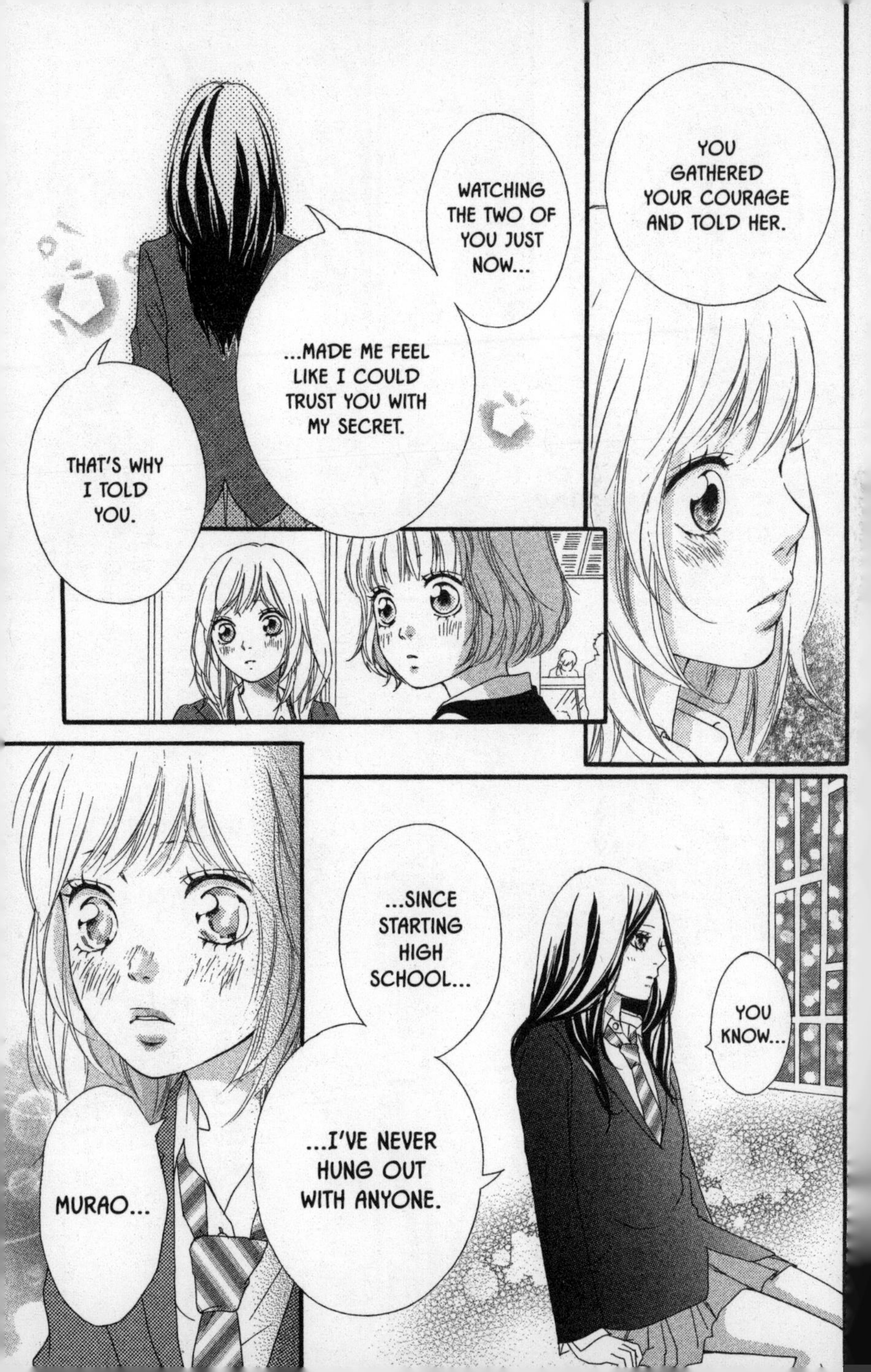
YOU GATHERED YOUR COURAGE AND TOLD HER.
WATCHING THE TWO OF YOU JUST NOW...
...MADE ME FEEL LIKE I COULD TRUST YOU WITH MY SECRET.
THAT'S WHY I TOLD YOU.
YOU KNOW...
...SINCE STARTING HIGH SCHOOL...
...I'VE NEVER HUNG OUT WITH ANYONE.
MURAO...

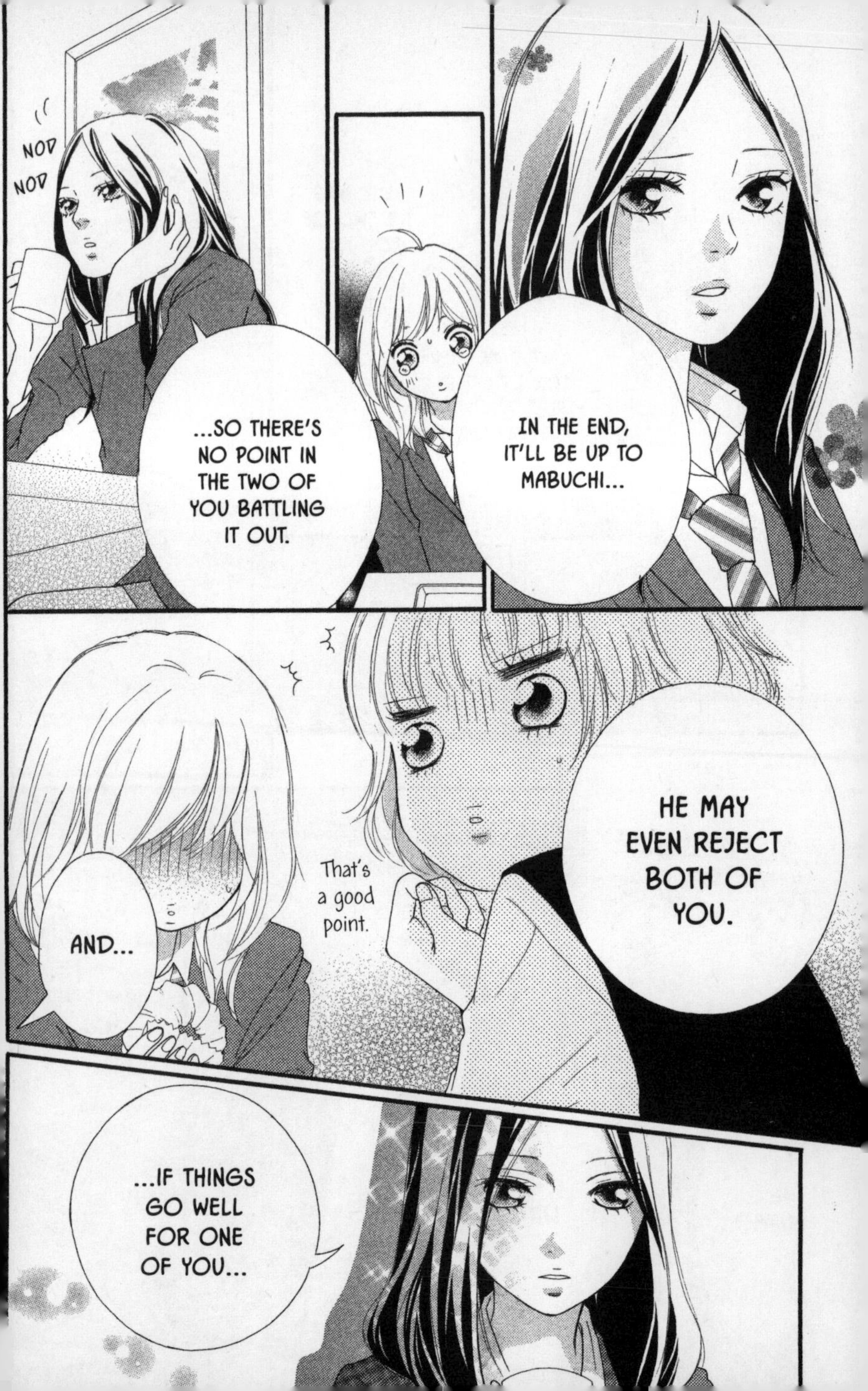
IN THE END, IT'LL BE UP TO MABUCHI...
...SO THERE'S NO POINT IN THE TWO OF YOU BATTLING IT OUT.
NOD NOD
HE MAY EVEN REJECT BOTH OF YOU.
That's a good point.
AND...
...IF THINGS GO WELL FOR ONE OF YOU...

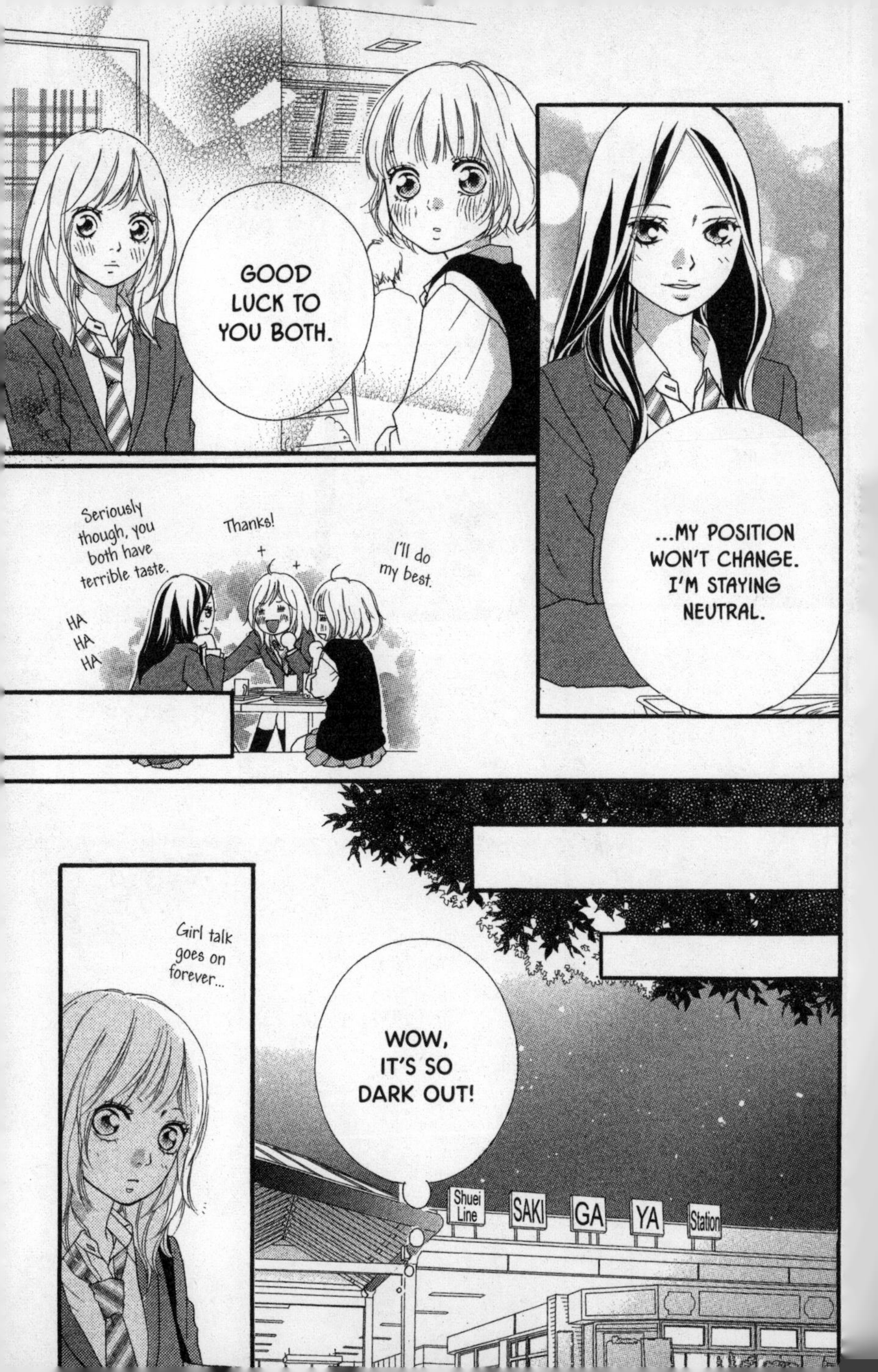
...MY POSITION WON'T CHANGE. I'M STAYING NEUTRAL.
GOOD LUCK TO YOU BOTH.
Thanks!
I'll do my best.
Seriously though, you both have terrible taste.
HA HA HA
WOW, IT'S SO DARK OUT!
Shuei Line
SAKI GA YA Station
Girl talk goes on forever...

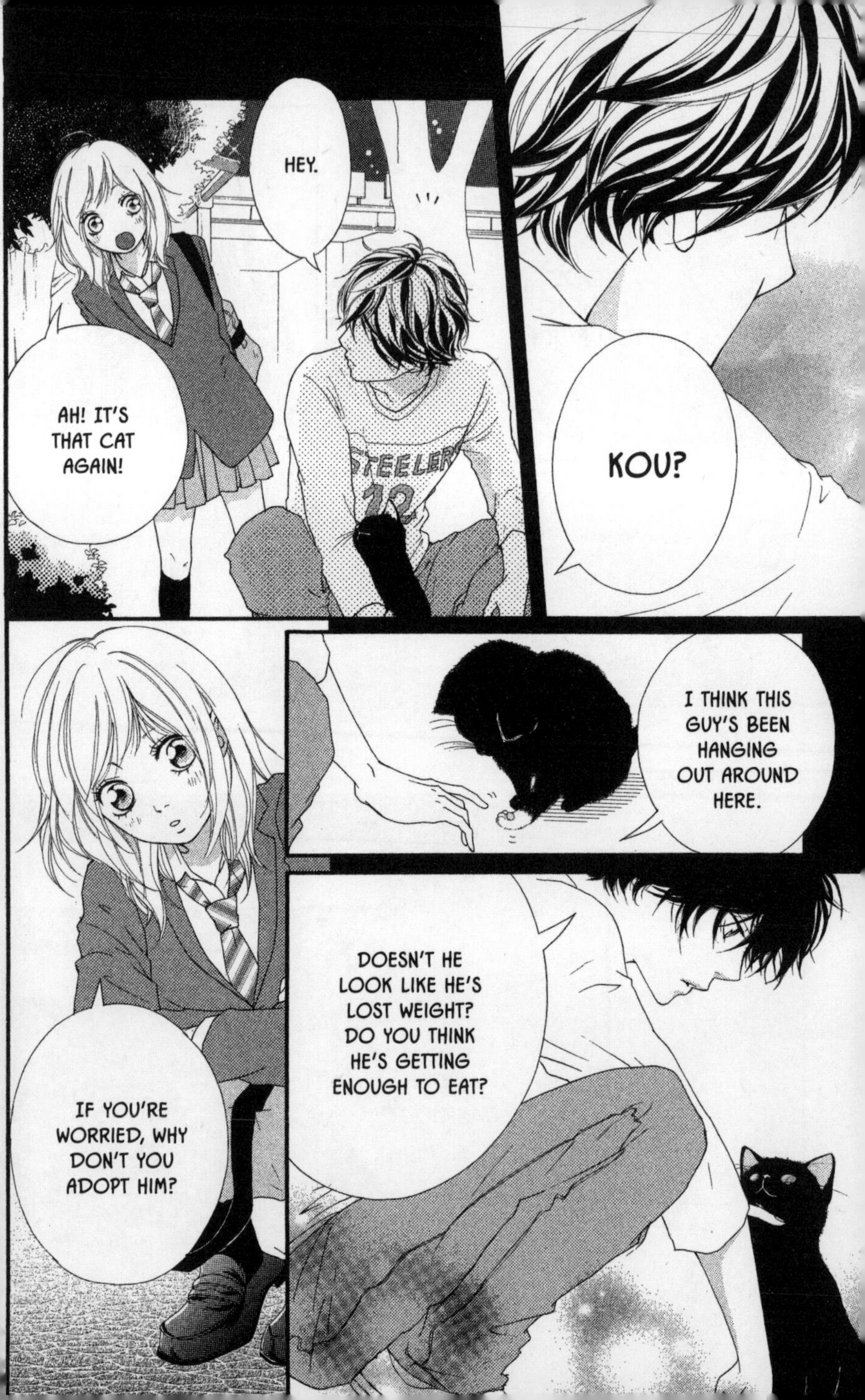
KOU?
HEY.
AH! IT'S THAT CAT AGAIN!
I THINK THIS GUY'S BEEN HANGING OUT AROUND HERE.
DOESN'T HE LOOK LIKE HE'S LOST WEIGHT? DO YOU THINK HE'S GETTING ENOUGH TO EAT?
IF YOU'RE WORRIED, WHY DON'T YOU ADOPT HIM?

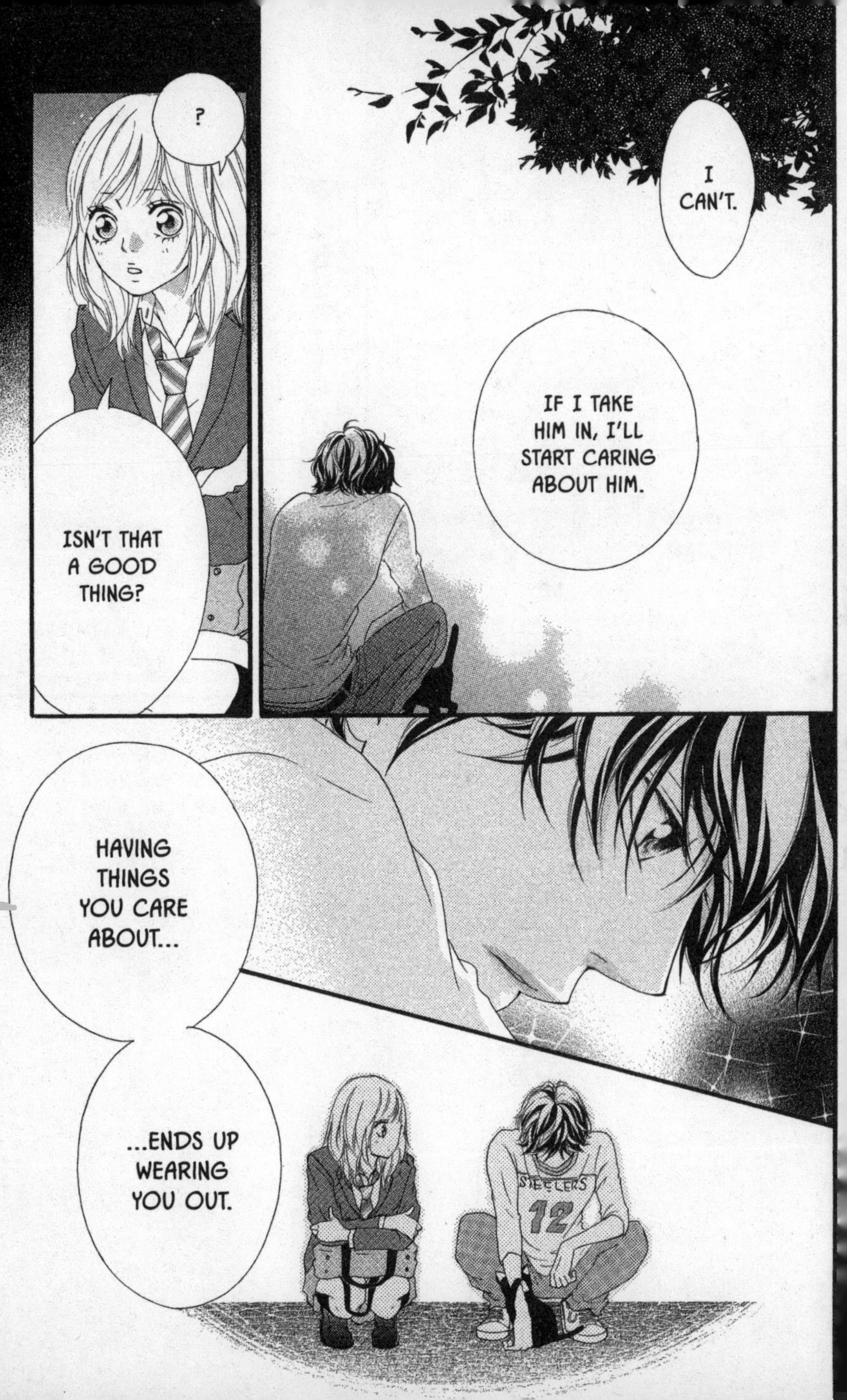
I CAN'T.
IF I TAKE HIM IN, I'LL START CARING ABOUT HIM.
?
ISN'T THAT A GOOD THING?
HAVING THINGS YOU CARE ABOUT...
...ENDS UP WEARING YOU OUT.
STEELERS 12

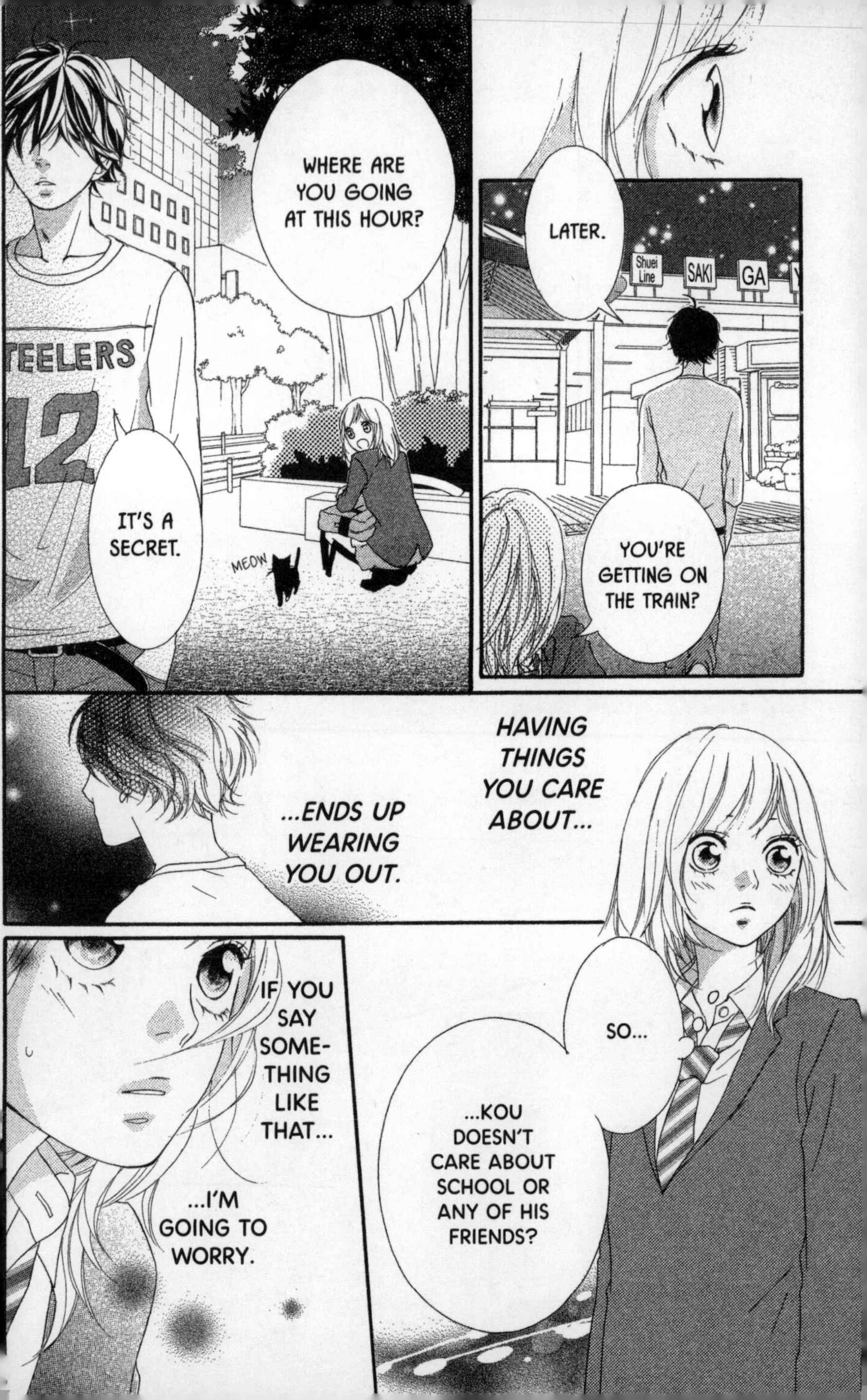
LATER.
Shuei Line
SAKI
GA
YOU'RE GETTING ON THE TRAIN?
WHERE ARE YOU GOING AT THIS HOUR?
IT'S A SECRET.
MEOW
HAVING THINGS YOU CARE ABOUT...
...ENDS UP WEARING YOU OUT.
SO...
...KOU DOESN'T CARE ABOUT SCHOOL OR ANY OF HIS FRIENDS?
IF YOU SAY SOME-THING LIKE THAT...
...I'M GOING TO WORRY.

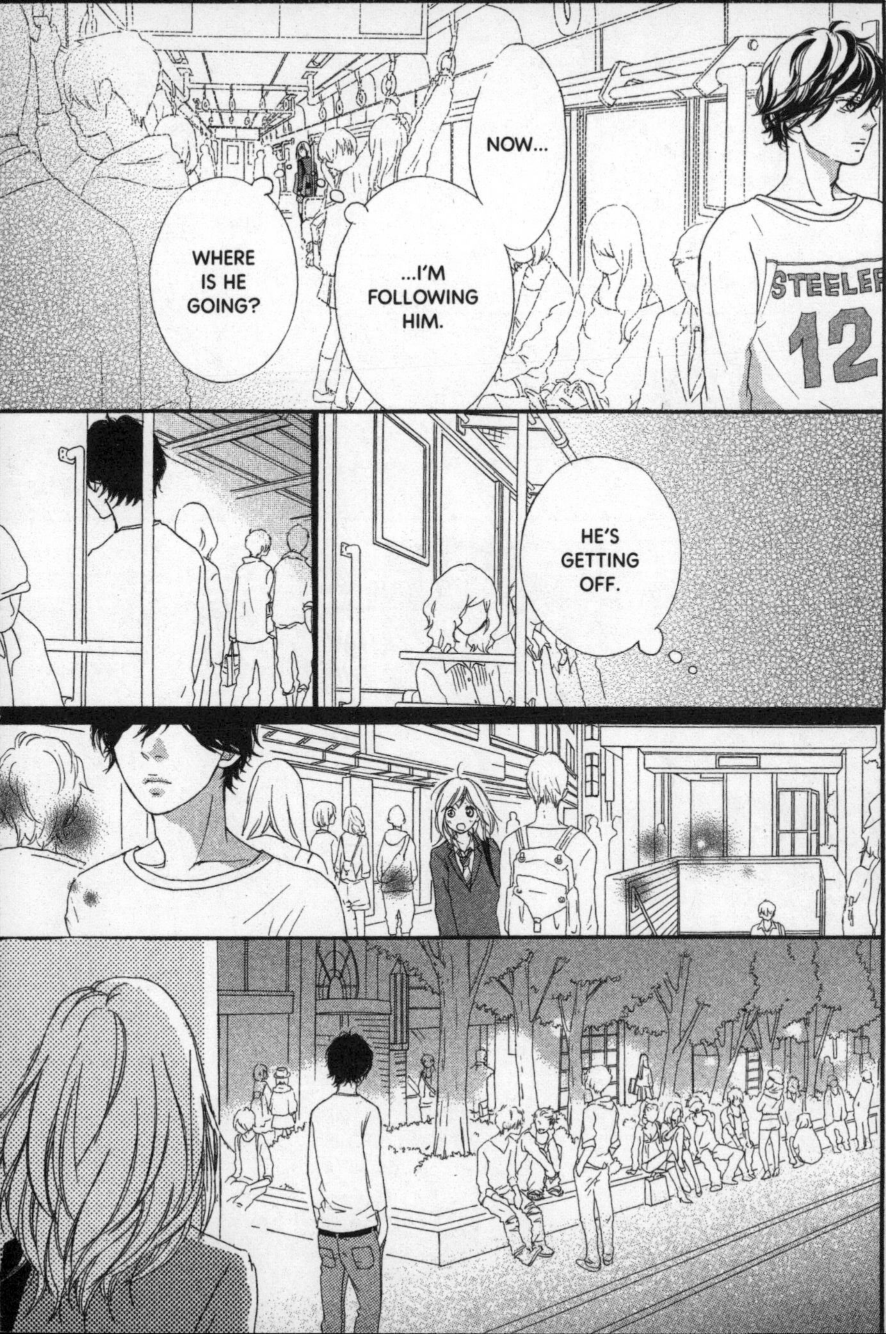
NOW...
...I'M FOLLOWING HIM.
WHERE IS HE GOING?
HE'S GETTING OFF.

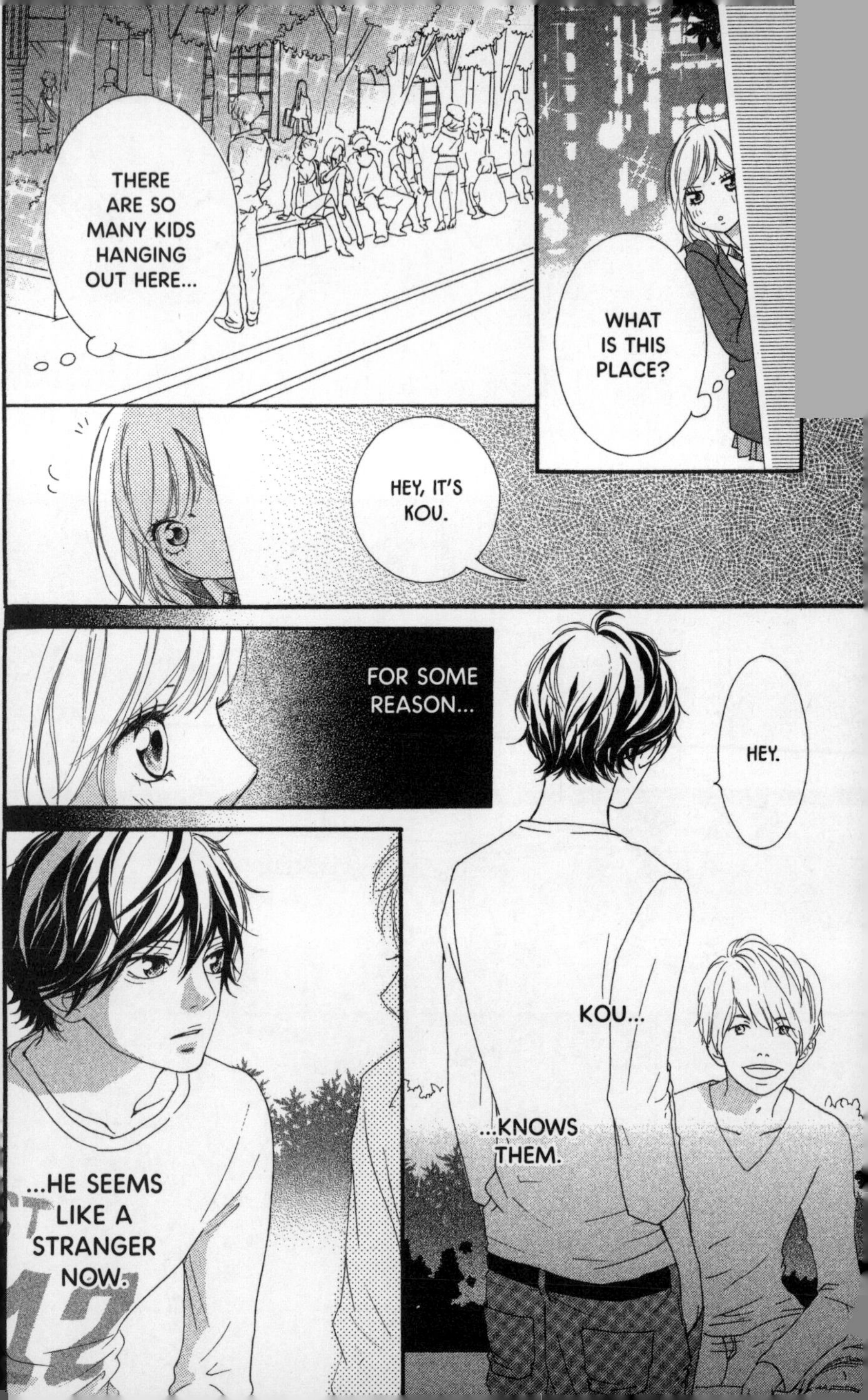
WHAT IS THIS PLACE?
THERE ARE SO MANY KIDS HANGING OUT HERE...
HEY, IT'S KOU.
HEY.
KOU...
...KNOWS THEM.
FOR SOME REASON...
...HE SEEMS LIKE A STRANGER NOW.

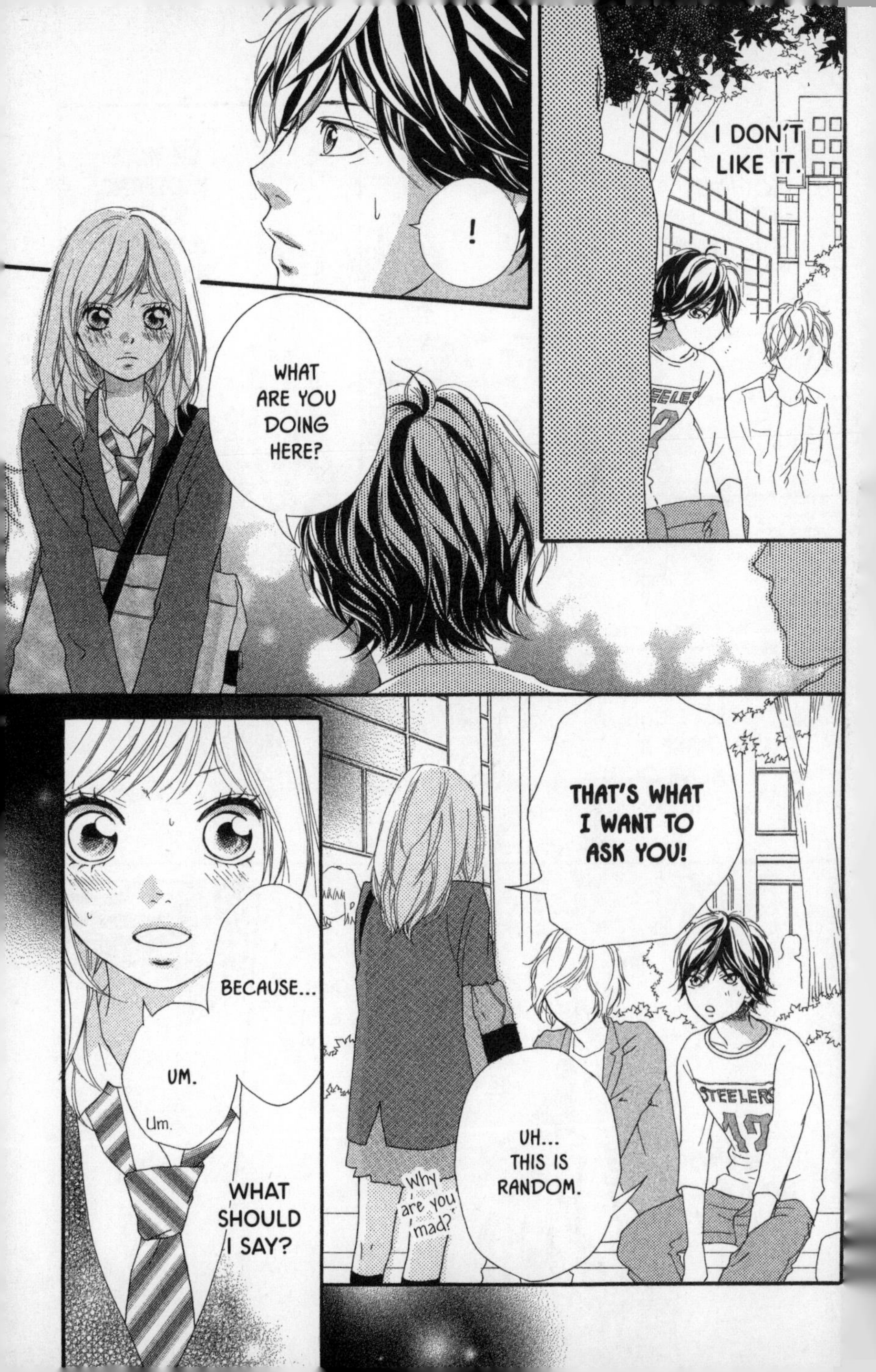

I DON'T LIKE IT.
!
WHAT ARE YOU DOING HERE?
THAT'S WHAT I WANT TO ASK YOU!
UH... THIS IS RANDOM.
Why are you mad?
BECAUSE...
UM.
Um.
WHAT SHOULD I SAY?

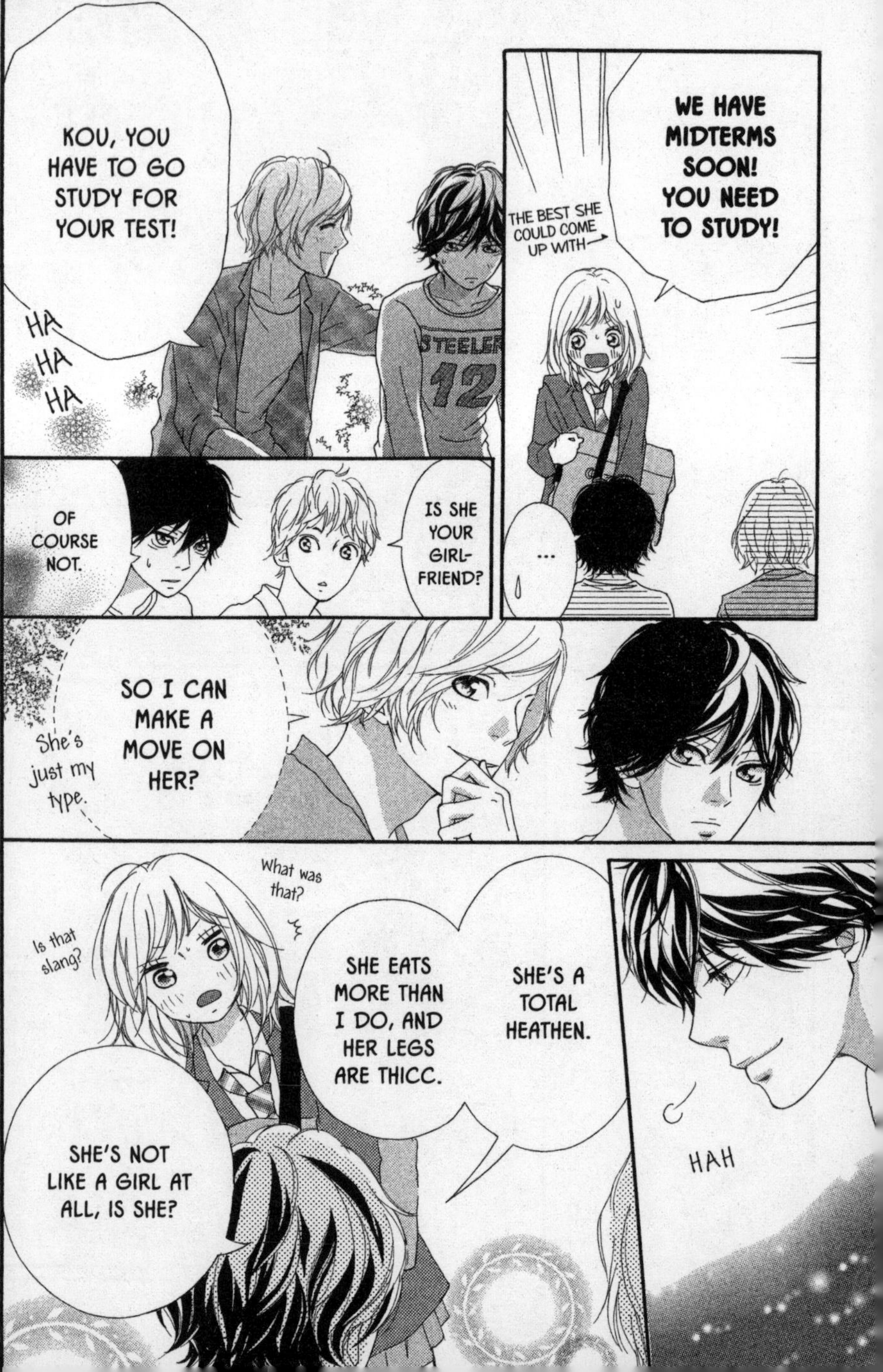
WE HAVE MIDTERMS SOON! YOU NEED TO STUDY!
THE BEST SHE COULD COME UP WITH
...
KOU, YOU HAVE TO GO STUDY FOR YOUR TEST!
HA HA HA
STEELER 12
IS SHE YOUR GIRL-FRIEND?
OF COURSE NOT.
SO I CAN MAKE A MOVE ON HER?
She's just my type.
HAH
SHE'S A TOTAL HEATHEN.
SHE EATS MORE THAN I DO, AND HER LEGS ARE THICC.
SHE'S NOT LIKE A GIRL AT ALL, IS SHE?
What was that?
Is that slang?

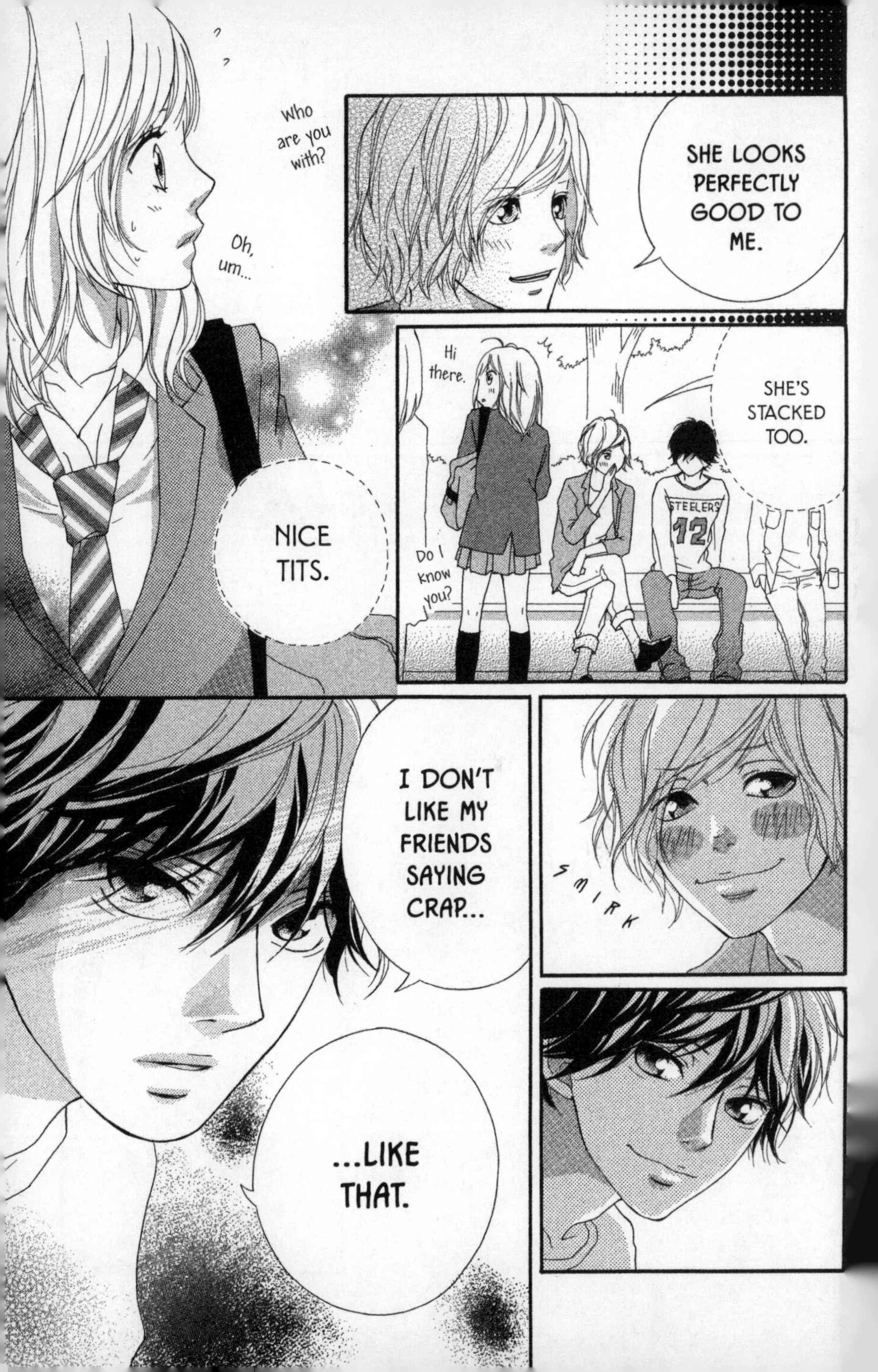

SHE LOOKS PERFECTLY GOOD TO ME.
SHE'S STACKED TOO.
Hi there.
STEELERS 12
Do I know you?
Who are you with?
Oh, um...
NICE TITS.
SMIRK
I DON'T LIKE MY FRIENDS SAYING CRAP...
...LIKE THAT.

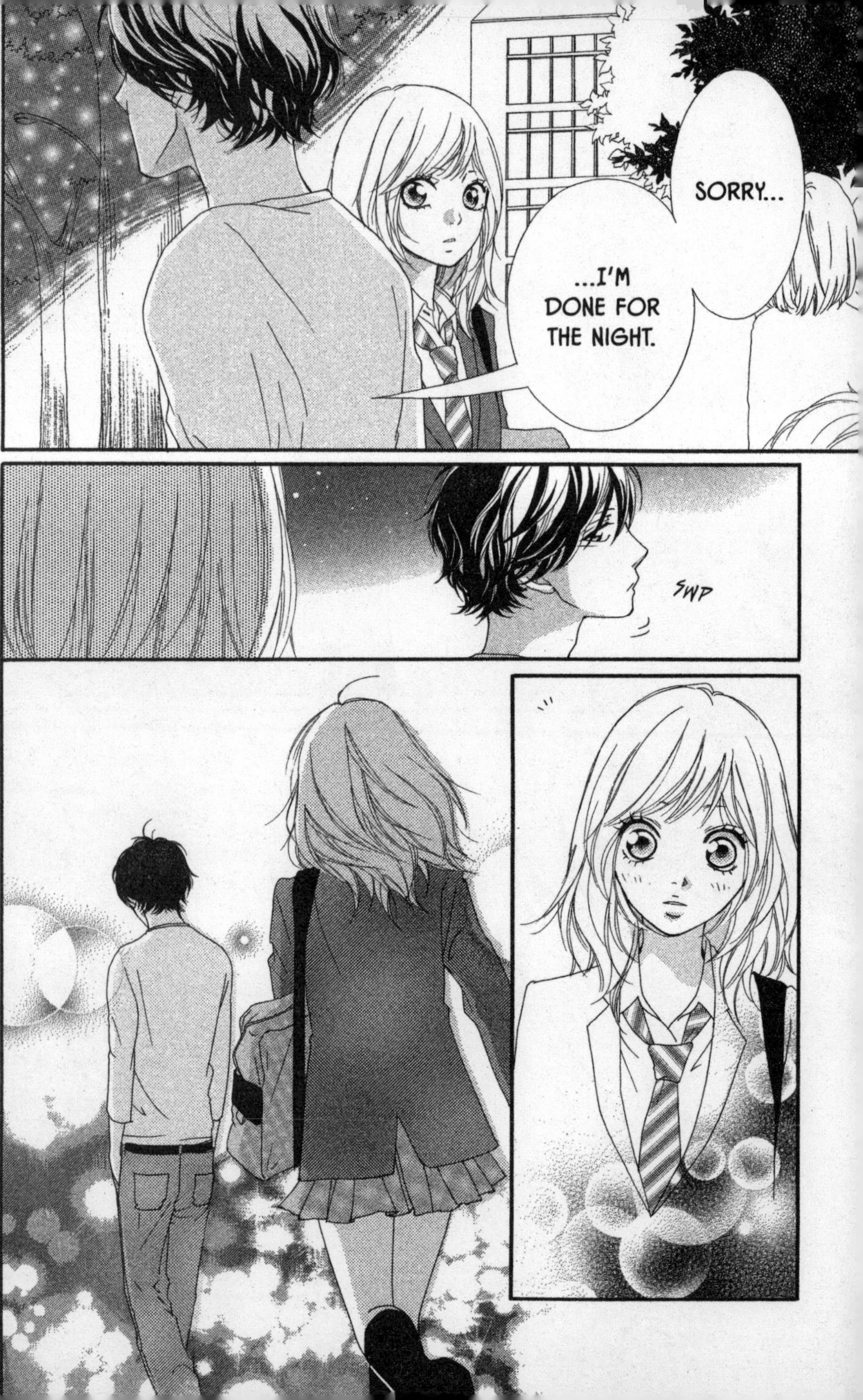
SORRY...
...I'M DONE FOR THE NIGHT.
SWP

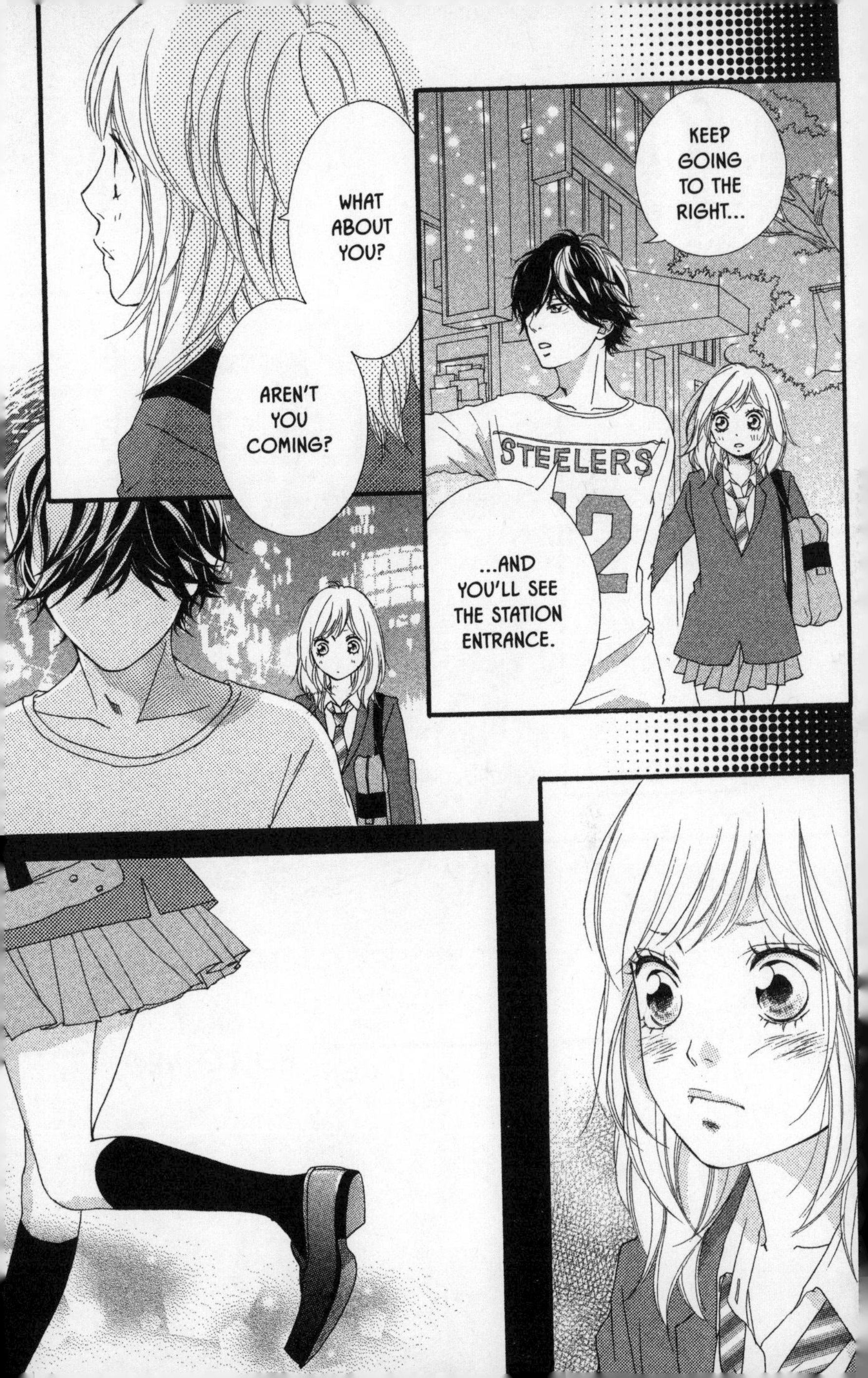
KEEP GOING TO THE RIGHT...
STEELERS
...AND YOU'LL SEE THE STATION ENTRANCE.
WHAT ABOUT YOU?
AREN'T YOU COMING?

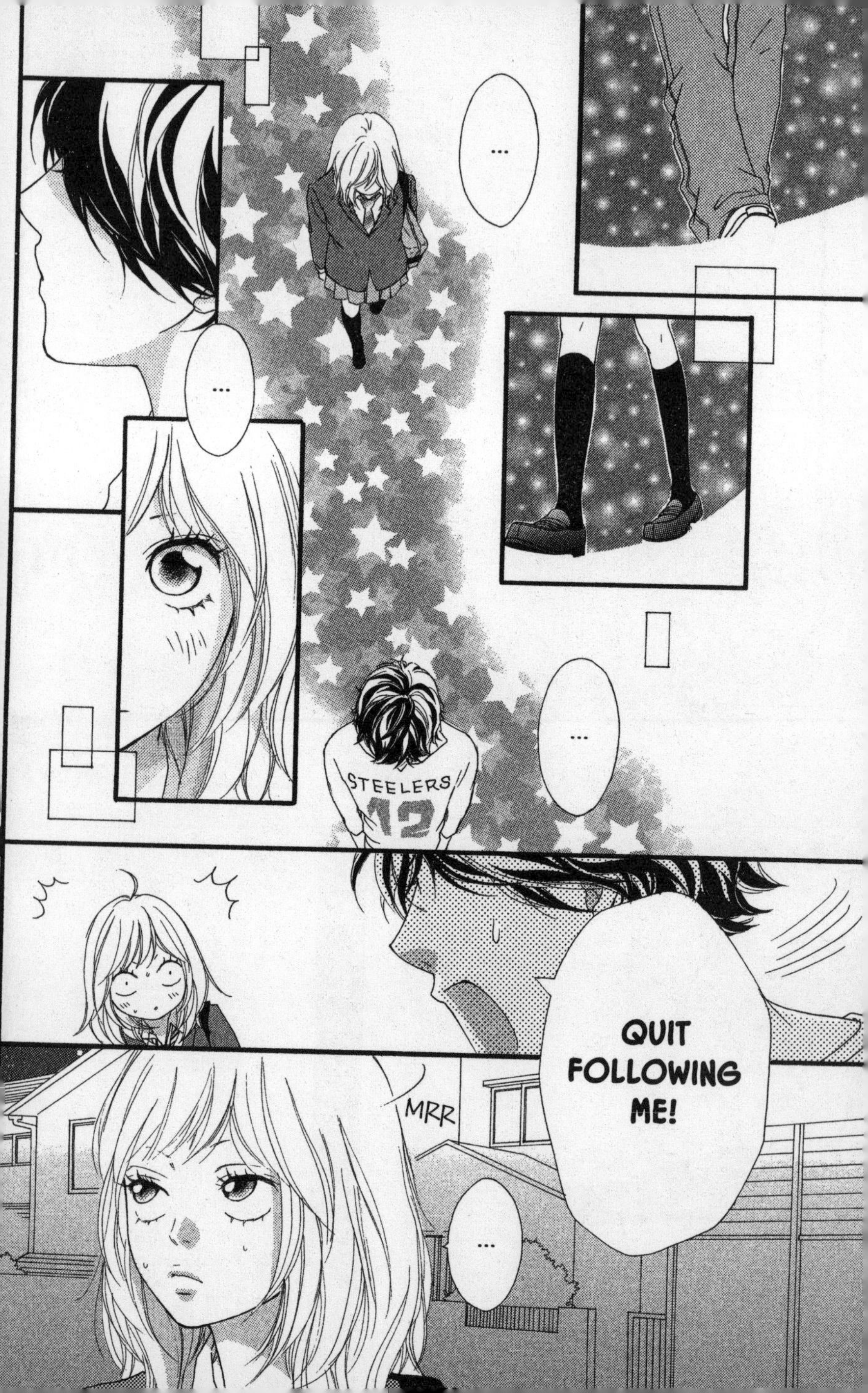
...
...
...
QUIT FOLLOWING ME!
MRR
...

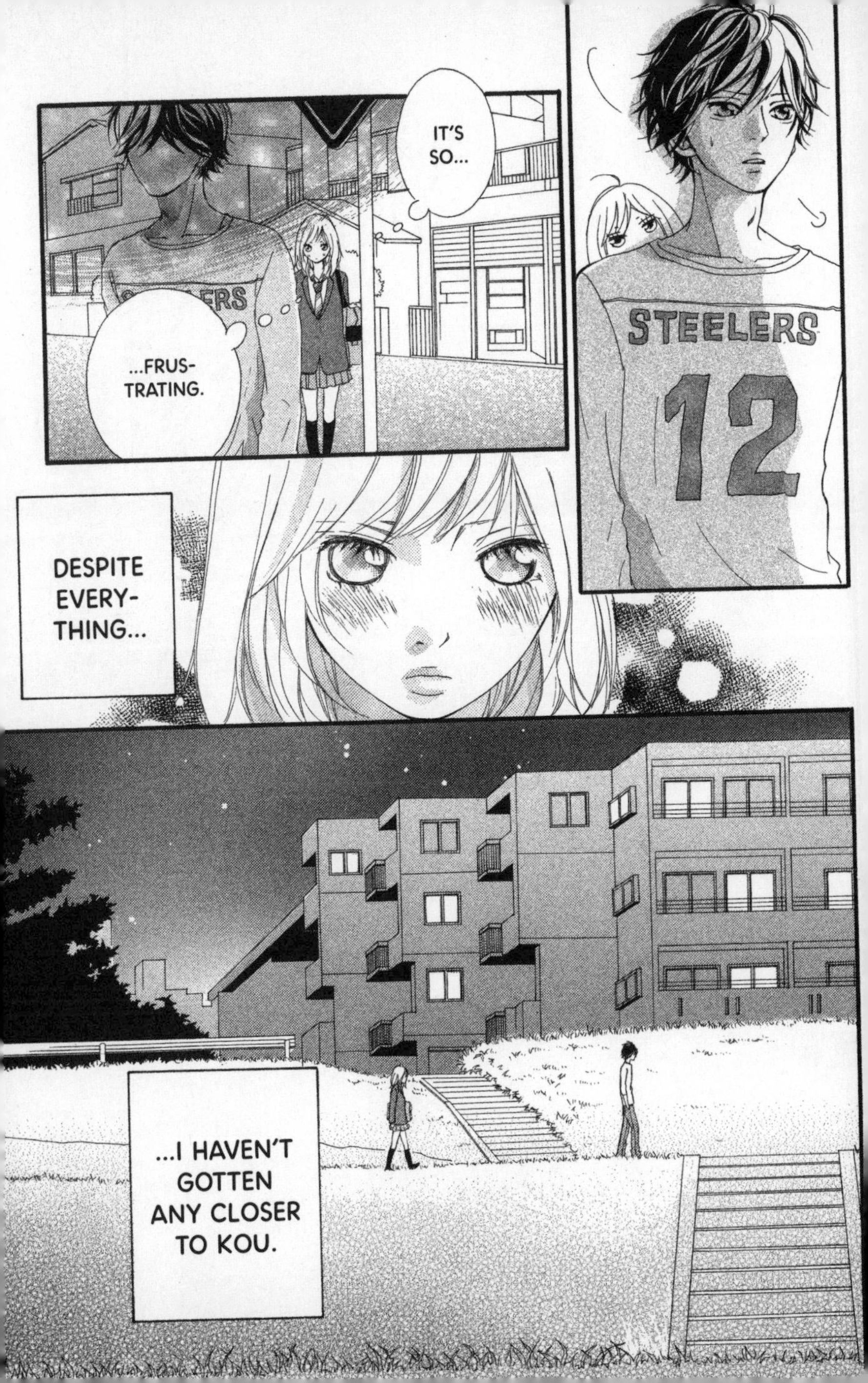
STEELERS
12
IT'S SO...
...FRUS-TRATING.
DESPITE EVERY-THING...
...I HAVEN'T GOTTEN ANY CLOSER TO KOU.

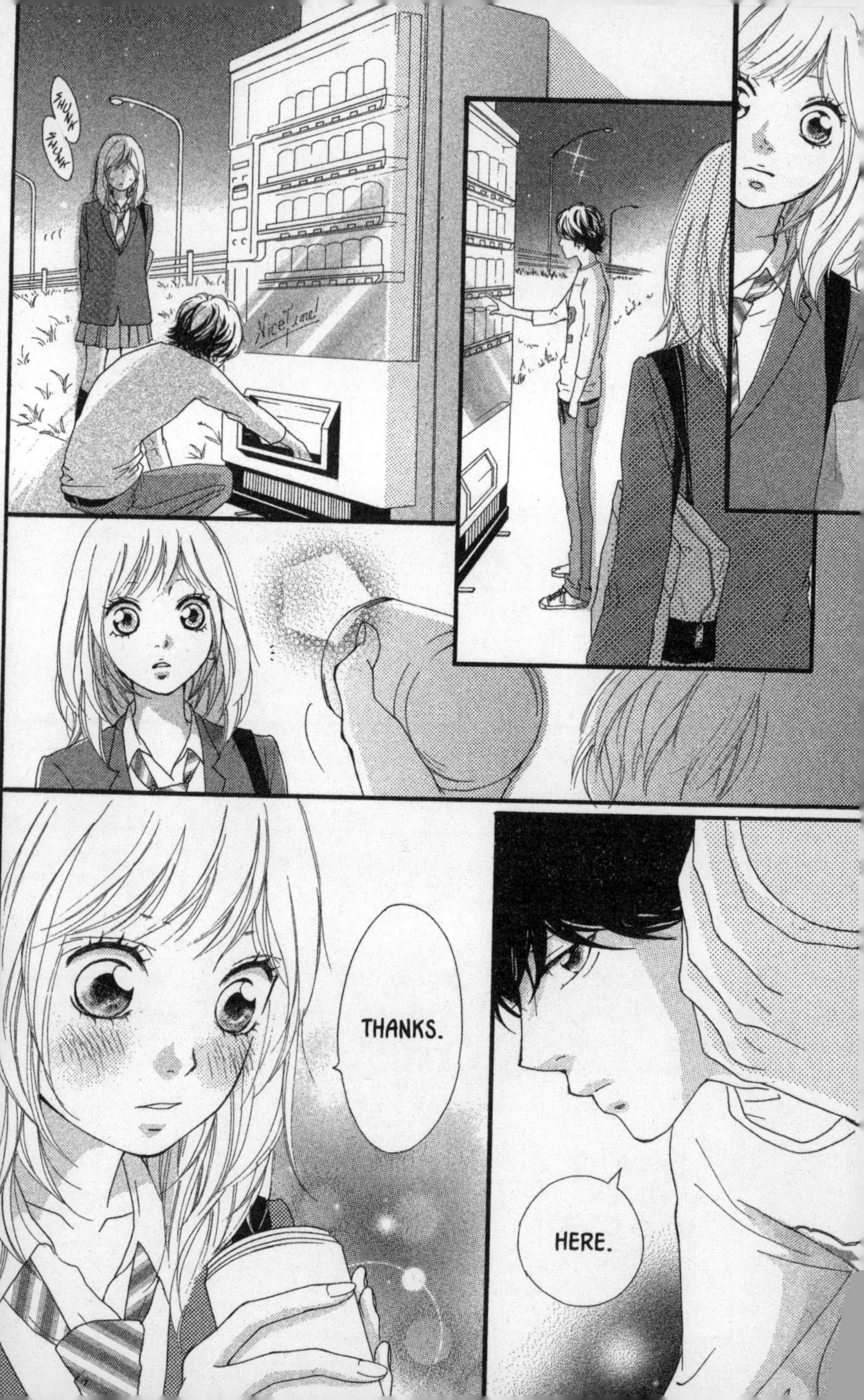
SHUNK
SHUNK
Nice Time!
HERE.
THANKS.

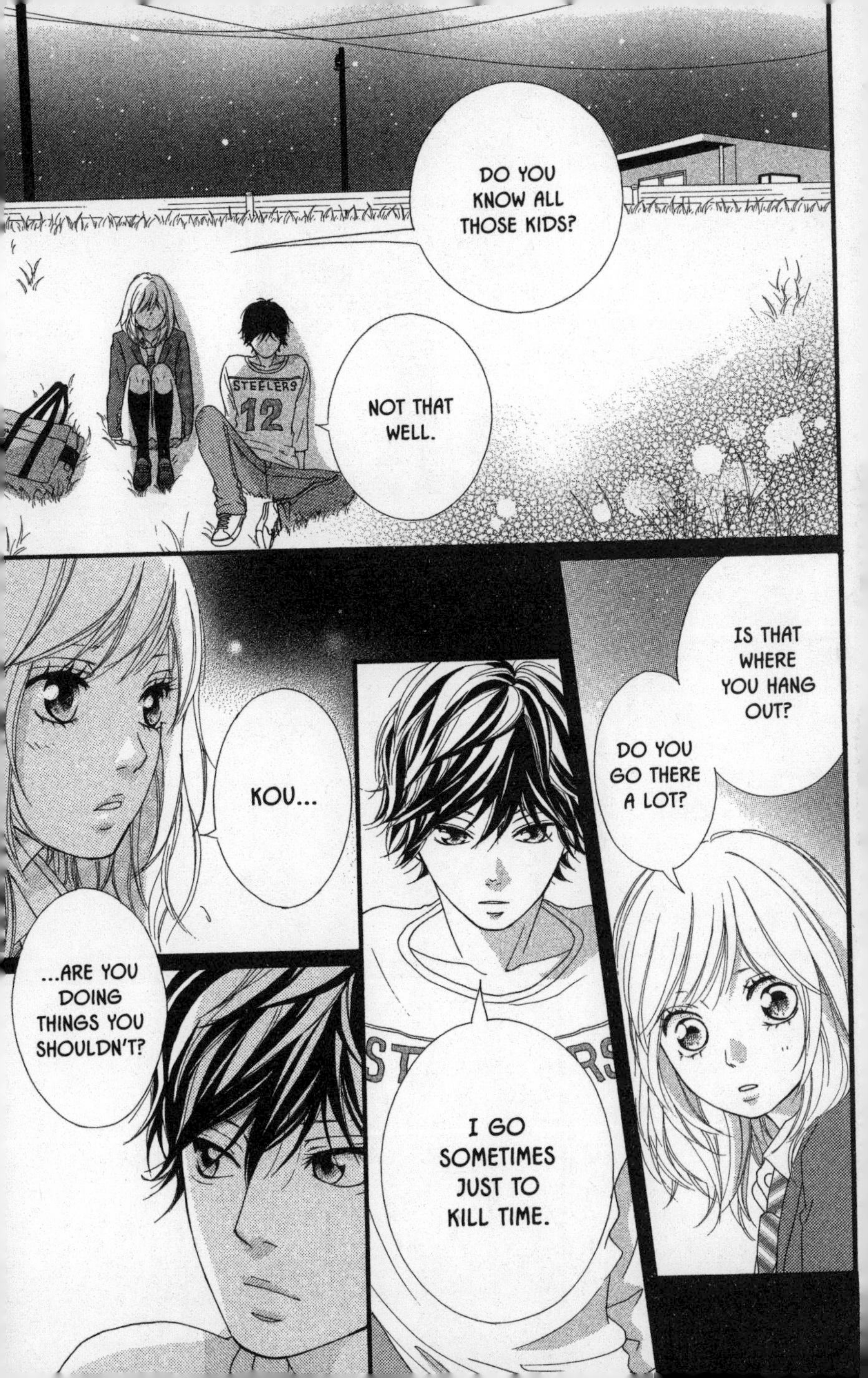
DO YOU KNOW ALL THOSE KIDS?
STEELERS 12
NOT THAT WELL.
IS THAT WHERE YOU HANG OUT?
DO YOU GO THERE A LOT?
I GO SOMETIMES JUST TO KILL TIME.
KOU...
...ARE YOU DOING THINGS YOU SHOULDN'T?

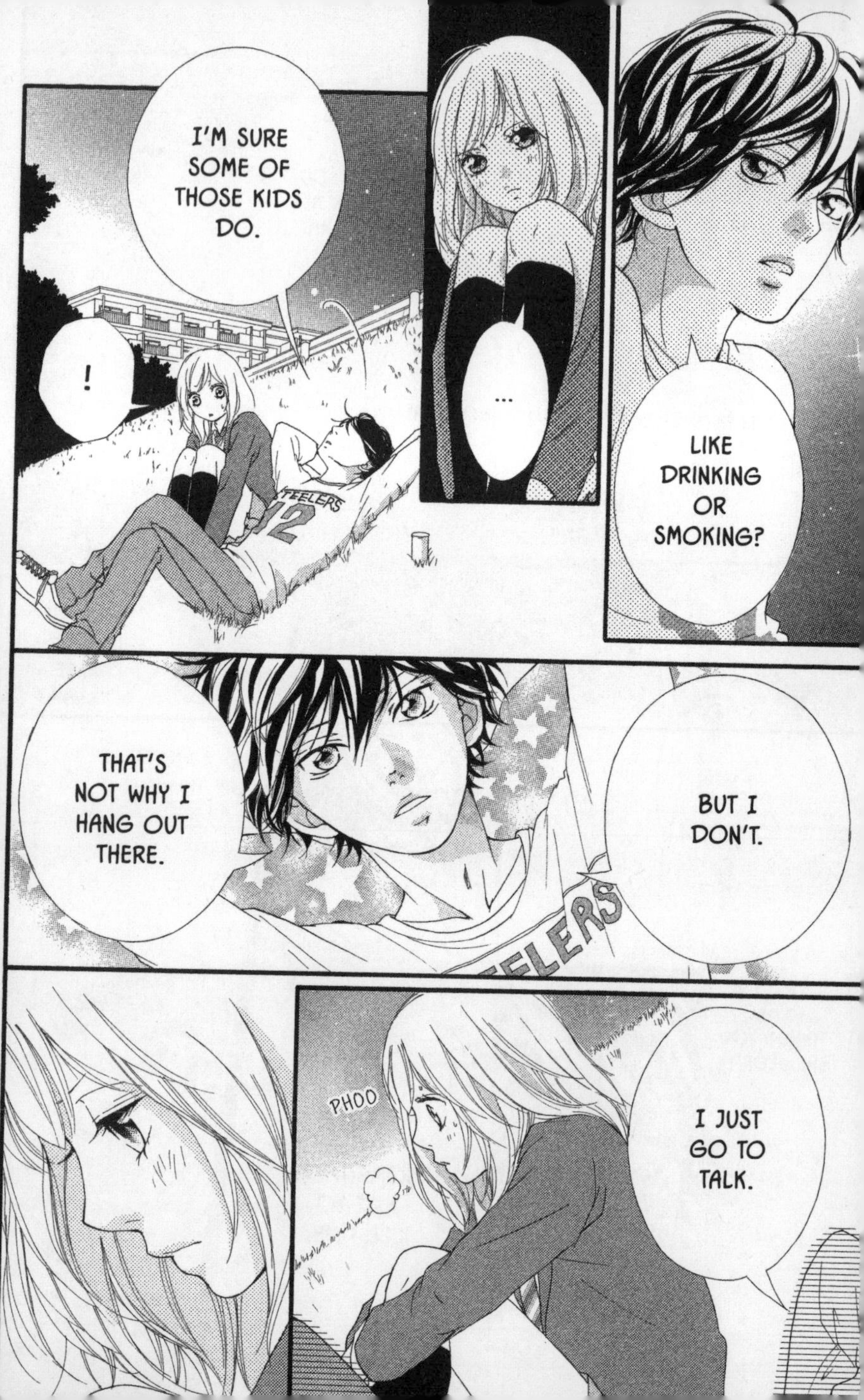
LIKE DRINKING OR SMOKING?
...
I'M SURE SOME OF THOSE KIDS DO.
!
BUT I DON'T.
THAT'S NOT WHY I HANG OUT THERE.
I JUST GO TO TALK.
PHOO

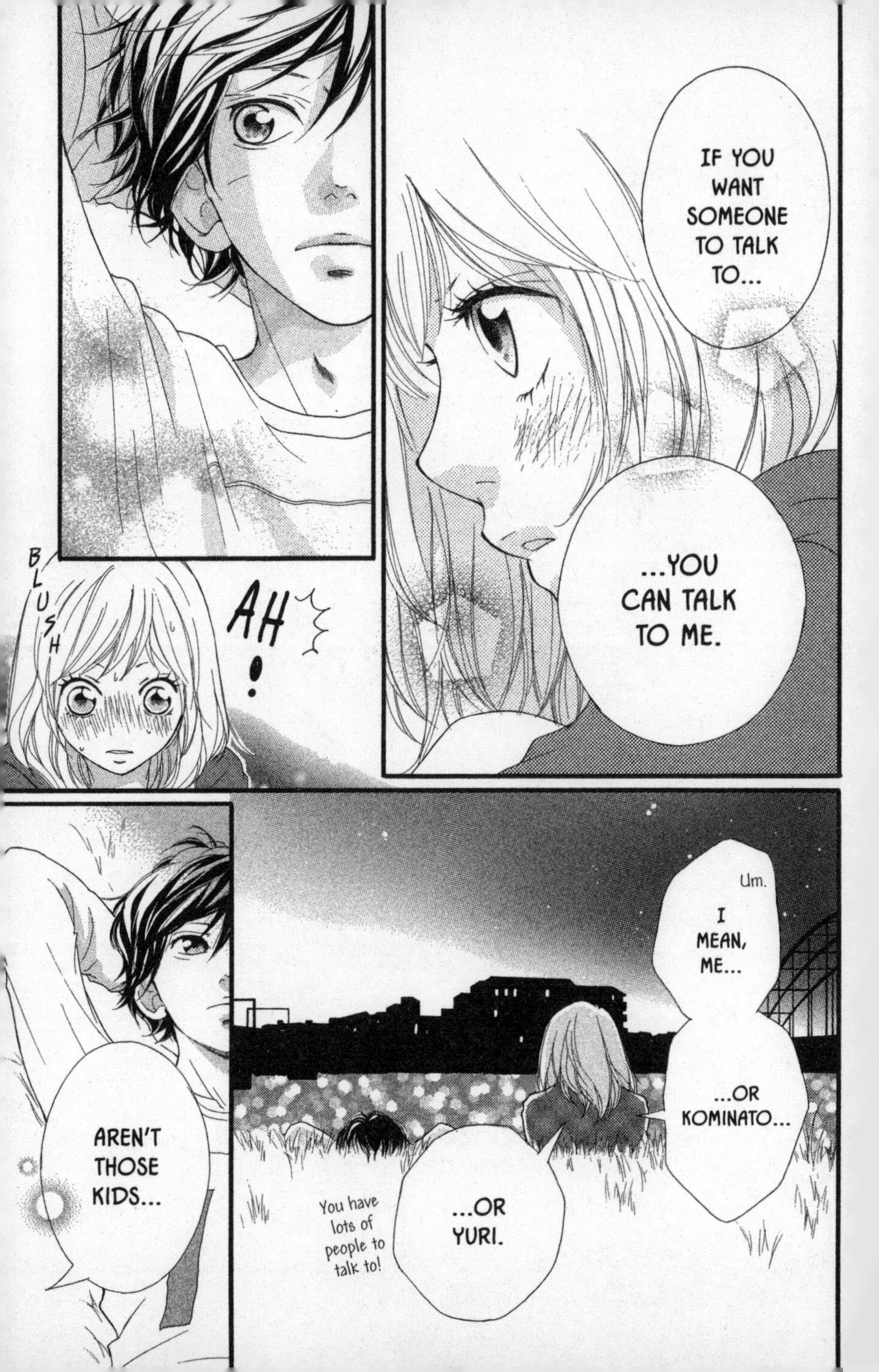
IF YOU WANT SOMEONE TO TALK TO...
...YOU CAN TALK TO ME.
BLUSH
AH!
Um.
I MEAN, ME...
...OR KOMINATO...
...OR YURI.
You have lots of people to talk to!
AREN'T THOSE KIDS...

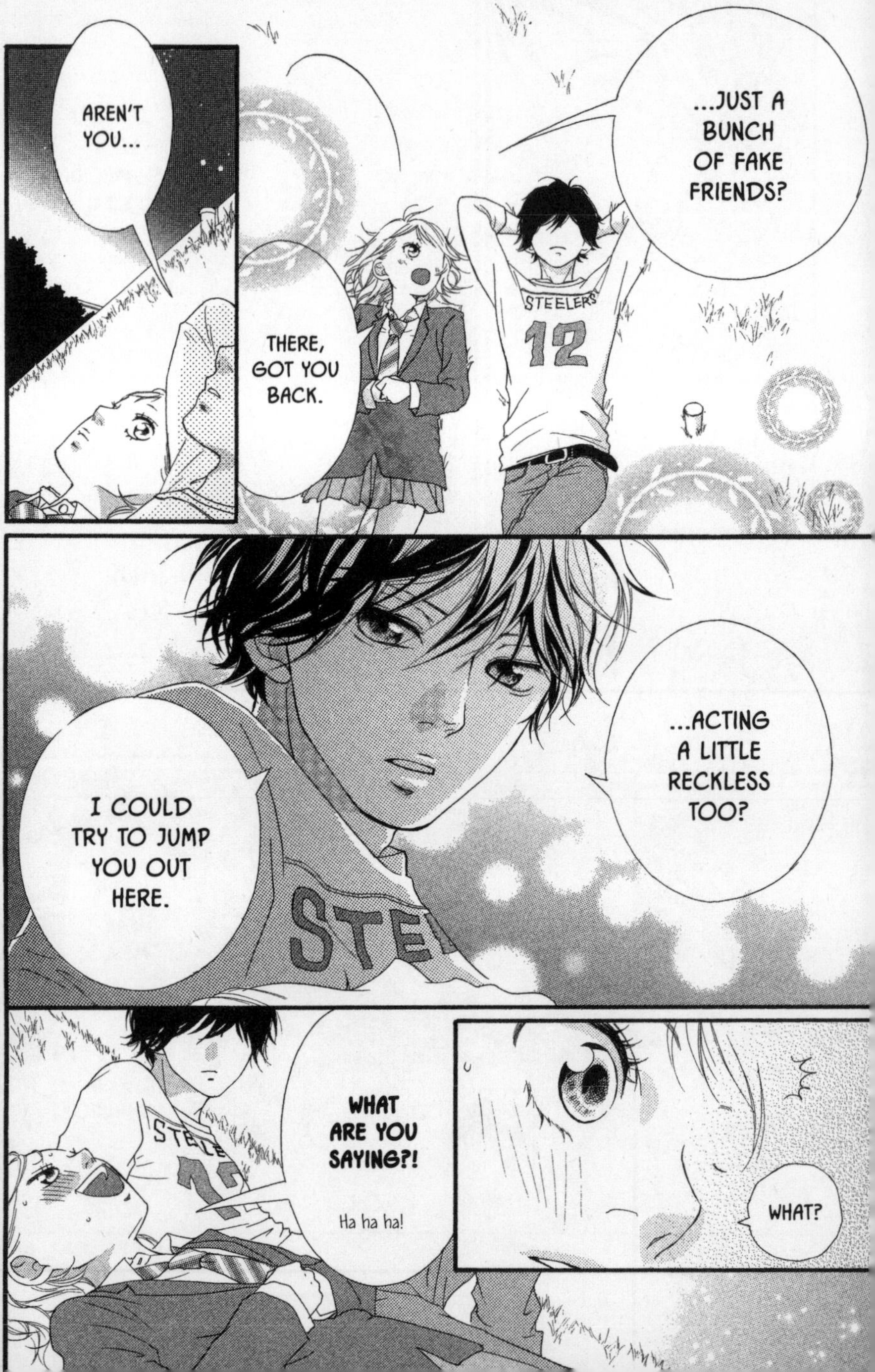
...JUST A BUNCH OF FAKE FRIENDS?
THERE, GOT YOU BACK.
AREN'T YOU...
...ACTING A LITTLE RECKLESS TOO?
I COULD TRY TO JUMP YOU OUT HERE.
WHAT?
WHAT ARE YOU SAYING?!
Ha ha ha!
STEELERS
12

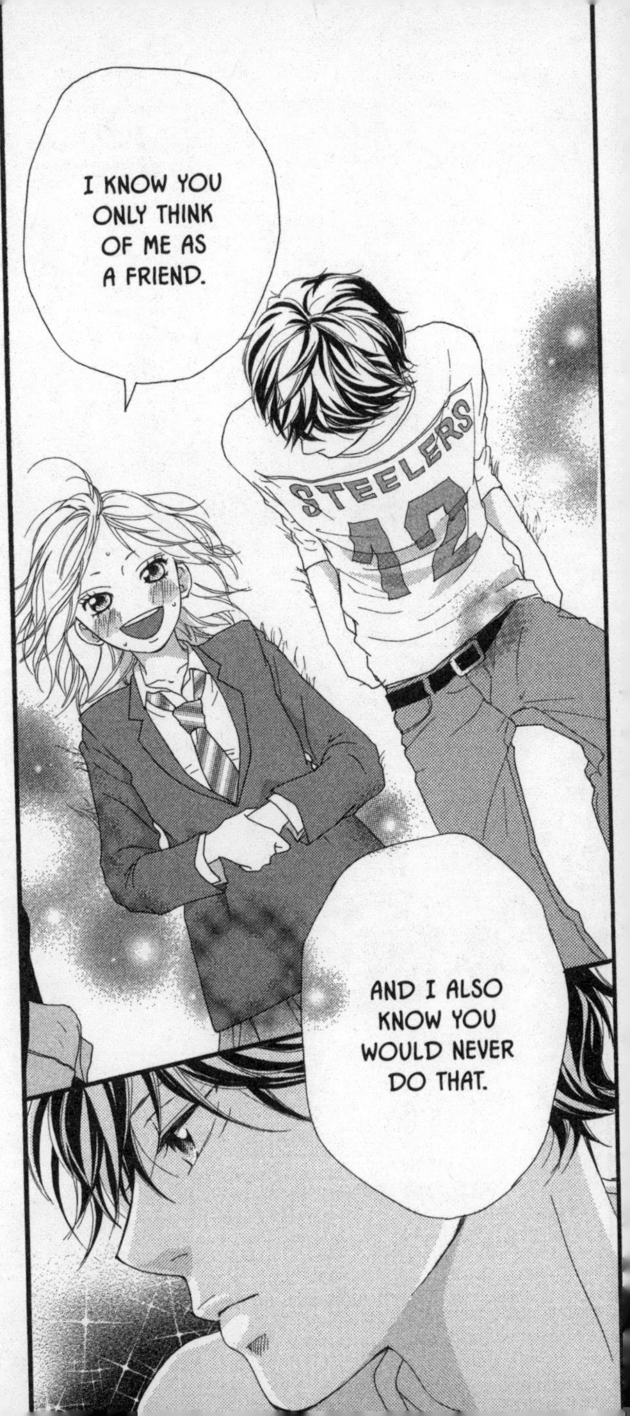
I KNOW YOU ONLY THINK OF ME AS A FRIEND.
STEELERS
12
AND I ALSO KNOW YOU WOULD NEVER DO THAT.

In *Betsuma* magazine we asked you to share ideas for Ramune swag and Mr. Tanaka's outfits. Thank you for your many suggestions! As my editor and I reviewed them, we laughed when we realized how many of Mr. Tanaka's outfits had been designed with appliqués. Who knew that appliqués could look so stupid and unstylish!! I could totally see Mr. Tanaka wearing them without any thought!! I'm going to take a closer look and decide on some Mr. Tanaka outfits to use! Of course I'll do the same with the Ramune swag! For those of you whose designs I use, please expect a signed illustration by me to be sent your way. ♡ I may be doing more of these calls for ideas in the future, so don't forget to check out *Betsuma* magazine.

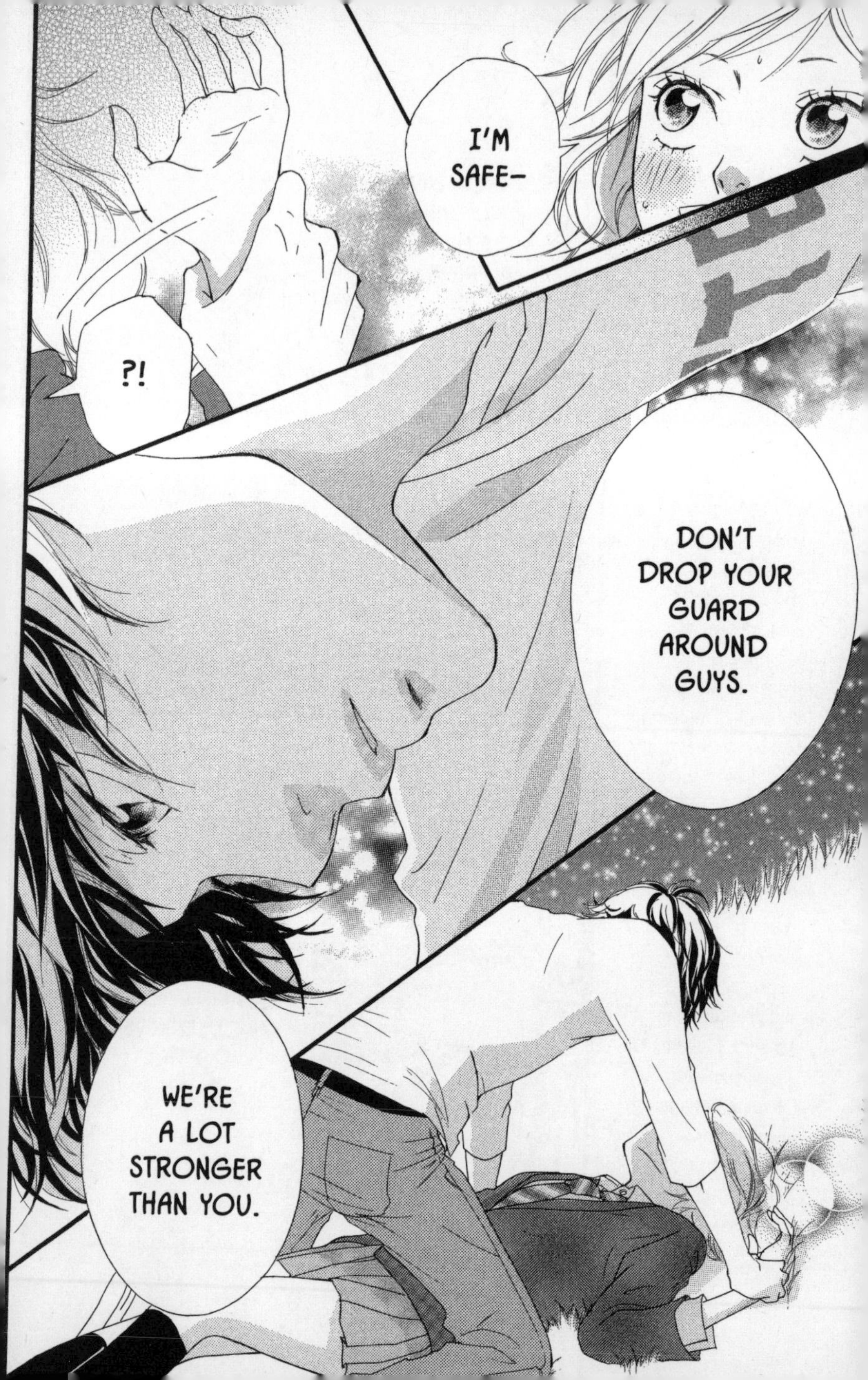
I'M SAFE—
?!
DON'T DROP YOUR GUARD AROUND GUYS.
WE'RE A LOT STRONGER THAN YOU.

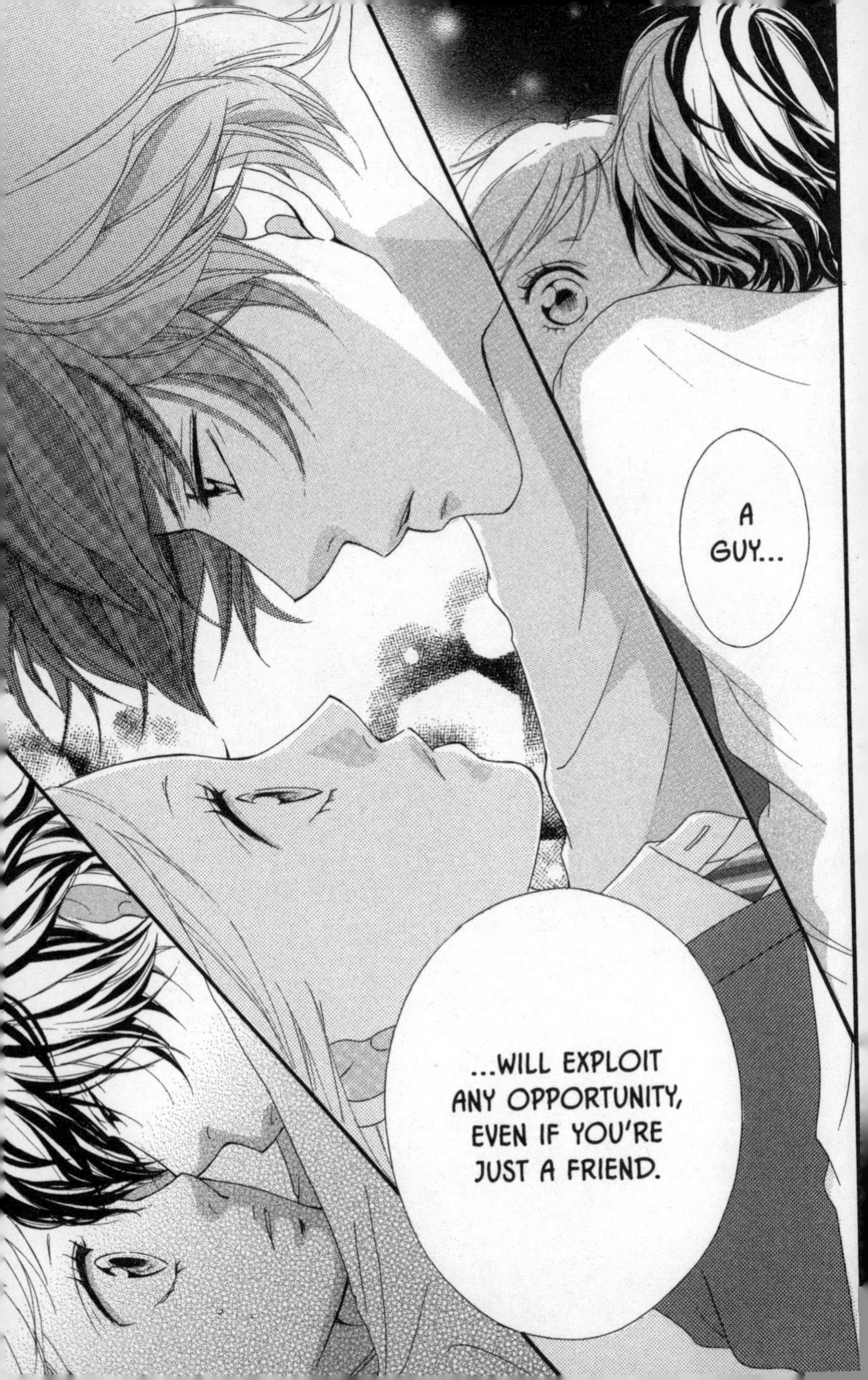
A GUY...
...WILL EXPLOIT ANY OPPORTUNITY, EVEN IF YOU'RE JUST A FRIEND.

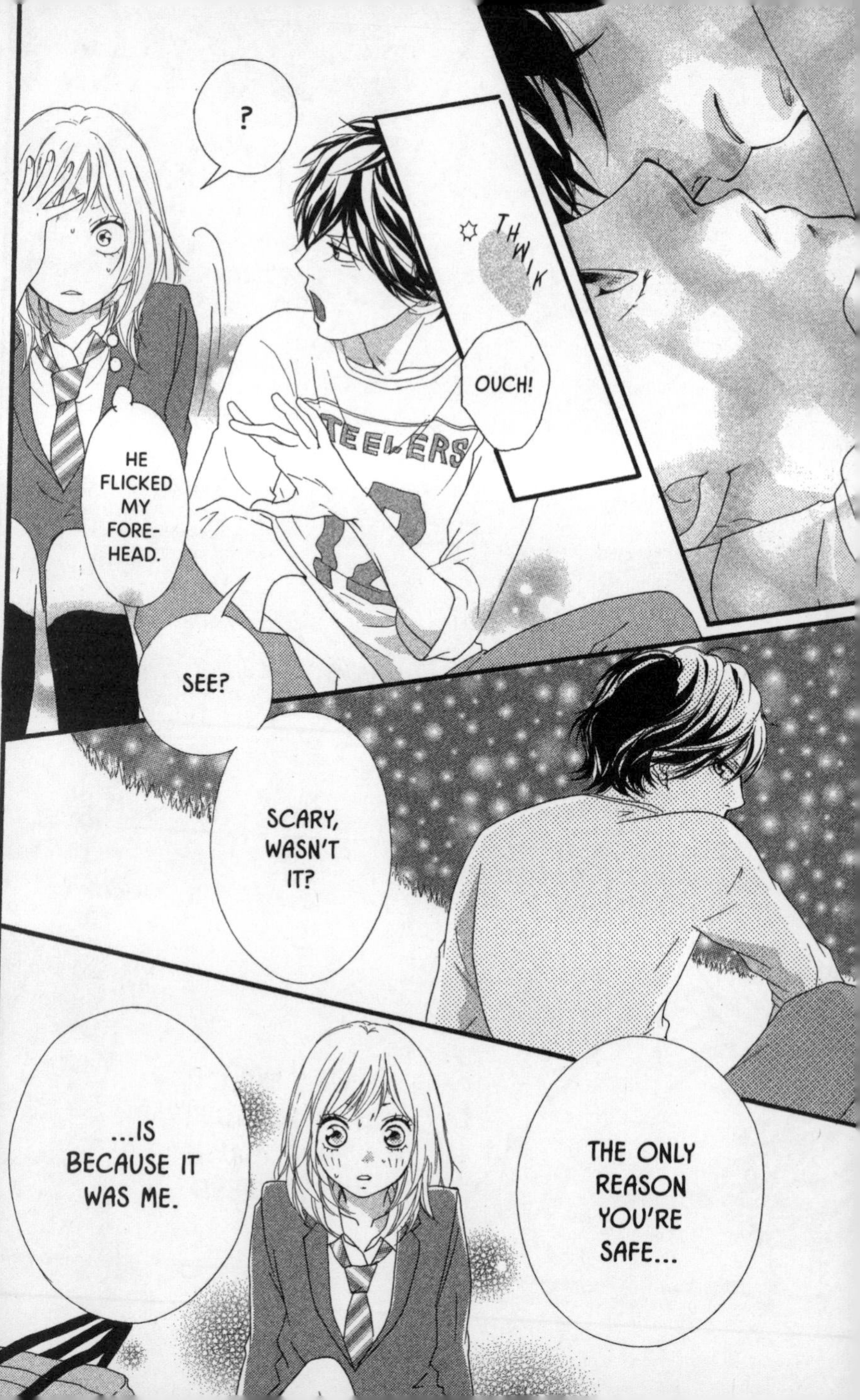
THWIK
OUCH!
?
HE FLICKED MY FOREHEAD.
SEE?
SCARY, WASN'T IT?
THE ONLY REASON YOU'RE SAFE...
...IS BECAUSE IT WAS ME.

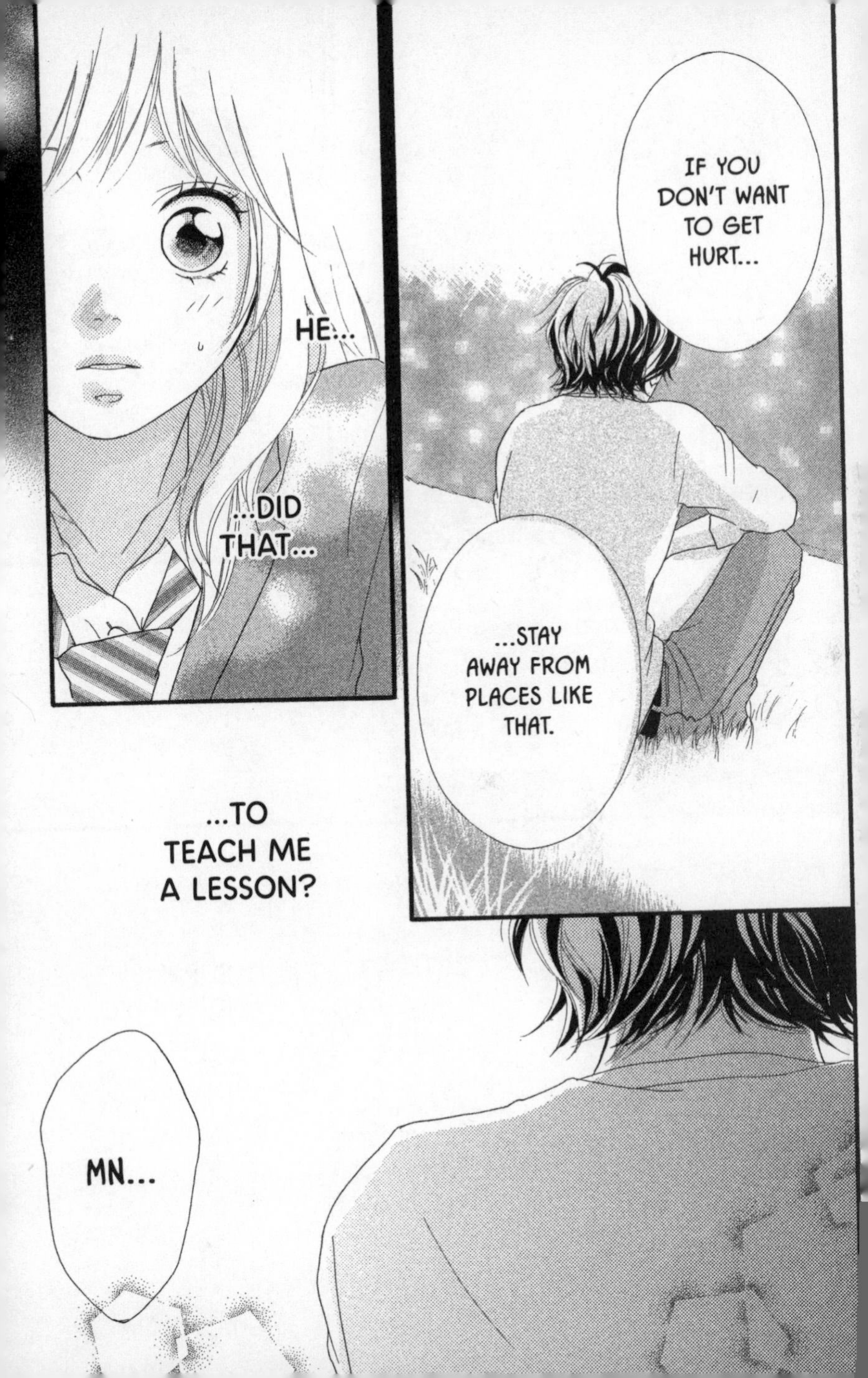
IF YOU DON'T WANT TO GET HURT...
...STAY AWAY FROM PLACES LIKE THAT.
HE...
...DID THAT...
...TO TEACH ME A LESSON?
MN...

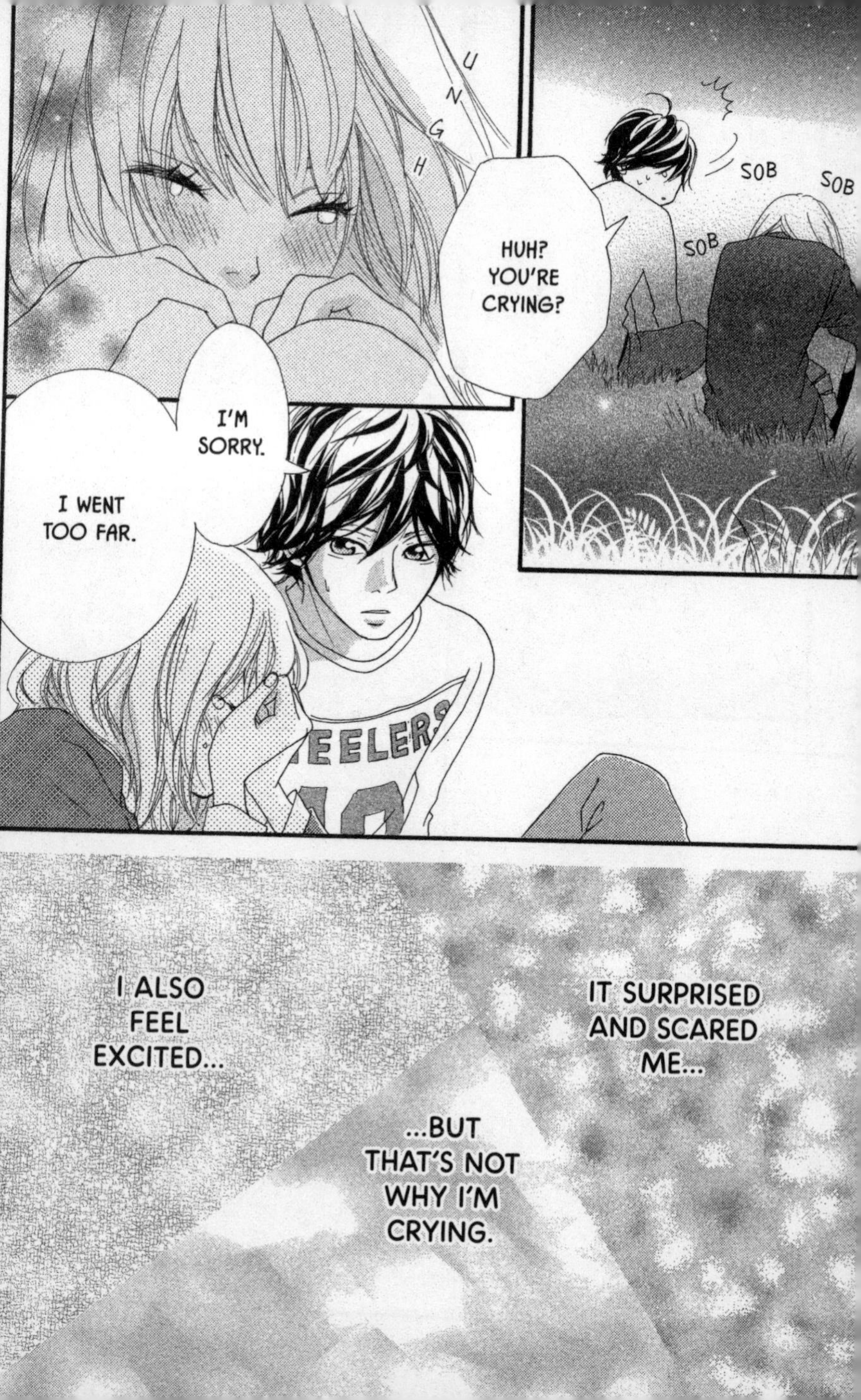
SOB
SOB
SOB
HUH? YOU'RE CRYING?
UNGH
I'M SORRY.
I WENT TOO FAR.
IT SURPRISED AND SCARED ME...
I ALSO FEEL EXCITED...
...BUT THAT'S NOT WHY I'M CRYING.

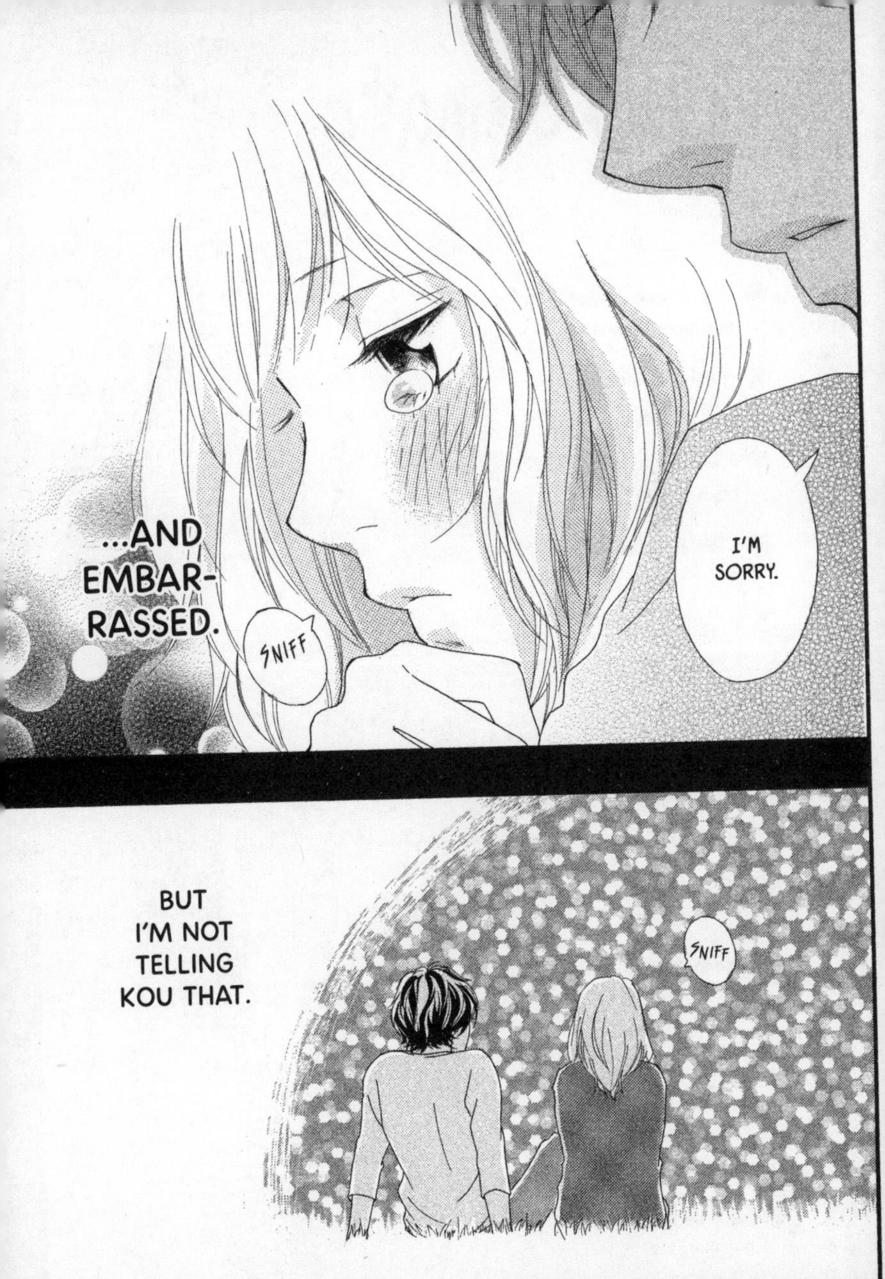
I'M SORRY.
...AND EMBAR-RASSED.
SNIFF
SNIFF
BUT I'M NOT TELLING KOU THAT.

Aya Kominato

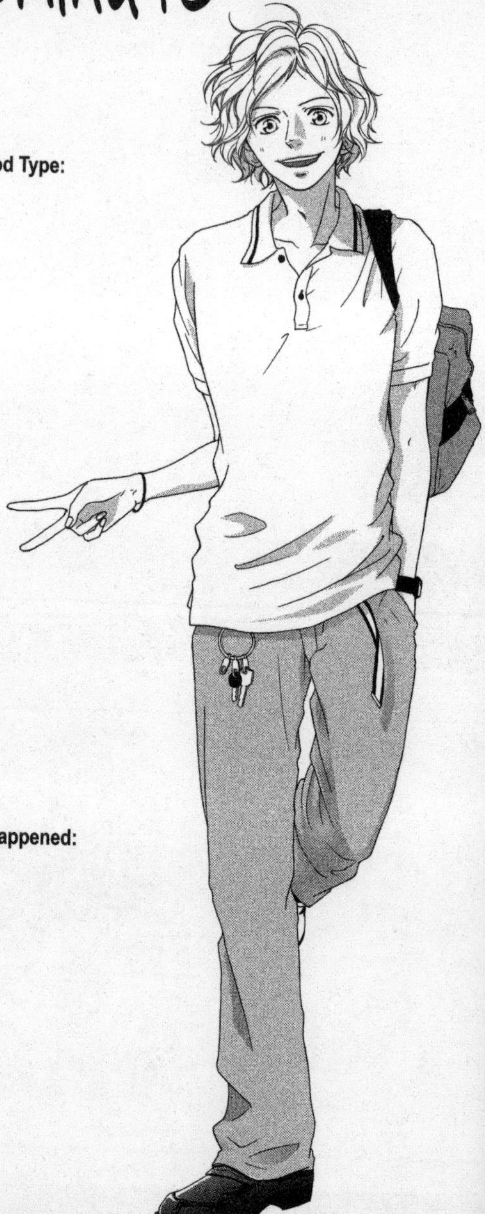

- **Birthday:**
  December 3rd
- **Astrological Sign, Blood Type:**
  Sagittarius, type A
- **Height, Weight:**
  5'10", 139 lbs.
- **Favorite Subject:**
  Math
- **Least Favorite Subject:**
  Art
- **Favorite Food:**
  Korean barbeque
- **Least Favorite Food:**
  Freeze-dried tofu
- **Favorite Music:**
  ONE OK ROCK
- **Siblings:**
  Younger sister
- **Age When First Crush Happened:**
  Second grade
- **Fun Fact:**
  I'm one-quarter French.
- **Favorite Snack:**
  Black Thunder chocolate
- **Favorite Drink:**
  Peach tea
- **Favorite Color:**
  Pink

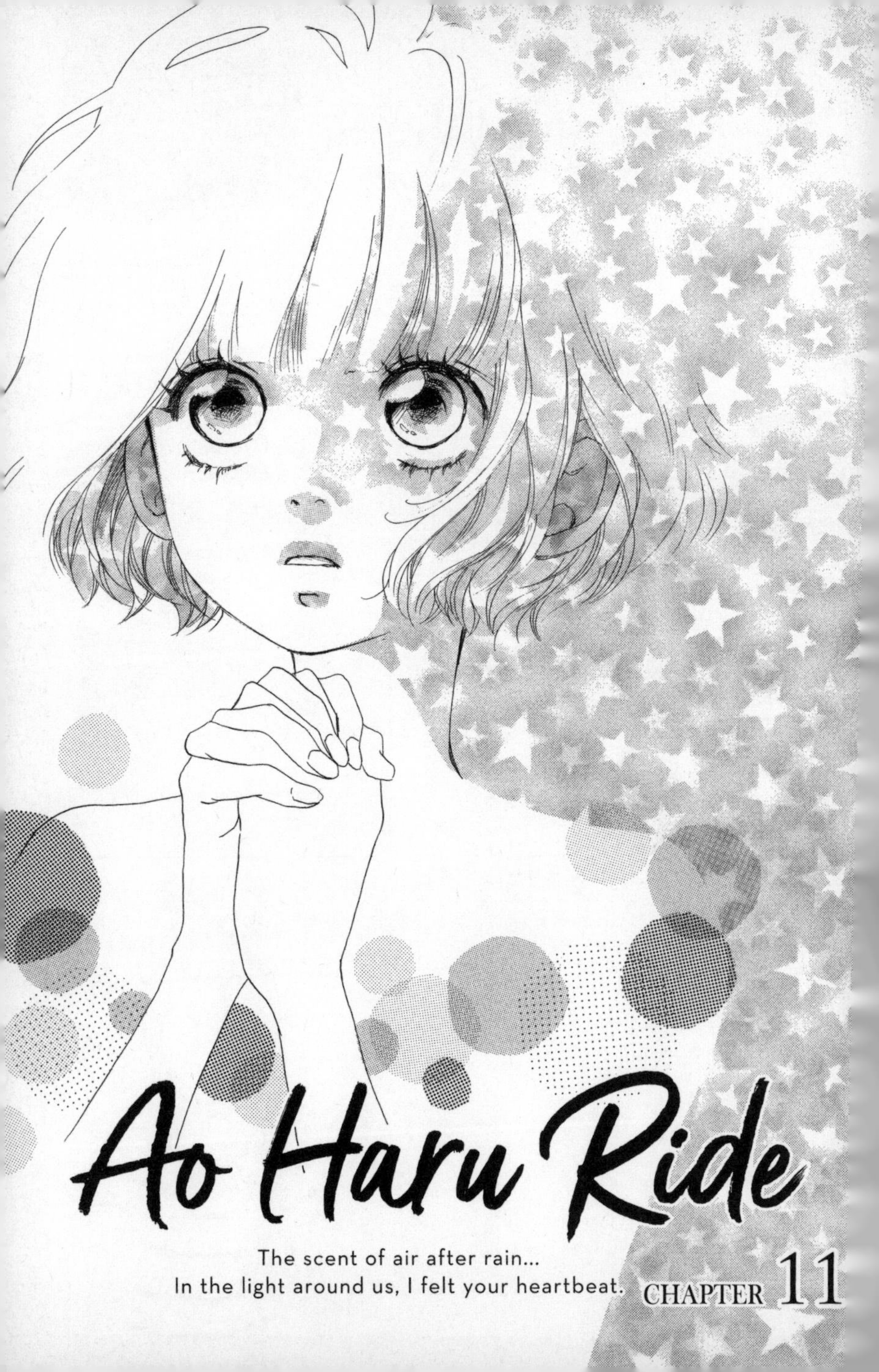
Ao Haru Ride
The scent of air after rain...
In the light around us, I felt your heartbeat.
CHAPTER 11

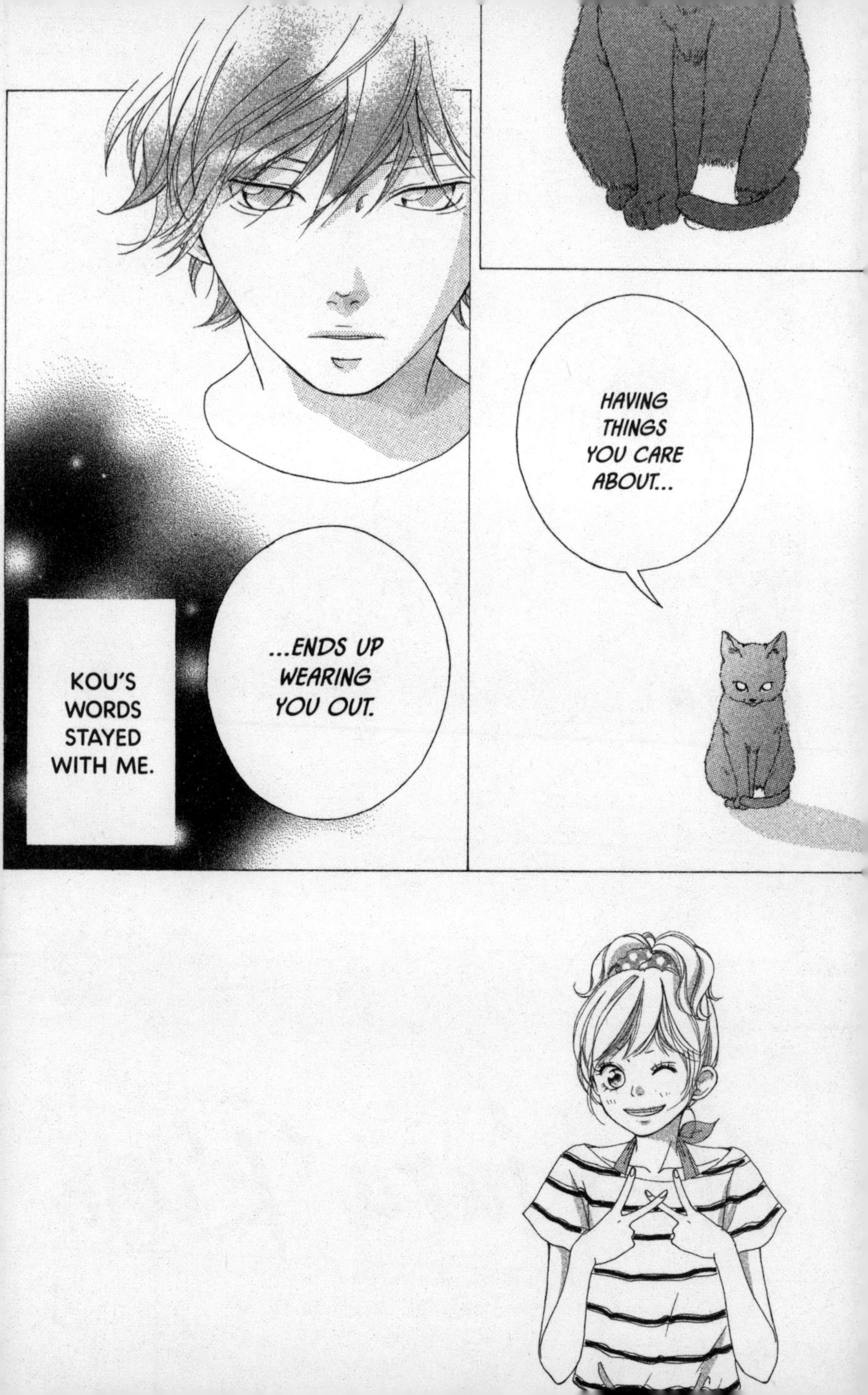
HAVING THINGS YOU CARE ABOUT...
...ENDS UP WEARING YOU OUT.
KOU'S WORDS STAYED WITH ME.

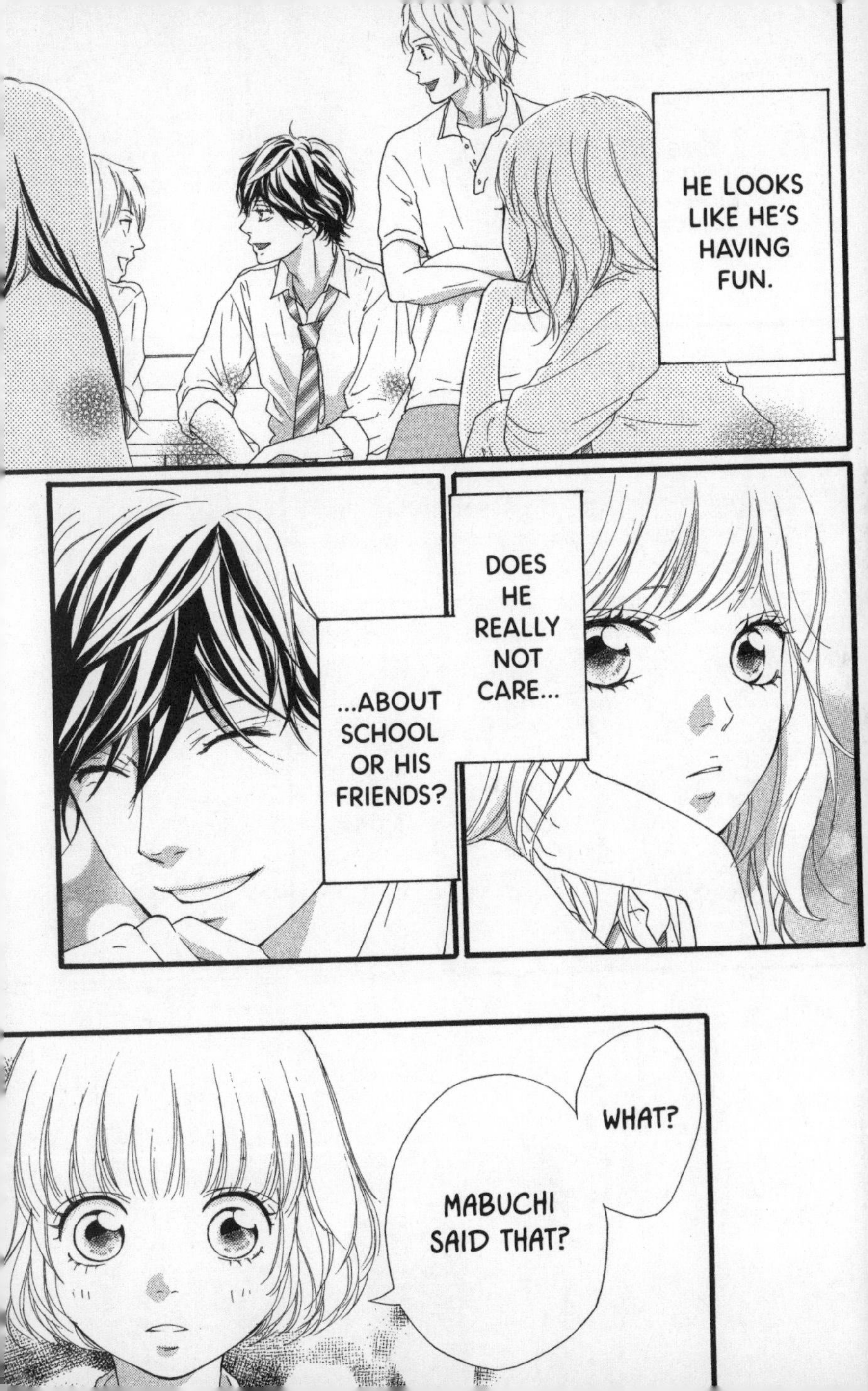
HE LOOKS LIKE HE'S HAVING FUN.
DOES HE REALLY NOT CARE...
...ABOUT SCHOOL OR HIS FRIENDS?
WHAT?
MABUCHI SAID THAT?

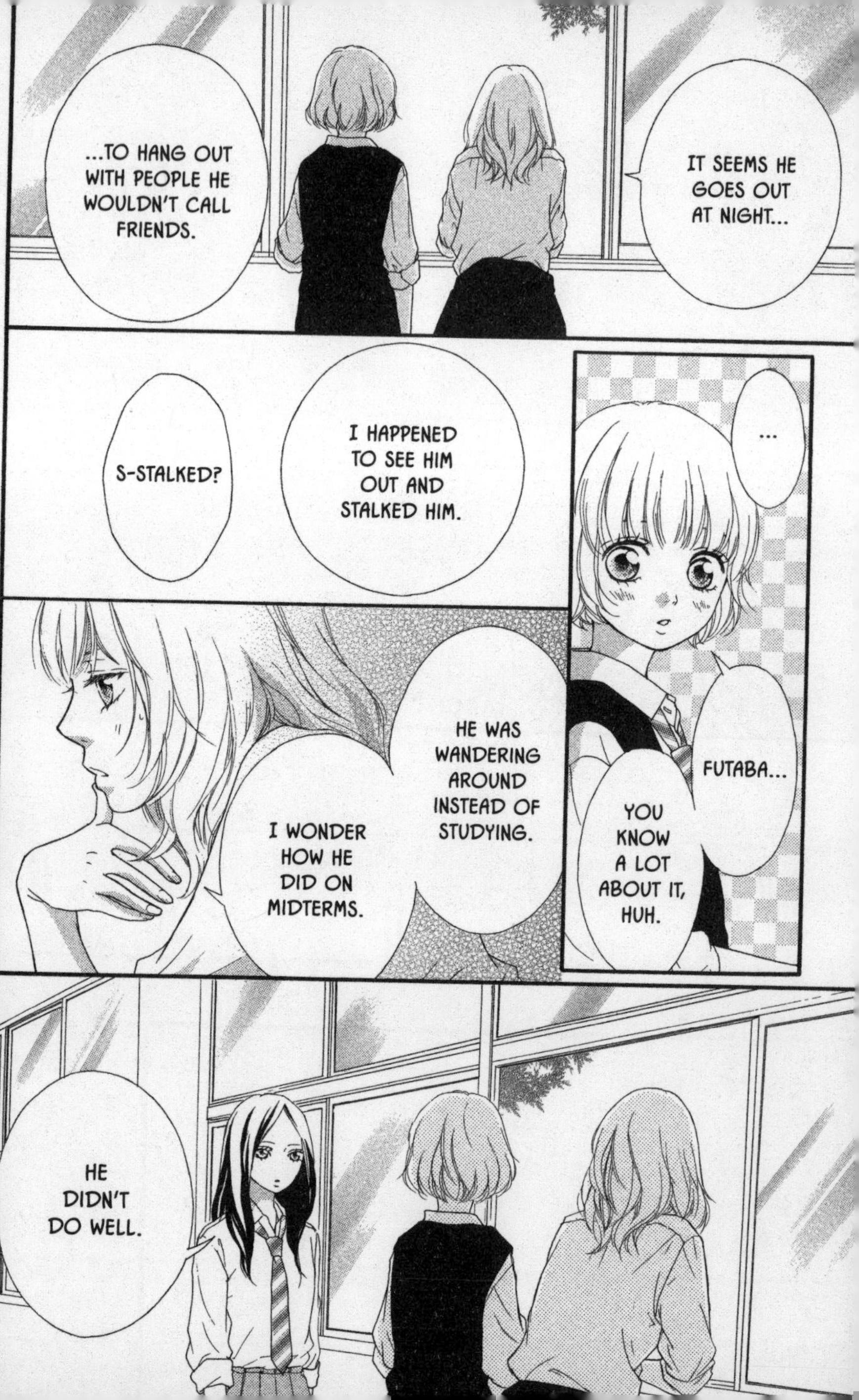
IT SEEMS HE GOES OUT AT NIGHT...
...TO HANG OUT WITH PEOPLE HE WOULDN'T CALL FRIENDS.
...
FUTABA...
YOU KNOW A LOT ABOUT IT, HUH.
I HAPPENED TO SEE HIM OUT AND STALKED HIM.
S-STALKED?
HE WAS WANDERING AROUND INSTEAD OF STUDYING.
I WONDER HOW HE DID ON MIDTERMS.
HE DIDN'T DO WELL.

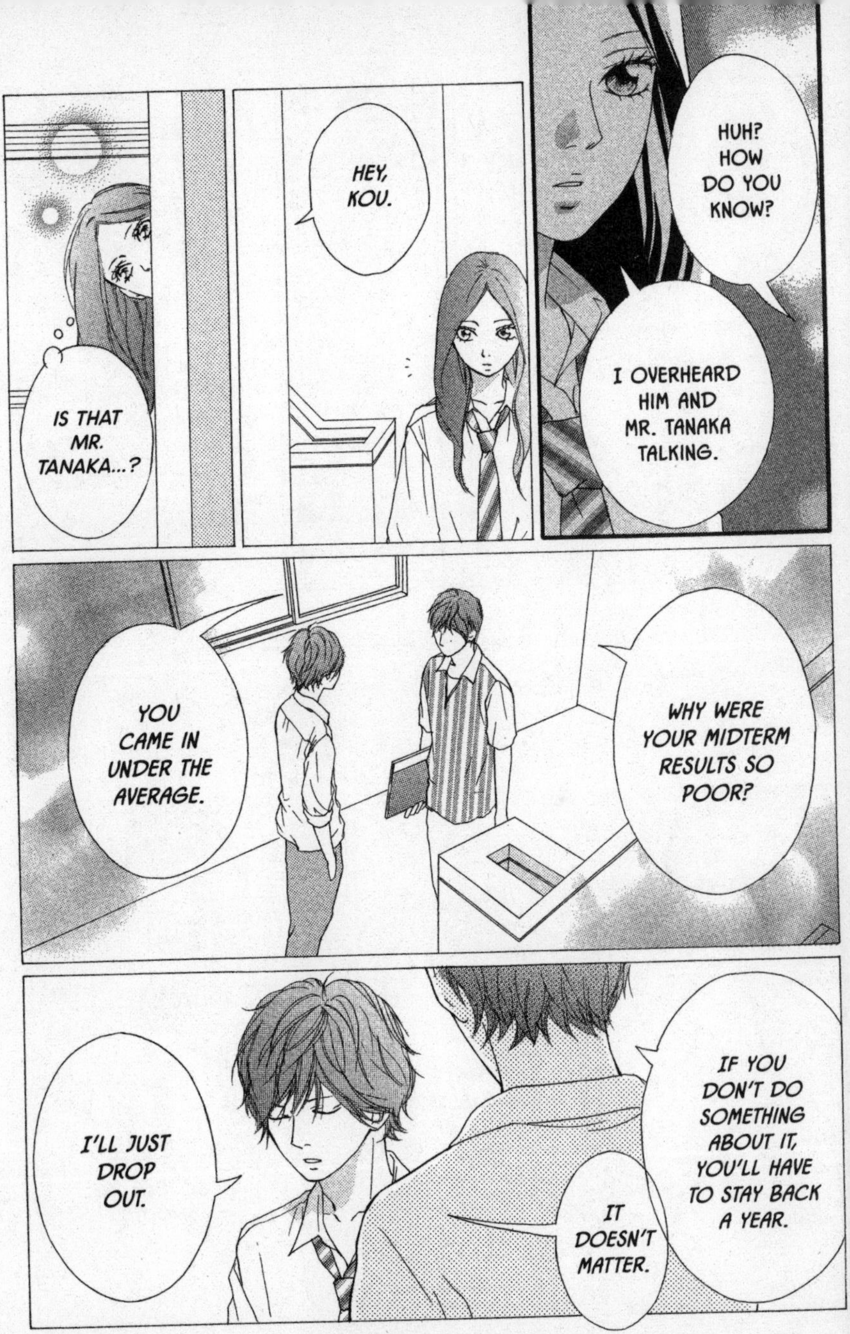
HUH? HOW DO YOU KNOW?
I OVERHEARD HIM AND MR. TANAKA TALKING.
HEY, KOU.
IS THAT MR. TANAKA...?
WHY WERE YOUR MIDTERM RESULTS SO POOR?
YOU CAME IN UNDER THE AVERAGE.
IF YOU DON'T DO SOMETHING ABOUT IT, YOU'LL HAVE TO STAY BACK A YEAR.
IT DOESN'T MATTER.
I'LL JUST DROP OUT.

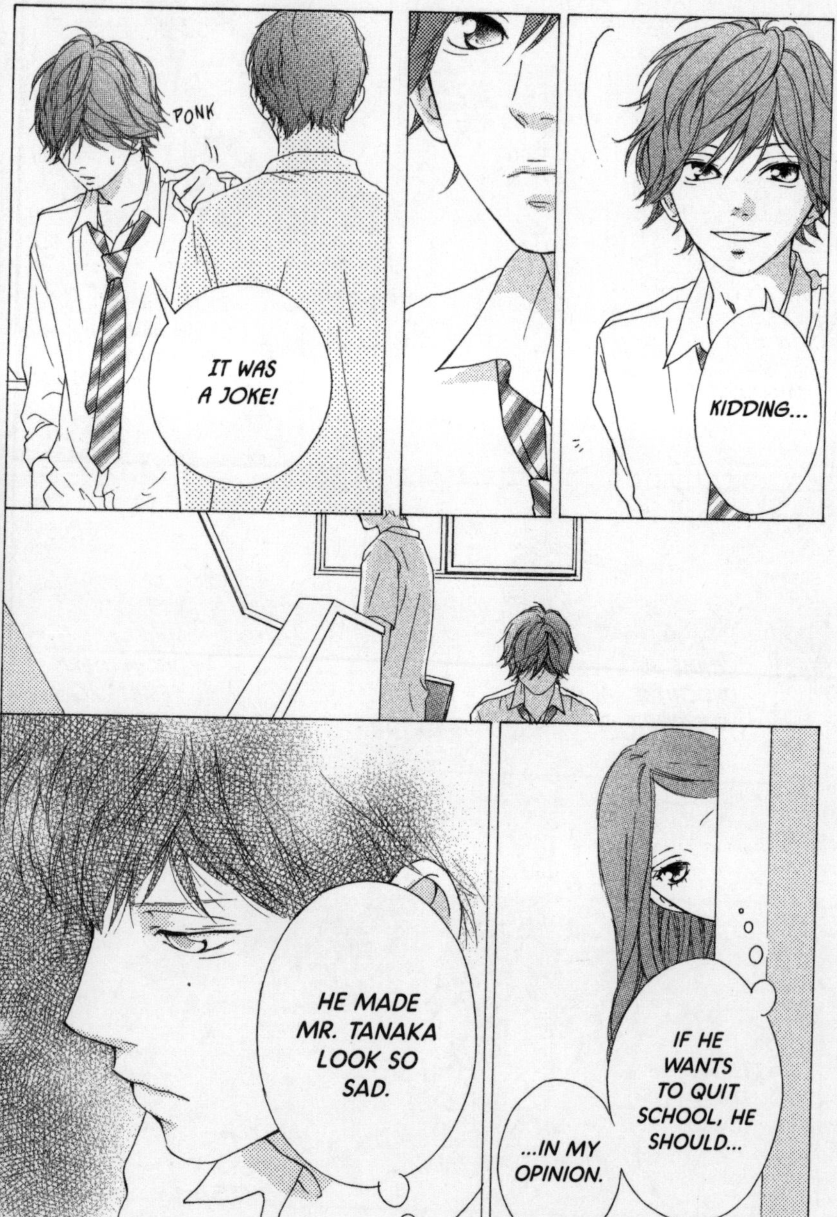
KIDDING...
PONK
IT WAS A JOKE!
IF HE WANTS TO QUIT SCHOOL, HE SHOULD...
...IN MY OPINION.
HE MADE MR. TANAKA LOOK SO SAD.

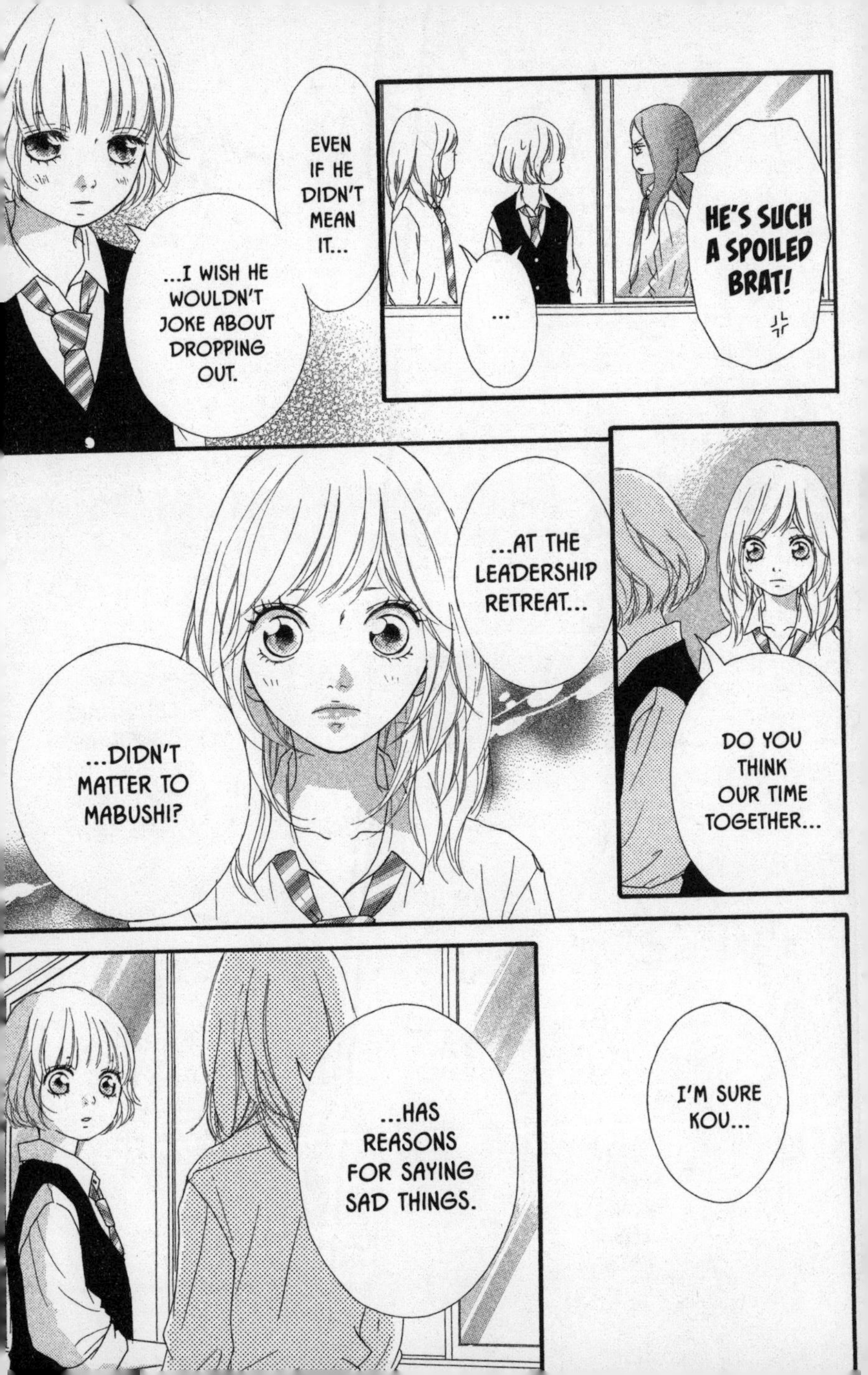
HE'S SUCH A SPOILED BRAT!
...
EVEN IF HE DIDN'T MEAN IT...
...I WISH HE WOULDN'T JOKE ABOUT DROPPING OUT.
DO YOU THINK OUR TIME TOGETHER...
...AT THE LEADERSHIP RETREAT...
...DIDN'T MATTER TO MABUSHI?
I'M SURE KOU...
...HAS REASONS FOR SAYING SAD THINGS.

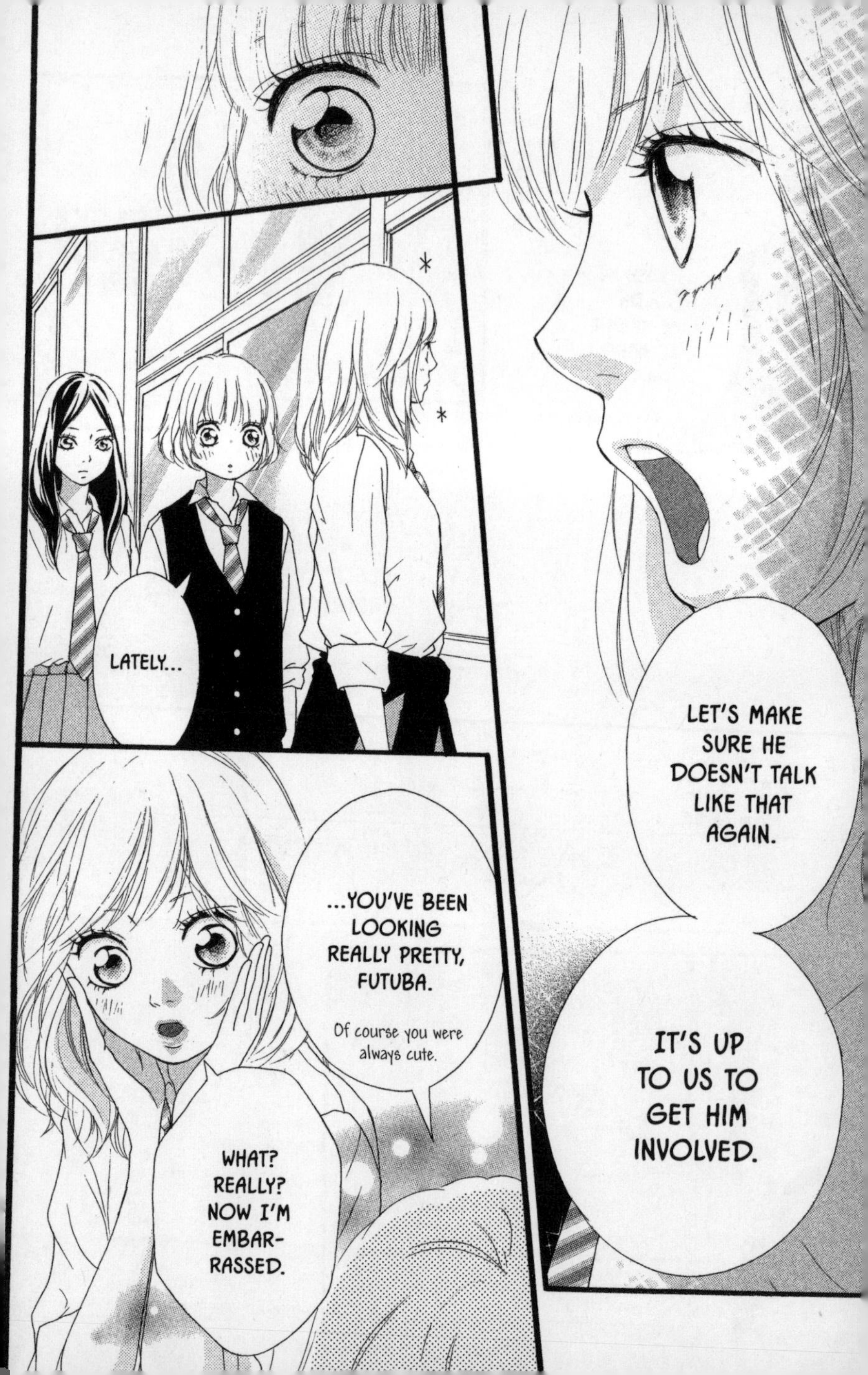
LET'S MAKE SURE HE DOESN'T TALK LIKE THAT AGAIN.
IT'S UP TO US TO GET HIM INVOLVED.
LATELY...
...YOU'VE BEEN LOOKING REALLY PRETTY, FUTUBA.
Of course you were always cute.
WHAT? REALLY? NOW I'M EMBAR-RASSED.

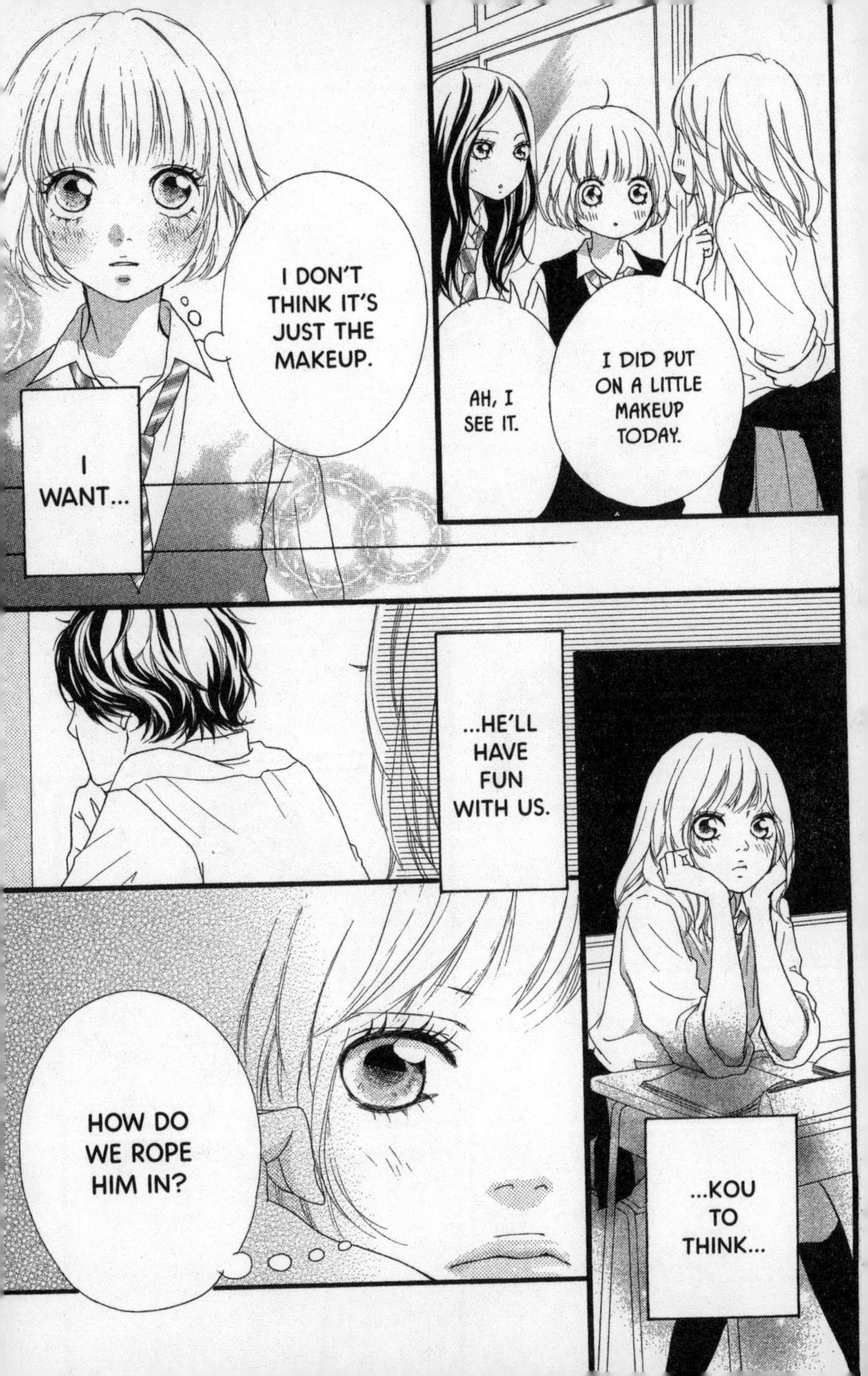
I DID PUT ON A LITTLE MAKEUP TODAY.
AH, I SEE IT.
I DON'T THINK IT'S JUST THE MAKEUP.
I WANT...
...KOU TO THINK...
...HE'LL HAVE FUN WITH US.
HOW DO WE ROPE HIM IN?

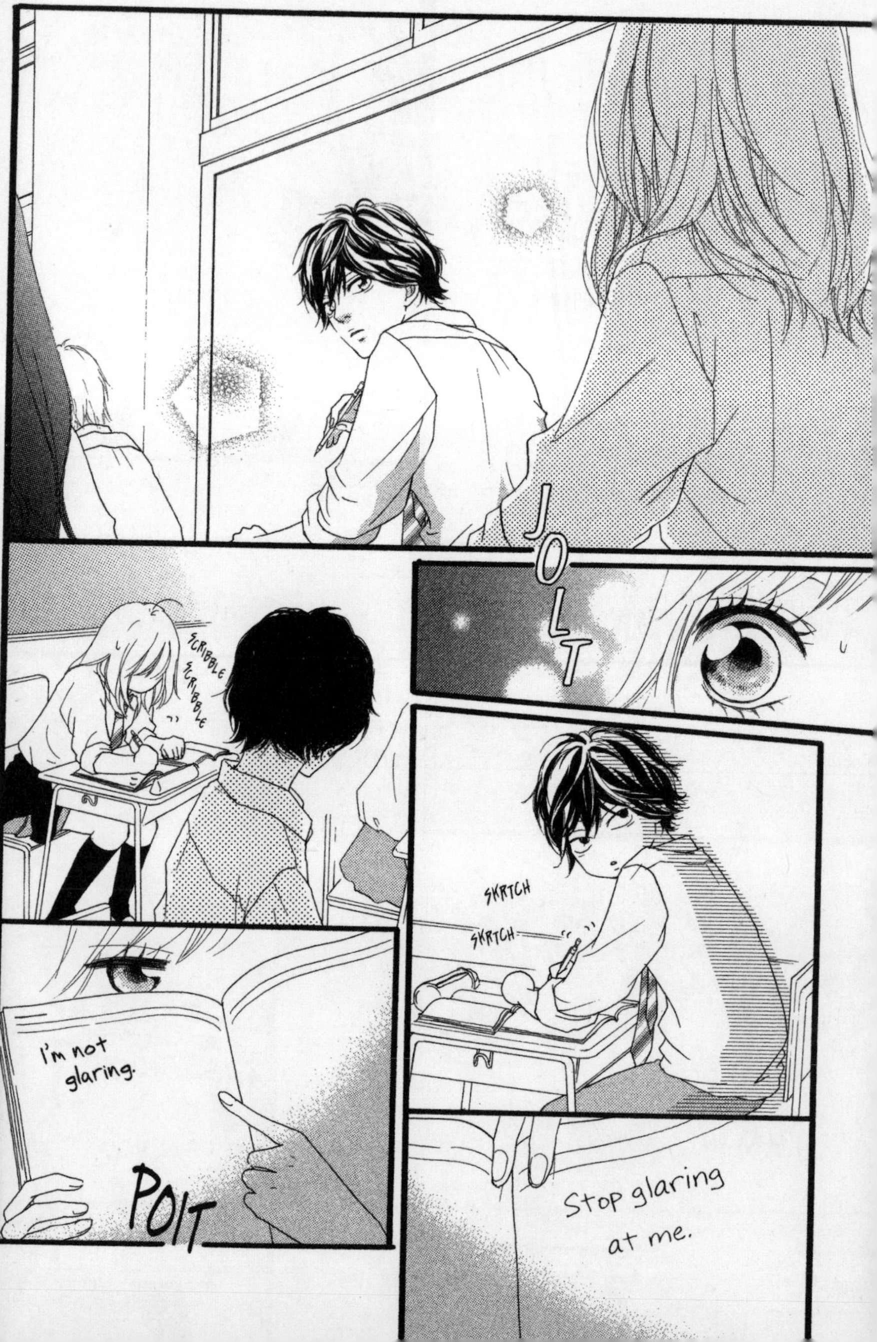
JOLT
SCRIBBLE SCRIBBLE
SKRTCH SKRTCH
Stop glaring at me.
I'm not glaring.
POIT

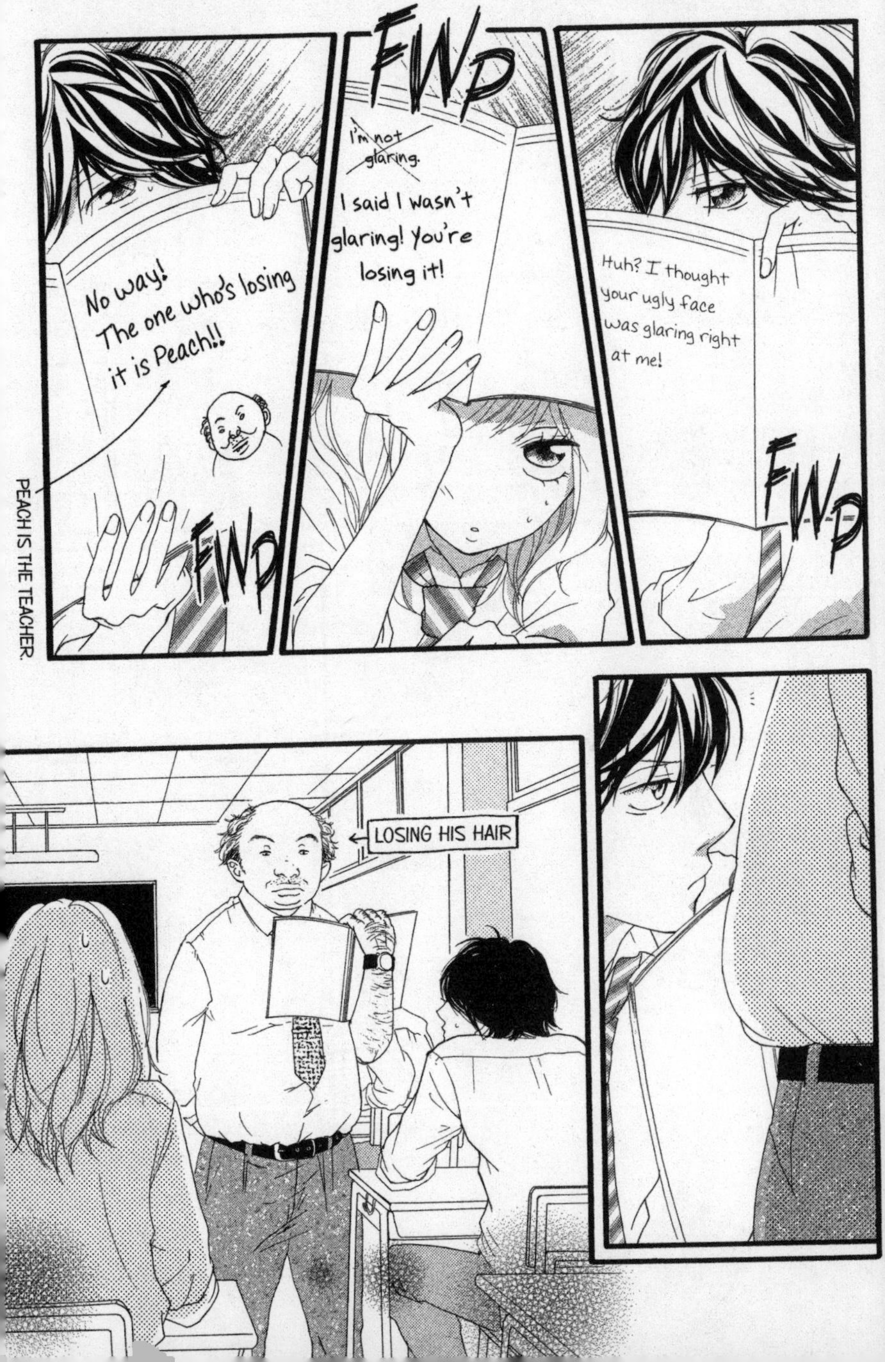
FWD
Huh? I thought your ugly face was glaring right at me!
FWD
I'm not glaring.
I said I wasn't glaring! You're losing it!
No way! The one who's losing it is Peach!!
FWD
PEACH IS THE TEACHER.
LOSING HIS HAIR

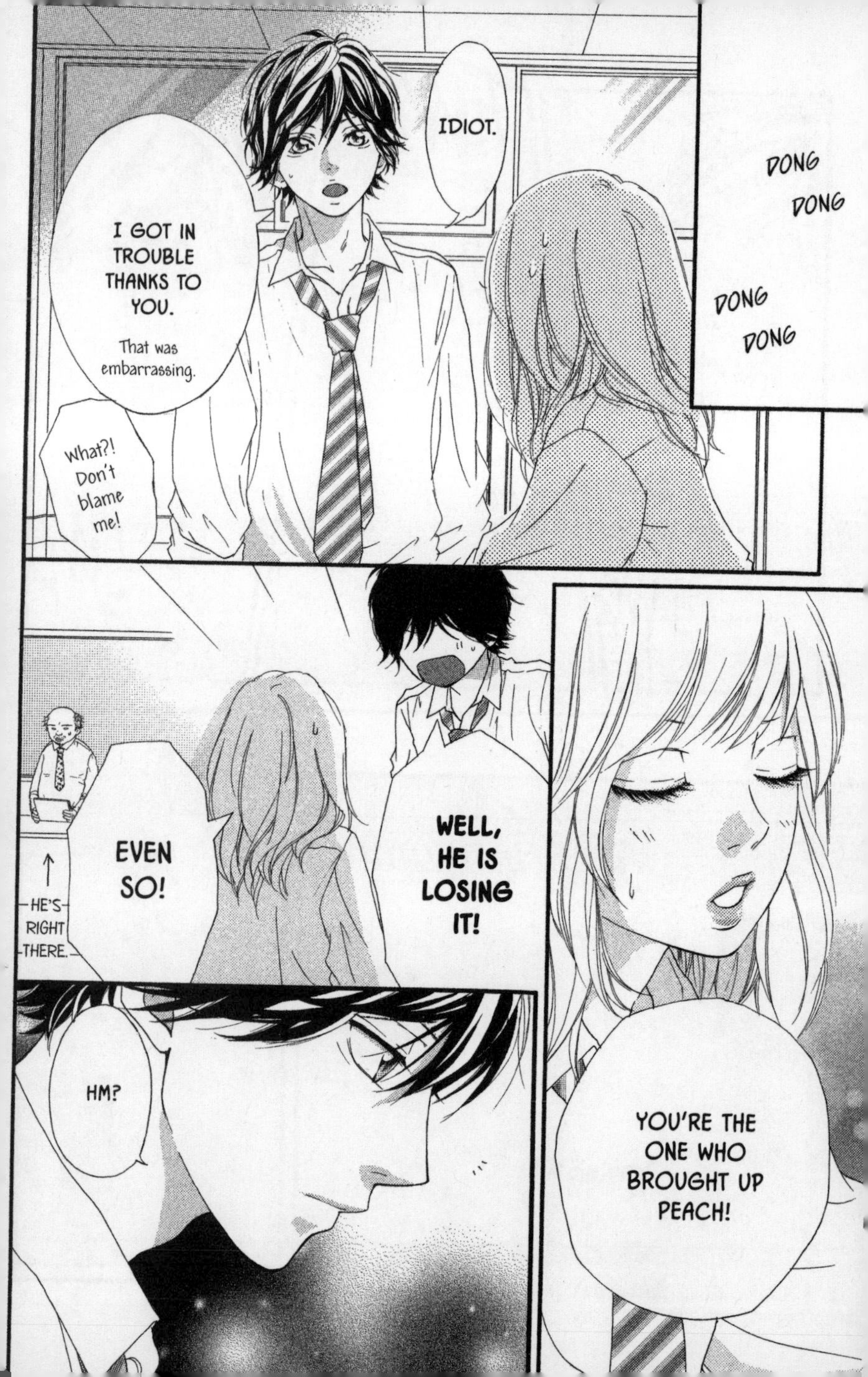
DONG
DONG
DONG
DONG
IDIOT.
I GOT IN TROUBLE THANKS TO YOU.
That was embarrassing.
What?! Don't blame me!
YOU'RE THE ONE WHO BROUGHT UP PEACH!
WELL, HE IS LOSING IT!
EVEN SO!
HE'S RIGHT THERE.
HM?

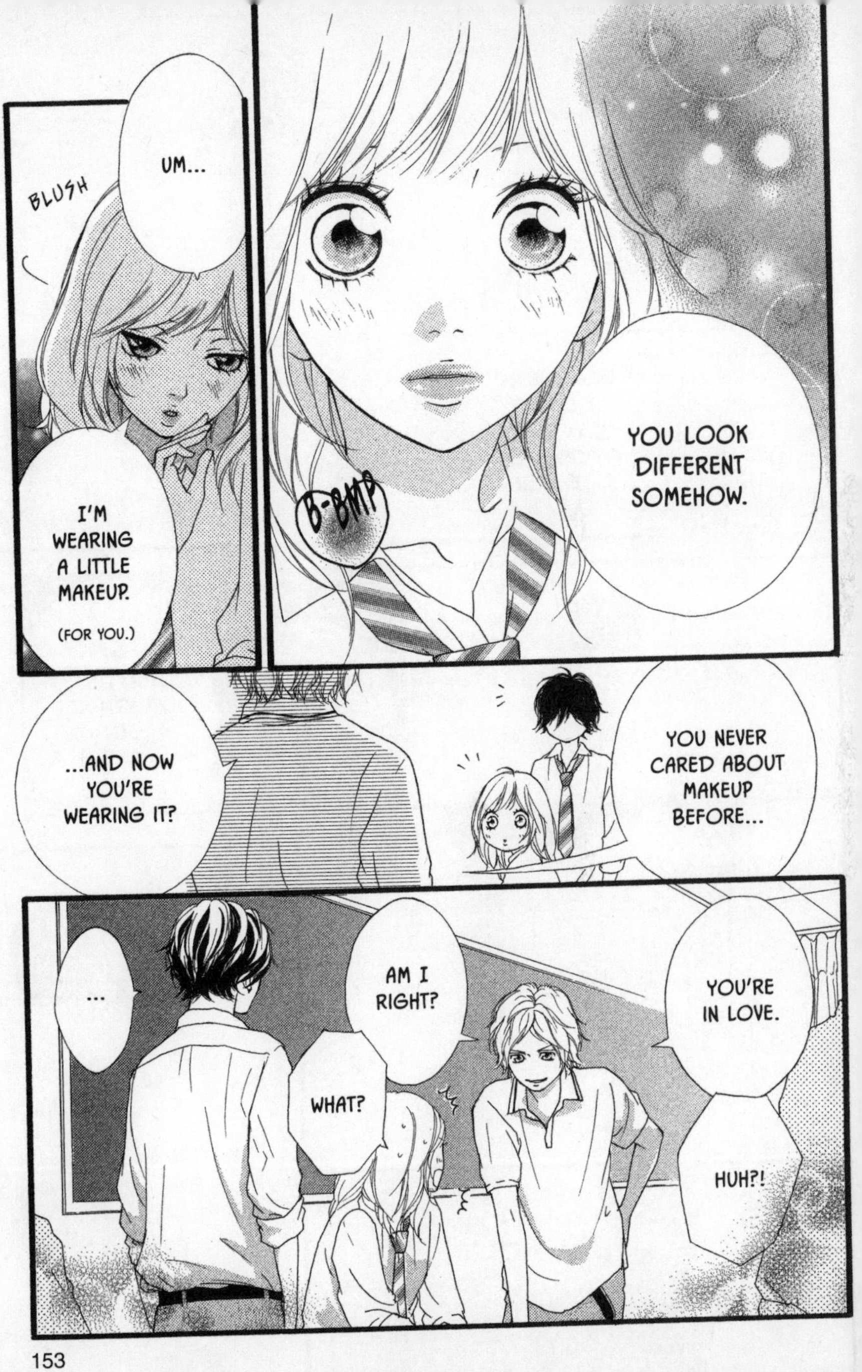
B-BMP
YOU LOOK DIFFERENT SOMEHOW.
UM...
BLUSH
I'M WEARING A LITTLE MAKEUP.
(FOR YOU.)
YOU NEVER CARED ABOUT MAKEUP BEFORE...
...AND NOW YOU'RE WEARING IT?
YOU'RE IN LOVE.
HUH?!
AM I RIGHT?
WHAT?
...

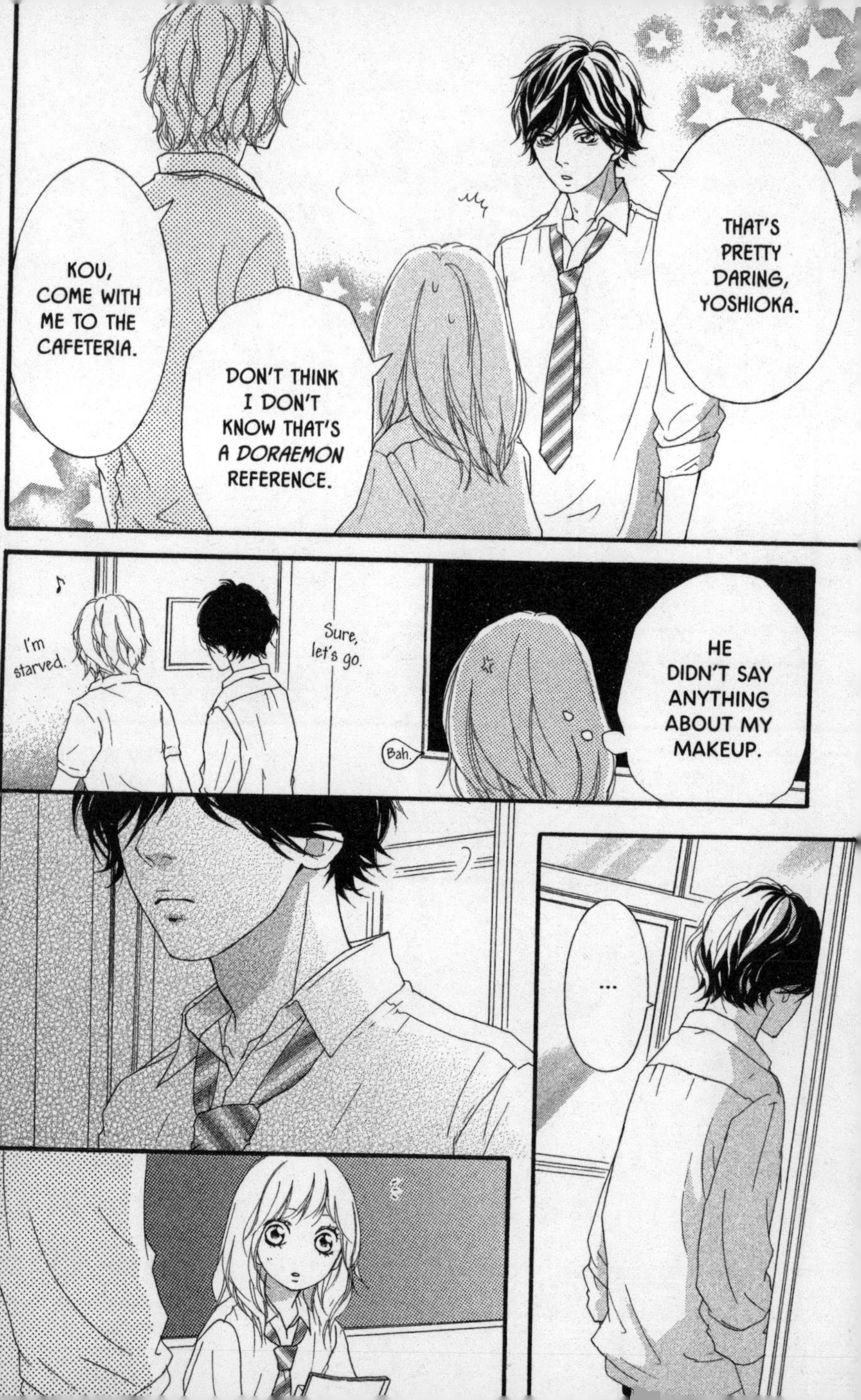
THAT'S PRETTY DARING, YOSHIOKA.
DON'T THINK I DON'T KNOW THAT'S A *DORAEMON* REFERENCE.
KOU, COME WITH ME TO THE CAFETERIA.
HE DIDN'T SAY ANYTHING ABOUT MY MAKEUP.
Bah.
Sure, let's go.
I'm starved.
...

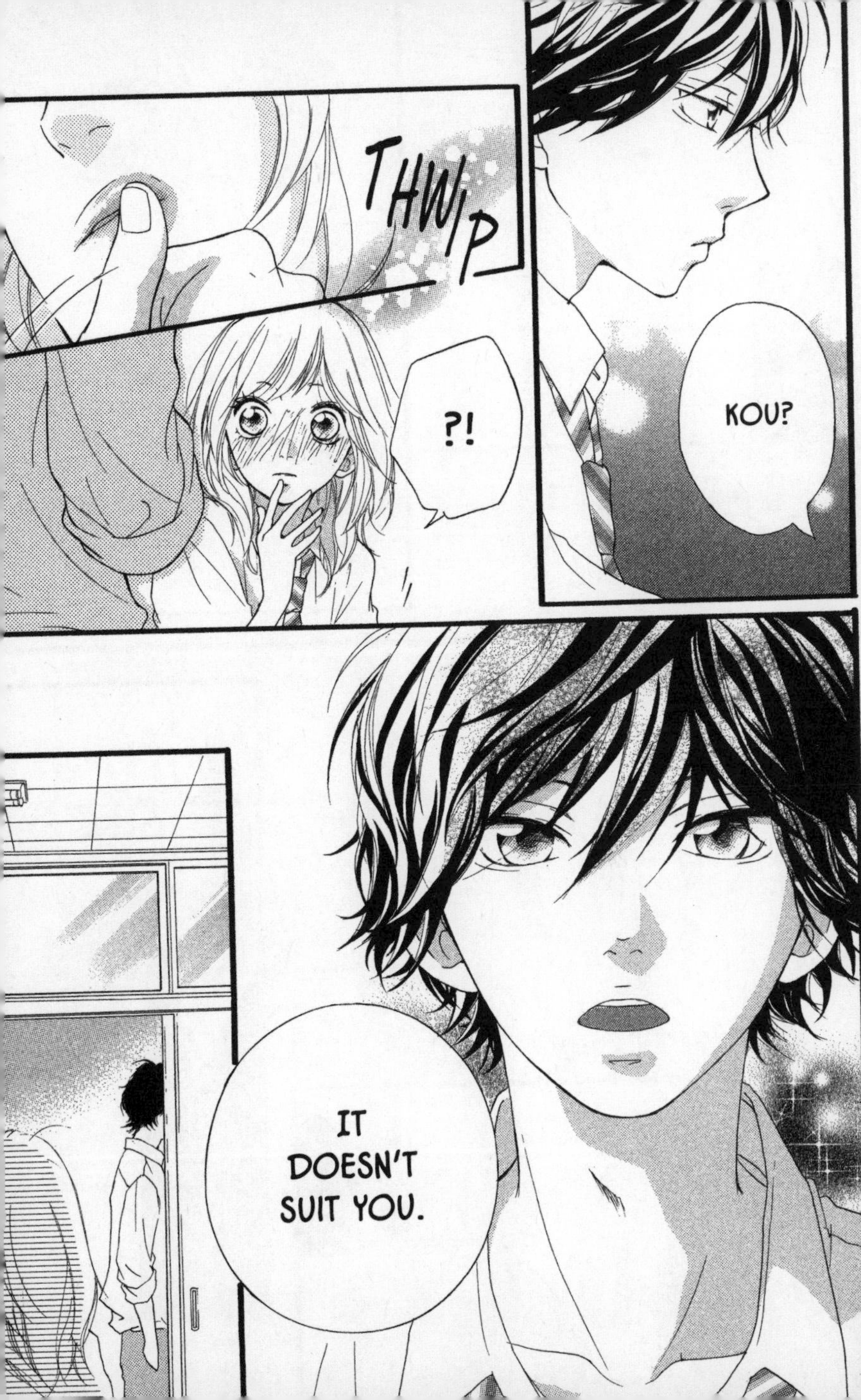
KOU?
THWIP
?!
IT DOESN'T SUIT YOU.

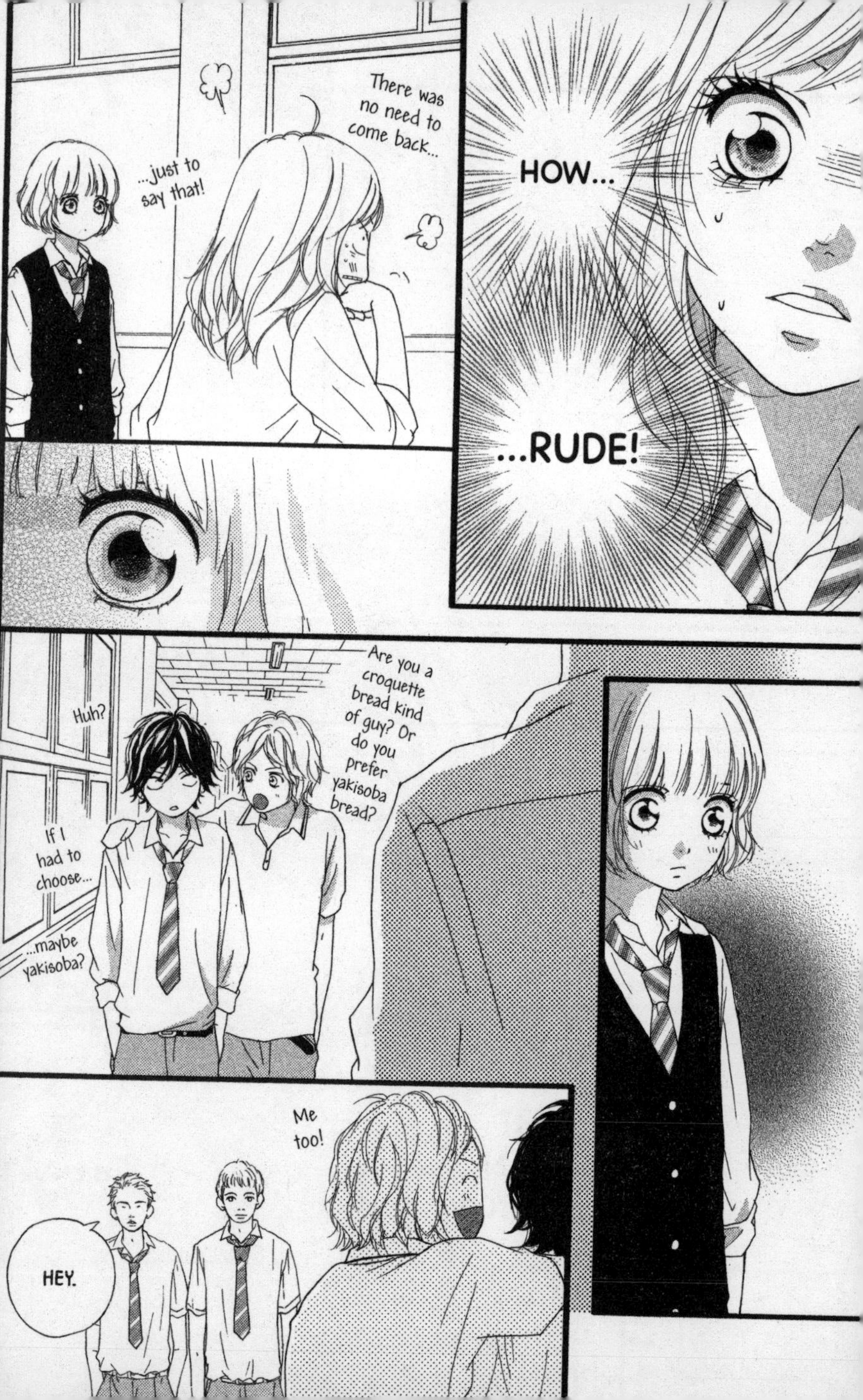
HOW...
...RUDE!
There was no need to come back...
...just to say that!
Are you a croquette bread kind of guy? Or do you prefer yakisoba bread?
Huh?
If I had to choose...
...maybe yakisoba?
Me too!
HEY.

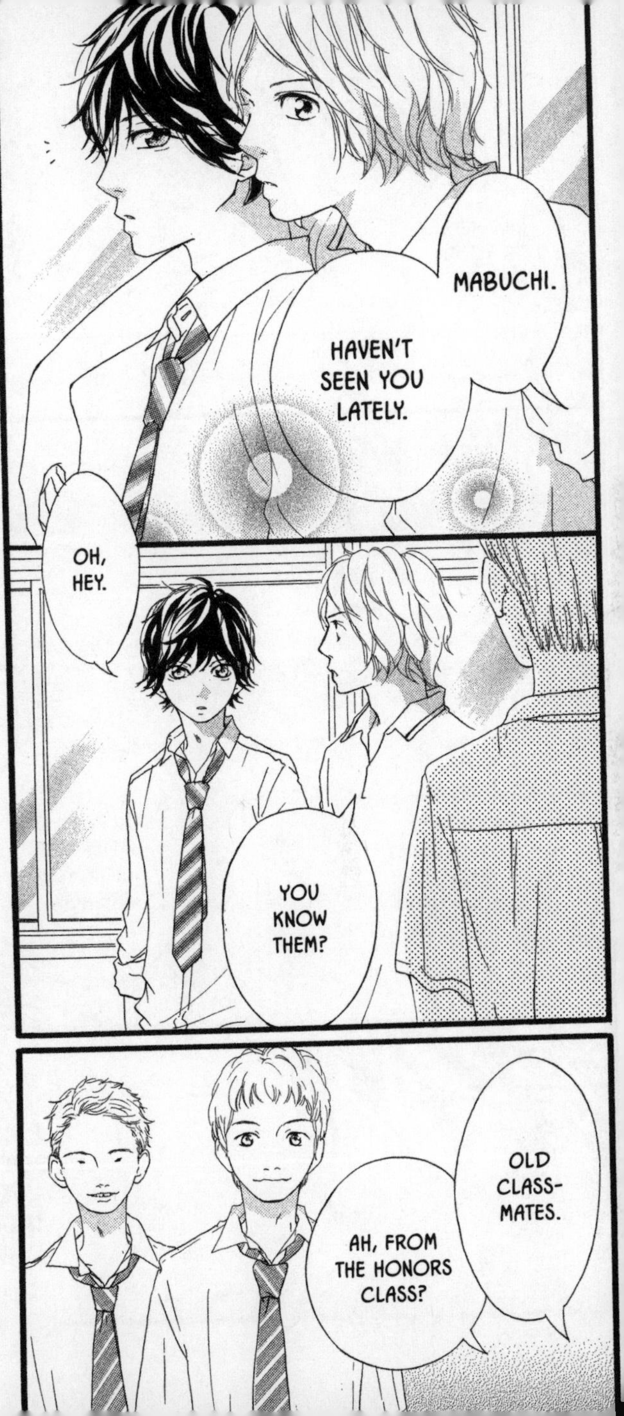
MABUCHI.
HAVEN'T SEEN YOU LATELY.
OH, HEY.
YOU KNOW THEM?
OLD CLASS-MATES.
AH, FROM THE HONORS CLASS?

I always appreciate and enjoy reading the letters you readers send me. When my heart is feeling splintered, I read your letters and they reinvigorate me. Somehow they've gotten me this far! I am truly appreciative!! Sometimes readers ask if I'll start a blog, but I probably won't. Sorry!! (Although there was a fake blog out there in the past, I've never written one.) I do use Twitter though, so please come take a look if you're interested: @sakisaka10. ♡ Most of the time my tweets are "yum," or "I'm tired," or "I'm in trouble." And here's the Twitter handle for the Betsuma Editorial Department: @betsuma_info. They should cover any *Ao Haru Ride* news that I forget to tweet. ♪ See you there! ★

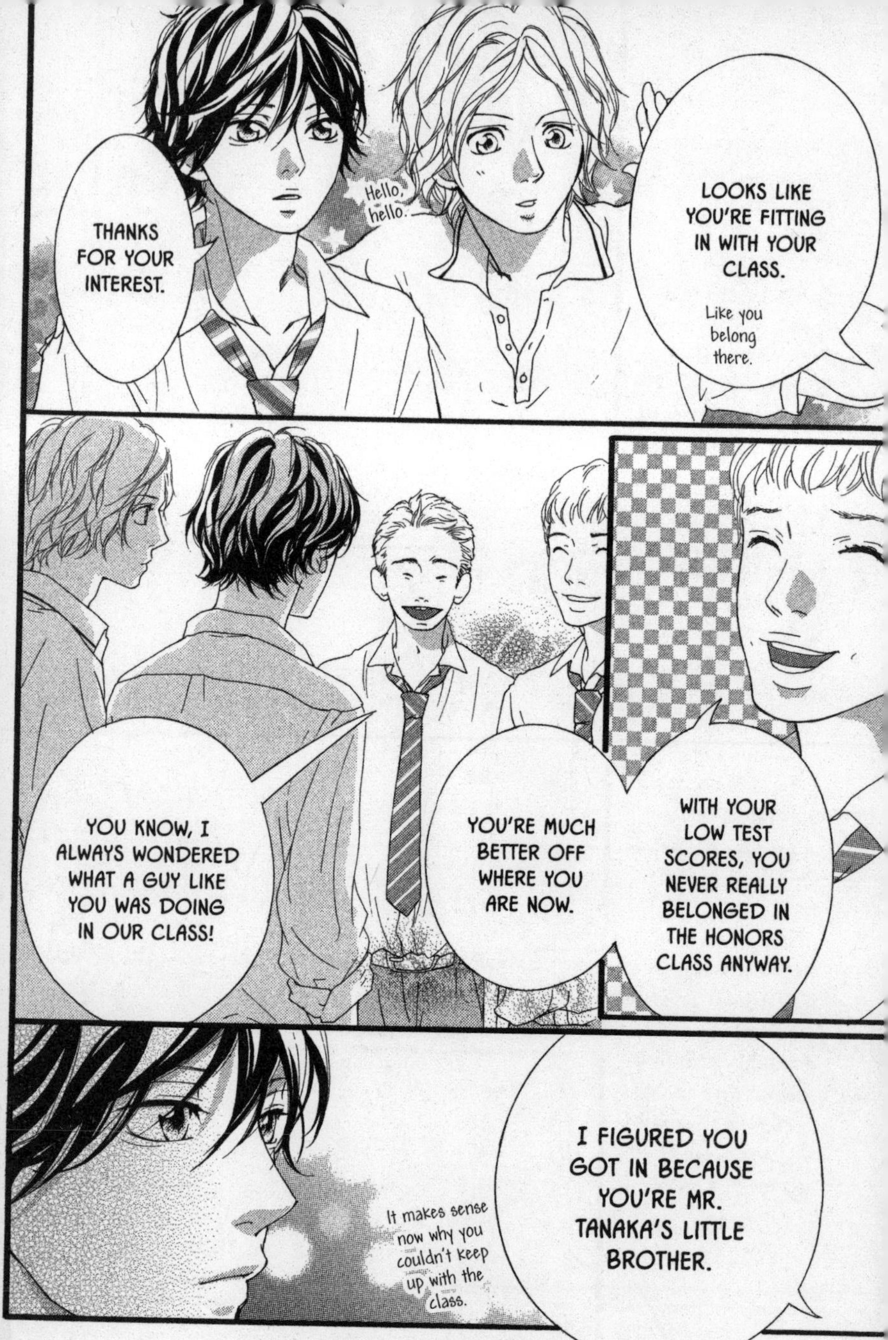
LOOKS LIKE YOU'RE FITTING IN WITH YOUR CLASS.
Like you belong there.
Hello, hello.
THANKS FOR YOUR INTEREST.
WITH YOUR LOW TEST SCORES, YOU NEVER REALLY BELONGED IN THE HONORS CLASS ANYWAY.
YOU'RE MUCH BETTER OFF WHERE YOU ARE NOW.
YOU KNOW, I ALWAYS WONDERED WHAT A GUY LIKE YOU WAS DOING IN OUR CLASS!
I FIGURED YOU GOT IN BECAUSE YOU'RE MR. TANAKA'S LITTLE BROTHER.
It makes sense now why you couldn't keep up with the class.

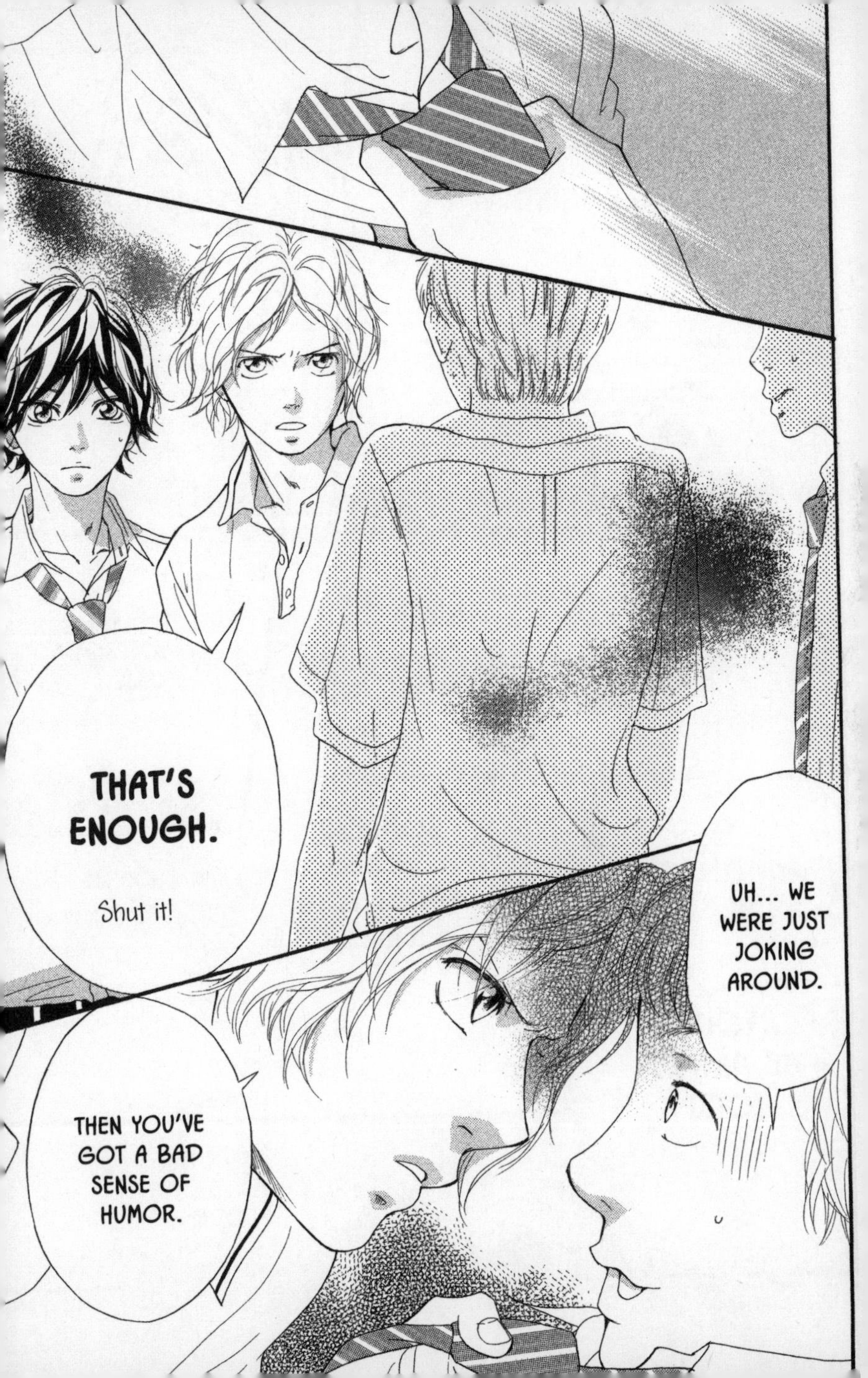
THAT'S ENOUGH.
Shut it!
UH... WE WERE JUST JOKING AROUND.
THEN YOU'VE GOT A BAD SENSE OF HUMOR.

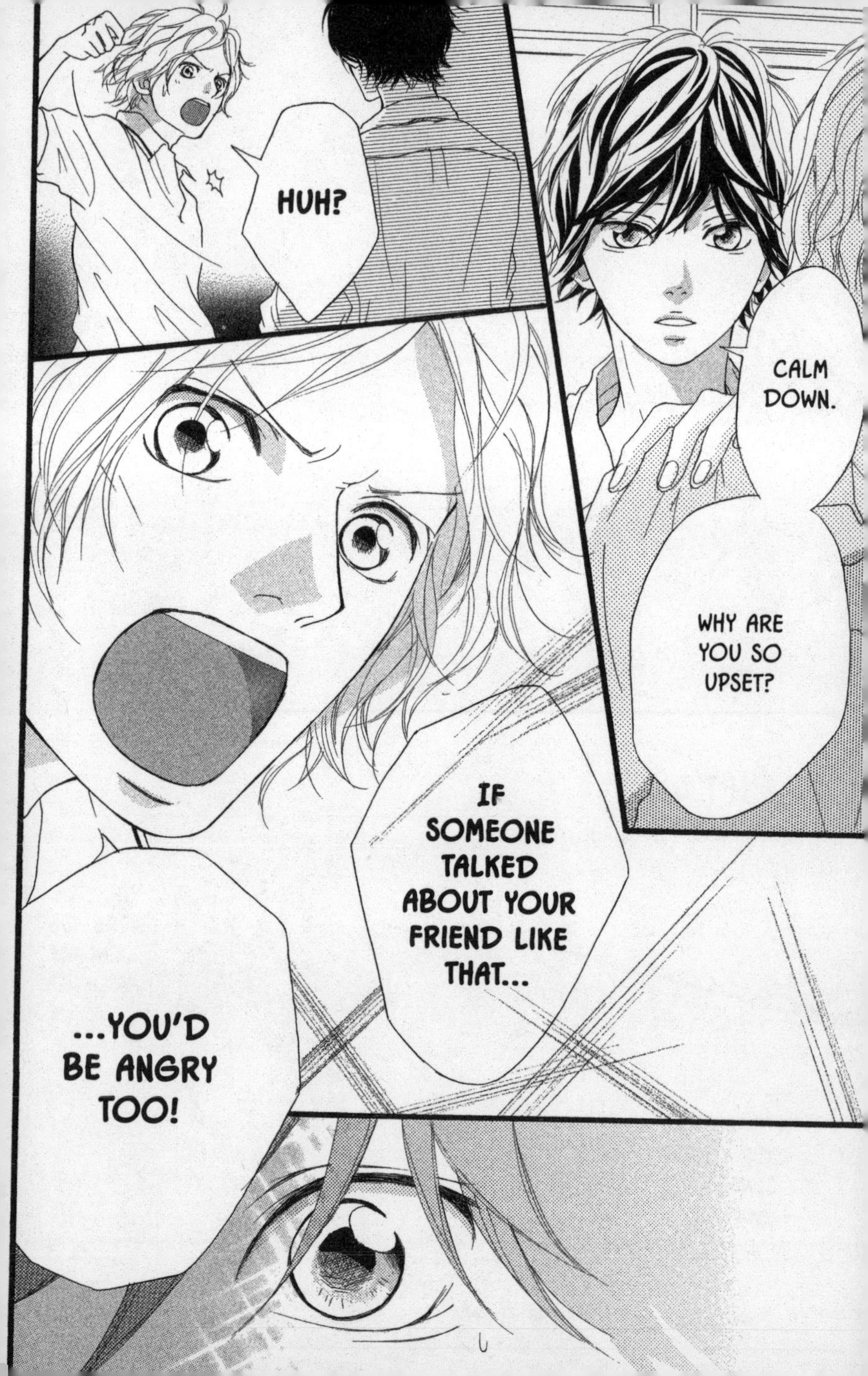
CALM DOWN.
WHY ARE YOU SO UPSET?
HUH?
IF SOMEONE TALKED ABOUT YOUR FRIEND LIKE THAT...
...YOU'D BE ANGRY TOO!

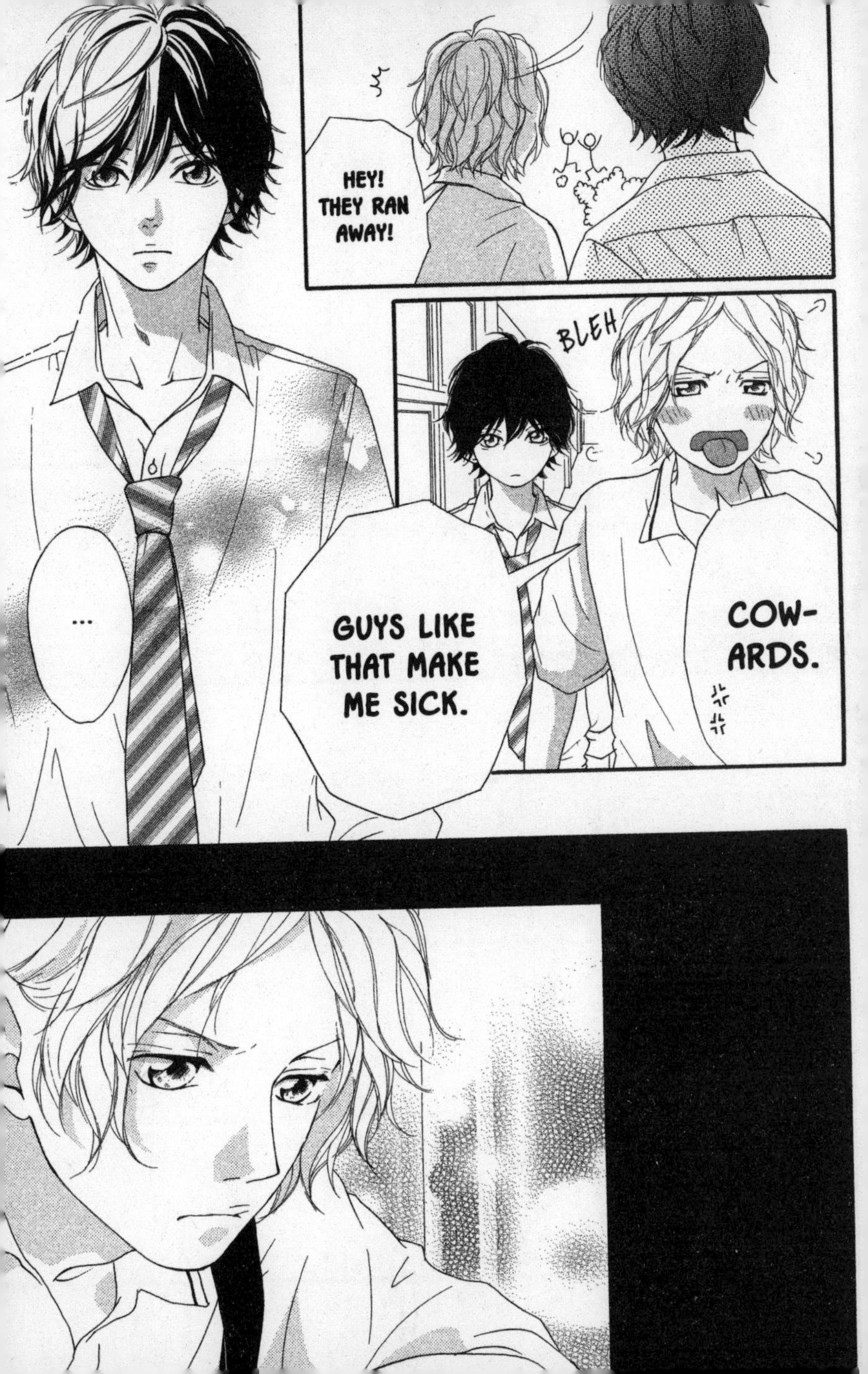
HEY! THEY RAN AWAY!
BLEH
COWARDS.
GUYS LIKE THAT MAKE ME SICK.
...

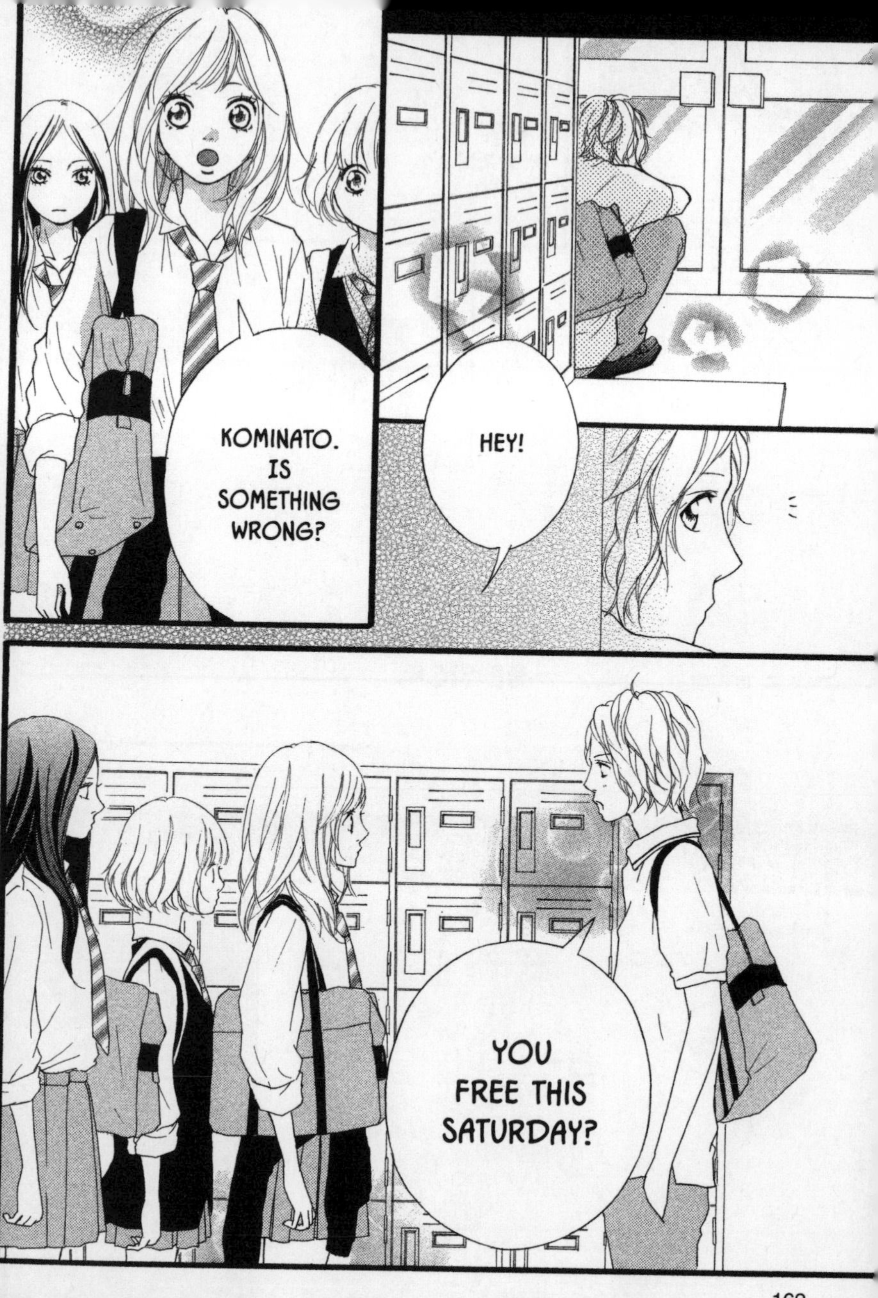
HEY!
KOMINATO. IS SOMETHING WRONG?
YOU FREE THIS SATURDAY?

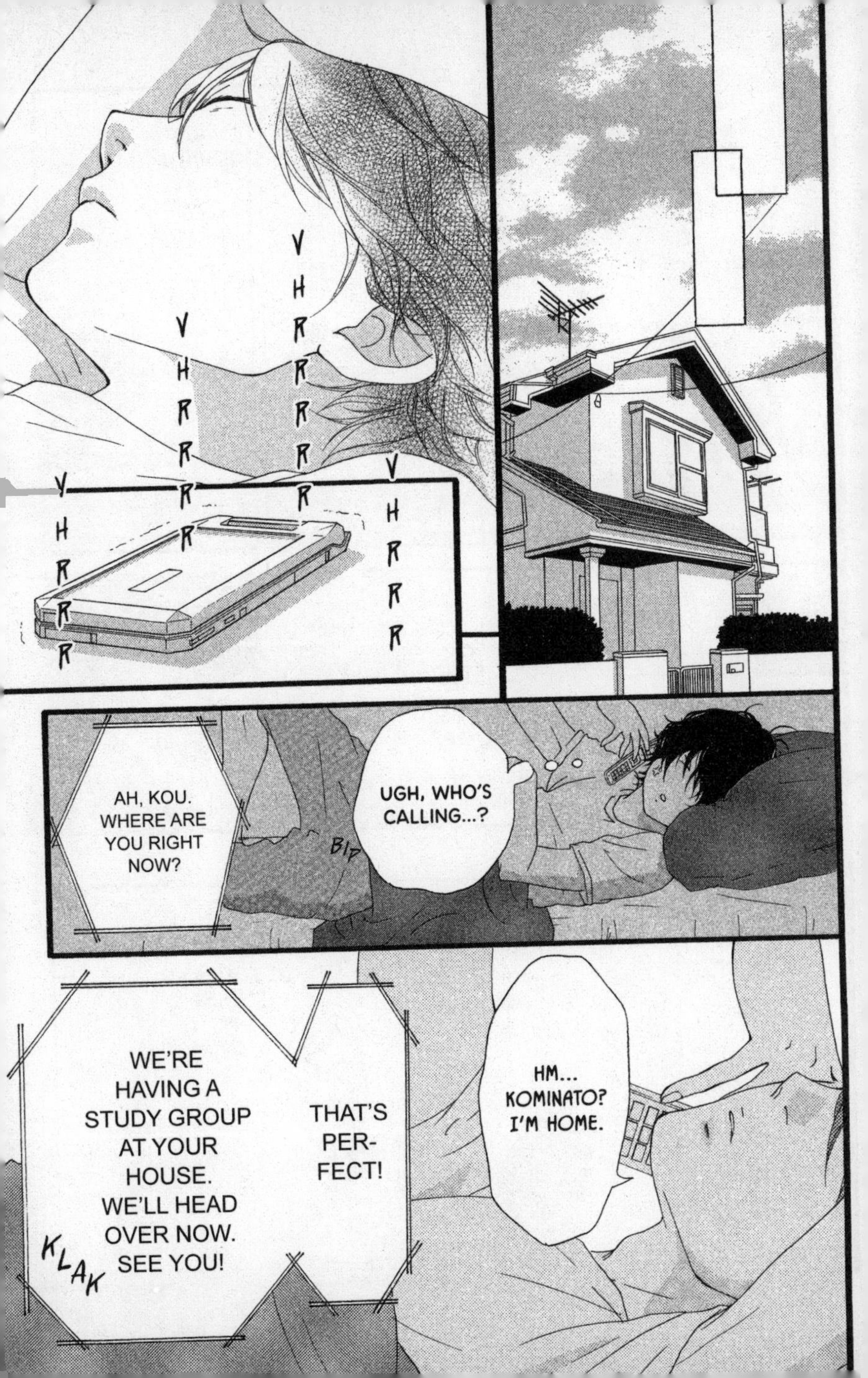
VHRRRRRR
VHRRRR
VHRRR
VHRRRR
UGH, WHO'S CALLING...?
BIP
AH, KOU. WHERE ARE YOU RIGHT NOW?
HM... KOMINATO? I'M HOME.
THAT'S PER-FECT!
WE'RE HAVING A STUDY GROUP AT YOUR HOUSE. WE'LL HEAD OVER NOW. SEE YOU!
KLAK

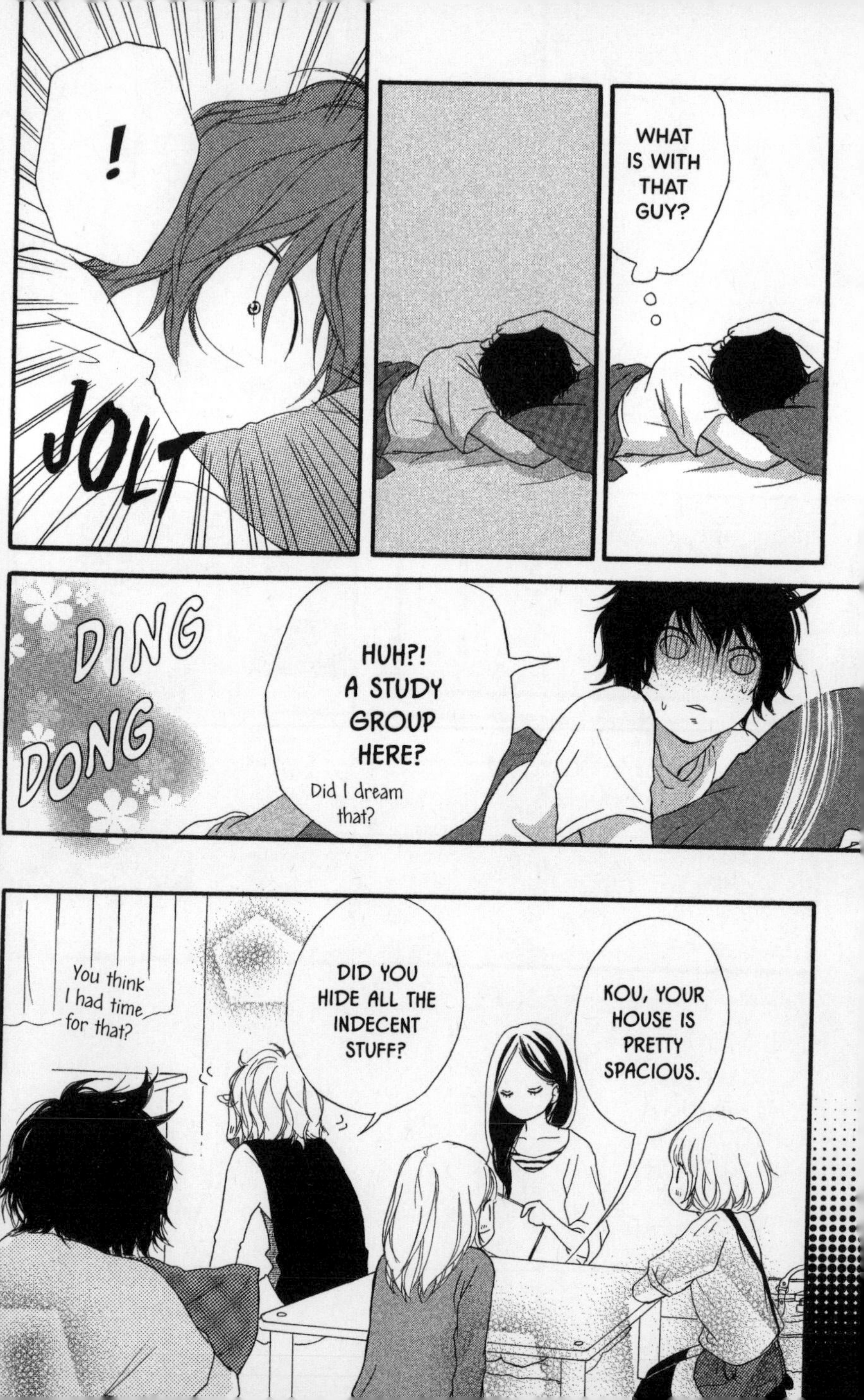
WHAT IS WITH THAT GUY?
!
JOLT
HUH?! A STUDY GROUP HERE?
Did I dream that?
DING DONG
KOU, YOUR HOUSE IS PRETTY SPACIOUS.
DID YOU HIDE ALL THE INDECENT STUFF?
You think I had time for that?

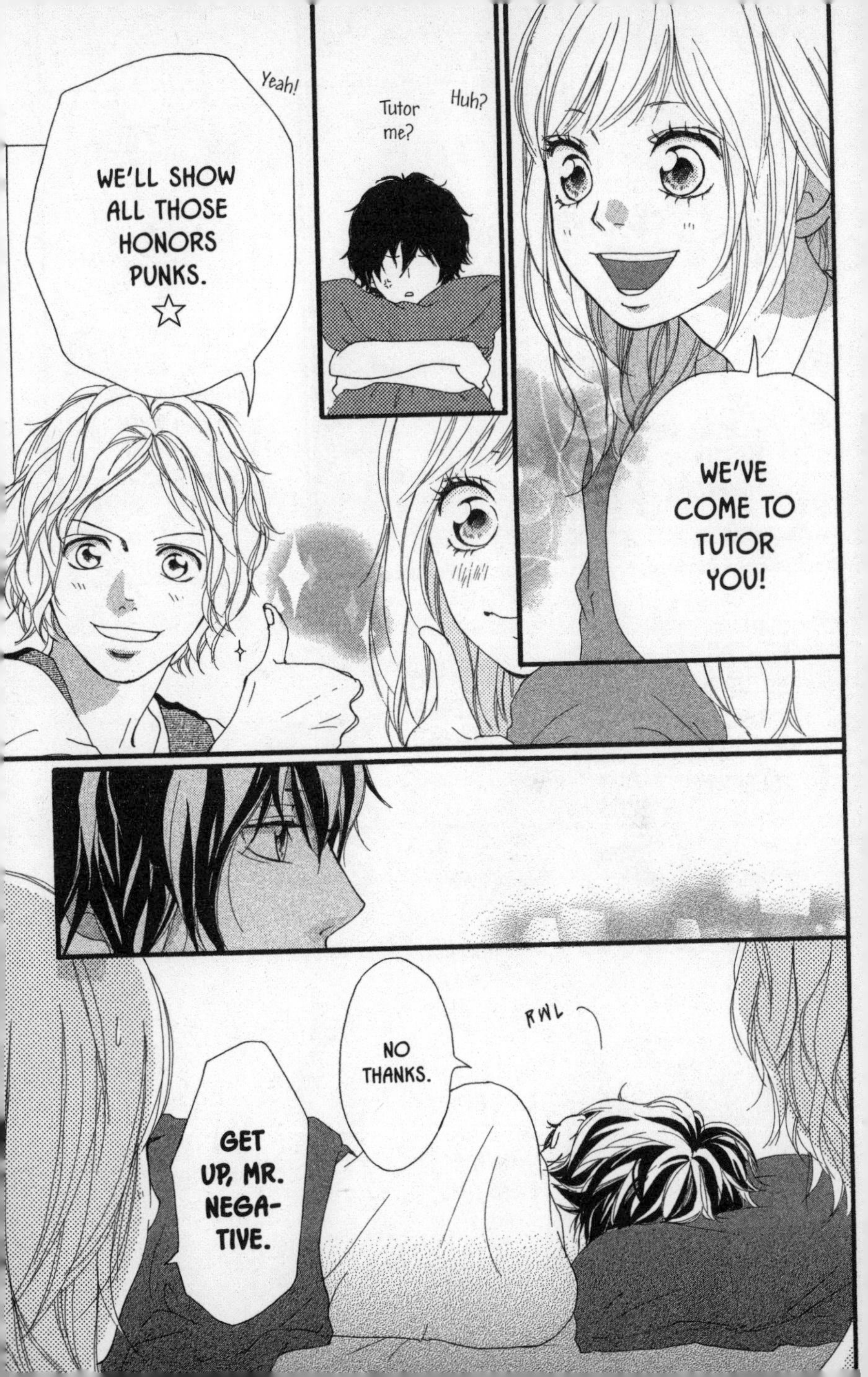
WE'VE COME TO TUTOR YOU!
Huh?
Tutor me?
Yeah!
WE'LL SHOW ALL THOSE HONORS PUNKS. ☆
RWL
NO THANKS.
GET UP, MR. NEGA-TIVE.

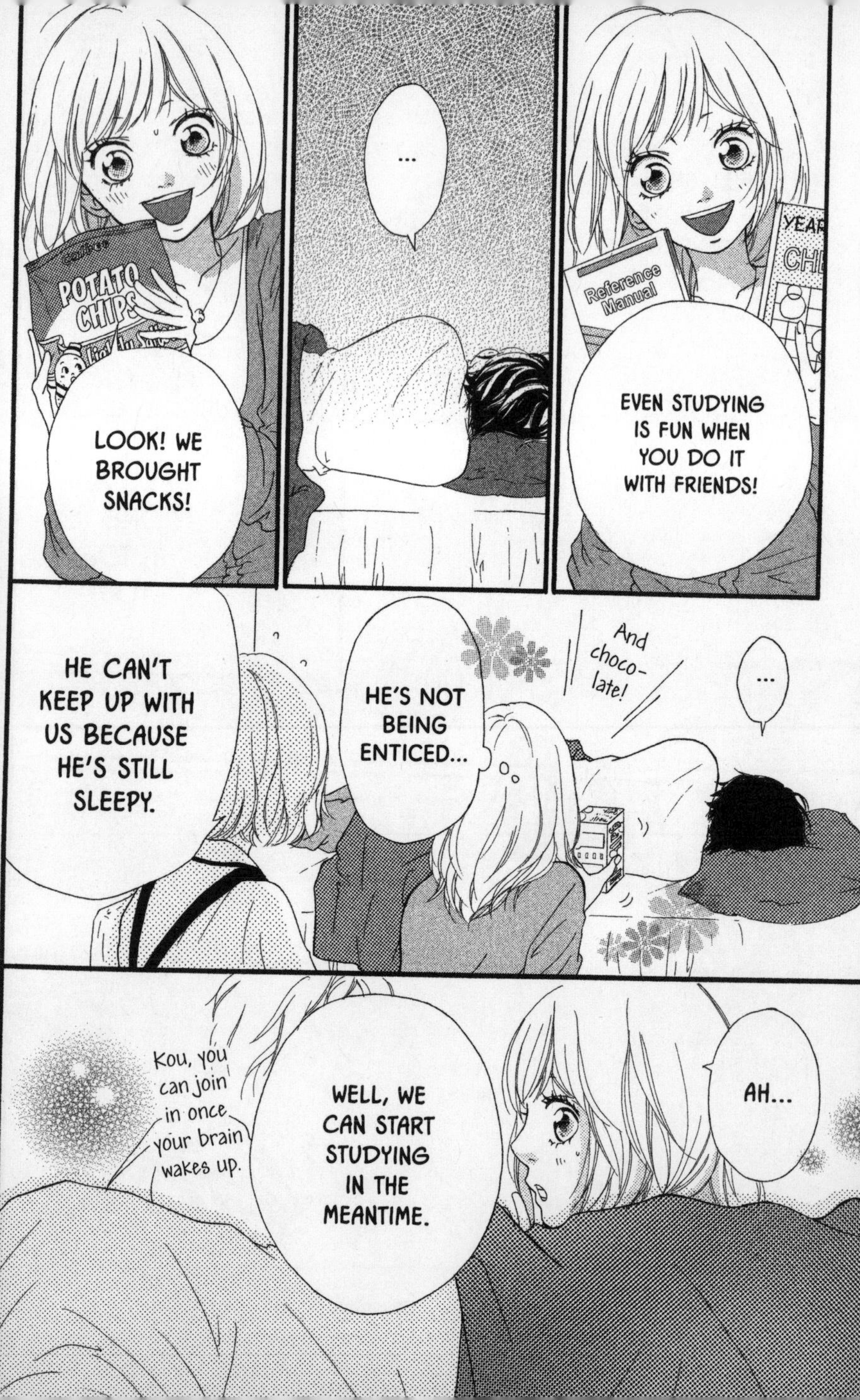
Reference Manual
EVEN STUDYING IS FUN WHEN YOU DO IT WITH FRIENDS!
...
POTATO CHIPS
LOOK! WE BROUGHT SNACKS!
...
And chocolate!
HE'S NOT BEING ENTICED...
HE CAN'T KEEP UP WITH US BECAUSE HE'S STILL SLEEPY.
AH...
WELL, WE CAN START STUDYING IN THE MEANTIME.
Kou, you can join in once your brain wakes up.

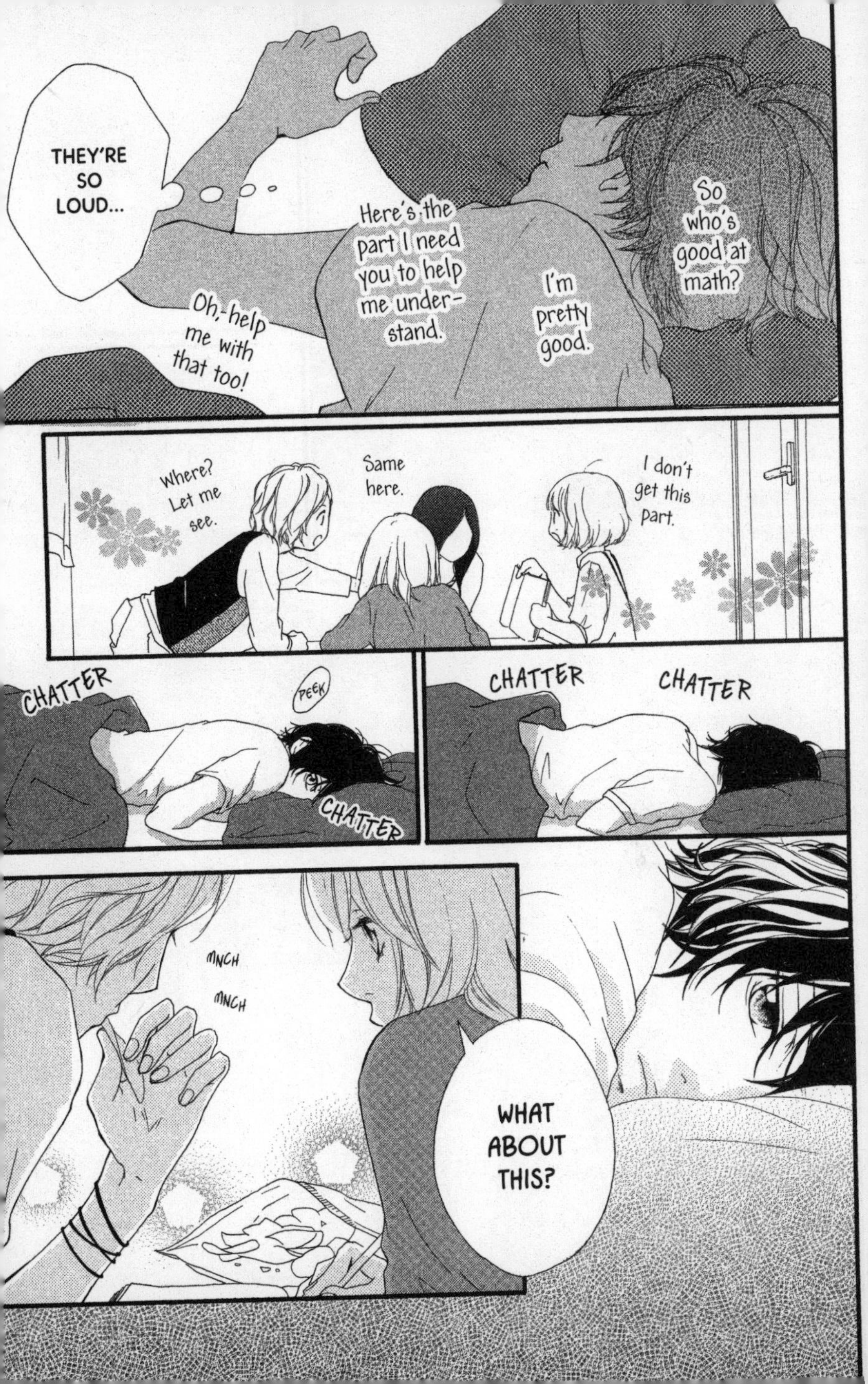
So who's good at math?
I'm pretty good.
Here's the part I need you to help me under-stand.
Oh, help me with that too!
THEY'RE SO LOUD...
I don't get this part.
Same here.
Where? Let me see.
CHATTER
CHATTER
PEEK
CHATTER
CHATTER
WHAT ABOUT THIS?
MNCH
MNCH

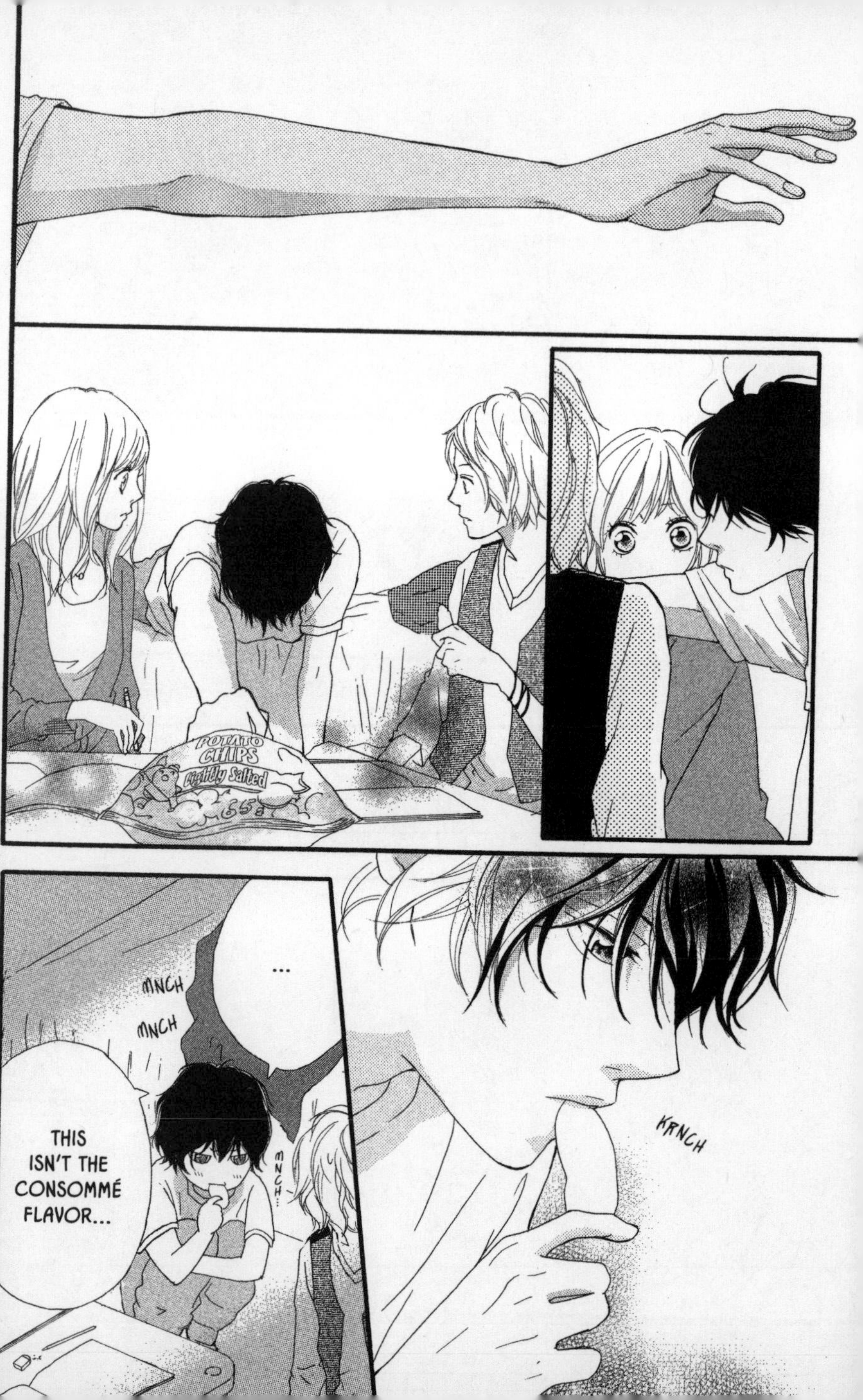
POTATO CHIPS
Lightly Salted
55g
KRNCH
...
MNCH...
MNCH
MNCH
THIS ISN'T THE CONSOMMÉ FLAVOR...

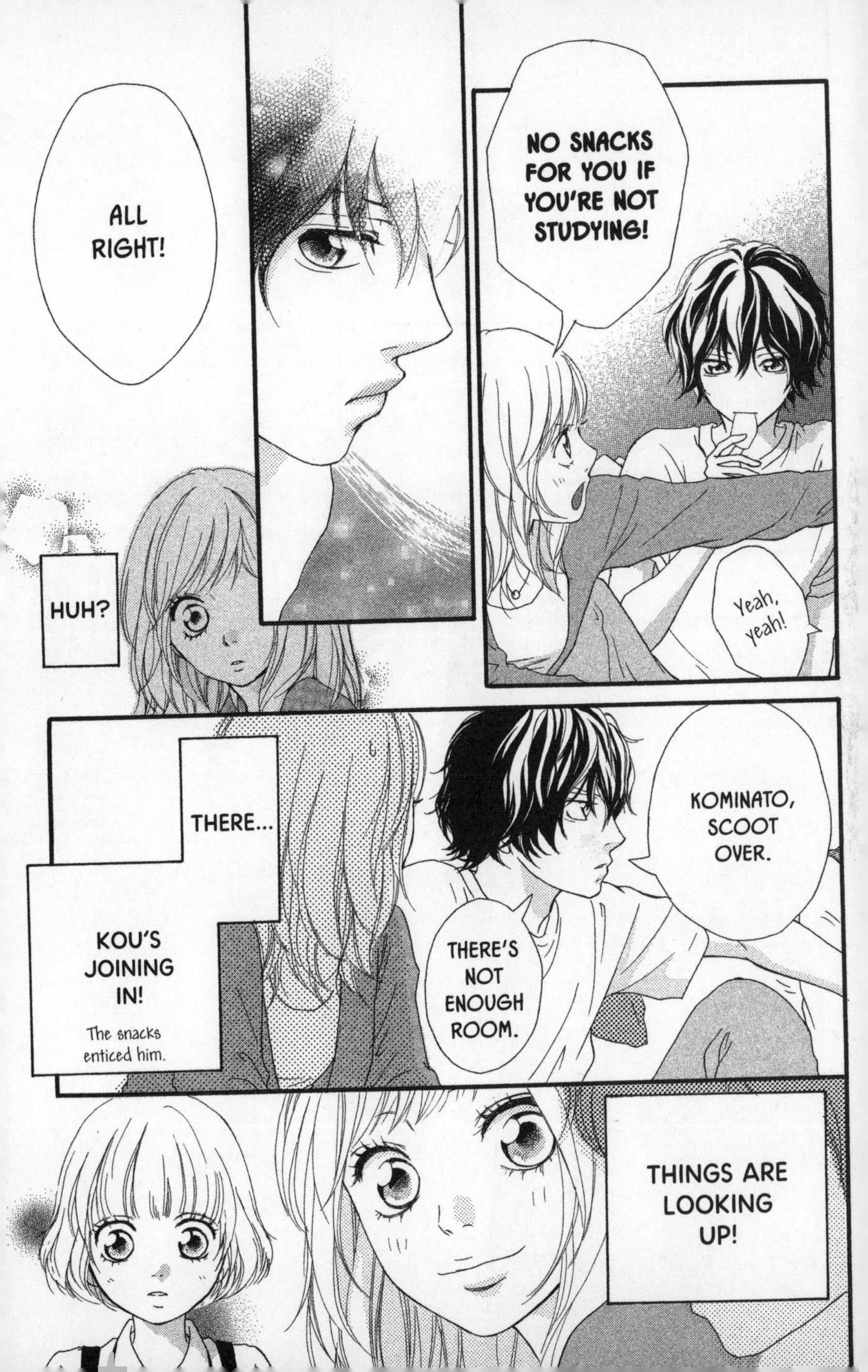
NO SNACKS FOR YOU IF YOU'RE NOT STUDYING!
Yeah, yeah!
ALL RIGHT!
HUH?
KOMINATO, SCOOT OVER.
THERE'S NOT ENOUGH ROOM.
THERE...
KOU'S JOINING IN!
The snacks enticed him.
THINGS ARE LOOKING UP!

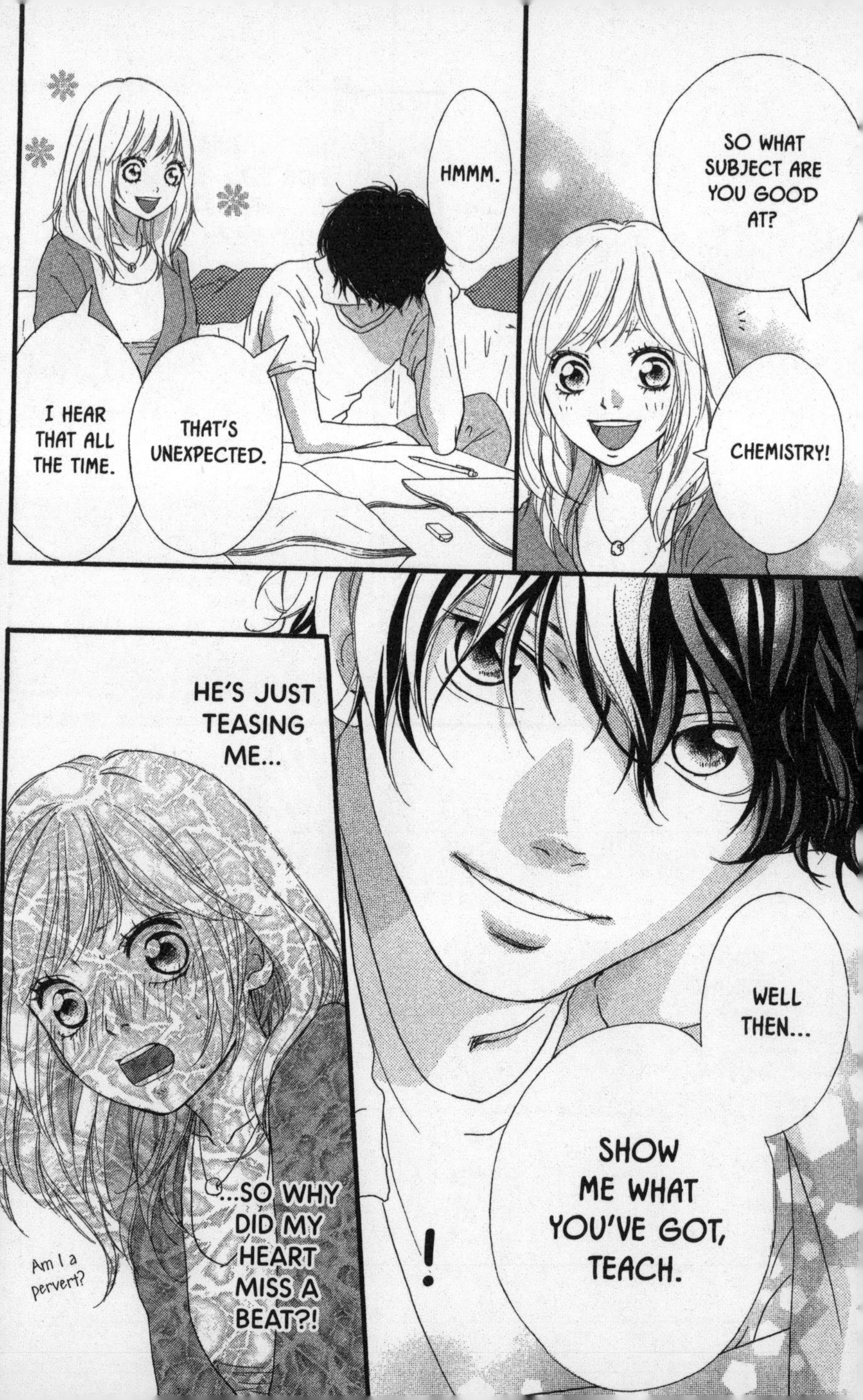
SO WHAT SUBJECT ARE YOU GOOD AT?
CHEMISTRY!
HMMM.
THAT'S UNEXPECTED.
I HEAR THAT ALL THE TIME.
WELL THEN...
SHOW ME WHAT YOU'VE GOT, TEACH.
!
HE'S JUST TEASING ME...
...SO WHY DID MY HEART MISS A BEAT?!
Am I a pervert?

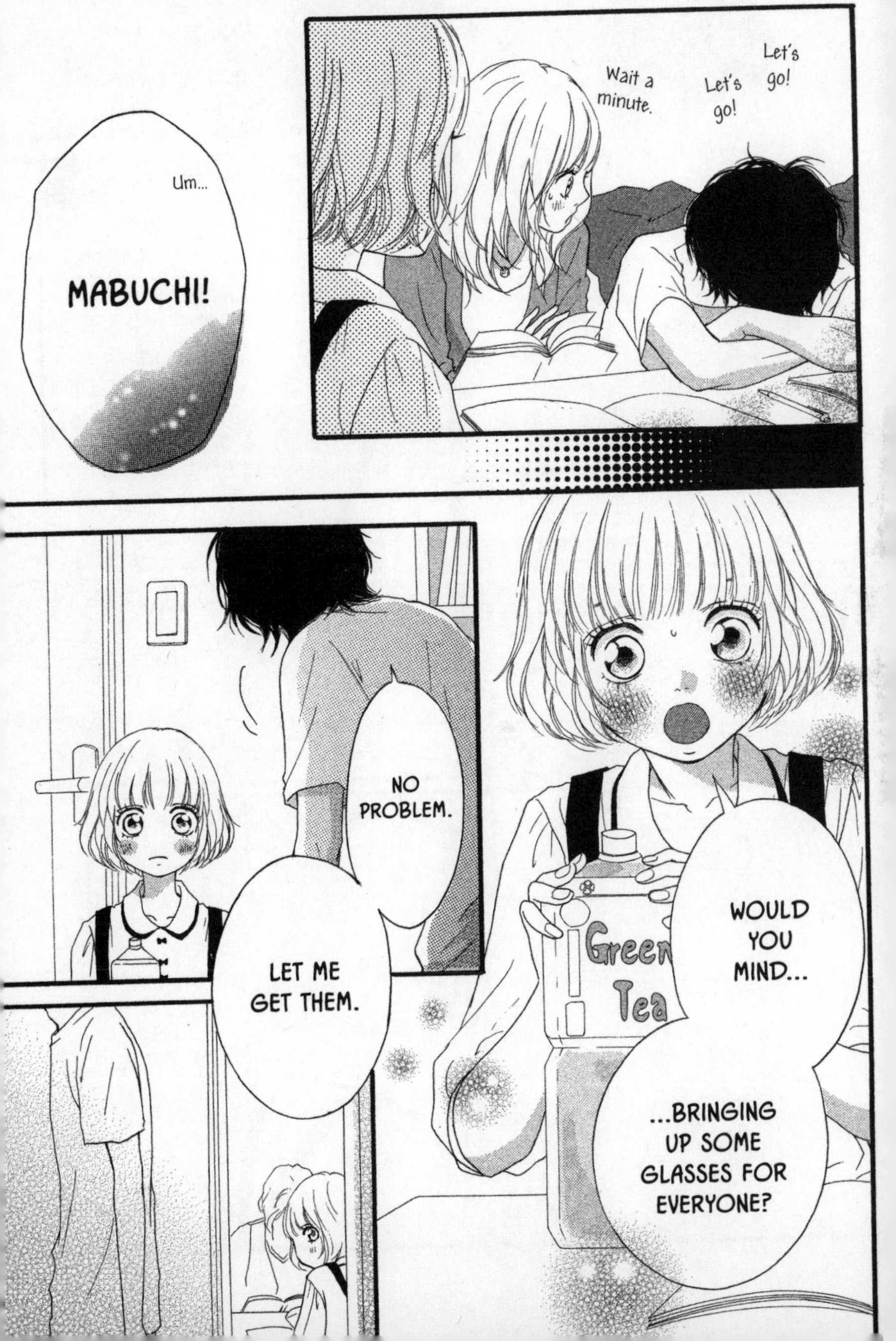
Let's go!
Let's go!
Wait a minute.
Um...
MABUCHI!
WOULD YOU MIND...
...BRINGING UP SOME GLASSES FOR EVERYONE?
Green Tea
NO PROBLEM.
LET ME GET THEM.

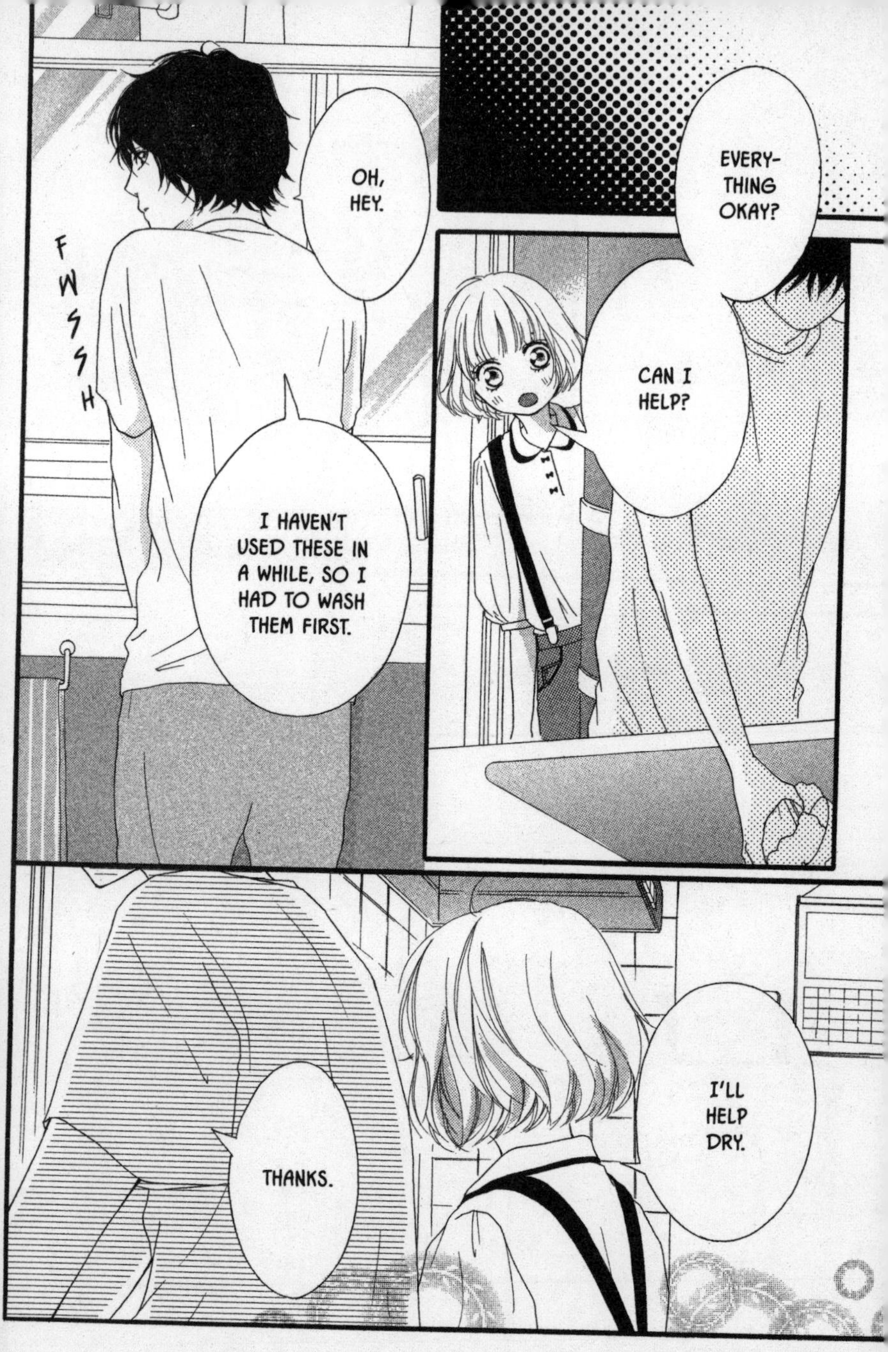
EVERY-THING OKAY?
CAN I HELP?
OH, HEY.
FWSSH
I HAVEN'T USED THESE IN A WHILE, SO I HAD TO WASH THEM FIRST.
I'LL HELP DRY.
THANKS.

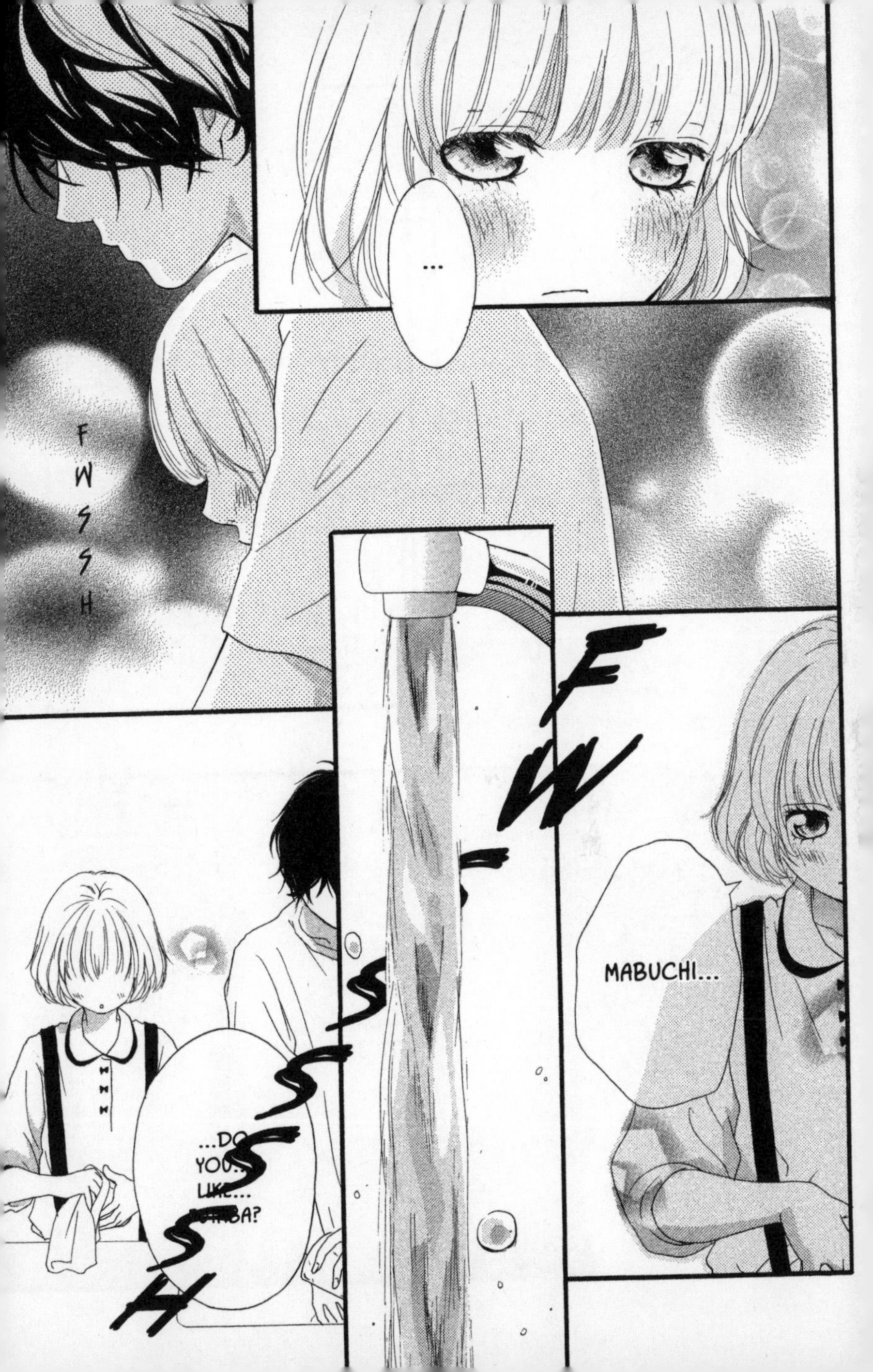
...
FWSSH
MABUCHI...
FWSSSH
...DO YOU... LIKE...

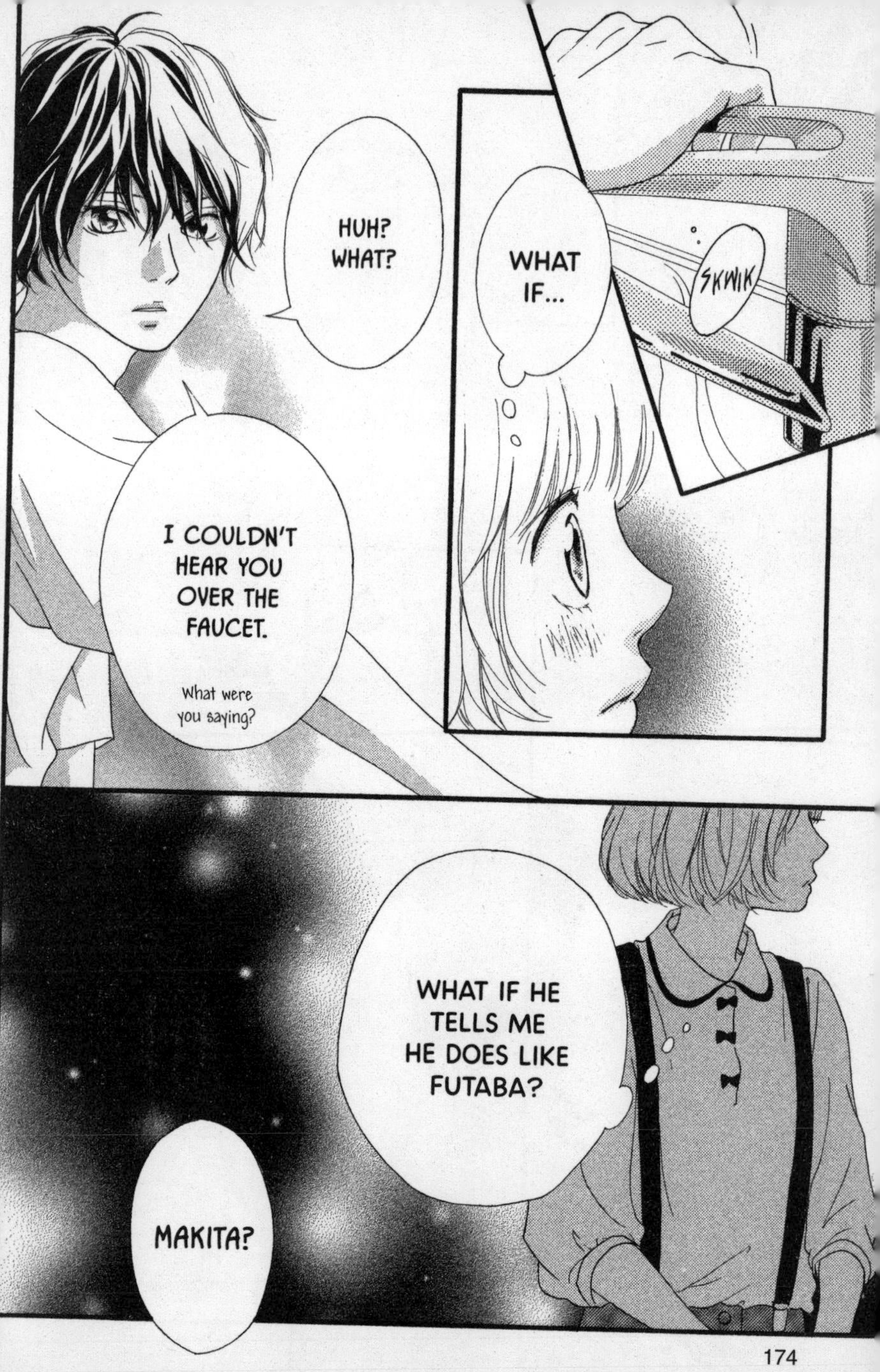
SKWIK
WHAT IF...
HUH? WHAT?
I COULDN'T HEAR YOU OVER THE FAUCET.
What were you saying?
WHAT IF HE TELLS ME HE DOES LIKE FUTABA?
MAKITA?

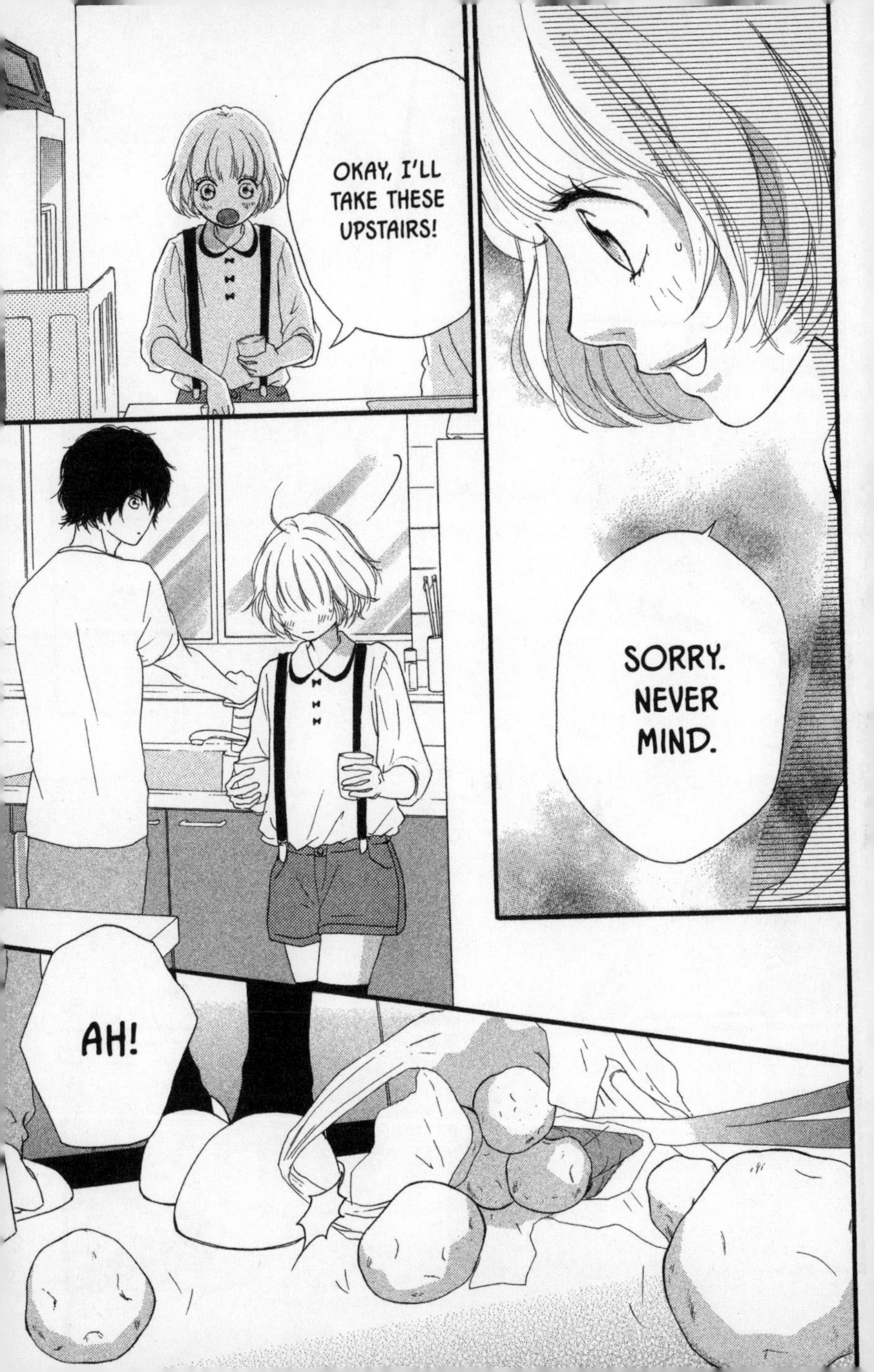
SORRY. NEVER MIND.
OKAY, I'LL TAKE THESE UPSTAIRS!
AH!

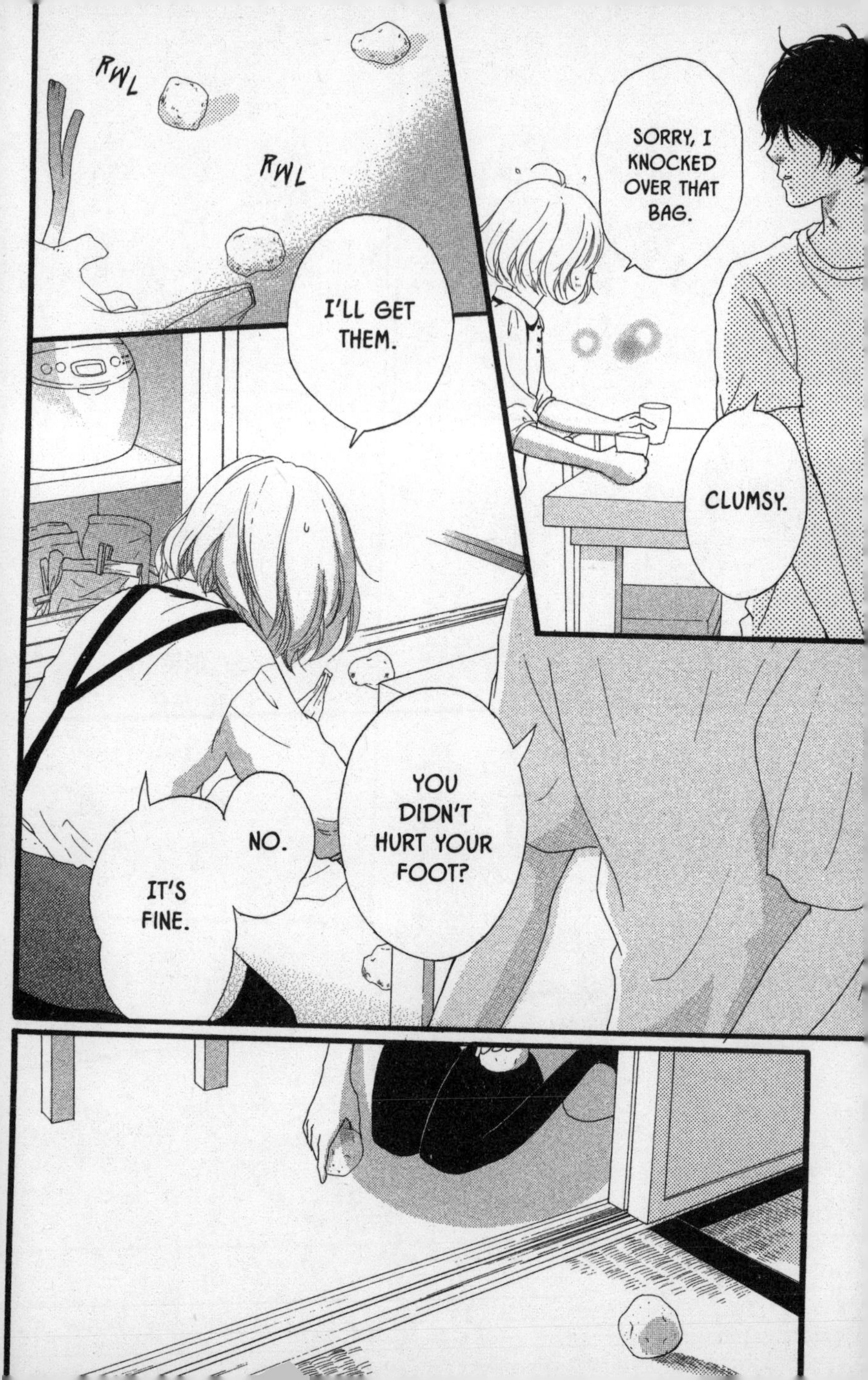
SORRY, I KNOCKED OVER THAT BAG.
CLUMSY.
RWL
RWL
I'LL GET THEM.
YOU DIDN'T HURT YOUR FOOT?
NO.
IT'S FINE.

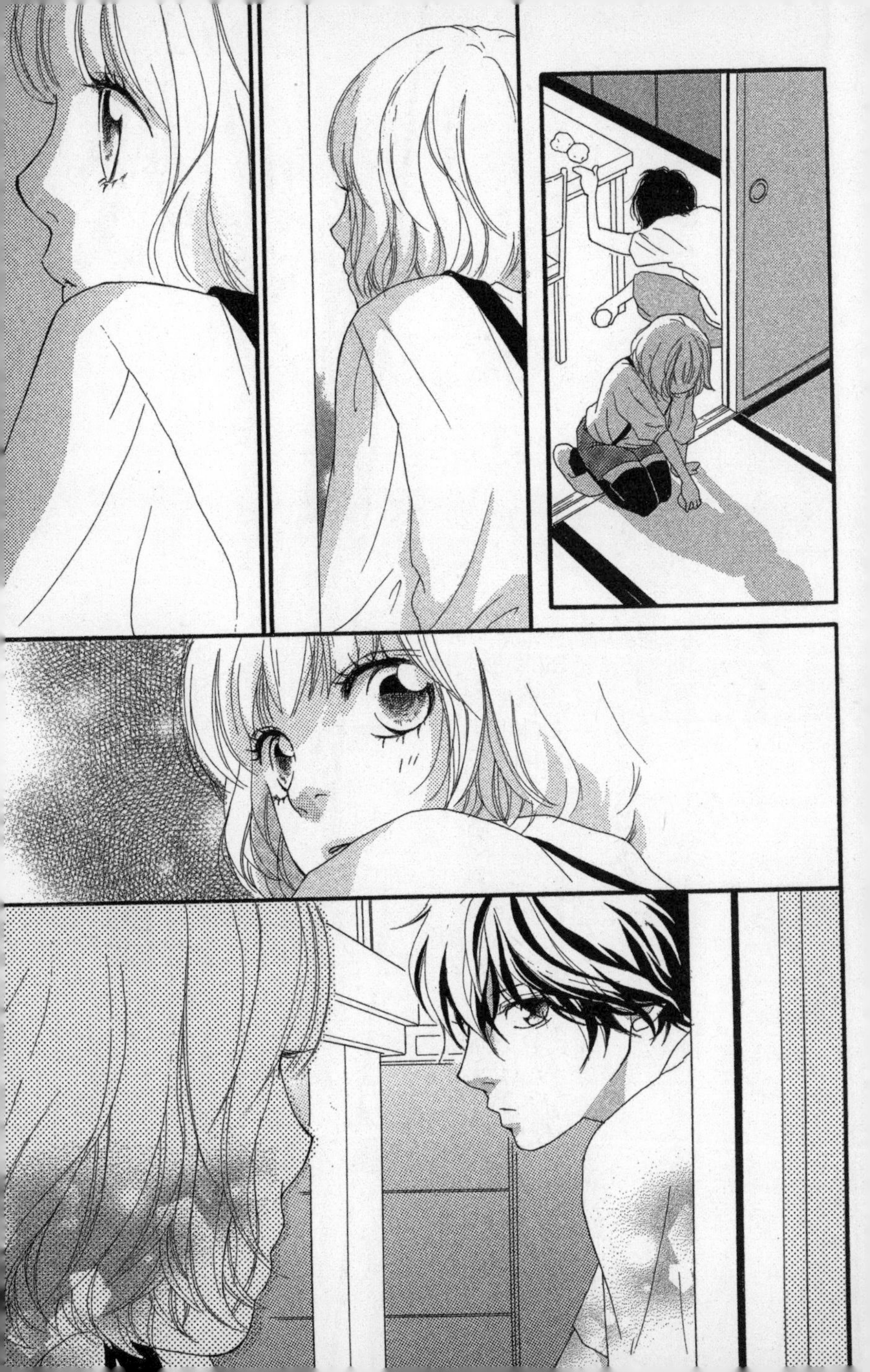

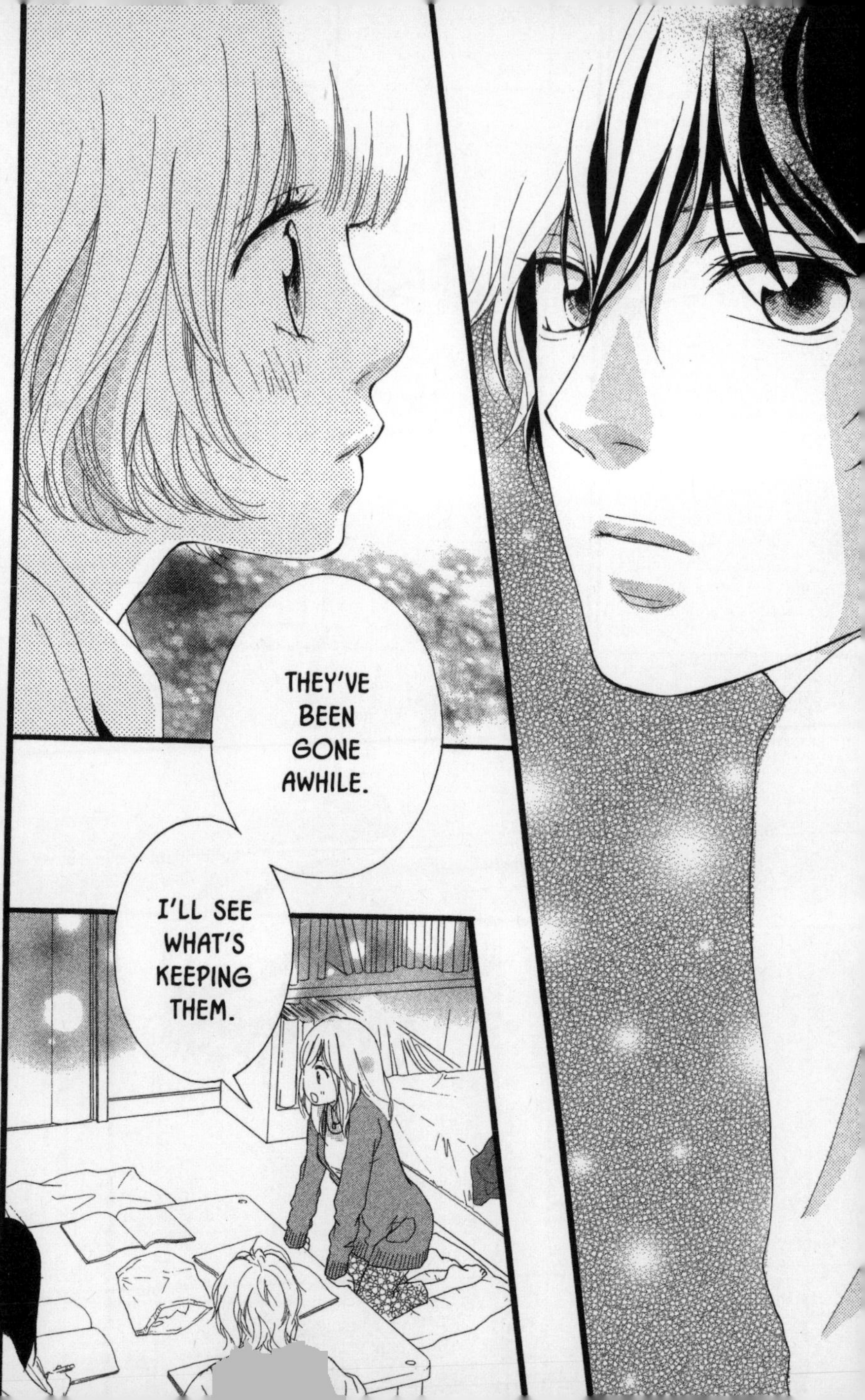
THEY'VE BEEN GONE AWHILE.
I'LL SEE WHAT'S KEEPING THEM.

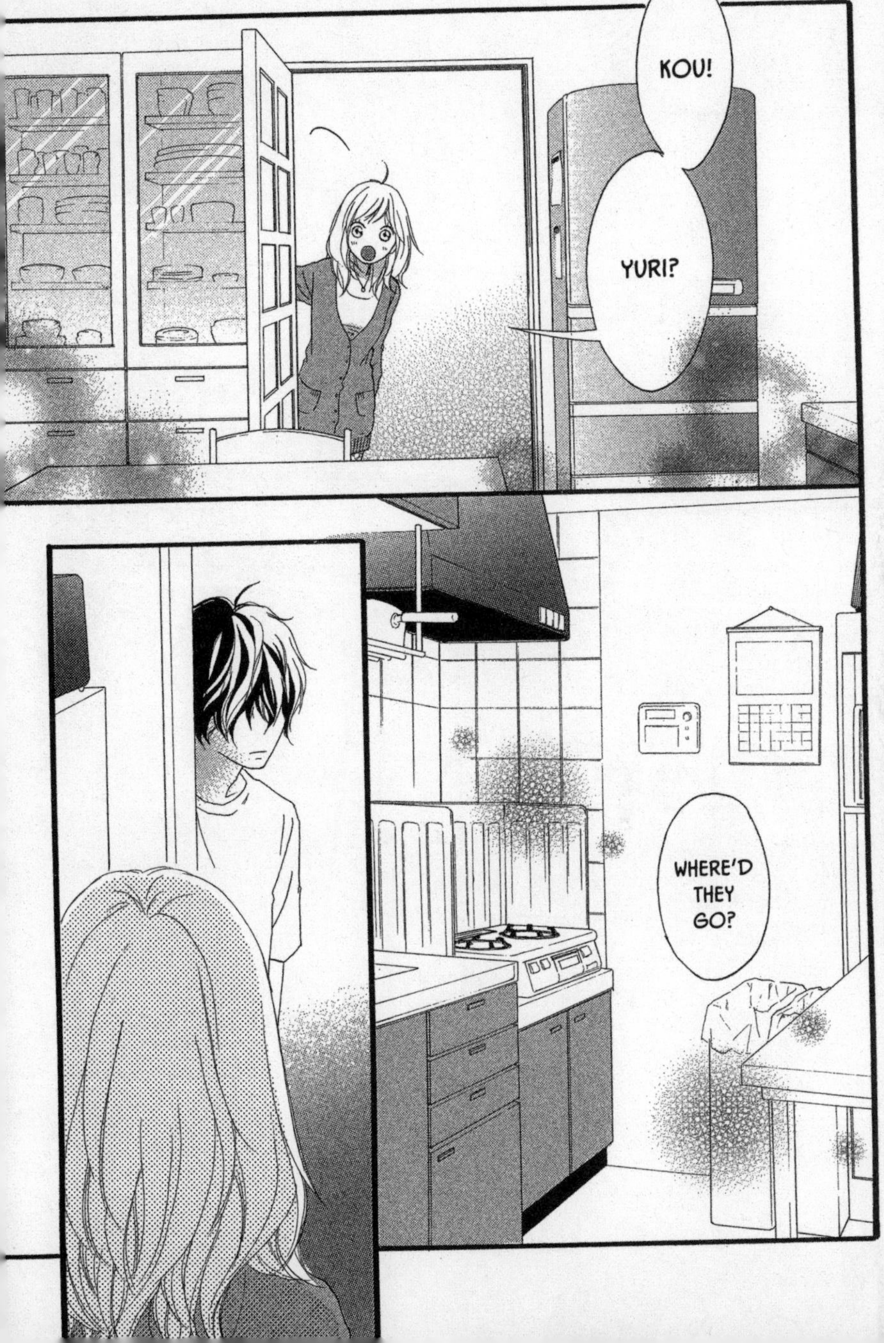
KOU!
YURI?
WHERE'D THEY GO?

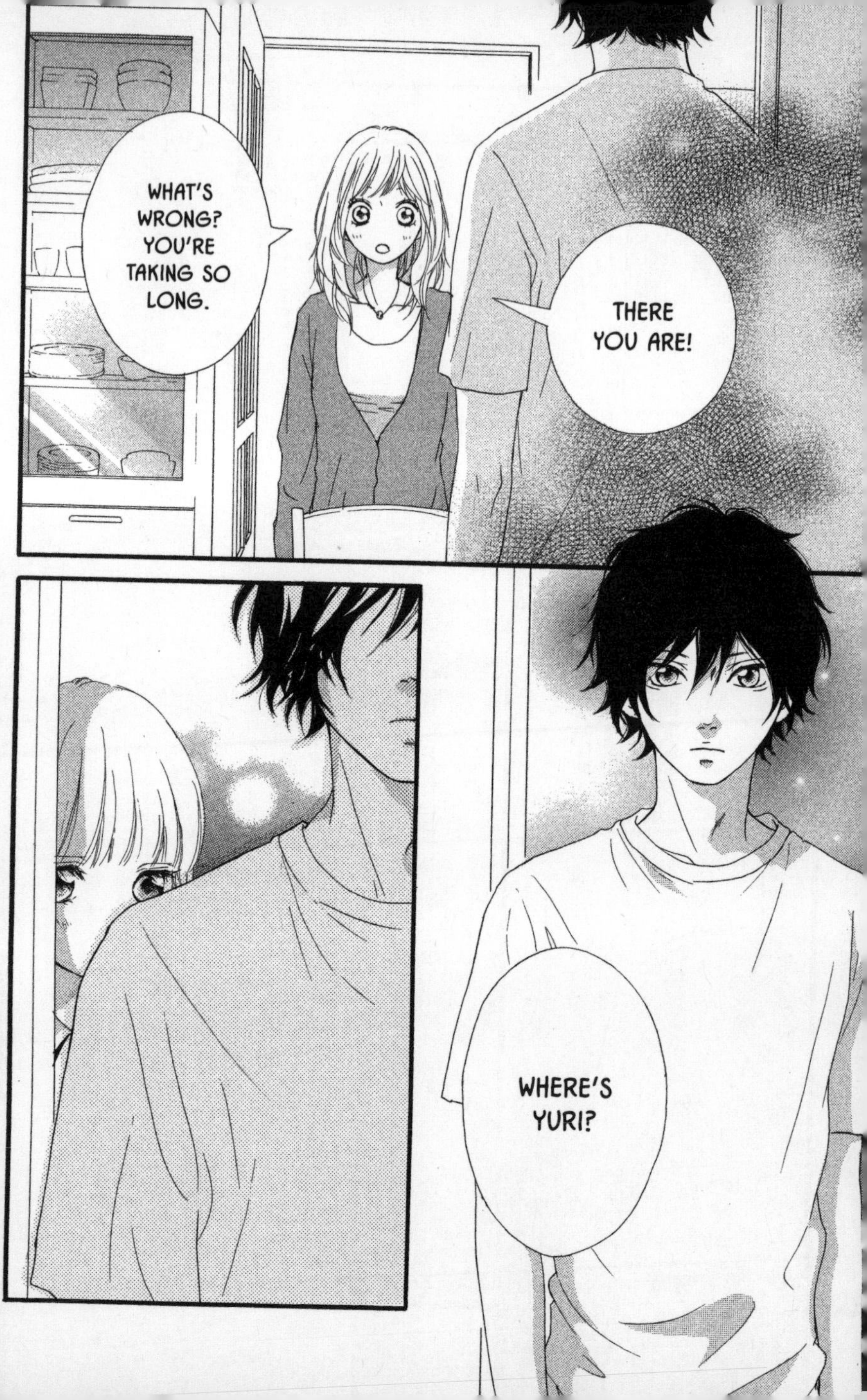
THERE YOU ARE!
WHAT'S WRONG? YOU'RE TAKING SO LONG.
WHERE'S YURI?

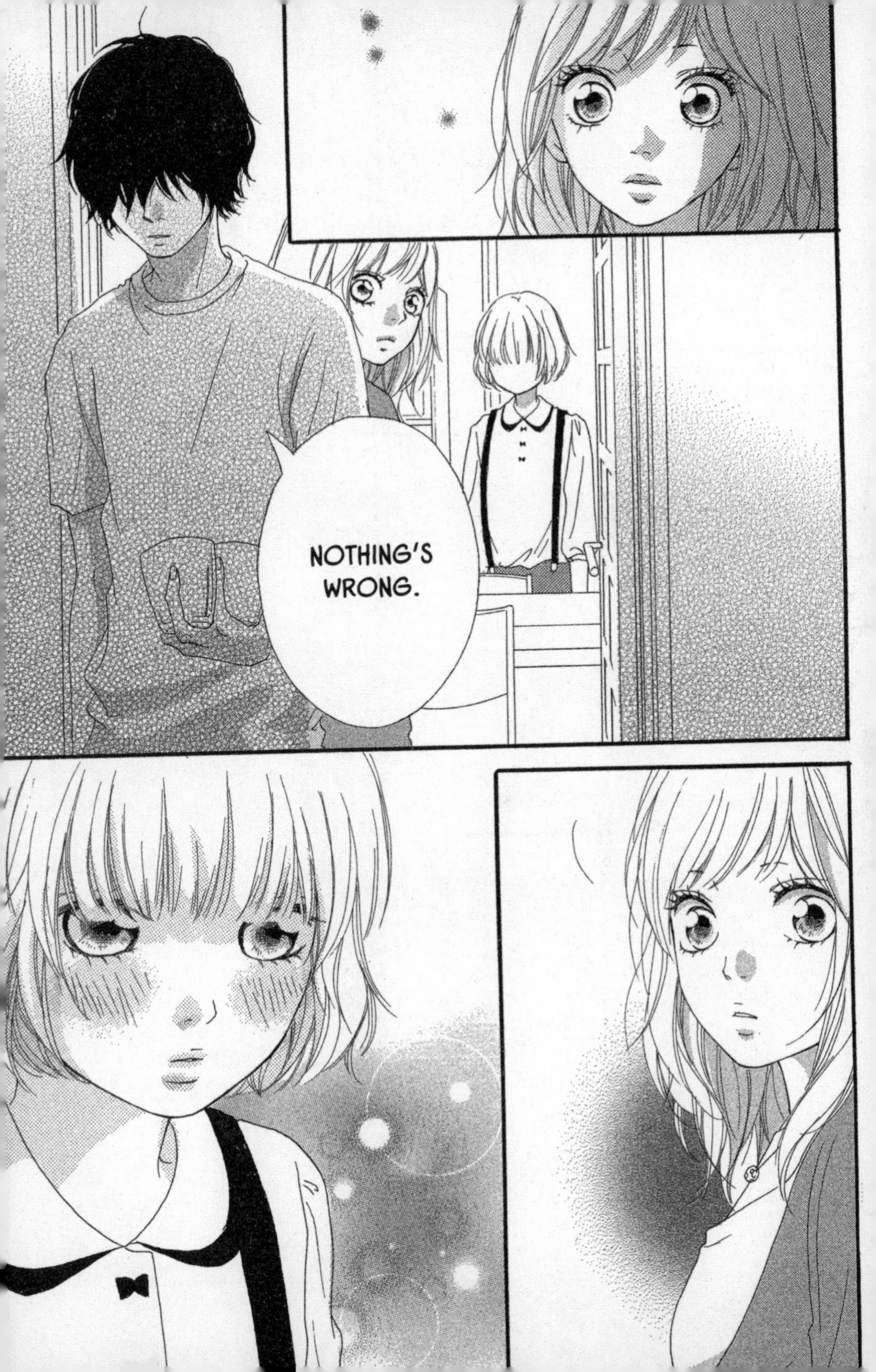
NOTHING'S WRONG.

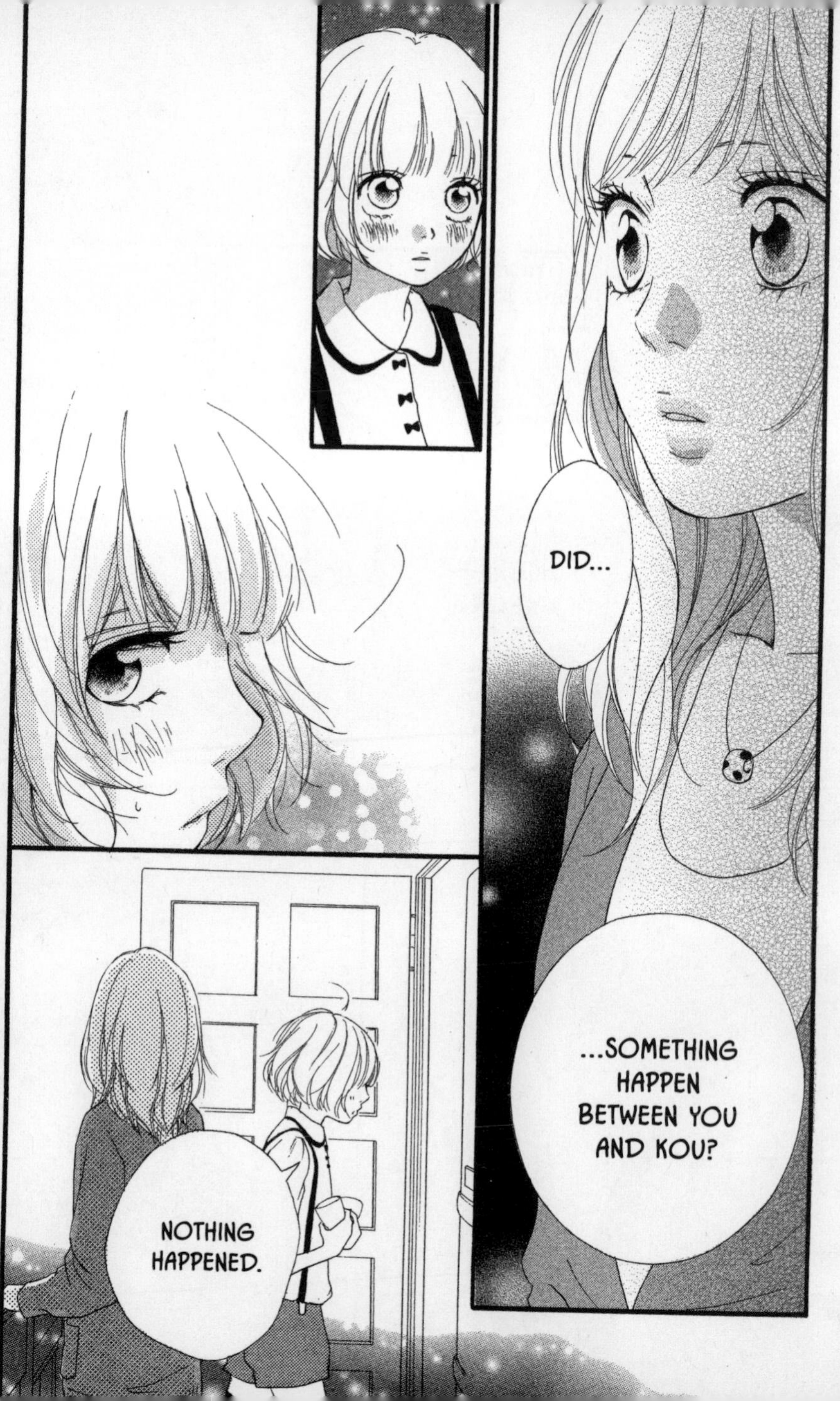
DID...
...SOMETHING HAPPEN BETWEEN YOU AND KOU?
NOTHING HAPPENED.

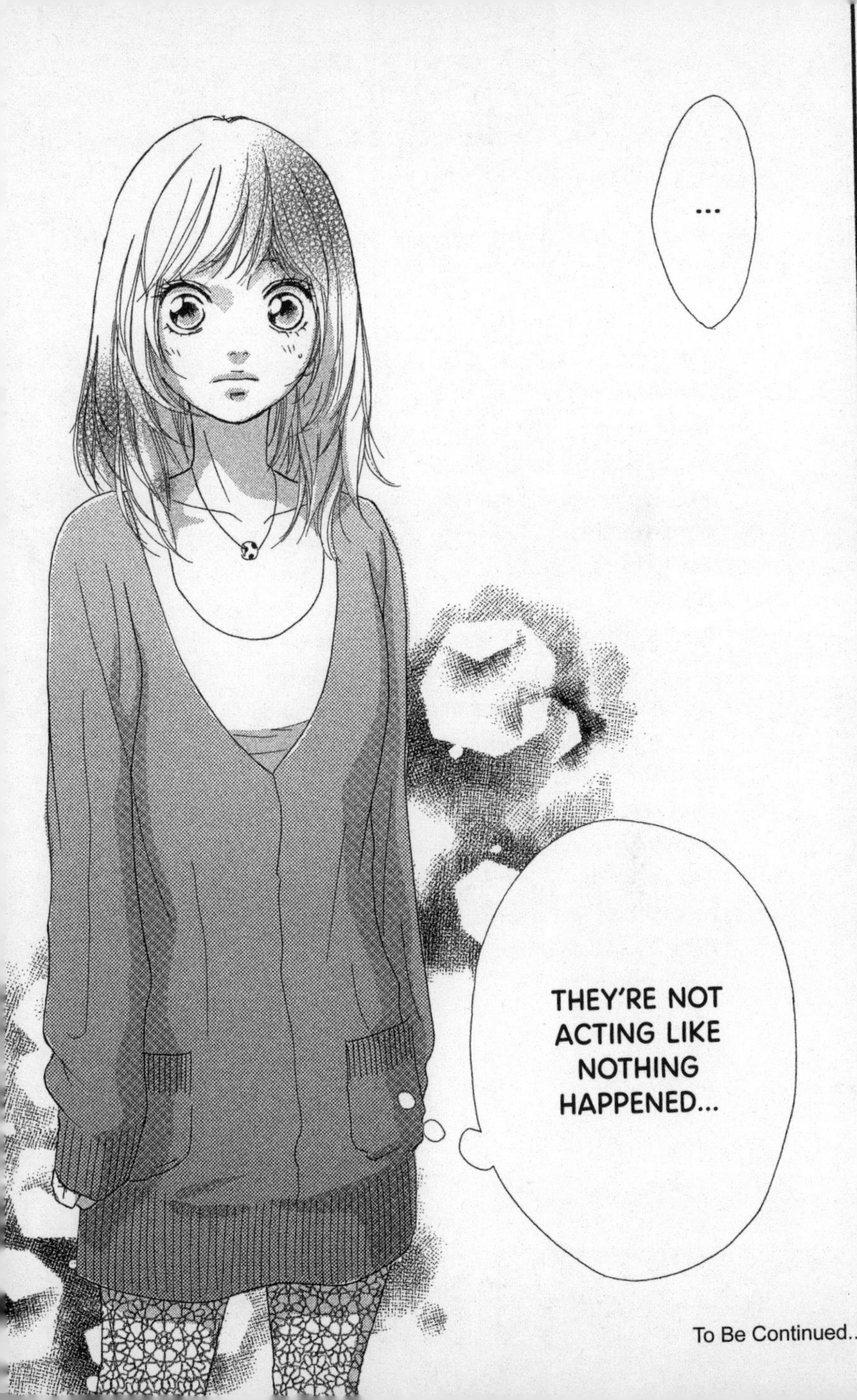
...
THEY'RE NOT ACTING LIKE NOTHING HAPPENED...

To Be Continued...

Before you read "Attraction of the Stars"...

I've written a bonus story for *Ao Haru Ride* called "Attraction of the Stars." It stars Shuko. When I got asked to write a bonus story, I was still fumbling my way through the main story (and I still am). I didn't want to sacrifice the main story, but I knew writing this would help me develop in some way. I went back and forth....and finally decided to write it. After I made the decision, I realized that I had not written a 16-page bonus manga since my debut! Having fewer pages requires that you cut anything that is not critical. But you still have to be able to show your style, and I realized that more pages can actually make storytelling easier. I learned a lot from this experience. How to make a story as interesting as possible in only a few pages is an essential skill. Working on this gave me a chance to revisit those basics. I hope you enjoy this *Ao Haru Ride* bonus story, "Attraction of the Stars."

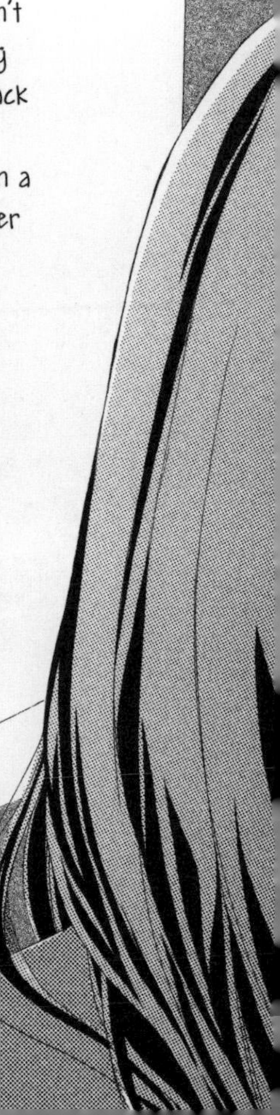

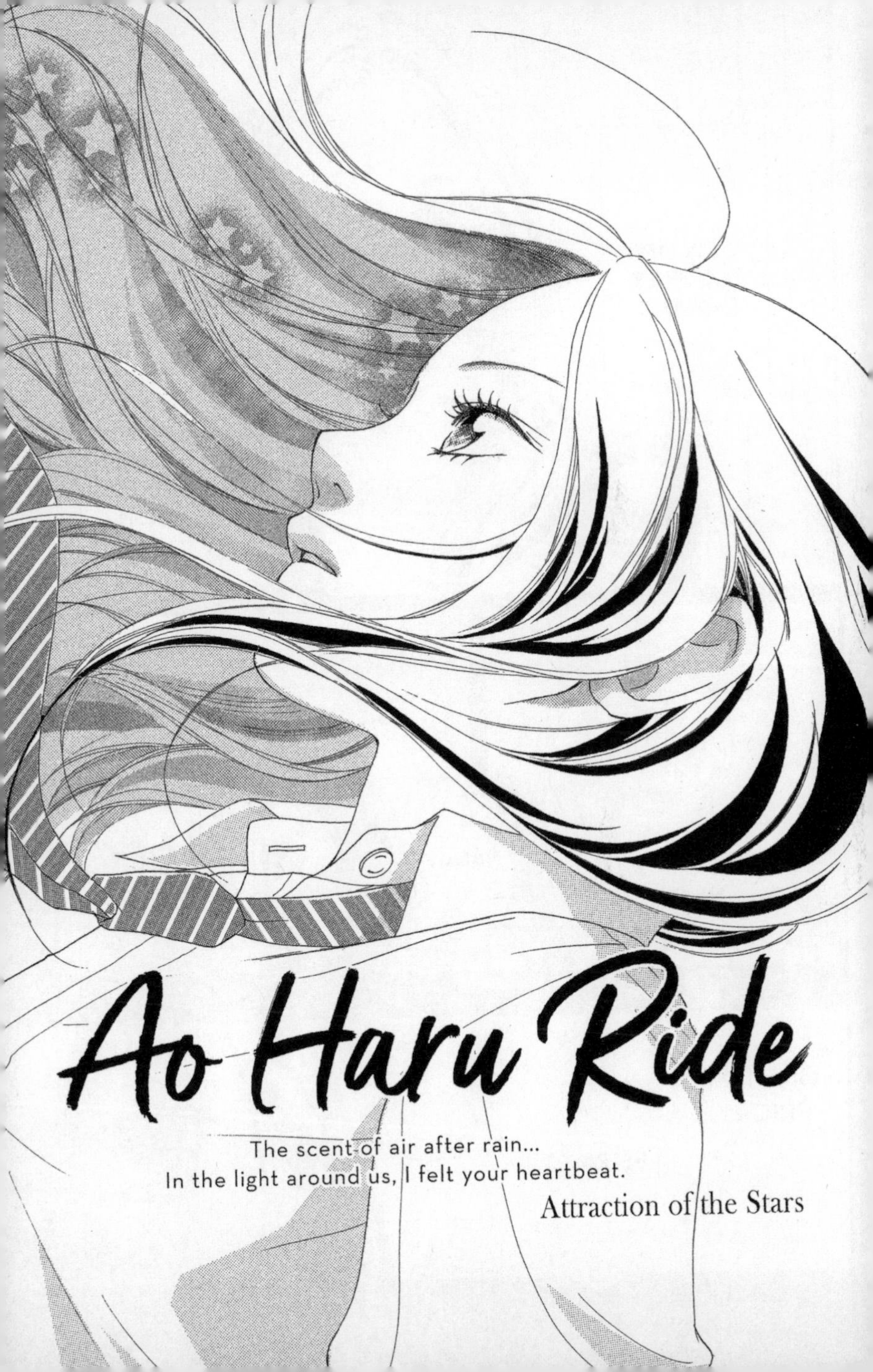
Ao Haru Ride
The scent of air after rain...
In the light around us, I felt your heartbeat.
Attraction of the Stars

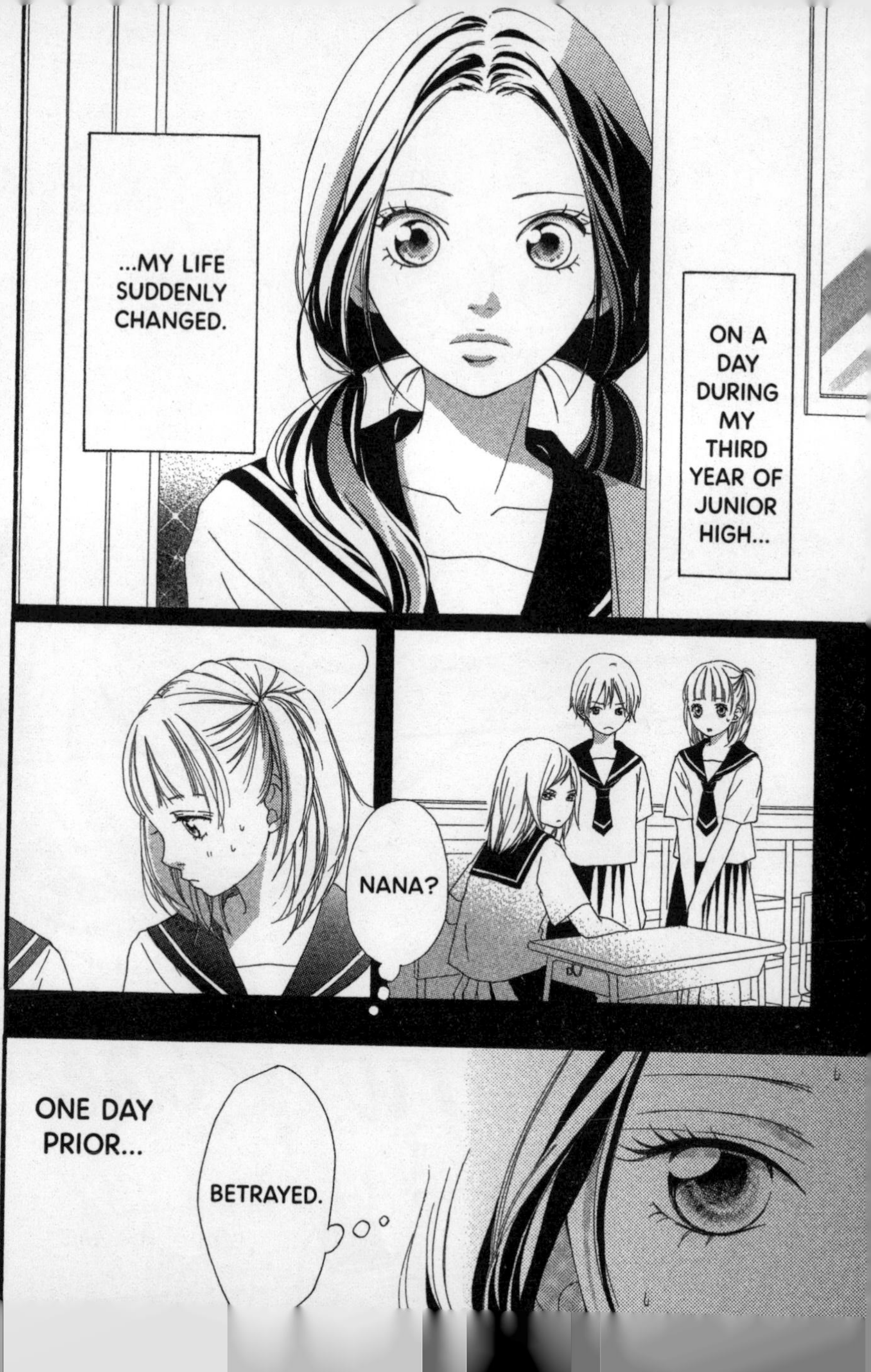
ON A DAY DURING MY THIRD YEAR OF JUNIOR HIGH...
...MY LIFE SUDDENLY CHANGED.
NANA?
BETRAYED.
ONE DAY PRIOR...

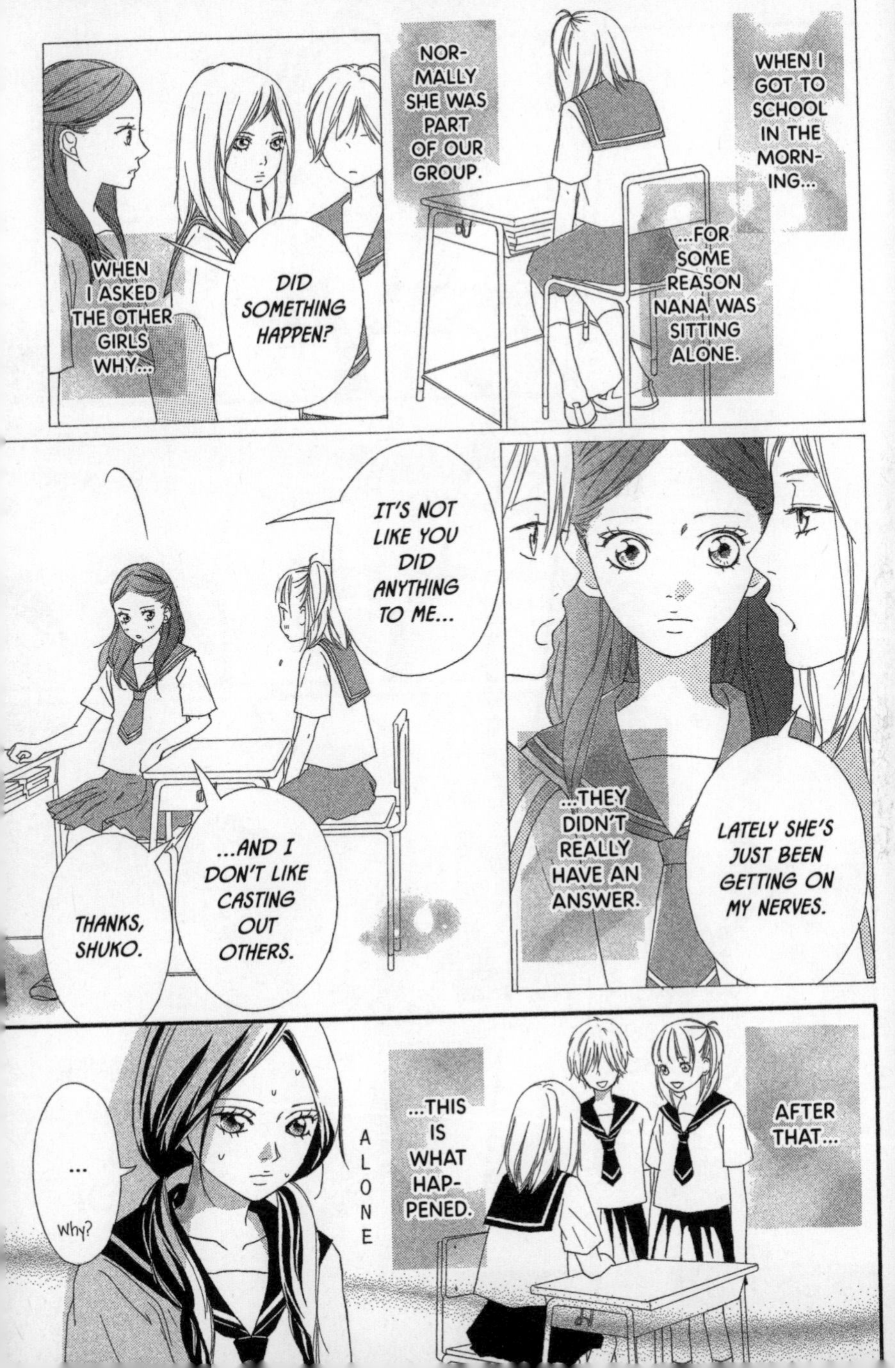
WHEN I GOT TO SCHOOL IN THE MORN-ING...
...FOR SOME REASON NANA WAS SITTING ALONE.
NOR-MALLY SHE WAS PART OF OUR GROUP.
WHEN I ASKED THE OTHER GIRLS WHY...
DID SOMETHING HAPPEN?
LATELY SHE'S JUST BEEN GETTING ON MY NERVES.
...THEY DIDN'T REALLY HAVE AN ANSWER.
IT'S NOT LIKE YOU DID ANYTHING TO ME...
...AND I DON'T LIKE CASTING OUT OTHERS.
THANKS, SHUKO.
AFTER THAT...
...THIS IS WHAT HAP-PENED.
ALONE
...
Why?

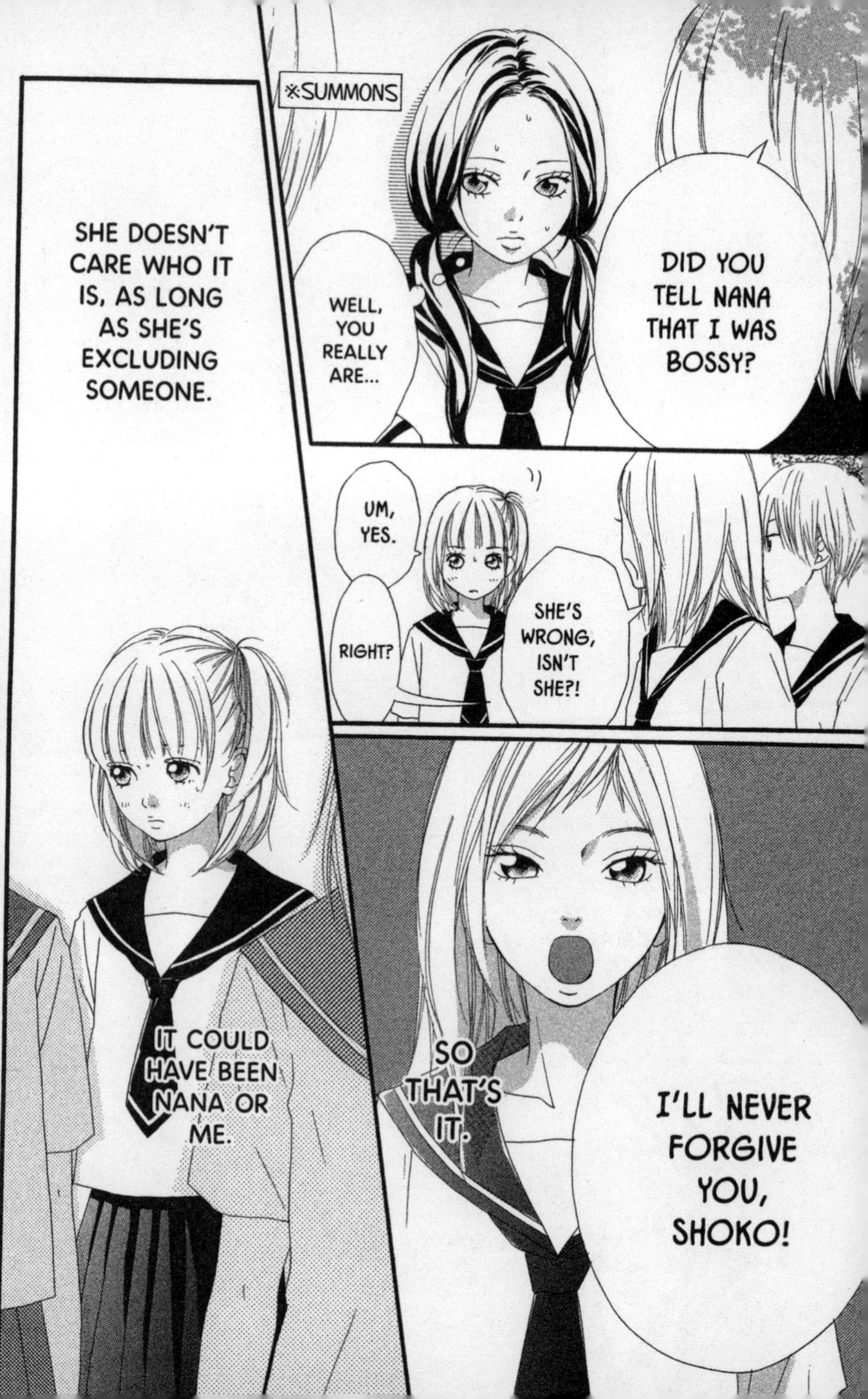
※SUMMONS
DID YOU TELL NANA THAT I WAS BOSSY?
WELL, YOU REALLY ARE...
SHE'S WRONG, ISN'T SHE?!
RIGHT?
UM, YES.
I'LL NEVER FORGIVE YOU, SHOKO!
SO THAT'S IT.
SHE DOESN'T CARE WHO IT IS, AS LONG AS SHE'S EXCLUDING SOMEONE.
IT COULD HAVE BEEN NANA OR ME.

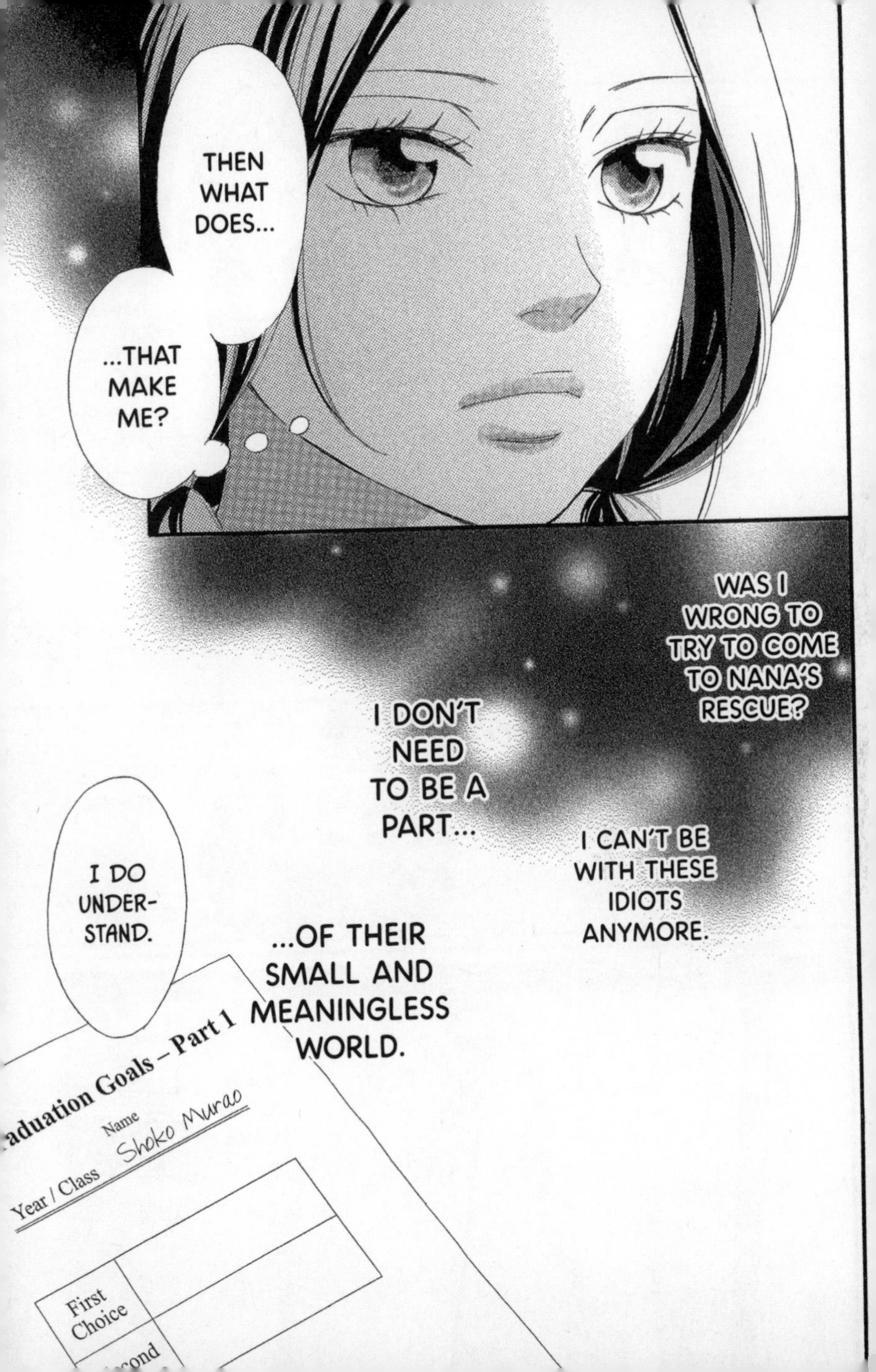
THEN WHAT DOES...
...THAT MAKE ME?
WAS I WRONG TO TRY TO COME TO NANA'S RESCUE?
I CAN'T BE WITH THESE IDIOTS ANYMORE.
I DON'T NEED TO BE A PART...
...OF THEIR SMALL AND MEANINGLESS WORLD.
I DO UNDER-STAND.
aduation Goals – Part 1
Name
Shoko Murao
Year / Class
First Choice
cond

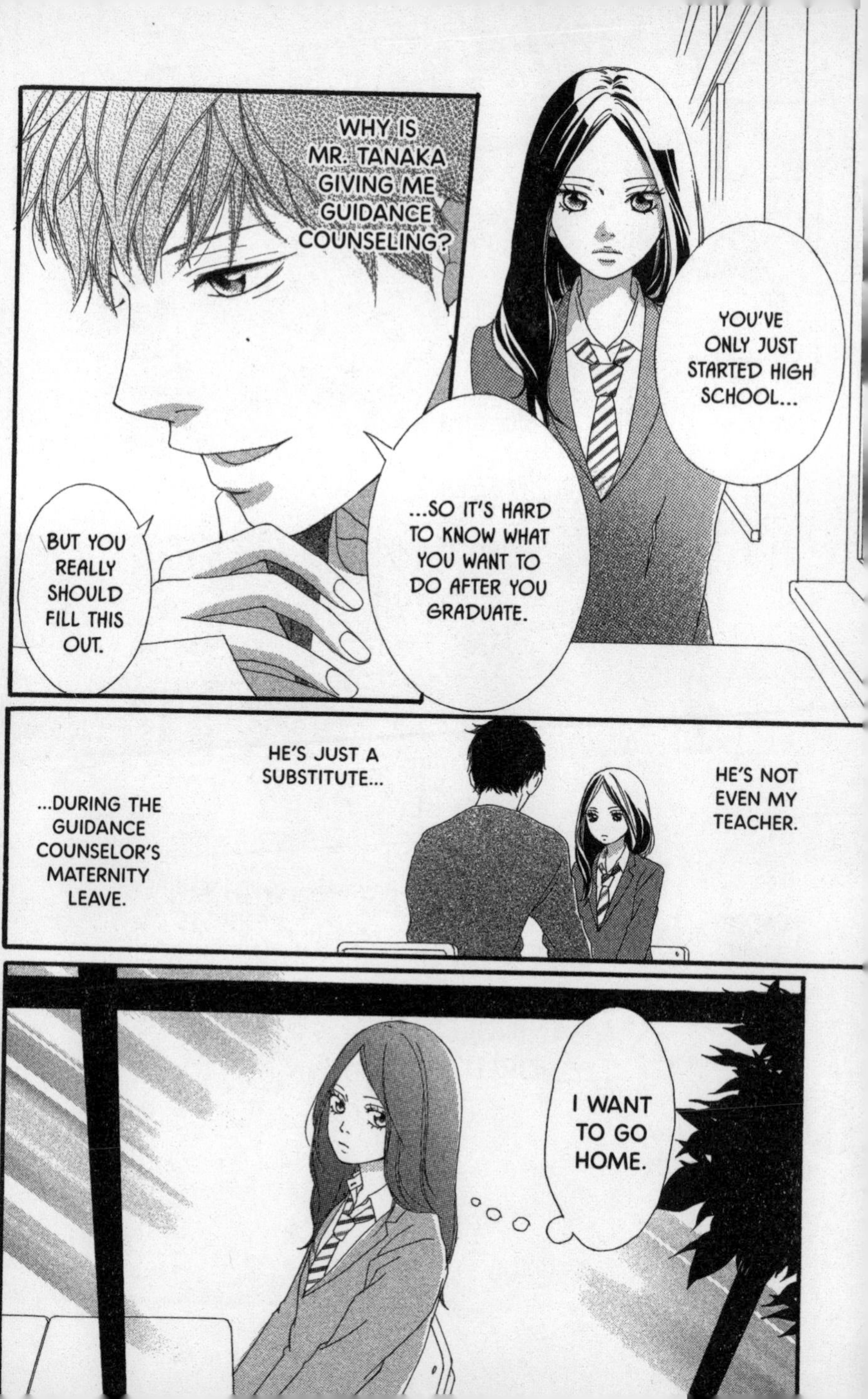
YOU'VE ONLY JUST STARTED HIGH SCHOOL...
WHY IS MR. TANAKA GIVING ME GUIDANCE COUNSELING?
...SO IT'S HARD TO KNOW WHAT YOU WANT TO DO AFTER YOU GRADUATE.
BUT YOU REALLY SHOULD FILL THIS OUT.
HE'S NOT EVEN MY TEACHER.
HE'S JUST A SUBSTITUTE...
...DURING THE GUIDANCE COUNSELOR'S MATERNITY LEAVE.
I WANT TO GO HOME.

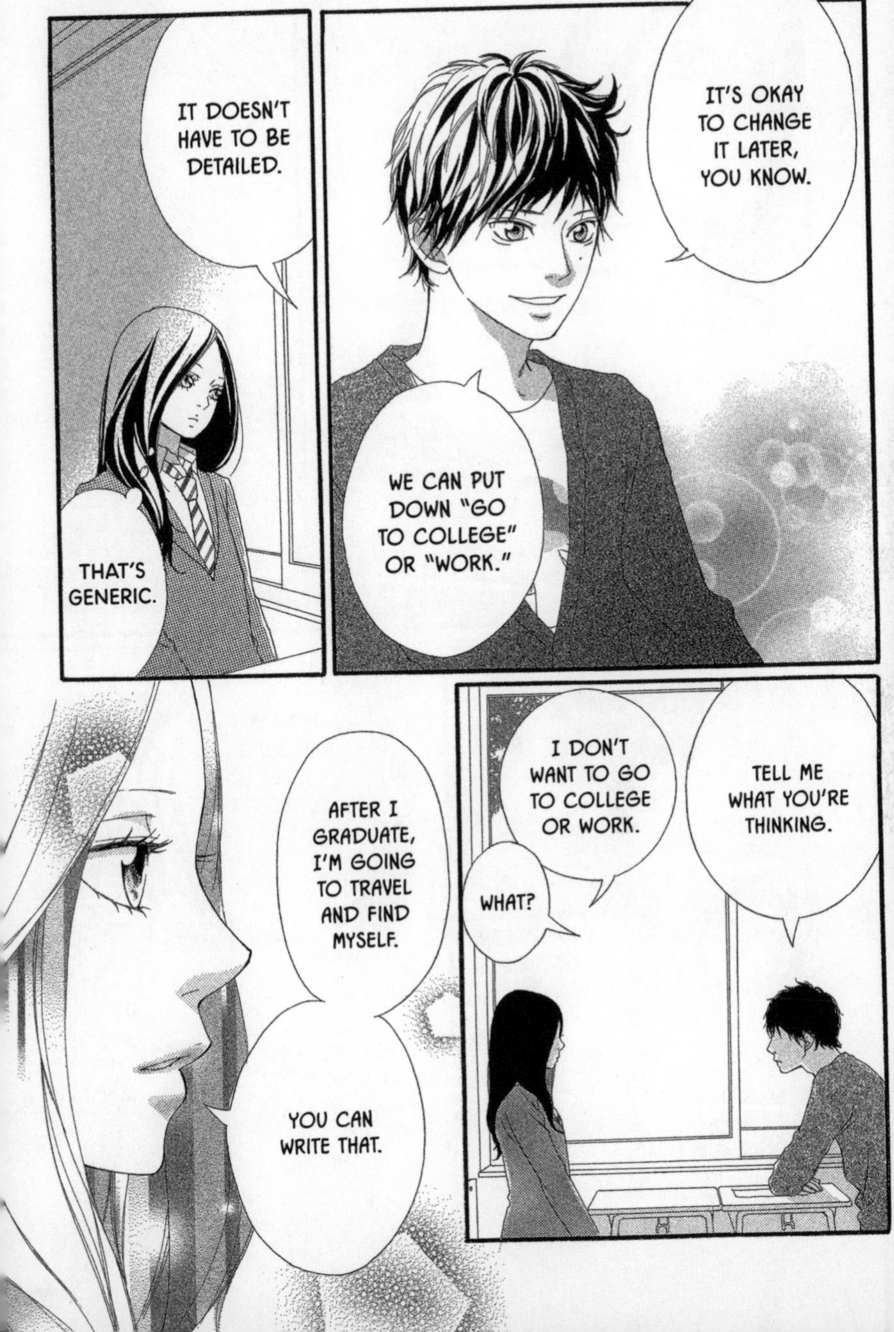
IT'S OKAY TO CHANGE IT LATER, YOU KNOW.
WE CAN PUT DOWN "GO TO COLLEGE" OR "WORK."
IT DOESN'T HAVE TO BE DETAILED.
THAT'S GENERIC.
TELL ME WHAT YOU'RE THINKING.
I DON'T WANT TO GO TO COLLEGE OR WORK.
WHAT?
AFTER I GRADUATE, I'M GOING TO TRAVEL AND FIND MYSELF.
YOU CAN WRITE THAT.

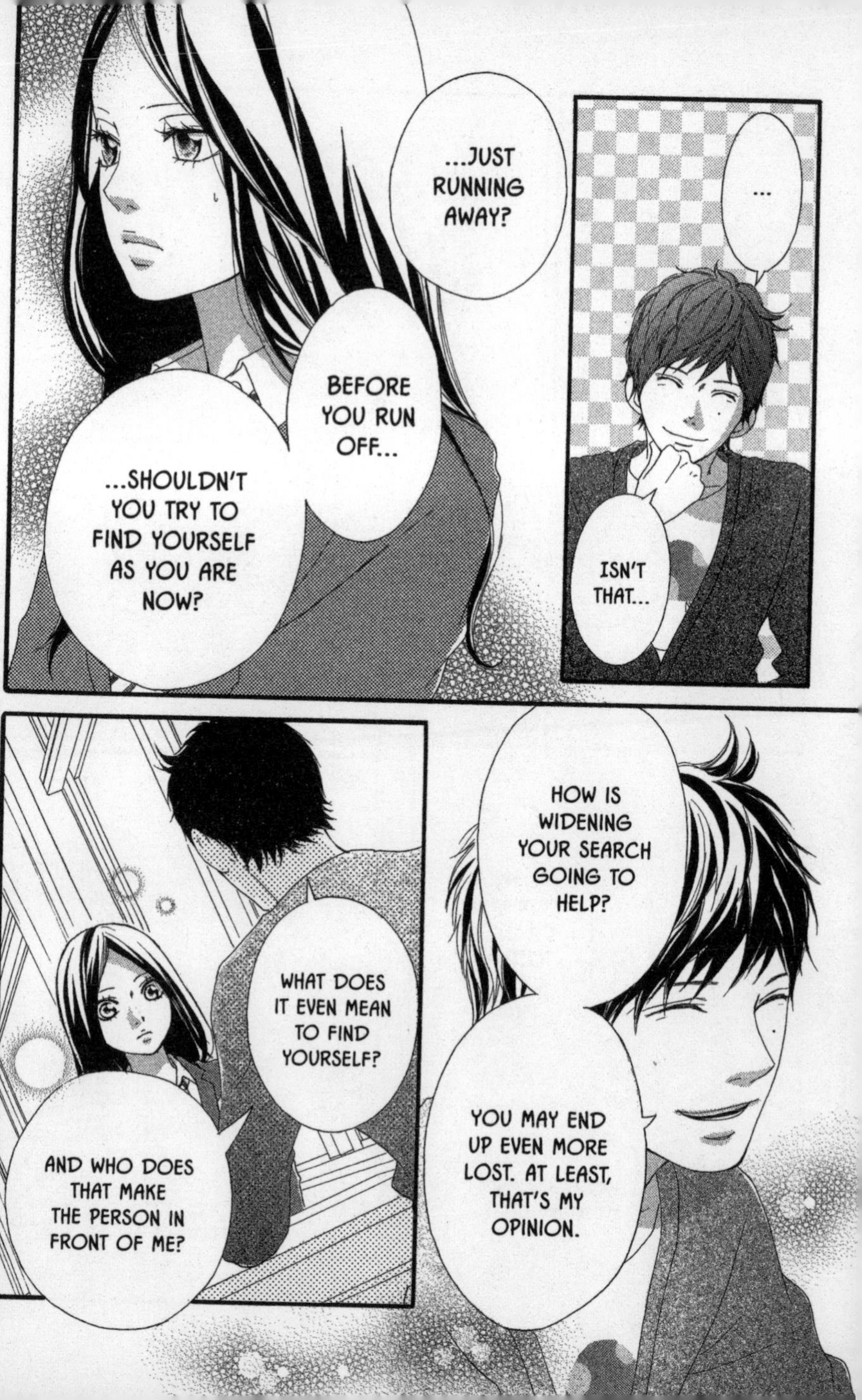
...
ISN'T THAT...
...JUST RUNNING AWAY?
BEFORE YOU RUN OFF...
...SHOULDN'T YOU TRY TO FIND YOURSELF AS YOU ARE NOW?
HOW IS WIDENING YOUR SEARCH GOING TO HELP?
YOU MAY END UP EVEN MORE LOST. AT LEAST, THAT'S MY OPINION.
WHAT DOES IT EVEN MEAN TO FIND YOURSELF?
AND WHO DOES THAT MAKE THE PERSON IN FRONT OF ME?

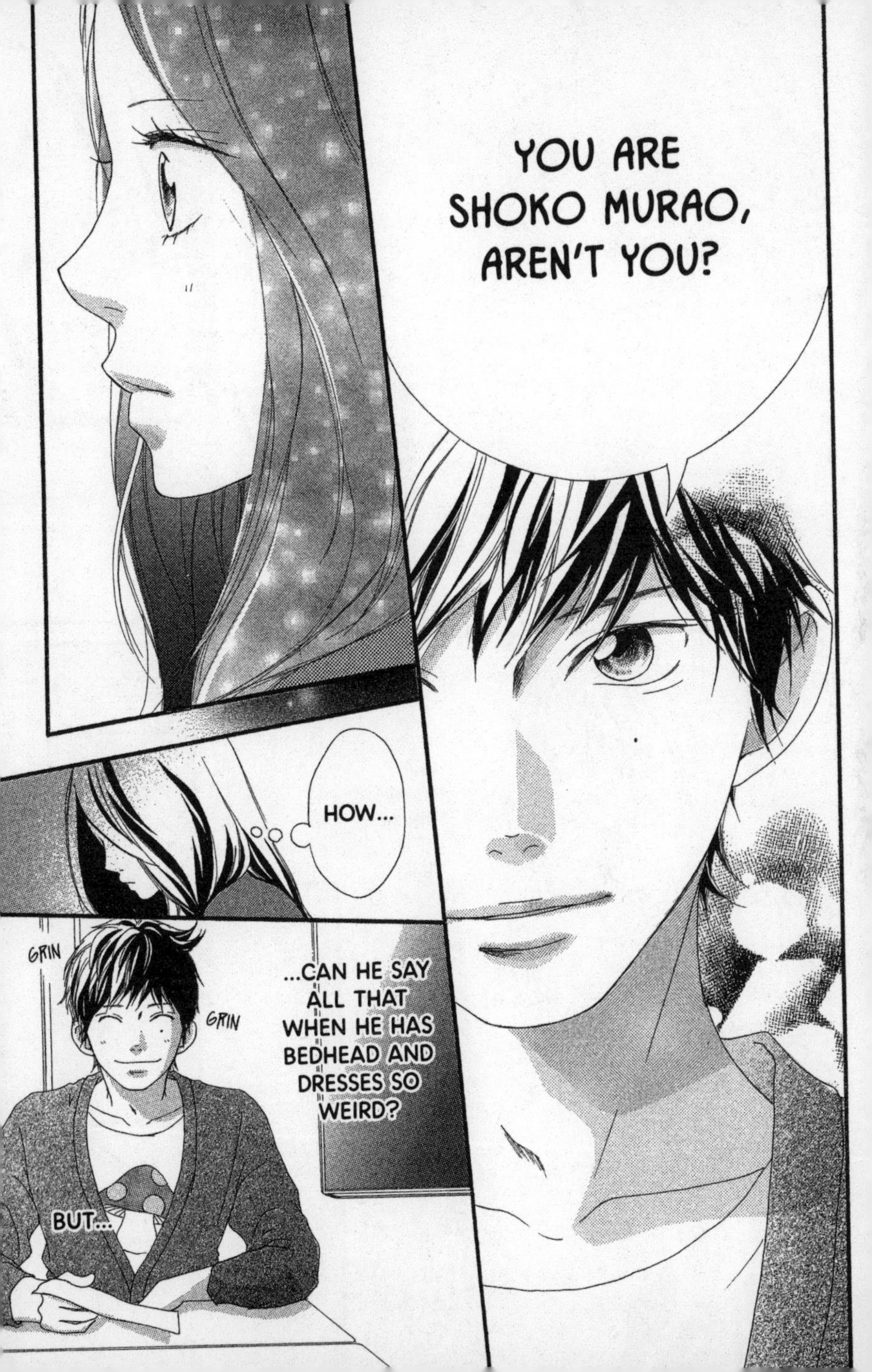
YOU ARE SHOKO MURAO, AREN'T YOU?
HOW...
...CAN HE SAY ALL THAT WHEN HE HAS BEDHEAD AND DRESSES SO WEIRD?
GRIN
GRIN
BUT...

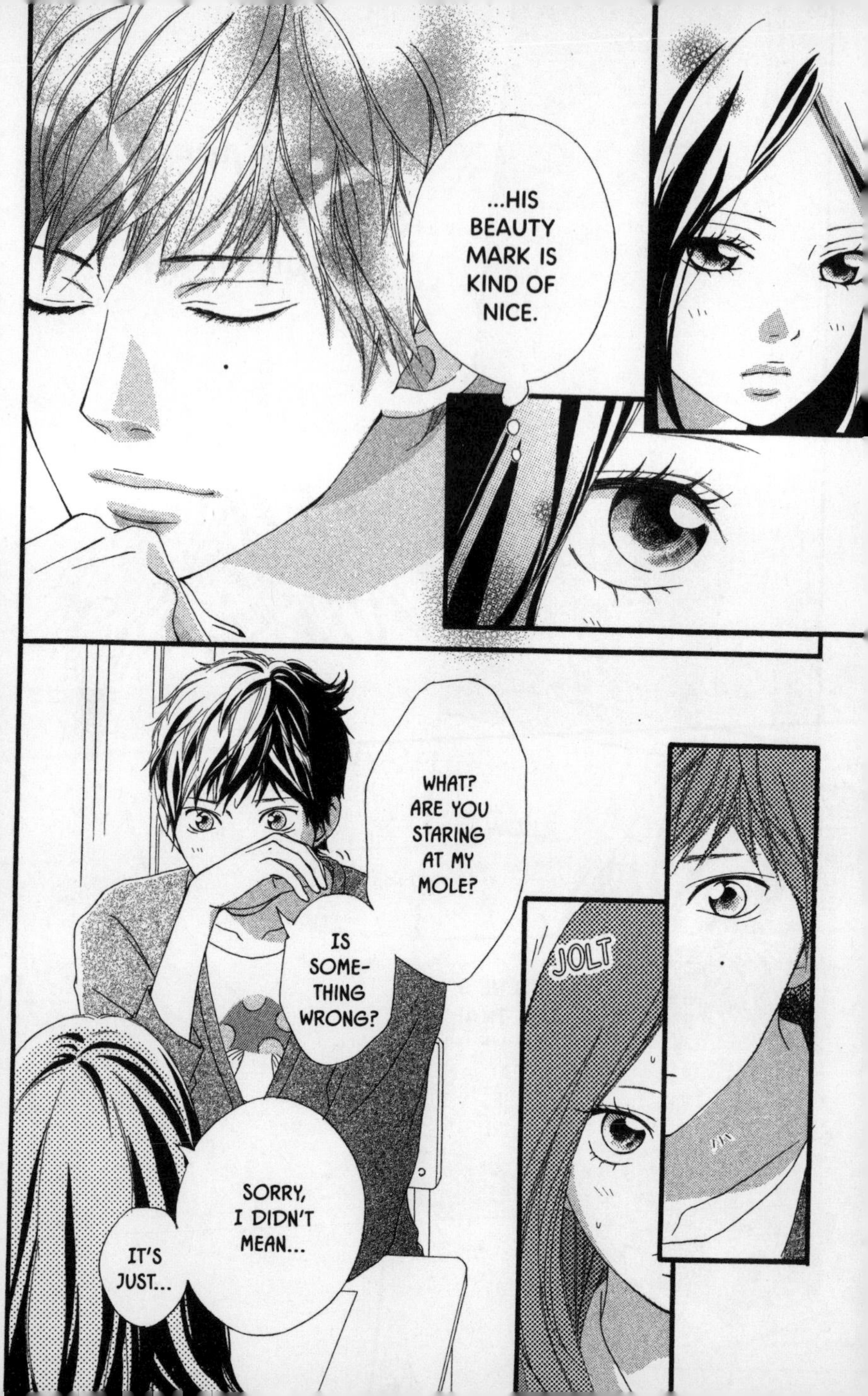
...HIS BEAUTY MARK IS KIND OF NICE.
JOLT
WHAT? ARE YOU STARING AT MY MOLE?
IS SOME-THING WRONG?
SORRY, I DIDN'T MEAN...
IT'S JUST...

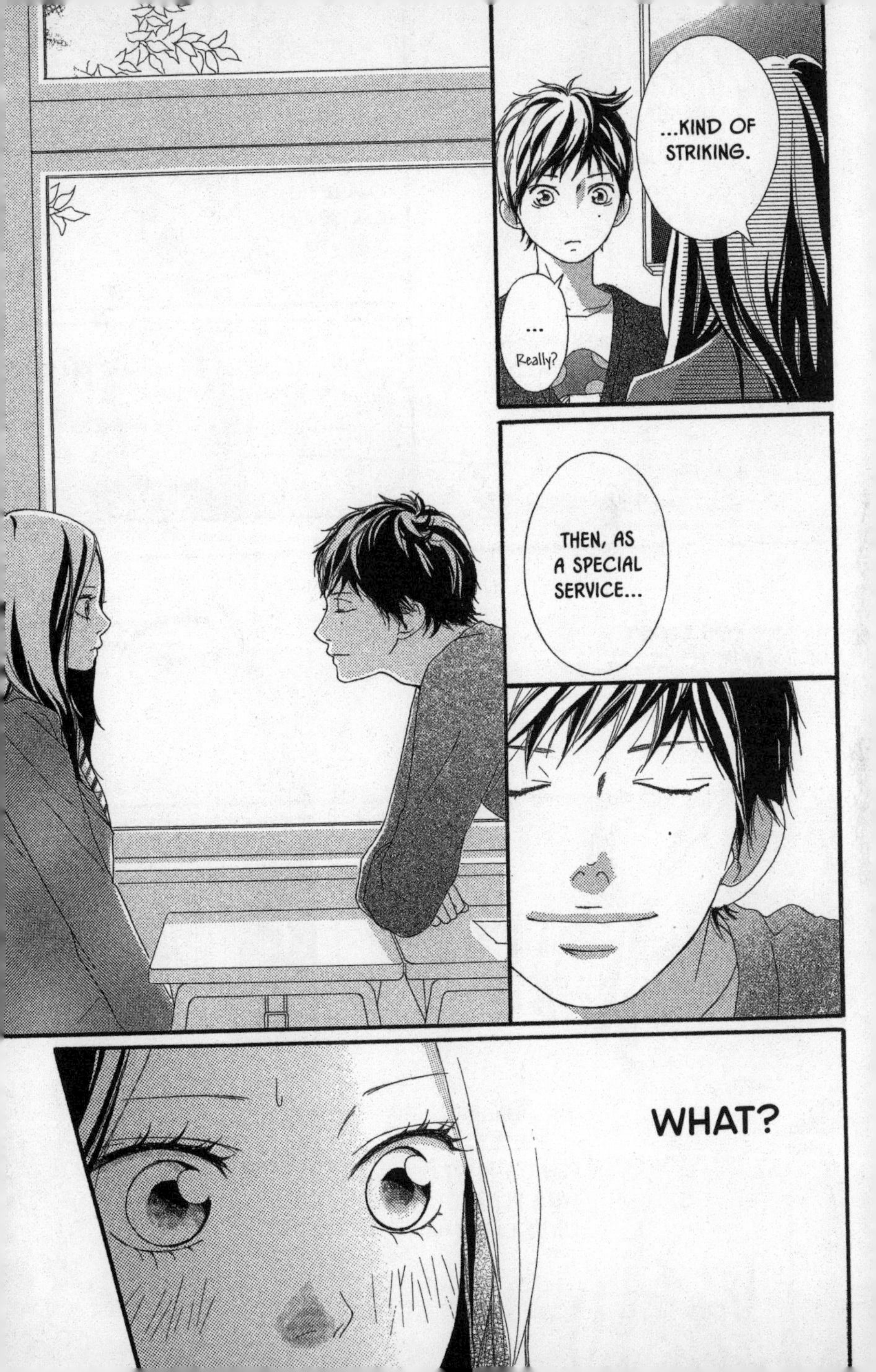
...KIND OF STRIKING.
... Really?
THEN, AS A SPECIAL SERVICE...
WHAT?

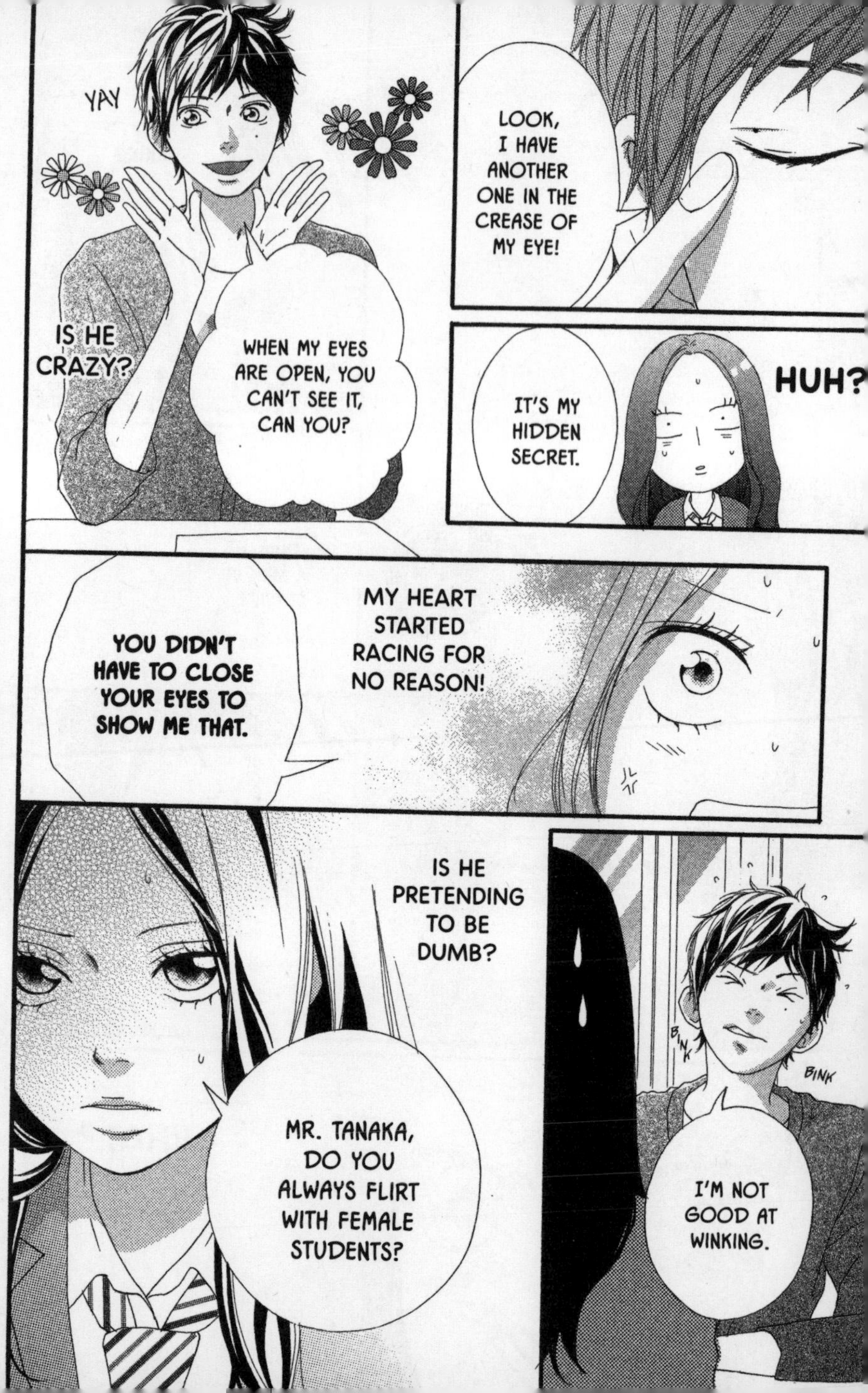
LOOK, I HAVE ANOTHER ONE IN THE CREASE OF MY EYE!
IT'S MY HIDDEN SECRET.
HUH?
YAY
WHEN MY EYES ARE OPEN, YOU CAN'T SEE IT, CAN YOU?
IS HE CRAZY?
MY HEART STARTED RACING FOR NO REASON!
YOU DIDN'T HAVE TO CLOSE YOUR EYES TO SHOW ME THAT.
BINK
BINK
I'M NOT GOOD AT WINKING.
IS HE PRETENDING TO BE DUMB?
MR. TANAKA, DO YOU ALWAYS FLIRT WITH FEMALE STUDENTS?

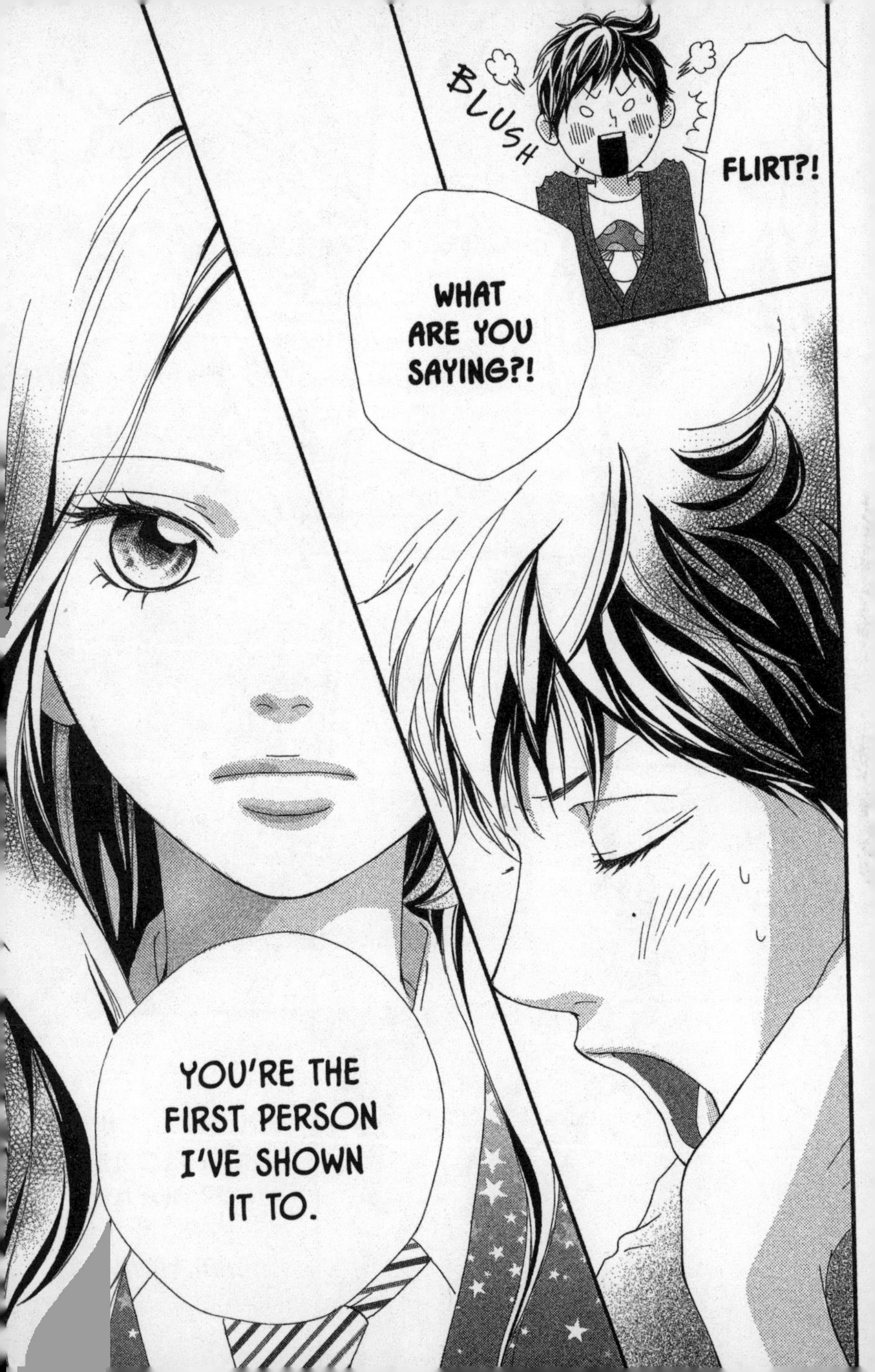
FLIRT?!
BLUSH
WHAT ARE YOU SAYING?!
YOU'RE THE FIRST PERSON I'VE SHOWN IT TO.

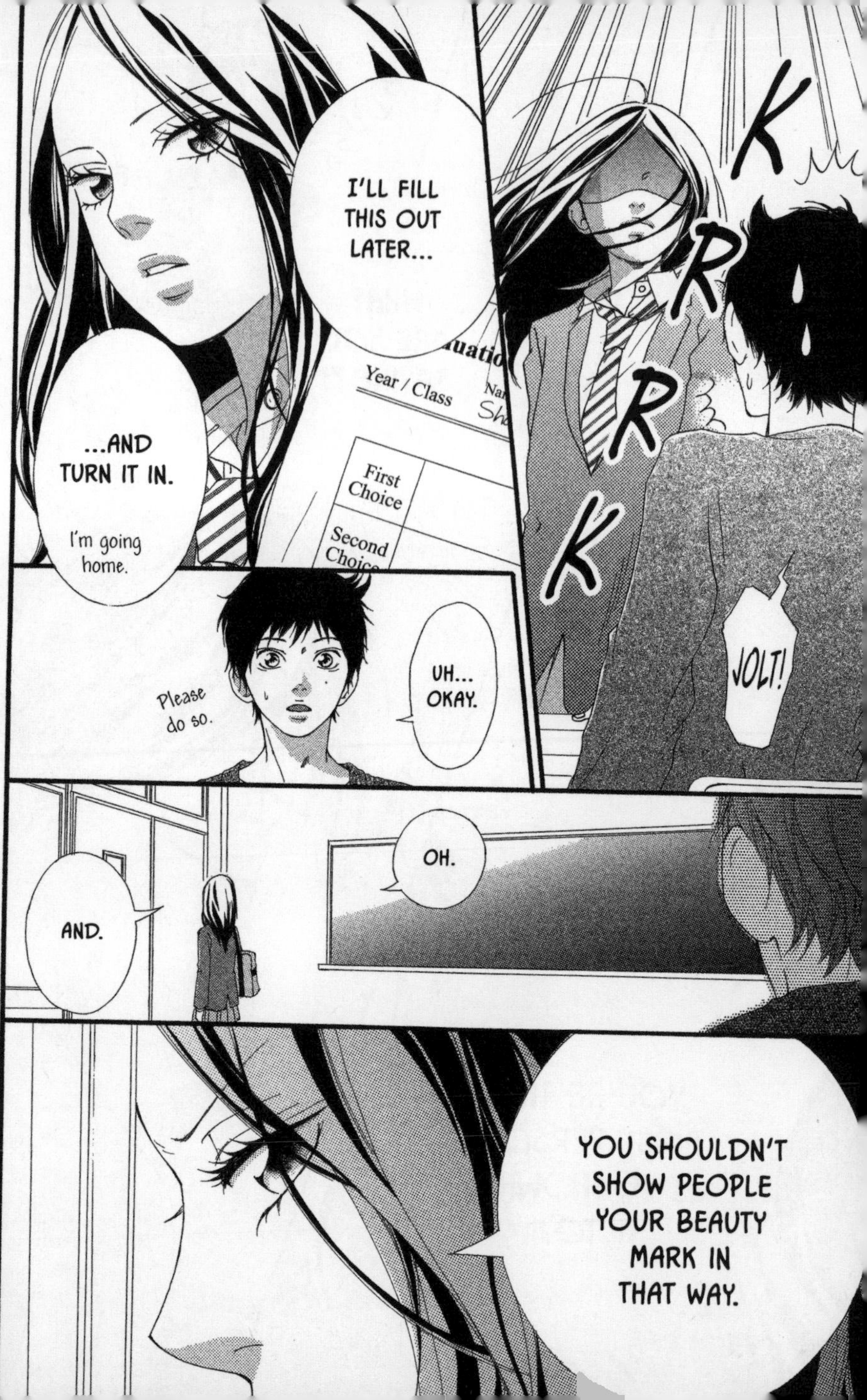
KRRK
JOLT!
I'LL FILL THIS OUT LATER...
Year / Class
First Choice
Second Choice
...AND TURN IT IN.
I'm going home.
UH... OKAY.
Please do so.
OH.
AND.
YOU SHOULDN'T SHOW PEOPLE YOUR BEAUTY MARK IN THAT WAY.

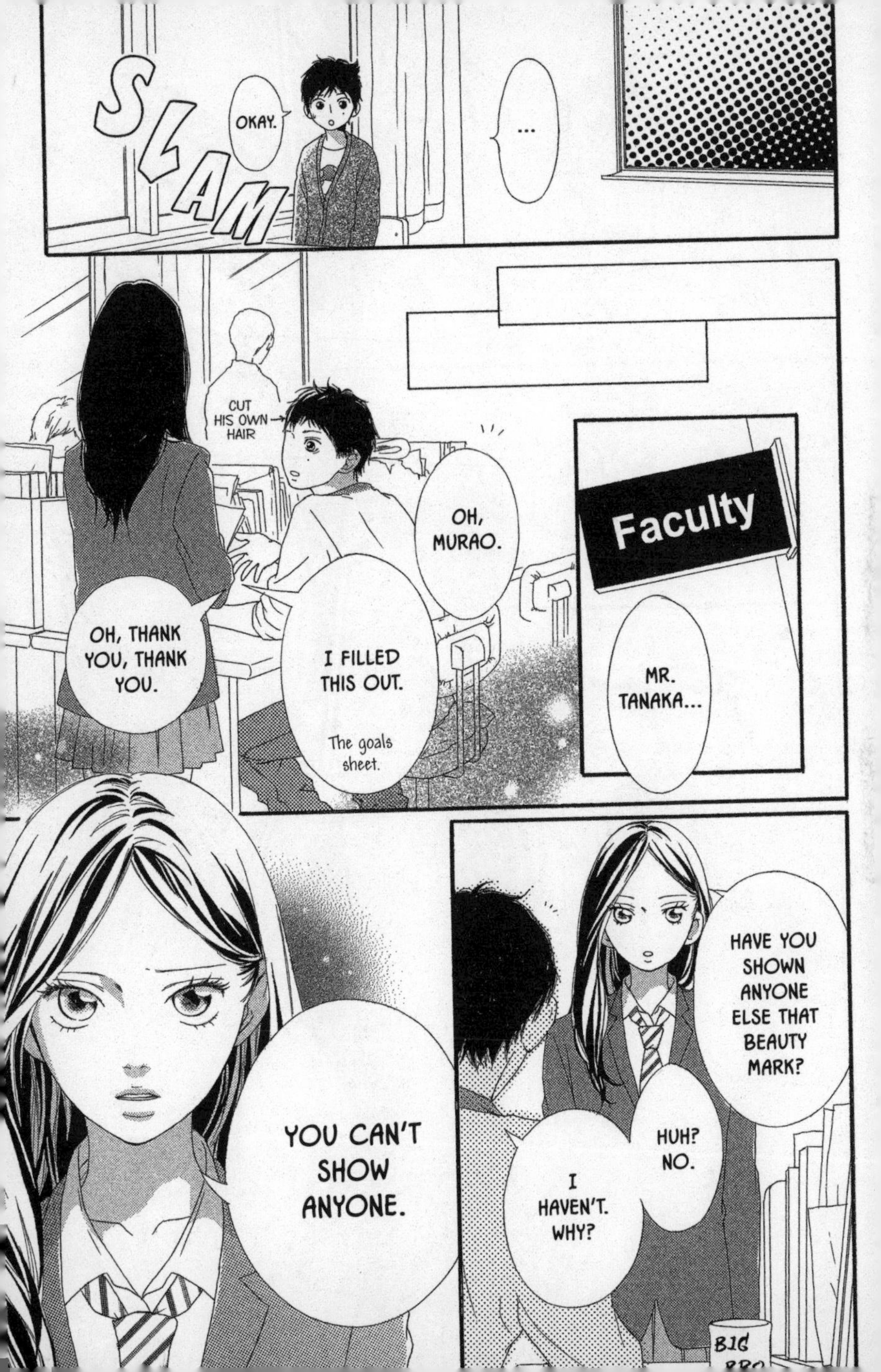
...
OKAY.
SLAM
Faculty
MR. TANAKA...
OH, MURAO.
I FILLED THIS OUT.
The goals sheet.
OH, THANK YOU, THANK YOU.
CUT HIS OWN HAIR
HAVE YOU SHOWN ANYONE ELSE THAT BEAUTY MARK?
HUH? NO.
I HAVEN'T. WHY?
YOU CAN'T SHOW ANYONE.

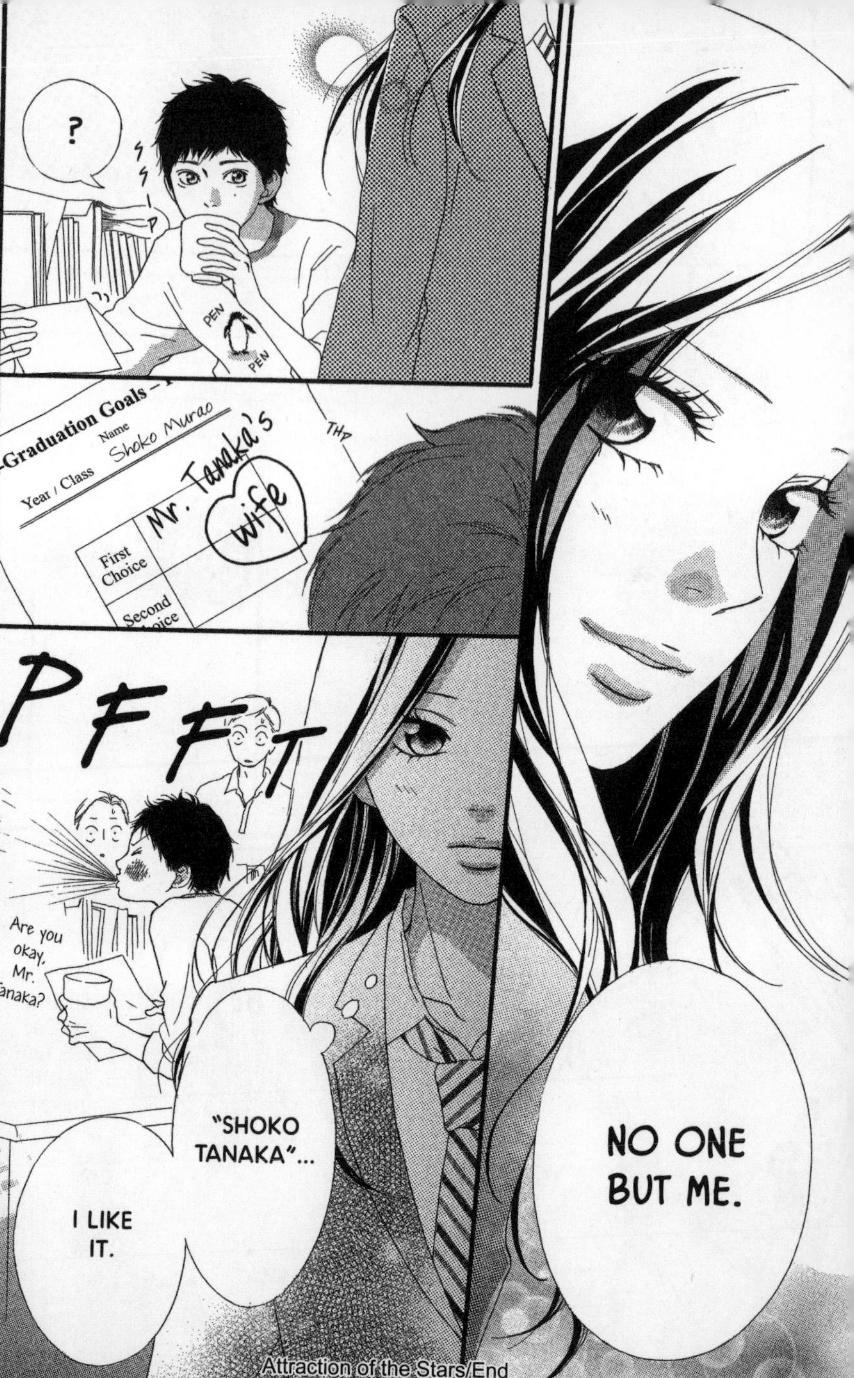
NO ONE BUT ME.
?
PEN
PEN
-Graduation Goals –
Year / Class
Name
Shoko Murao
First Choice
Mr. Tanaka's wife
Second
THP
PFFT
Are you okay, Mr. Tanaka?
"SHOKO TANAKA"...
I LIKE IT.

Attraction of the Stars/End

AFTERWORD

Thank you for reading to the end!

Have you ever fallen for the same person a close friend
has? In my case, we weren't as close as Futaba and Yuri,
but I did have a crush on the same person as another
pretty good friend in my class. I didn't hear about it
directly from her, so we were both free to like him without really worrying about each other. It was more like "if
something happens and one of us gets together with him,
that's just how things go because we both like him..." But
if that friend were my best friend, I don't think I would
have taken it as lightly... I don't even want to think about
it. I would be so conflicted. And I would also be in love.

Good luck, Futaba and Yuri. I hope you readers will watch
over them as well. And with that, thank you always for
your support! See you next time!

By the way, back to the boy I was talking about... After
some time, the other girl got asked out by somebody else,
and by that time I didn't like him anymore, so nothing
ever came of it. His moment of popularity ended without
him ever knowing about it.

 Io Sakisaka

You know, when I visited the shrine during the New Year (2011), my fortune said I was destined for "very bad luck" this year. But when I look back, it was a relatively peaceful year. Phew!

Or...perhaps something bad happened, and I simply forgot about it? I guess you could say "phew" about that too!

If you ever pull a fortune that forecasts "very bad luck," I suggest that you not worry too much because everything will be fine!

IO SAKISAKA

Born on June 8, Io Sakisaka made her debut as a manga creator with *Sakura, Chiru*. Her works include *Call My Name*, *Gate of Planet* and *Blue*. *Strobe Edge*, her previous work, is also published by VIZ Media's Shojo Beat imprint. *Ao Haru Ride* was adapted into an anime series in 2014. In her spare time, Sakisaka likes to paint things and sleep.

Ao Haru Ride

VOLUME 3
SHOJO BEAT EDITION

STORY AND ART BY **IO SAKISAKA**

TRANSLATION **Emi Louie-Nishikawa**
TOUCH-UP ART + LETTERING **Inori Fukuda Trant**
DESIGN **Shawn Carrico**
EDITOR **Nancy Thistlethwaite**

AOHA RIDE © 2011 by Io Sakisaka
All rights reserved.
First published in Japan in 2011 by SHUEISHA Inc., Tokyo.
English translation rights arranged by SHUEISHA Inc.

The stories, characters and incidents mentioned
in this publication are entirely fictional.

Printed in the U.S.A.

Published by VIZ Media, LLC
P.O. Box 77010
San Francisco, CA 94107

10 9 8 7 6 5 4 3 2 1
First printing, February 2019

PARENTAL ADVISORY
AO HARU RIDE is rated T for Teen and
is recommended for ages 13 and up.
This volume contains the petulance of youth.

viz.com   shojobeat.com

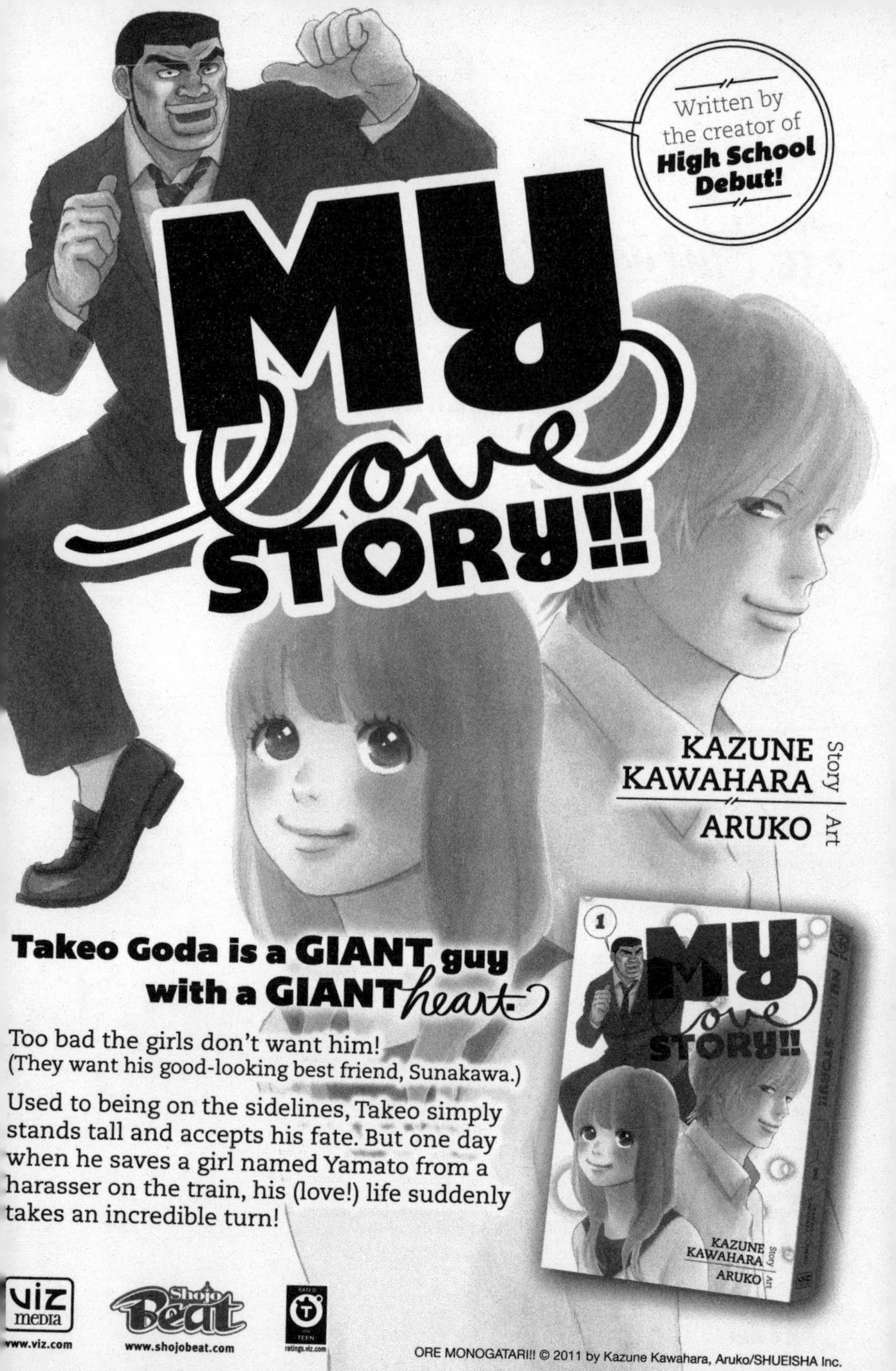
Written by the creator of High School Debut!
MY love STORY!!
KAZUNE KAWAHARA Story
ARUKO Art
Takeo Goda is a GIANT guy with a GIANT heart.
Too bad the girls don't want him!
(They want his good-looking best friend, Sunakawa.)
Used to being on the sidelines, Takeo simply stands tall and accepts his fate. But one day when he saves a girl named Yamato from a harasser on the train, his (love!) life suddenly takes an incredible turn!
1
MY love STORY!!
KAZUNE KAWAHARA Story
ARUKO Art
viz media
www.viz.com
Shojo Beat
www.shojobeat.com
RATED T TEEN
ratings.viz.com

Honey
So Sweet

Story and Art by *Amu Meguro*

Little did Nao Kogure realize back in middle school that when she left an umbrella and a box of bandages in the rain for injured delinquent Taiga Onise that she would meet him again in high school. Nao wants nothing to do with the gruff and frightening Taiga, but he suddenly presents her with a huge bouquet of flowers and asks her to date him—with marriage in mind! Is Taiga really so scary, or is he a sweetheart in disguise?

SHORTCAKE CAKE

CAKE

STORY AND ART BY
suu Morishita

An unflappable girl and a cast of lovable roommates at a boardinghouse create bonds of friendship and romance!

When Ten moves out of her parents' home in the mountains to live in a boardinghouse, she finds herself becoming fast friends with her male roommates. But can love and romance be far behind?

RATED TEEN

VIZ

STOP!

YOU MAY BE READING THE WRONG WAY.

In keeping with the original Japanese comic format, this book reads from right to left—so action, sound effects and word balloons are completely reversed to preserve the orientation of the original artwork.